Rock 'n' Roll SOCCER

THE SHORT LIFE AND FAST TIMES OF THE NORTH AMERICAN SOCCER LEAGUE

IAN PLENDERLEITH

WITH A FOREWORD BY RODNEY MARSH

ICON

First published in the UK in 2014
by Icon Books Ltd, Omnibus Business Centre,
39–41 North Road, London N7 9DP
email: info@iconbooks.com
www.iconbooks.com

This edition published in the UK in 2016 by Icon Books Ltd

Sold in the UK, Europe and Asia
by Faber & Faber Ltd, Bloomsbury House,
74–77 Great Russell Street,
London WC1B 3DA or their agents

Distributed in the UK, Europe and Asia
by Grantham Book Services,
Trent Road, Grantham NG31 7XQ

Distributed in Australia and New Zealand
by Allen & Unwin Pty Ltd,
PO Box 8500, 83 Alexander Street,
Crows Nest, NSW 2065

Distributed in South Africa
by Jonathan Ball, Office B4,
The District, 41 Sir Lowry Road,
Woodstock 7925

Distributed in Canada
by Publishers Group Canada,
76 Stafford Street, Unit 300,
Toronto, Ontario M6J 2S1

ISBN: 978-190685-085-2

Typeset in ITC Legacy by Marie Doherty

Printed and bound in the UK by
Clays Ltd, St Ives plc

For my dad, Robert Plenderleith, who had the great but truly terrible idea to take his six-year-old son to Sincil Bank in 1971

In memory of soccer writer David Wangerin (1962–2012)

About the author

Ian Plenderleith is a British football writer and journalist who finished this book at the end of a fifteen-year spell in the United States. He is the author of the critically acclaimed football short story collection *For Whom The Ball Rolls*, and has written about football in the UK, Germany and the US for publications including the *Guardian*, *Soccer America*, the *Wall Street Journal* and *When Saturday Comes*. He lives in Frankfurt am Main, Germany.

Rodney Marsh won nine caps for England between 1971 and 1973 and made over 400 league appearances for Fulham, QPR and Manchester City. After moving to the USA and the Tampa Bay Rowdies in 1976, he was instrumental in helping both his team and the North American Soccer League look for a few heady years like they were going to revolutionize the US sporting landscape.

Contents

Author's note

This is an analysis, not a complete history, of the North American Soccer League. The book does not cover every team season by season, and the events and games described are only in a very rough chronological order. There are dozens of players, coaches and owners not mentioned in this book, but Colin Jose's book *A Complete Record of the North American Soccer League* will answer any statistical question that might arise while reading. The internet will more than likely help too. Because the League's cities, team names, rules and structure changed constantly, I have added two appendices for reference. Appendix A (page 405) lists the cities and the names of the teams they hosted in any given year. Appendix B (page 407) lists the finalists and the scores of the championship game or games.

I call football 'soccer' throughout, simply to avoid confusion and differentiate it from American football. I refer to a team's coach knowing that we in the UK would call that same person a manager. Again, this is to differentiate the coach from the general manager (GM) – every US sports team has a GM, who is generally in charge of buying players and managing the budget for buying players. He also tends to act as more of a team spokesman than the coach. Simply put, the GM manages the team, and the coach coaches it. Or, at least, that's the theory.

When referring to the NASL as 'the League', a capital L is used to differentiate it from any other league. An MVP is Most Valuable Player, which depending on the context means 'man of the match' or 'player of the season'. An All-Star XI is announced at the end of every US sports league's season to honour those judged to be the best eleven players in the league that year – it is generally considered to be a big deal. The term 'franchise' is used liberally and interchangeably with 'club' and 'team', not because I supported the FA's decision to move Wimbledon FC to Milton Keynes (I didn't, and still don't), but because in the 1970s especially, US soccer teams really were franchises, as mobile and vulnerable as under-performing branches of a fast food chain. Quotes in the present tense are from interviews conducted by the author, quotes in the past tense are from archival research.

Picture credits for images in the plate section appear alongside the individual images. Where images appear uncredited we have been unable to trace the copyright holder; anyone whose copyright has been inadvertently infringed is invited to contact the publisher.

Foreword

by Rodney Marsh

History may have largely forgotten the North American Soccer League, but it wasn't forgettable to those of us who were there. I joined the appropriately named Tampa Bay Rowdies from Manchester City in 1976 when the NASL was on the rise, following in the footsteps of world greats Pelé and Eusebio. My very first day at the Rowdies pretty much set the tone for what was to come. I walked into the secretary's office to find her on the phone to the local police station, negotiating to get two of our players out of jail. Apparently a couple of Tampa's Scottish lads had enjoyed a boisterous night out and ended up behind bars.

Yes, the NASL had a reputation as something of a party league for ageing pros. The last time that Pelé came to play in Tampa for the New York Cosmos in 1977, it was a massive game, built up for weeks beforehand. Our marketing executive sent a limo to the airport to pick him up, along with their colourful striker Giorgio Chinaglia, to be taken straight to a press conference at a TV station. In the back of the limo were two beautiful cheerleaders holding a bottle of Chivas Regal on a silver tray. The story goes that the two players never made it to the press conference, and in fact were not seen at all for several hours. Next day, the Rowdies won 4–2 in front of 45,000 fans.

Yet no one who played in the NASL disputes that we all took the soccer very, very seriously, and that included Pelé. The Rowdies developed an intense rivalry with the Cosmos, and I had my personal battles with the great Brazilian. In one game he went ballistic at me for what he thought was showboating (he was right – it was). In another game he scythed me down and provoked a fifteen-man brawl. Most painful of all, after I nutmegged him once he came up to me and ruffled my hair – a sporting gesture by the revered icon. Except that no one could see that he'd gouged my ear with his fingernail and opened up a bleeding wound.

Off the field, Pelé was always the perfect gentleman, but on the field he would throw the elbow and harass the referee. He was not only the greatest player in the world, but a proper winner, and the vast majority of those who played both with him and against him in the NASL approached the game with just as much commitment.

Pelé and football's other household names like Johan Cruyff and Franz Beckenbauer were a perfect fit for America, where I quickly learned that people generally love a super-star as much as they love a big event. I still today look at the English mentality and its desire to slag off a star and destroy him as quickly as possible. In the US, I found a country that not only celebrated its stars, but enjoyed them too. Like many other British players at the time I felt more relaxed in a place where I could express myself freely, both on and off the field.

Of course there was a lot of craziness as well. In my NASL career I was a player, coach and finally part-owner of the Rowdies. Before the final season in 1984 we met to discuss possible rule changes, and somebody suggested each team should have a designated number 9 who would be allowed to punch the ball in open play. I burst out laughing, and told them FIFA would never allow it. We actually took a vote on it, and it tells you something about the adventurous mindset of some of the owners that the idea suffered only a narrow defeat.

Those owners were the same men, women and corporations who lost millions of dollars in a league that ultimately didn't make it. Some were clueless jokers out to make a fast buck, but many were courageous investors who genuinely thought that soccer had a future in the US. Beyond all the razzmatazz and the great players, it was their cash and enthusiasm that helped lay the foundations for soccer's massive presence today across North America. The millions of young kids now playing across the US and Canada are the enduring legacy of a trend kick-started by the global game's biggest names, and the hundreds of European and South American pros who joined them.

I've always felt that there's been the need for a relevant, definitive book about the NASL that would capture the essence of the League and its true place in both US and world soccer history. This book finally does justice to the story of the remarkable rise and fall of a wild and uniquely glorious league that dared to be different, and had a hell of a good time along the way.

Rodney Marsh

Introduction

'This sport will take off. There is absolutely no
way that it will not bypass everything else. This
country will be the centre of world soccer. In the
80s there will be a mania for the game here. There
will be three to five million kids playing it. The
North American Soccer League will be the world's
No. 1 soccer league. And it will be the biggest
sports league in the USA.'

—North American Soccer League Commissioner*
Phil Woosnam, 1977.[1]

No one ever accused the North American Soccer League
Commissioner Phil Woosnam of lacking optimism. It was, after
all, the former Aston Villa forward's drive and diligence that
had rescued the nascent professional soccer league from the
brink of extinction after just one year of play in 1968. Less than
ten years later under his stewardship, the League was not only
succeeding and expanding beyond the wildest of expectations,
but was turning into a roller-coaster phenomenon that really
might fulfil Woosnam's brash and bullish forecast: number one
sport in America, number one soccer league in the world. Yet
again, the Yanks were coming with their arrogance, their money,
their revolutionary vision and their self-belief, sweeping aside a
century of tradition as they stormed forward into a shiny future
that was splashed with character, colour and cool.

---

* North American term for chairman, president, chief, honcho, big boss.

1

A few months after Woosnam's bold forecast, the New York Cosmos beat the Fort Lauderdale Strikers 8-3 in a sold-out NASL playoff game at Giants Stadium, New Jersey. The attendance was 77,691, and the Cosmos starting line-up featured Pelé, Franz Beckenbauer, Carlos Alberto and Giorgio Chinaglia. The NASL was at its zenith, and this single game sums up everything the League stood for – a huge crowd, tons of goals and some of the biggest names in world soccer. There were celebrities in the stands and leggy cheerleaders on the touchline. What could possibly go wrong? It's easy to ask that question now with a knowing smile. Arguably of more interest are the things that went right.

In the 1970s, Pelé, Johan Cruyff, Eusebio, George Best, Gerd Müller and Beckenbauer all played in the same league. Forty years later, that legendary constellation seems almost unreal. Yet, this was the product which the NASL attempted to sell to a sceptical audience – the world's greatest players representing start-up teams unknown both at home and abroad. The NASL was a project way ahead of its time. It was a big-money glamour league that aimed to entertain, while generating cash. In that respect, it was the Champions League and the English Premier League rolled into one. Pelé had already retired from soccer in 1974, but he chose to come back the following year for one league only. The pugnacious NASL offered the kind of outrageous, multi-million dollar deal that no European team had the courage to put on the table, yet it pointed to the eventual path of European club soccer at its highest level.

European attitudes towards US soccer have always been informed by a sense that the Yanks don't know what they're doing when it comes to any sport that won't stop the action for commercial breaks. It was no different in the 1970s. The British press looked down on the pom-pom presentation, the plastic pitches, the garish uniforms, and the alien points system that was set up to encourage more goalscoring. More goals? How distasteful! When the NASL declined, there was a sense of both relief and *schadenfreude* in Europe, shared by a majority of the professional sports establishment in the USA. The NASL was up against incredible odds – it had to compete against American football, baseball and basketball at home and with the conservative soccer traditionalists abroad. Yet its vision of the game has persevered, while at the time it flourished for a few short years in conspicuous contrast to the grim European game. In Britain especially, crowds were plummeting thanks to widespread hooliganism, while tactics were increasingly geared towards results with little thought paid to thrilling the fans.

Woosnam's fantasy may have been realized if the NASL had had the money and the management to carry the League through for just a few more years. After all, the National Basketball Association struggled through the same decade before establishing itself in the mainstream of US sport and culture in the 1980s. The National Football League, despite gridiron's long history, had only recently become a massive, major-league movement thanks to a lucrative television contract and the ease of air travel. In the post-Second World War years, the most popular US sports were baseball, boxing and horseracing, all followed avidly on the radio, but the latter two had declined in popularity as American football rose. As far as soccer was concerned in the 1960s when plans were first discussed for a new professional league, the North American sports market was an open field with a large share of the cash and the audience still up for grabs. If it had pulled through, we could now be looking at Woosnam's alternative: a league firmly established as the best in the world, whose success has carried Canada and the US to the top of the international game. Players flocking to North America from Europe, Africa and Latin America to play for the globally known brands whose games are transmitted to Europe, Africa, Asia and South America by satellite every weekend from February to November. The League having stolen a jump on the old capitals of soccer, baffled as to why they didn't feel the imminent gusts of change. FIFA having begrudgingly upped sticks and relocated to midtown Manhattan, dwarfed by the NASL's 24-floor tower across the road on Sixth Avenue (with a pneumatic chute installed beneath for the efficient transfer of brown envelopes).

If you were designing a prototype for a brand new, modern soccer league, you would place the most image-conscious, most skilful, most brand-friendly players with the clubs in the biggest, most glamorous cities. The ensuing media coverage would guarantee the crowds, and so sponsorship revenue and a fat television deal would automatically follow. Celebrities and politicians would start to show their faces in the stands as sure as ticks on a stray dog. Your league might look like the Premier League, or the periodically mooted European Super League. It would look something like the top half of North America's first division in the late 1970s, a league that got too much right to ignore.

'In Britain there is certainly room for radical thought about a more modern approach to the needs of the fans, better communication,' wrote the *Sunday Mirror* journalist Ken Jones in the late 1970s. 'The United States will one day emerge as a major power in the soccer world. There is a lot to be done, a lot to learn, a long road to travel, but please send up a few fireworks along the way. Light the sky with your ambition, energy and initiative. Soccer needs America.'[2] In *The Observer*, Hugh McIlvanney also pleaded the US case: 'It would be foolish to look upon soccer in the US as a sort of threat,' he wrote in 1977, 'when it might so easily provide a marvellous infusion of freshness. Given the present condition of British football, we should be the last people to take an excessively didactic attitude about what is happening here.'[3]

These were rare positive voices to be heard about US soccer in the supercilious European media. They recognized the potential in America's verve and hunger, and the fact that Europe badly needed a few 'fireworks' up its backside to liven up its act. Such perspectives have been lost in the standard narrative of the NASL as a failure, or through contemporary assessments by the likes of the *Guardian*'s David Lacey, who dismissed the NASL as 'a glossy but third rate competition'.[4] Like Elvis, though, the NASL only *ended up* a failure – there was plenty of good and influential material long before the Vegas years and the body found in the bathtub.

In the quick-fire, instant-image era of the internet, there's a standard photograph that tends to turn up whenever there's a discussion about the NASL – a picture of the shirts worn by the Colorado Caribous during the 1978 season, the ones with the leather cowboy fringe all the way across the chest. Ha ha, *that's* how stupid the NASL was. Remember, the league that beat its chest in the 1970s and told the world to watch out, then crashed like Lynyrd Skynyrd's private jet? What's missing from that facile summation is the *life* of the North American Soccer League, and its crucial role for both US and world soccer beyond the 1970s. The stories of the myriad players who moved thousands of miles to start up a brave new league at a time when most players stayed firmly put in their home countries. What it was like to play with and against Eusebio and Pelé, or to share a dressing room with a domineering character like Johan Cruyff. What it meant to be thrown into a world of six-lane highways, five-hour flights to away games, and to take to the field on the back of an elephant while trying to remember the instructions you'd only half understood from your Yugoslavian coach. Then, after the game, you'd get to meet a famous rock star. 'People assume that my greatest thrill last year was winning the [NASL] championship,' said the New York Cosmos' young English midfielder Steve Hunt in 1978. 'They're wrong. It was meeting Mick Jagger.'[5]

The NASL introduced the idea that a soccer game could be an event and a spectacle, not just two teams meeting to compete for points. You weren't herded into the stadium by policemen waving wooden batons. You were a customer, not a criminal or a public nuisance. You arrived at the stadium two or three hours early to grill hot dogs and chug down beer with your mates in the car park while listening to a ramped-up radio. Then, well refreshed and whooping in that way unique to hyper-enthusiastic US sports fans, you'd enter a newly constructed, futuristic, multi-purpose stadium – the same impressive dome where the city's baseball and American football teams played. The players were introduced by name and were greeted with raucous music and dancing girls as they ran out on to the field, one by one, waving to the crowd. There might be a soul star singing 'The Star-Spangled Banner' (Lou Rawls was a regular part of the NASL's pre-game routine) before the cheerleaders raised their well-honed legs in formation, some rockets decorated the night sky, and the match ball would descend in the arms of a man with a parachute on his back, dressed up as a clown. Manufactured atmosphere, some might argue. Others might argue in return, innovative marketing techniques aimed at wooing a new generation of sports fan.

Once the game started you could watch a version of soccer easily recognizable as the real thing, but which promoted scoring, played down defensive duties, and refuted the virtues of a hard-fought 1–1 draw. That's why the NASL instigated the shootout – not because drawn games were 'un-American', but because they were unsatisfactory to a US crowd. Why bother going to a game if neither side was going to win? Why deny the fans that moment of climactic glory or crushing disappointment? Then if a cheerleader congratulated the biggest name on the soccer planet with a kiss after he won the game with a coolly taken shootout conversion ... hey, relax dude, that's just how we roll with the game here.

Woosnam and the NASL had the courage to initiate a new way forward for the game. It took two decades for the rest of the world to embrace, but then the biggest soccer leagues on the planet became an extension of what the NASL had begun. The redevelopment of European club soccer owes a substantial debt to what is commonly disdained as North America's farcical, hubristic attempt to found its own national league. During the NASL years, television revenue became an indicator of a league's health. The League abolished the price ceilings for what players could earn. For better and worse, it revolutionized the idea of what a soccer club could be. It played games in modern, all-seater stadiums. In the Cosmos, it created an all-conquering giant that everyone loved to hate. In an era of bleakness, austerity and violence in Europe, it found a way to make professional soccer fun. That it took FIFA, UEFA and the biggest European leagues so long to catch up demonstrates just how out of touch they were. The NASL at its brief peak might have been a product of the brash, loud and shameless 70s, but then and now it's the league of the future.

1 Atlanta, 'Champions of England'

'America? They can't play the bloody game over there!'
—Ron Newman, future NASL coach, in 1967.

The front-page, capitalized headline on the *Birmingham Evening Mail* was unequivocal: US CLUB WANTS TO BUY VILLA.[1] This was almost 40 years before Randy Lerner took over the Birmingham club in 2006, when the interest of American millionaires in English top-flight clubs was no longer quite so shocking. In November 1968, however, it was beyond radical. England were world champions, and the only foreign players in English soccer were from Scotland, Ireland and Wales. The Americans did not even play the game, did they?

In Atlanta, they did. By the time of the *Mail*'s headline, the Atlanta Chiefs had been playing it for two whole years. Only that summer they had taken on the English league champions, Manchester City. They had the backing of the Atlanta Braves baseball team, making them, in the words of *Mail* reporter Dennis Shaw, 'the wealthy American soccer club'. And it quoted the team's chief executive Dick Cecil as saying 'we would only be interested in taking full control', stressing that the organization had 'vast financial resources'. Villa, struggling for cash, were certainly interested enough to open talks.

Mr Cecil was asked by the newspaper, somewhat understatedly, if he didn't think that US control of an English soccer team 'would raise eyebrows', to which Cecil responded puckishly, 'Rather like our taking over the *Queen Mary**.' However, he stressed that the team would still be English-run. 'We would not expect to come over with a boatload of Americans and think we had all the answers to English football. We think we would have something to offer by American methods in some spheres. Remember we are businessmen. We would not want to be regarded as a lot of American millionaires coming in to throw money around unwisely.'

The takeover never happened, possibly because it was 30 years too early, and because Villa eventually found other sources of money more comfortably close to home. In the late 1960s, the English league was not ready for American businessmen with fancy new ideas about making money out of soccer. In England, there were still some vestiges of the Corinthian ideal, although any rejection of American business values probably stemmed more from a parochial distaste for the upfront approach of the brazen Yanks. We'll take old money, but not new. Meanwhile, the game was there to be played, not exploited, and it was backed by almost a century of tradition. If a team was having money troubles, it would get through somehow. Glorious old teams like Aston Villa would not be allowed to die overnight.

Dick Cecil will only give a knowing smile when asked today if the Chiefs were making a realistic bid for Villa. At a time when the fledgling US game was looking for every chance to make itself public in a bid to sell soccer, the headline alone could be counted as a great result (he later told the *Daily Mail*,

---

* UK transatlantic passenger ship that had been retired the previous year to Long Beach, California, to become a hotel, restaurant and tourist attraction, a victim of the aviation age.

'A link with Aston Villa would have given soccer in America tremendous impetus'). In 1968, with the backing of baseball cash and the optimism of Phil Woosnam, Villa's under-rated Welsh forward who was nearing the end of his career, Atlanta was the pioneer in an ambitious drive to permanently alter the American sporting landscape. In England, foreign ownership was too much, too soon. In the United States, change was a constant, and its limits were unknown.

English champions, bad losers

Manchester City's assistant manager Malcolm Allison didn't take his team's defeat to Atlanta well. Prior to the game on 27 May 1968, he had been sanguine, while the local media touted City as champions of England and thus possibly the best team in the world – a deductive leap that, in the name of publicity, few in either camp would have bothered to dispute. 'The stadium is a beautiful facility and the pitch is fine with us,' Allison said.[2] 'It won't make a bit of difference to us playing on part of a baseball infield. It'll be just like playing on a frozen field in England. And we've played in all kinds of conditions.' He even pre-empted excuses about City struggling after a long, hard season, because it just meant 'we really don't need that much practice'.

His players were more cautious. Tony Book, looking back at an already demanding tour (City had so far played and drawn with Dunfermline Athletic, twice, in Toronto and New Britain, and then beaten the Rochester Lancers 4–0) conceded that 'the team is a little tired, since we've had to really play in these games. It seems everyone wants to beat us.' With City missing some key players on international duty, the game could be a close one. Should that happen, he added, 'it could be a great thing for soccer. It would be great for the game, because everyone back home and over the world is watching soccer in America. And we all want it to succeed here.'[3]

Book's comments reflect that City, to their huge credit, willingly co-operated in selling the exhibition game to the Atlanta public, arriving in the city a few days in advance, showing up at various banquets and receptions in their honour, and generally doing their part to talk up the coming game and soccer in general. In spite of the rigours of a demanding tour at the end of a long and extremely successful English season, manager Joe Mercer at least gave the impression that his side was taking it all seriously enough. 'Although we don't quite know what to expect, you can bet we won't be complacent,' he said.[4] 'I haven't seen the Chiefs play, but I do know some of their players and what their capabilities are.' Francis Lee also cautioned that 'they just might give us a pleasant, or unpleasant, surprise.'[5]

Pleasantly, or unpleasantly, City lost 3–2 in front of 23,000 raucous fans, and Allison's reaction was far from gracious. 'They couldn't play in the Fourth Division in England,' he said.[6] 'The boy that kicked the last goal was offside too. They played well. We played poorly. It's as simple as that. It happens sometimes in England. The Third and Fourth Division sides come up and beat the First and Second Division teams. They just want the game more. The Chiefs had more to gain tonight than we did. We played like we didn't really want to win the match.'

The game itself, though, was a proper contest, and in spite of the purportedly offside third goal, City keeper Ken Mulhearn conceded that his team's penalty goal through

Francis Lee should probably not have been given either. 'I was surprised,' he said. 'I really didn't think they would be that fast. I knew they had the soccer skills, but the speed surprised me.' He compared Atlanta with the better teams from the English Second Division.

What also surprised the local media was the passion of the crowd as they reacted to the home side's comeback from an early goal scored by City's Tony Coleman. 'The play on both sides was brilliant, fierce and fiery,' wrote the *Atlanta Constitution*. 'The Chiefs opened with every intent on winning and hammered at the British goal on numerous occasions.' They equalized through Englishman Graham Newton – a former bit-part player with Walsall, Coventry and Bournemouth – then hit late goals through Kaizer Motaung (who later returned to his native South Africa with the team's name to found the Kaizer Chiefs), and the Zambian Freddy Mwila – Allison's 'offside' goal. Lee's penalty in the 88th minute was too little, too late to prevent defeat.

Mercer's analysis was much more generous than Allison's. 'We were beaten fair and square on the night,' he said. 'We're going to Chicago next and somebody has got to catch out for it [the loss].' The Chiefs' player-coach Phil Woosnam exulted: 'The boys did it. They really played well together and it was a real team effort. They worked the ball well and really went after them.' He wasn't about to say anything too rash, though, being aware of the need to temper local expectations and the American penchant for hyperbole. 'We're not First Division now just because we won one game. That does not make us the world champs.'[7] Striker Ray Bloomfield, a former England Youth international who had been persuaded by Woosnam to move to Atlanta from Aston Villa, was moved to say, no matter what happened to soccer in the US now, 'I shall never forget tonight.'[8]

The local press, however, which thanks to Woosnam's tireless lobbying was giving the new team generous coverage in its sports pages, could see that this was a friendly game with some significance. Columnist Jesse Outlar wrote that the Chiefs 'attacked the Marvels* as though the World Cup were at stake, instead of a mere exhibition score. When it was over, excited boosters [fans] mobbed the Chiefs, proving that soccer is not only a highly emotional game in Latin America and London. Those 23,141 customers could not have cheered louder Monday night if the Braves had won the seventh game of the World Series.' For an American sportswriter, that really was the ultimate accolade.

The paper's most forthright columnist, Furman Bisher – a sporting version of H.L. Mencken whose views were rarely less than entertaining – wrote with some retrospective irony that the game 'was another fight for independence. Once again Our Side was the frontier and Manchester was the aggressor. We were the bush-league, Manchester the classic bully. We were the pitiful minority, Manchester the tyrant.' The win meant that 'our colonials still have a streak going, beginning with the Revolutionary War and carrying on down through the Ryder Cup, the Walker Cup, the Wightman Cup and the cup that runneth over.' Meanwhile, Eric Woodward wrote for a UK audience in *Football Monthly*, 'The score, 3–2, could not reflect the enthusiasm the game detonated among a crowd of 23,141 – at least two-thirds of whom were seeing professional soccer for the first time.' No one could now dispute that soccer would 'sweep the States' when a crowd of this size,

---

* The Atlanta press repeatedly referred to City as 'The Manchester Marvels'.

way above the League norm, 'literally abandoned their seats in this no-standing Atlanta Stadium to stand and yell themselves hoarse for 90 minutes ... The noise at times made Liverpool's Kop sound like a cathedral choir in comparison.'[9] It should be noted, however, that the fulsome Woodward worked for the Chiefs as an administrator.

While Atlanta's burgeoning soccer community glowed, City left town to continue their long tour. They lost to Borussia Dortmund in Chicago, twice drew with Dunfermline *again*, in Vancouver and LA (both games ended 0–0, so they weren't making soccer converts at every stop), then went down 3–0 to the Oakland Clippers. Next it was on to Mexico, to play Atlante in the Aztec Stadium, but the game was cancelled because Atlante claimed that City had broken the terms of their contract, which stated that they were supposed to field their championship-winning team. Mercer told them this was physically impossible due to injuries and absences – the situation had become so bad that Allison had played in the second half in one of the Dunfermline friendlies, affording the entire bench the opportunity to hurl abuse at him in 'the true Allison style'[10] – and so the game never happened. A second game scheduled against another Mexican first division team, America, was also cancelled.

You'd think after a gruelling domestic season and eight games across North America, that would have been the cue to take a flight back to Manchester. The squad was threadbare, players were enduring games in pain, and they were missing two key men, Colin Bell and Mike Summerbee, both off on international duty with the England team. Yet clearly something still rankled about that defeat in Atlanta. When the games in Mexico were cancelled, City called the Chiefs. Do you fancy a rematch? With the chance of another gate four times above their home average, Atlanta were more than happy to oblige and host the English champions a second time. The rematch was set for 15 June. They had nothing to lose, and plenty of publicity to gain.

Unwanted twins – the NASL's painful birth

> 'It was the late 60s, the Vietnam war was wind-
> ing down, there was a lot of rebellion, a lot of
> "we want to do things differently", the long hair
> – well, soccer fit that trend.'
>
> —Dick Cecil, former Chief Executive,
> Atlanta Chiefs[11]

It's not enough to state that the Atlanta Chiefs were a North American professional soccer team in their second year of existence, because that very existence was both extraordinary and precarious. Although the Chiefs were backed by the wealth of the Atlanta Braves and their owners, professional soccer's new start in the US had already almost choked to an embarrassing, early death. A few months after the Manchester City games, it would almost do so again. Its survival on both occasions owed much to Atlanta, a city in the state of Georgia that is twice the size of Scotland, but where in the mid-1960s a total of six private schools played soccer prior to the founding of the Chiefs.

Professional soccer's presence in the USA was to some extent fortuitous. The live transmission of the 1966 World Cup final had accelerated the imaginations of several wealthy men who had made money out of sport, and who for some time had been considering the formation of a professional, nationwide soccer league. This was in part thanks to the economically favourable climate of the 1960s, and also because several European teams touring the US in the previous decade had pulled in large crowds for one-off friendlies that gave a deceptive picture of the country's level of soccer interest. The United States Soccer Football Association (USSFA – and from 1974 shortened to the United States Soccer Federation/USSF) was also interested in the idea of a coast-to-coast pro league, and let it be known that it was ready to listen to proposals. The putative owners were not sentimental about American sporting tradition, and did not care about creating a new rival to baseball or American football – if there was space for a viable new sport, they would be happy to exploit it. The baseball owners like those of the Braves, for example, had new, multipurpose stadiums that needed more teams and events, and if soccer was going to fill an empty date on the calendar and bring in cash, there was no American businessman or woman alive who was going to get wet-cheeked about stagnating baseball gates and the thought of fewer dads taking their sons to the ball game for peanuts and crackerjack.

Basketball and ice hockey were, in the mid-1960s, not yet firmly established in the US, while even baseball, the generally accepted 'national pastime', was sensitive to the 'threat' in advance of professional soccer's nationwide return to the US (the first attempt, in the 1930s, had foundered due to administrative factionalism, geographical distances, and the advent of the Great Depression).[12] Perhaps baseball commissioner William Eckert was so defensive because many young fans at this time were eschewing his sport on the fairly reasonable grounds that it was boring compared with American football.

When anything happened to affect baseball's position, he stated, 'I am naturally concerned and will look into it.' Eckert opposed soccer due to potential damage to the field; 'conflict of interest and possible anti-trust implications'; the dilution of baseball promotion 'by efforts to sell a new sport during the baseball season'; and finally, as a sort of catch-all whinge that got to the real point, 'financial damage to baseball as a whole'.[13] This combination of pseudo-threatening waffle and statutory objections ignored the guiding business principles of all those who invested in North American sports teams, which were – as outlined by Eric Midwinter in his 1986 analysis of sport's over-commercialization, *Fair Game* – that teams are located in cities 'with the same calculating eye to profit as might attend the decision to site a supermarket in an acceptable catchment area'.[14] When it doesn't work, the supermarket is shut down or relocated.

Dick Cecil, the man behind the Villa takeover talks, remembers the day he saw England versus West Germany, two months after interested owners of the possible National Professional Soccer League (NPSL) had met for the first time at the New York Athletic Club. While for many Englishmen the match would have been the culmination of a lifetime's devotion to soccer, it was Cecil's first ever glimpse of the game. 'We had a baseball game,' he recalls. 'We turned on the TV and the players started watching the game. It probably had more word of mouth reaction than any game I'd ever seen to that point. People were calling people and saying, "Are you watching this game? It's a hell of a game."' There were lots of goals, and 100,000 people in a stadium, and the game was being broadcast around the world. It's easy to see how that might have been seductive to businessmen used to making money out of sport.

Writer Chuck Cascio put it succinctly in his 1975 book *Soccer USA*. 'Bucks. That's what did it,' he wrote. 'Thoughts of millions of green bucks were generated by the 1966 World Cup games in England, and before you could say "Pelé", three new professional American soccer leagues were formed.'[15] American media coverage widely quoted the large amounts of revenue generated by the healthy attendances at the tournament's games, and these were perhaps interpreted out of context. The world's best players at the time – Pelé, Eusebio, Bobby Moore, Bobby Charlton and the emerging Franz Beckenbauer – had all been captured in one place, in a country where soccer was the overwhelmingly established national game. While their nose for business had no doubt made men like Lamar Hunt, Jack Kent Cooke, William Clay Ford and William Randolph Hearst II comfortably rich and more, their missing sense for what placed a love of sport in people's hearts led them down a dark alley where they promptly got mugged.

The three gestating pro leagues were chiselled quickly down to two before a ball was kicked, but that was still one league too many. The NPSL, including the Atlanta Chiefs, was a 'proper' league, in the sense that all its teams recruited their own professional players. The United Soccer Association (USA – only a cynic would say this was a crass marketing appeal to patriotic sentiment), caught on the hop by the NPSL's announcement that it would start play in 1967, decided that it could not afford to start one year later in 1968, so hastily supplanted entire professional teams from various European and South American cities to selected North American locations to play out a twelve-game season, followed by a championship final. At best, the teams could be termed second choice for what now looks like a prototype World Club Championship.

Participants included Stoke City (the Cleveland Stokers), Wolverhampton Wanderers (the LA Wolves), Aberdeen (the Washington Whips) and Dundee United (Dallas Tornado – well, at least they both begin with a 'D'). Without very much rhyme or reason, Uruguay's Montevideo became the New York Skyliners, Bangu of Brazil camped in Houston, Texas, while Cagliari masqueraded as the Chicago Mustangs.

To call it a United States professional soccer league is giving the USA way too much credence. It was an extended summer tournament for randomly available and not especially famous clubs, which just happened to be played in the US. Although, when you watch the highlights of the LA Wolves beating the Washington Whips 6–5 in the final in LA, there's little doubt that the teams were, by then, taking it seriously. A final's a final, after all. Never mind that an eleven-goal game in Britain would have immediately raised suspicions of a fix.

Yet on the recommendation of the USSFA, FIFA had sanctioned the USA, not the NPSL, which became now, by a process of elimination, an 'outlaw' league unrecognized by soccer's international governing body. To render even more absurd the landscape of the brave new soccer world, it was the internationally ostracized NPSL that managed to secure a ten-year national television contract with the Columbia Broadcasting System (CBS), albeit a contract with numerous get-out clauses for CBS if soccer didn't attract enough viewers.

'Jobs for the boys'

Why did the USSFA choose the imported league? In short, money (again). The USSFA wanted to charge each team in any new and officially recognized professional league a $25,000 fee (the previous fixed fee for teams at any level of US soccer was just $25), and also to take a share of gate receipts (5 per cent) and TV money (25 per cent). The NPSL said no way, while the USA, led by Jack Kent Cooke, said yes. 'Jobs for the boys' was seemingly another factor. In late 1966, the NPSL hired the former secretary of the Scottish FA, Sir George Graham, to come over and help them get started, and in a letter home to 'my dear Willie' (a William Gallagher, role unspecified, but possibly a former colleague at the SFA) Sir George opines that when two separate groups showed an interest in starting a professional league, the USSFA 'thought they saw a real chance to pick up a stack of dollars for nothing!' When Kent Cooke's USA agreed to the USSFA's terms, 'the immediate result was that two of the leading USSFA negotiators, both of them past presidents, became associated with this Cooke group [the USA], one of them as president, the other as "legal advisor", with his son also connected with them.' However, because the NPSL didn't then slip away and die as expected, 'today things here are in a most dreadful mess'. Graham wrote that he was brought over to the US to negotiate between the two parties, but that the NPSL now wouldn't negotiate with the USSFA because they 'cheated us, they lied to us, they misled us, and we have no faith whatsoever in any dealings with them.'[16]

Both leagues had offices in downtown New York, and each had its own commissioner, remembers journalist Paul Gardner, who has been covering soccer in the US for over half a century. 'Anyone could have told them it wasn't going to work, but they [the businessmen and investors] weren't the sort of guys who were going to back down. They nearly ruined the whole thing before it got off the ground. The soccer was not good. Do I remember any outstanding games from that year? No.'[17] Another problem, he adds, was that the media had little idea of how to report the game. The journalists sent to cover games 'were low-level people, or being put out to grass, and the soccer beat ranked very low on the scale of desirable jobs in sports departments. That was [sports editor] Dick Young's threat to the young writers at the *Daily News* – "Get that right or I'll put you on soccer".' The revered English football journalist Brian Glanville was understandably sceptical.[18] 'We don't yet know whether there is room even for one soccer league in America,' he wrote in the *New York Times*. 'English managers like Harry Catterick of Everton and Ron Greenwood of West Ham, who've taken their clubs to the US, don't think so. But it is perfectly sure there is no room for two.'

As an employee of the Atlanta Braves, Dick Cecil had been charged with bringing teams and events into the Braves' new stadium. He flew to a meeting of interested baseball team representatives, businessmen and former politicians initiated by Bill Cox, the ex-owner of the Philadelphia Phillies who had been banned from baseball for life for betting on his own team. Together they formed the NPSL, and when the USA was sanctioned by FIFA, 'we decided to go ahead anyway,' says Cecil. 'We got the TV contract with CBS, which was a big blow to the other guys. We were just happy as hell because of CBS.'

Why did CBS choose to cover an unsanctioned league? 'I'm damned if I know,' he says. 'I think they looked at us like this – we were starting a league with real players and not with teams from abroad. The other league was rent-a-team. I didn't know who the hell FIFA was and I didn't care. I came out of an environment where you go sign players, and instead of the US we had the whole world to attack.' Presumably CBS didn't care who FIFA was either, setting a pattern of conflict with Zürich that would last for almost the next two decades.

Securing television rights was already seen as a key to any league's success in the US, well over two decades before the idea caught on in Europe that screens transmitting games directly to almost every home on the continent could generate masses of revenue for clubs and owners. Bill McPhail, vice-president for sports at CBS, said, 'Sure we're taking a risk. We don't think soccer will ever replace baseball or football. It may never catch on at all. But we've signed a long-term contract and I don't think we'll pull out unless it's absolutely a disaster.'[19]

Once the NPSL was formally founded, the next challenge was to start a league from scratch. The owners of the ten teams – four of which were in the same cities as USA teams – lured a number of foreign coaches to New York for interviews, and at this meeting the fate of the future NASL was decided. Phil Woosnam, an inside right with Orient, West Ham and Aston Villa (described by Villa and Atlanta teammate Ray Bloomfield as 'a midfield maestro, he was like a bloody spider. I didn't realize how good he was until I marked him in a game'[20]), talked to Dick Cecil, and the two men hit it off immediately. Cecil managed to persuade the St Louis franchise, which was about to hire Woosnam, that Atlanta, with its dearth of any kind of ethnic population, badly needed an English speaker as its coach. 'This was American football country,' says Cecil, 'and the first thing we made a philosophical decision on was that the head coach and the players had to speak English, because we had one hell of an educational process to go through.'

Woosnam agreed to come to Atlanta. He went back to England and found that he had been offered the chance to play for Chelsea, but decided to stick to his word, even though

23

he was yet to sign a contract and was venturing into uncharted soccer territory. Cecil says it was a fledgling sign of Woosnam's vision for soccer in the US that he turned down the chance to play for the London side. 'I think he really wanted to be the big fish. If he'd stayed in England, he'd just have been one of many. He was a very bright man, he excelled in math, he was educated, and he was ... I'm not sure he was liked by a lot of people, but he was respected by almost everybody.' Despite 'massive disagreements on a lot of things', because Woosnam wasn't realistic from a business point of view, the two men set about recruiting players from around the world.

Cecil gives the credit for putting the team together to Woosnam and his 'big resources' (that is, his huge network of contacts in the game), as well as his incredible work ethic. Letters sent to Cecil from Woosnam as he travelled around Africa and the UK recruiting players testify to his inexhaustible diligence and superb organizational skills. 'At long last mission accomplished,' he wrote to Cecil from Zambia at midnight on 12 December 1966. 'This afternoon Zambian government sanction officially confirmed and tonight players signed are Zoom [Samuel Ndhlovu], Emment [Kapengwe] and Howard [Mwikuta].' Then he was leaving for Nairobi to sign another Zambian, Freddy Mwila, before heading to Ghana to contact another player, and then 'we will be meeting British players in England on Sunday 18th.'[21]

Woosnam was joined on the team by midfielder Vic Crowe, who had been a Welsh international and Villa teammate. They also signed Peter McParland, a prolific goalscorer for Villa in the late 1950s who had netted five of Northern Ireland's six goals at the 1958 World Cup (one fewer than Pelé got at his breakout tournament). McParland calls his move to Atlanta 'an exciting sort of time at the end of my career. I felt like I had the knowhow to help build up the League and my team. They didn't have to sell it to me. There was nothing like going out there to take a look – I decided straight away.'[22] Ray Bloomfield remembers that 'Phil took a lot of younger players he knew had talent – a mixture. The reason I went with Phil was that he said the NASL was going to be the biggest thing in the world, that I'd be playing with Bobby Moore and Geoff Hurst. Phil genuinely believed it. I thought it would enhance my career.'[23]

Another important recruit for the League's future was Ron Newman*, who two years later ended up exporting Woosnam's missionary zeal in Atlanta to Dallas, where he became coach of the Tornado. Fresh off the plane in 1967, he says that he was impressed by how 'everything was new. Everything was huge.' Had he been sold on the idea of spreading the soccer gospel to the US heartlands? He admits that it may have been something else that swayed him when he met the Braves' baseball representatives at a hotel in London. 'We had lobster,' Newman says. 'I'd never had lobster before, we couldn't afford that.'[24]

Woosnam's three Zambians ('Zoom' never made it) were joined by Willie Evans from Ghana. Two Jamaicans, a Trinidadian and a Swede joined various Welsh- and Englishmen, who were all treated very well and moved into apartment buildings in Williamsburg Village, according to McParland. 'They were excellent players,' says McParland of the Zambians Kapengwe and Mwila. 'We had a decent standard of players – they didn't go for the top men, they went for a

---

* Newman became the only NASL coach to win the Coach of the Year award more than once. In fact, he won it three times: 1971 (Dallas), 1977 (Fort Lauderdale), and 1984 (San Diego).

standard they wanted to try and work on, and build up from. I thought it was quite decent in the first season and in the second season they improved. In the second season in 1968 we [the Chiefs] won the whole thing' (the Oakland Clippers, a team made up chiefly of Yugoslavs and Costa Ricans, had won the sole NPSL title in 1967).

By that second season, though, neither the USA nor the NPSL existed. Seeing sense and, more to the point, seeing how much money they were losing, the leagues began merger talks before the 1967 season was even over. Before the start of the 67 season, one of the Braves' owners, Bill Bartholomay, had said that the NPSL did not 'foresee a battle between the two leagues.'[25] *Atlanta Journal* writer Bob Hertzel wrote in the same article: 'Both leagues are run by responsible people, on sound financial footing and there is a good possibility of a merger in the future. Bartholomay, however, stated that he hoped both leagues would be able to continue to operate, profitably, on their own.'

This was dreamy thinking, or bluff. Crowds for both leagues in 1967 were mediocre. In the traditional soccer stronghold of St Louis, an impressive 21,000 showed for the Stars' first home game against Oakland. After that, it drew around 5,000–7,000 for most games. Elsewhere, the picture was similar, with gates of roughly 3,000–6,000 for most teams, except in Chicago, where the recruitment of some Poles and Germans to appeal to local ethnic groups was a risible failure – three times the team pulled in paltry three-figure crowds at massive Soldier Field, while many low-scoring games reflected a game far removed from the thrills and atmosphere of the 1966 World Cup final. Not even the radical points system devised by Woosnam and Cecil – six points for a win, three for a draw, and a bonus point for every goal scored up to three – was yet having a noticeable effect on the kind of positive play it was deemed would attract Americans used to higher scoring sports. 'I don't think it failed,' says Cecil in defence of the system. 'We accomplished an increase in scoring, though not to the degree we wanted – we didn't get many 6–5 games, but we got people going after the three goals.'[26]

'Building a toilet in the desert'

The print press, however, was being generous to the new game. Even Furman Bisher, described by Dick Cecil as 'a curmudgeon', and who had the previous year derisively referred to the city's new soccer team as the Atlanta Kickapoos, was happy to give them a chance. Woosnam had taken Bisher and several other reporters over to England to watch a League Cup semi-final between West Ham United and West Bromwich Albion at Upton Park in February of 1967, and judging by the thoughtful columns that followed, it must have worked. The *Atlanta Constitution* sports editor Jesse Outlar wrote of the 2–2 second leg that 'Soccer is action-crammed from the first whistle to the final second. Any sport with as much movement as soccer should prove popular in the United States once the public is exposed to such players as Bobby Moore and Geoff Hurst.' He was also astonished at the match-day squad of twelve players, with only a single sub, and he vouched for the fact that soccer is a contact sport and that players must be 'in top physical condition'.[27] A month earlier, Bisher had conceded that soccer was indeed coming, even though he wrote that playing the sport in Atlanta was like 'building a restroom in the middle of the desert.'[28]

When the Chiefs played their first game, a 3–2 friendly win over the Baltimore Bays, Jim Minter of the *Atlanta Journal* wrote that soccer was 'a tremendous game, which at first view one is tempted to describe as more exciting even than basketball, baseball or football.' Would America accept it? 'It's difficult to see how it can miss,' said Minter. 'The pace is compelling, it is easy to watch and understand, and it creates a place for the little man, rapidly being pushed out in football and basketball, and to an extent in baseball.'[29]

The players and coaches who taught the unsuspecting Americans about the virtues of this new sport they were getting, like it or not, made the issue of size one of several simple talking points to stress that soccer was a democratic sport. Anyone could play it, unlike basketball (mainly tall), American football (the larger the better), or hockey (tough). Unlike football, baseball and hockey, you didn't need tons of expensive equipment. Girls and women could play it too – even though, at this point in soccer's history, female participation was woefully low around the rest of the world. All you needed was the basic equipment. Although, as Ron Newman found out, even getting a ball and goalposts was a challenge. Having told his eight-year-old son, who had been distraught at moving to a non-soccer country, that he could form his own youth league, Newman found himself faced with more enthusiasm than he'd expected, and had to follow through.

'I'd worked five or six years in the docks as an apprentice and so I was a carpenter,' says Newman. 'I used to joke that there had been two very important carpenters in history – Jesus Christ and me. So I got the job of making a set of goalposts, because there were no goals. I made the goals, and Saturday morning came around, but somebody had ripped the goalposts down and broken them into bits. Anyway, we hammered in two goals in the end without a crossbar, but that was the start of my exploits in seeing what had to be done in a country like the US. There was nothing there. Nothing. But after a year things got bigger and more kids came around – it grew and grew and grew. So when I left [Atlanta] for Dallas after a couple of years I handed it over to the YMCA and they started the Summer Soccer League.'[30] The YMCA is still the largest youth soccer league in the Atlanta area.

Newman and all his teammates were sent out by Woosnam to schools across the greater Atlanta metropolitan area as part of their brief to promote the game. In 1967, 12,000 school-children went through the Chiefs' soccer clinics, while 42 area high schools had begun to play the game,[31] though there were plenty of misunderstandings along the way. One teacher, recalls Newman, was eager to know how they managed to stay upright on the ice. A clinic Newman did at Atlanta's Farm Prison was so successful that Woosnam sent the whole team back there for a game. 'They marked out a field on the exercise yard,' says Newman. 'We got changed and I'm walking across the exercise yard and all these prisoners recognized me, and my teammates didn't realize that I'd been there before, so all these hoodlums are greeting me: "Hey Ron, buddy, great to see you again, how are you doing?" So all my teammates thought I'd been in jail before. But that kind of visit got us a lot of publicity.'

While all this activity was slowly alerting the natives to soccer's creeping presence, the NPSL and the USA continued to talk. The need to form a single league was hastened by the English Football Association's announcement in October 1967 that it would ban for one year any of its players who appeared in the NPSL, because that league was unsanctioned by FIFA. Woosnam, who had committed himself to another year in Atlanta, and who was openly conceding that the survival of both leagues depended on a merger, observed that if other countries followed the FA's lead, 'it practically brings to a standstill our recruiting of players in other countries.' He said the NPSL had been called 'rebels, outlaws. We're undesirable characters ... and the names have stuck a little bit.' It would become a familiar feeling for the future League Commissioner throughout the 1970s.[32]

By the end of the year, though, the NPSL had settled with FIFA out of court after maintaining that FIFA's non-recognition of the NPSL was illegal under the Sherman Antitrust Act.* 'What we'll get is recognition by the USSFA and, through them, FIFA,' said Cecil, adding that 'this opens the door to the total development of amateur and professional soccer in the United States.' One month later, the English FA rescinded its threat to ban players who had played in the NPSL, and the two leagues settled on a merger, ending up with seventeen teams for the 1968 season in the newly named North American Soccer League. Some cities with two teams had one removed elsewhere (one Chicago team moved to Kansas City and one LA team went to San Diego), while the New York Skyliners and Toronto City folded to leave space for the Generals and the Falcons respectively. Less satisfactorily, though, the merged league continued with joint commissioners, Dick Walsh of the defunct USA and Kenneth Macker of the equally extinct NPSL. Clearly, there was still a reluctance to let go of their thoroughly flawed creations.

---

* For more on the NPSL's historic, hysterical encounter in Zürich with a volatile Sir Stanley Rous, see Chapter 7.

While Walsh was claiming, 'I don't see any weak franchises' in the nine-team Eastern Conference,[33] in Atlanta the financial news was sobering for the Chiefs' paymasters at the Atlanta Braves, even as they continued to espouse their faith in soccer's long-term future. Furman Bisher reported that the Braves' $480,053 net income for 1967 was $300,000 lower because of the Chiefs. But the feisty columnist had clearly warmed to Woosnam, whom he called 'such an honest, sincere, devoted man that you would like to see him succeed, provided that we can prevent mayhem, rioting and mass murder.'[34] Yet the 1968 season began inauspiciously when games on the second weekend of the season – the home opener for half the League's teams – were cancelled due to the assassination of Dr Martin Luther King Jr. Chicago pulled in just 336 fans for an early game against Atlanta. Broadly, the gates were much as before, across the four-figure range. Even an 11,000 opening night crowd for Atlanta in a 2–1 win over Detroit was declared a let-down by Woosnam, who had written a column in the *Atlanta Journal* before the season urging Atlanta to become a true global city by embracing the one 'worldwide' sport.[35] Following the Detroit game, he said, 'I think there is more soccer interest in Atlanta than that. I was sure the quality of our play would warrant a bigger crowd.'[36] It seems the perennial optimist had been hoping for 20,000 people, but this disappointment was nothing compared with the Houston game the following month – a rainy night saw the gate slump to just over 2,000 as the Chiefs won 3–1 and took the Conference lead. A week later they tried a double-header with the Braves, but the baseball crowd was 15,202 compared with 3,880 for the Chiefs. 'The big crowd picked the wrong game,' wrote the increasingly sympathetic Furman

Bisher.[37] The Chiefs had won 4–1, while the Braves had been beaten by the LA Dodgers.

Even just six weeks into the first NASL season, co-commissioner Walsh was already finding it hard to talk up the League's financial state in the face of poor crowds. 'Everybody is going to take a hard look at it [the overall situation] at the end of the year,' he said. 'Nobody expected to finish in the black this year, yet there is nobody that is shaky at this stage.' Bill Bartholomay maintained that 'the League is still suffering merger pains ... but they will heal in time.' Nonetheless, the *Atlanta Journal* pointed out that the Chiefs' break-even gate of 15,000 was 'now negative', and that many were openly saying that the Chiefs 'could be something of an albatross around the Braves' necks.'[38]

Then, for diversion, Manchester City came to town. They lost, they left, and, as previously noted, the reigning English league champions decided to come back again for a second attempt to beat the Chiefs.

Sky Blue thinking – 'We'll get them this time'

> 'The first time we played them, we had something to prove. Now they feel like they do. We feel like we have even more to prove this time. We have beaten them once, now, to see if we can do it again.'
>
> —Phil Woosnam[39]

City's return to Atlanta was a publicity godsend to the Chiefs. They had beaten the best team from the country of soccer's soul, its home and its heartland, and now that team was coming back for revenge. Looked at soberly, it was merely a final game on a meaningless summer tour before the serious business of a new English season and the challenge of the European Champions Cup. If you wanted to enter into the spirit of the challenge, though (and why wouldn't you? What's the point of sport otherwise?), you could look at this as a dramatic face-off between an emerging club from the potentially global powerhouse of the sport's future, and the benchmark of the game's quality and tradition from the oldest running domestic league of all. If City didn't care, why were they here? And why were they so vocal ahead of the second game?

'We intend to go home on a happy note, and that is one of the reasons we will be coming to Atlanta early,' said Joe Mercer.[40] Malcolm Allison generously upgraded the Chiefs from his earlier derogatory 'Fourth Division' assessment to a 'good Third Division side. But we do want to redeem ourselves a bit for the first game.'[41] A few days later, he added, 'We didn't run in the last game like we should have. We'll run better this time, I assure you. The last time, we practised in the daytime. This time, we're practising at night and are being a little stricter with the boys. We want to go home on a successful note.'[42] More provocative was a guest column in the *Atlanta Journal* entitled 'Manchester City Will Massacre Chiefs' by the deputy sports editor of the *Manchester Evening News,* George Dowson. 'You will need more than a posse of Minutemen to help stem the tide of revenge and dented pride that will come hurtling down on the Chiefs' goal,' wrote Dowson from the safety of Lancashire.[43] 'I say now that City will not only beat the Chiefs, they will massacre them.' City fans, he wrote, were 'not only angry that their team has been beaten, but that their heroes should fall to opponents they consider should not even be on the same field.' When the result of the first game had come through to the newspaper's office, he added, 'we had the audacity to query it. The result should have read: Atlanta 3 City 12.' Dowson forecast that City would win by three, four or even five goals. Francis Lee was just as confident, blithely predicting that, 'we should get four or five goals, I think.'

It's difficult to tell how much of this was genuine hubris, and how much it was City gamely playing along with the pre-match hype. Did George Dowson really meet a lot of 'angry' City fans in the pubs and on the streets of Manchester that summer? For the Chiefs, though, there's no question that Allison's remark about their place in the English pyramid rankled, as several of those involved still recall his quote almost half a century later. Phil Woosnam tried to look at it with his mathematical sense of logic: 'It's really not a question of whether we're First Division, or Fourth Division or Sixth Division,' he said. 'We beat them, we outplayed them. Certainly they didn't have three of their better players, but then that simply means that we're only three players away from being the best team in England, doesn't it?' Welsh goalkeeper Vic Rouse reiterated that Allison's statement 'was just sour grapes. After all, what did he build a champion out of? I'll tell you what, Fourth Division players.' Atlanta's English defender John Cocking, who had come from amateur soccer, warned that 'they had better thrash us this time, or everyone will know for sure how close we are to them in calibre.'[44]

The trash talk did its job and an even bigger crowd than before, of 25,000, showed up for the return game. There had been reports in the Atlanta media that City had sent for their stars, so badly did they want to win, but in truth neither Colin Bell nor Mike Summerbee came out to join their team. Mike

Doyle, who had been missing from the US tour while on duty with the England Under-23s, had in fact flown over for the previous game with the Oakland Clippers, only to be sent off after eighteen minutes for arguing with the referee about an earlier red card for his teammate Tony Coleman. Playing with only nine men, City had held out until close to the finish. City's official brochure, titled *We Are The Champions,* took the view that the Clippers, featuring eight Yugoslavs, had taken exception to physical contact and had 'retaliated by shirt-pulling and spitting'. And one of the Clippers' goals was scored when the Oakland centre forward had 'held [keeper] Ken Mulhearn in a head-lock.' So it wasn't just Malcolm Allison at the club who was inventive with post-match excuses.

There is surviving footage of the second Chiefs–City game, and the press reports of a loud crowd are not exaggerated. When the commentary stops for advertising breaks, but the film keeps running, you can hear the cheesy organ – which ruins so many ice hockey games in North America – attempting to incite an already animated crowd. The organ, however, is superfluous, as there is a huge roar every time the Chiefs win a tackle and launch an attack. In the early stages the game moved from end to end without either side discernibly dominating. Both teams had early goals disallowed for offside. There were a lot of long balls, and a lot of lost possession. Gradually, both teams started to get some shots on goal, and then in the 28th minute the Chiefs won a penalty, though it was not clear why. The TV commentator stated that a City player was 'detected holding as that cross pass was coming in from the side-lines by John Cocking'. Phil Woosnam would later counter City's objections to the kick by saying that the call was fine because Graham Newton was kicked in the forehead. In any case, Freddy Mwila converted the kick to give Atlanta a 1–0 lead. Mwila almost scored again five minutes later, forcing Mulhearn into a fine save low to his left, then a neat move between Stan Bowles and Francis Lee ended with the latter shooting straight at Chiefs' keeper Vic Rouse. Half-time: Chiefs 1 City 0.

Atlanta forward Peter McParland came into the game after half-time, and testifies that the City players were taking the game very seriously. 'I had trouble with the centre half – the captain Tony Book,' he recalls. 'He was very determined, and he was a bit aggressive, and I didn't like his approach. I warned him that I'd give him some back. It was Allison, the main man, that threw the challenge down for the second game. We were all out to try and turn them over, which we did. Book was hitting me, tackling me rather hard and whatever, and I didn't like his challenges, and I did give him a warning. He was trying to show he was the master and all that.'[45]

City equalized through Chris Jones on a pass from Harry Dowd, but the Chiefs regained the lead through their star South African Kaizer Motaung, who together with the Zambians Mwila and Kapengwe absolutely dominated the midfield and produced the game's best footballing moments. Woosnam came on as a substitute with 20 minutes to go and seemed to be enjoying himself too, combining well with McParland on several occasions and creating numerous chances for Kapengwe. As McParland hints, the game began to get very testy, and although City pushed forward again towards the end, the Chiefs continued to play with three up front, and most of the English champions' attacks broke down in and around the penalty area. One overwhelming characteristic of the game was that the Chiefs did most of the passing, while City resorted to the long ball. Much in the style of a lower-division English team, it might be said. Final score: Chiefs 2 City 1.

'I felt sorry for them that they were thrown into that situation with the challenge,' says McParland. 'We were determined to do well, so that was the main thing, that we were able to get a grip of them. It was nice to be able to beat an ex-manager – Vic [Crowe] and Phil [Woosnam] and myself had all worked with Joe Mercer.' Despite his tussles with Book, there was no animosity after the game, he says. 'We were real happy that we'd beaten them and had a little get-together with the City lads after the game at the stadium, and had a chat as they were going home the next day. It wasn't a case of smirking at them, it was just friendship.'[46]

Even after a second loss, Malcolm Allison avoided any kind of concession to his vanquishers. 'The referee's played a good game,' he said, referring to the Chiefs' penalty kick. Yes, he admitted, the Chiefs played better. However, 'we played better too. We play 42 games during the season. Let them play 42 games in all kinds of weather and then you can tell.' Asked if the Chiefs could play in English Division Two, Allison replied, 'If they could play a whole season in the Third Division and win it, then they might be able to play in the Second Division.' His pre-match claims that City would get four or five goals had been just to 'get the attendance up'.[47]

Two weeks later, *Manchester Evening News* columnist Dowson had the chance to appeal for clemency. 'I stand before you a chastened and much-enlightened man,' he wrote in a second guest column for the *Atlanta Journal*, after being swamped by letters and match report cuttings from Atlanta fans. 'It is evident that City were outplayed and that the Chiefs were worthy winners.' Having now joined the Chiefs' fan club, he then quoted Joe Mercer as saying, 'Without a doubt Atlanta is the most soccer-minded City in the US, and I must compliment everybody connected with the Chiefs for their enthusiasm and endeavour. I was immensely impressed with the way they are selling the game there, promoting it in such a spectacular manner.' But Mercer also said he would never again 'attempt such a long tour with such a tight schedule'.[48]

Indeed, with such a tiny, injury-hit squad, City's tour was sporting insanity. Losing or failing to win so many games had done little for their reputation back home, and while they were gone Manchester United had beaten Benfica in the European Cup final, hugely overshadowing City's feat of topping the first division the season before. 'After the game is before the game', as the German coach Sepp Herberger once observed. City returned home knackered and bruised, their jaunt a far cry from the revenue-generating, image-building summer US tours that their latter-day counterparts now undertake with a squad of 30 expensive, richly compensated internationals.

Dick Cecil is generous to City for playing along and, in the final analysis, as realistic as Malcolm Allison about the standard of his team. 'You know what summer tours are – half vacation, half play the younger players,' he says. 'They didn't bring their full team. And we beat them 2–1, which was as humiliating as hell for them. We were heady as hell about it, and then we played Santos and they beat us [5–2 – 'They took us apart,' says McParland]. We were probably Third or Fourth Division standard at the time, if that. Phil liked to think we were Third Division. The reason we drew so well was that the players spent so much time out in the community. They were out there being ambassadors for the game. Phil was so involved, he was truly the missionary for the game in this country.'[49]

Atlanta's midfielder Ray Bloomfield says, 'I know for a fact those [City] boys wanted to win that second game. I'm not saying we would have won the English league, but we could give anyone a game. I knew all those boys in that team.' Yet like Cecil, he concedes that the Santos game a couple of weeks later brought everyone back down to earth. 'That was the nucleus of the team that won the 1970 World Cup,' he says. 'They were on a different planet; there was no comparison between them and Manchester City.'[50]

'The League was dead'

Following their triumphs over City, the Chiefs became the first North American Soccer League champions in 1968, lifting the trophy after beating San Diego 3–0 in front of 15,000 home fans in the playoff final second leg. The League, however, almost croaked that winter, and was only saved by the industry of Woosnam, who was hastily appointed as the League's sole commissioner, working out of an office in the bowels of the Atlanta stadium with the help of former *Daily Express* journalist Clive Toye. Paul Gardner, not unkindly, calls them 'two guys who were too stupid to know what was going on, or were too devoted in the face of adversity',[51] but they saved the NASL from premature death after numerous owners pulled out, alarmed at their losses, the low average crowds of 3,400 in huge stadiums (20,000 was the average needed to break even), and suddenly unprepared to stay in soccer for even the medium term. The 1969 season kicked off with just five teams – Atlanta, Kansas City, Dallas, St Louis and Baltimore – and without a TV contract, after CBS too gave up due to poor ratings. One third of the season, eight games, was again played by representatives from England (Villa, West Ham, Wolves) and Scotland (Dundee United – back in Dallas – and Kilmarnock), with the 'real' teams taking over in early June for a sixteen-game league campaign, with no playoffs. For the third successive season, American professional soccer seemed to be starting from a base of nothing.

'The League was dead' at the end of 1968, says Cecil. Importing the English and Scottish clubs again was 'just to keep it alive. I'm not even sure why.' The following year Woosnam moved out of his stadium cubby-hole and into an office downtown. 'Phil's job was to find owners,' says Cecil, 'and he did a hell of a job; he kept the League going. We dropped out in 1973; we'd lost six million dollars by that point. That's not much by today's standards, but it was a million a year. But I think what the original Chiefs did was to set a model for the rest of the country. I helped put the Seattle Sounders together originally [in 1974], and the ownership group. Places like Portland and San Jose and other places that didn't have ethnic populations – we were the model. Ron Newman in Dallas too.'[52]

In the early 1970s the NASL kept its head down, gradually expanding its teams, its crowds and its coverage. The title changed hands season by season, reflecting a lack of stability and a high turnover of mainly low-profile players from the same British, eastern European, Caribbean and Central American countries, although St Louis was a rare exception in fielding teams largely made up of US players (manfully struggling on until it finally quit in 1977). According to Ray Bloomfield, who stayed with Atlanta until 1970, and then

played with the Dallas Tornado until 1973, there was a significant drop in the quality of play following the League's near
collapse at the end of 1968. 'In 1967 and 68 there wasn't a lot
of difference between us and the English teams,' he says. 'But
from 1969, when it went down to five teams and we all had
to work other jobs to make a living, it was semi-pro standard
until Phil built the League back up.'[53]

A sudden jump to fifteen teams in 1974 (from nine the
year before) had its basis in the drive of Woosnam's belief and
boundless optimism, and the doggedness of his blunt but
cheerful sidekick, Toye. To save money, many of its players
came on loan from those English Third and Fourth Divisions
derided by Malcolm Allison, and Paul Gardner agrees with
Bloomfield that this was reflected in the standard and style of
play. Yet over time not only Woosnam, but also Dallas owner
Lamar Hunt persuaded many rich friends and associates to
invest in teams where saner men would have turned their
backs and zipped their wallets. Hunt reputedly persuaded
construction bigwig Tom McCloskey, for example, to found
the Philadelphia Atoms when McCloskey hit him up for nine
tickets at the 1973 Super Bowl.

Other factors, according to NASL veteran and former
Liverpool player John Best, were the League's and the owners' stringent austerity measures, and the accumulation of
hard work on the part of the players, both on the field and in
the community. This, he says, resulted in 'a true expansion in
attendance, in general coverage, and in the presence of professional soccer. The players by then had gone out and made
many, many appearances both as individual players and as
whole teams.'[54]

The constitution of the ownership was also changing,

with sports entrepreneurs beginning to give way to major corporations. Following a chance encounter at the 1970 World Cup between Woosnam and Nesuhi Ertegun, a soccer-loving Turkish-American executive at Atlantic Records, the latter's parent company Warner Communications formed the New York Cosmos in 1971 and appointed Clive Toye as general manager. Not that anyone paid too much attention to this personnel move until four years later, when Toye, to the surprise, delight and consternation of various parties, succeeded in signing a three-time World Cup winner from Brazil named Edson Arantes do Nascimento.

Season-by-season overview

1967

The Yugoslav-dominated **Oakland Clippers** won the 'outlaw' ten-team National Professional Soccer League, beating the Baltimore Bays 4–2 over the course of a two-legged championship game. Crowds averaged less than 5,000, and though pay and conditions were good, and the standard of play was generally deemed to be quite decent, few virgin US soccer spectators would have known who or what they were watching. In the championship game of the twelve-team, FIFA-backed United Soccer Association, the LA Wolves (of Wolverhampton) beat the Washington Whips (of Aberdeen) 6–5 after extra time. Healthy five-figure crowds in Houston, where Bangu of Rio were pretending to be the Houston Stars, took the USA's average gate close to 8,000.

Fun facts: Cesar Menotti, who would coach Argentina to their 1978 World Cup title, scored four goals for the New York Generals in the NPSL. The USA's Dallas Tornado would stay in the same city with the same name until 1981 – the NASL's most durable team.

1968

The rival leagues merged to become the seventeen-team North American Soccer League. The Manchester City-conquering **Atlanta Chiefs** beat the San Diego Toros in a two-legged final to take the first championship, winning the second game 3–0 in front of a home gate of almost 15,000. When large, well-funded squads of foreign players were set against crowds far lower than expected (the average gate was just shy of 4,700), the resultant negative figures caused a dozen teams to fold at the end of the season.

Fun facts: The Dallas Tornado famously – and inexplicably – went on an extensive, months-long pre-season world tour. The team's almost exclusively European players were ordered to wear American cowboy gear in public, even though they had yet to set foot on US soil. Exhausted, they drew three and lost eighteen of their first 21 NASL games, and ultimately managed just two victories in the 32-game season.

1969

The **Kansas City Spurs** won the five-team single division (Baltimore, Dallas, Atlanta and St Louis were the other four), with no championship game.

Fun facts: Kansas City was represented by Wolves for the eight-game, pre-season 'international cup competition', which they topped as well, so they won a double, of sorts. Crowds were just as poor as for the international club games as they were for the regular NASL games, but when the Baltimore Bays (West Ham) beat the Dallas Tornado (Dundee United) 6–1, three World Cup winners got on the score sheet – Geoff Hurst, Bobby Moore (both future NASL players) and Martin Peters. Trevor Brooking grabbed a hat-trick.

1970

Six teams, made up of two divisions of three, with a two-leg championship game that saw the **Rochester Lancers**, in their first season, beat another newcomer, the Washington Darts, 4–3 on aggregate (Baltimore had folded).

Fun facts: the Lancers, despite being champions, got through three coaches this season, but were boosted by signing a trio of Ghanaians – Frank Odoi, Gladstone Ofori, and Yeo Kankam – for the run-in and the championship games. Rochester also topped the attendance league, though their average gate was only just below 5,000. Counted in the league standings for all teams were games against touring sides like Coventry City and Hertha Berlin.

1971

Eight teams, two groups of four – the new teams were Montreal, Toronto and the Cosmos, while Kansas City quit. The cost of a new franchise doubled to $25,000. The **Dallas Tornado** beat Atlanta in a three-game championship series.

Fun facts: Biggest gate of the season by a long shot was almost 20,000 for an early August Cosmos 3–2 home win over Rochester at Yankee Stadium. It also happened to be a double-header with Colombian champions Deportivo Cali playing Santos of Brazil, featuring the quite good Pelé ... League average gate: just over 4,000.

2 Pelé vs Eusebio: 'Hot property getting mobbed'

'I've been in the League for a long time and I can
remember when we used to play for a six pack.
Now it's different. You lose a game, and those
Warner Communications vice-presidents are
down there in the locker room, looking you over.'
—New York Cosmos goalkeeper Shep Messing[1]

When the dollar-packing founders of the North American
Soccer League looked at the brimming English stadiums of
the 1966 World Cup and translated those crowds of white,
male heads into a positive number at the bottom of a balance sheet, they were probably expecting to recreate the sights,
sounds and healthy numbers of that tournament within the
short time span demanded by eager capitalists seeking swift
returns on their down payments. Yet most of those vision-
challenged investors had long since given up the idea of making a fast buck out of soccer when, almost nine years later – at
Nickerson Field, a 12,500-capacity college stadium in New
England – anything that even remotely mirrored the 1966
World Cup came to pass in North America. When it did, no
one was ready, while the game itself – later annulled – ended in
a riot after the most famous player in the world scored a goal
and was mobbed by an enthusiastic but out-of-control crowd.
Under the protection of his quick-thinking bodyguards, Pelé
had to be stretchered from the field with a knee injury. Mostly
due to good luck, no one else was hurt.

The Boston Minutemen played the New York Cosmos in June 1975 shortly after both teams had signed players who were – almost beyond argument – the greatest players in the world. In the 1960s, that is. And more specifically, at the time of the 1966 World Cup, where a group game between Portugal and Brazil had represented the last time that Pelé (now of the New York Cosmos) had played against Eusebio (now of the Boston Minutemen) in a meaningful, competitive game. Now here they were, facing off in a league that had so far made headlines only for its audacity in existing at all, and for the struggles and setbacks it had suffered during its nascent years. Except that now, at the precise marquee moment when the NASL had the chance to replicate the glory of the world stage, it was caught unawares. Seemingly, it had occurred to no one that a 12,500-seat stadium would not suffice to meet the demands of a night that should have been hyped in advance as a major turning point in the League's history.

In the late 1960s, various entrepreneurs had lured Pelé's club Santos to New York to play Eusebio's club Benfica, and the two men were naturally given top billing on the posters that advertised these friendly games. So the attraction of their opposition, which was purely a sporting rivalry, was not unknown even in the United States. Prior to those exhibition spectacles, however, the two players had met on three competitive occasions, and so far the honours were just about even.

In 1962, South American club champions Santos met European champions Benfica in the Intercontinental Cup, at that time a two-legged, home and away affair. Benfica had won the European Cup earlier that year, beating the Spanish champions Real Madrid 5–3 in a final that saw the nineteen-year-old Eusebio score the last two goals. When they travelled to Rio de

Janeiro in September for the first game, they narrowly lost to Santos, 3-2, with Pelé scoring twice. It was in the second leg in Lisbon, however, that the mighty Brazilian showed Europe that what they had seen at the 1958 World Cup had been more than just a teenage flash. Scoring a hat-trick, and assisting on the other two goals, Pelé took his team to a 5-0 lead, before Eusebio and his teammate Santana scored two woefully late consolation goals. Penetrating the Benfica defence time and again, Pelé seemed an unstoppable force, a brutal, beautiful combination of power, speed and technical perfection.

If this was Pelé at his absolute peak, at the very top of the world game, then four years later in England, at Goodison Park in Liverpool, it was Eusebio's turn to step under the lights. Pelé had started Brazil's tournament with a goal in a win over Bulgaria, but the eastern Europeans had kicked him out of the game, much to the fury of the Brazilian press, and so he had missed the second game against Hungary, which Brazil lost. In the final game at Goodison, the world champions needed to at least draw with, and preferably beat, the in-form Portuguese, who had already won against Hungary and Bulgaria. Pelé, though not fully fit, was brought back into the line-up, presumably based on the belief that, as a miracle-worker, he would be able to pull through. The Portuguese, however, targeted him from the start, and before half-time Pelé had been crocked again, thanks in large part to the lenient refereeing of the fussy but ineffective Englishman, George McCabe. In the second half, in the days before even a single substitute was allowed, Pelé hobbled around with his right knee in a bandage. Even then, he managed a few perfectly placed passes with his left foot, despite the fact he was playing at around 30 per cent of his real capacity.

Eusebio at one point was seen sympathizing with Pelé after a bad foul from one of his Portuguese teammates. The two men were not just extraordinary footballers, but genuine gentlemen. Pelé, in frustration at the foul play of the Portuguese, did eventually lose his rag and charged an opposing defender, a retaliatory offence that nowadays would yield a straight red card. By that point, however, Eusebio had won the game with a virtuoso display of poise, acceleration, and explosive shooting. His dribbling and close control in this game are mesmerizing, and the endless latter-day discussions about whether Lionel Messi and Cristiano Ronaldo are among the all-time greats could be silenced by a look at the elastic Eusebio in his prime, who has the main assets of both. Against Brazil, he registered no fewer than seventeen goal attempts, creating the first in Portugal's 3–1 win, and then scoring twice himself. He finished the tournament as top scorer with nine goals, helping his country to its best ever finish in third place. His overall career statistics are astonishing – he made 301 domestic league appearances for Benfica and scored 317 goals, while in the course of winning his 64 caps for Portugal, he scored 41. The win over Brazil at the 1966 World Cup was not even his boldest feat at that tournament – in the quarter-final against North Korea, with the Portuguese 3–0 down, Eusebio scored four consecutive goals in leading his country's comeback to an eventual 5–3 win.

When you look at the stature, the quality and the prolific histories of these two players, it seems borderline surreal that their next meaningful encounter should take place in the NASL, a full nine years after that World Cup game in northern England. Maybe this was why the League itself failed to realize the significance of the match. The great moments of American sporting history, after all, were rarely made on a midweek night in early summer in a Massachusetts college stadium. There were no television cameras there that night, despite the fact this was Pelé's first away game since his surprise unveiling the month before as New York's newest recruit. The Minutemen's previous home crowd, against Seattle on June 6, had been 2,104. It should be noted, though, that along with several other teams, the Minutemen had been generally pulling in more at the gate than in previous seasons. Their crowds for the first two games of the 1975 season had been closer to the 7,000 mark, while in the 1974 season the corresponding fixture against the Cosmos had seen a gate of almost 11,000. Coached by the straight-talking Austrian Hubert Vogelsinger, and starring the consistent Nigerian former West Ham striker Ade Coker, Boston had developed into a decent team. Their signing of Eusebio was actually something of a puzzle.

Not getting caught in a Playboy club

Like Pelé, Eusebio had come to the NASL just the month before, but without any of the fanfare of Pelé's multi-million dollar contract, and certainly on a comparatively smaller salary – the *Toronto Star* reported that Eusebio would be paid $1,000 per game. Still, that wage was enough to cause unease in the Boston dressing room, where most players were still on peanuts and holding down part-time jobs to supplement their soccer money. In New York, under the auspices of Cosmos' owners Warner Communications, Pelé could be paraded as a superstar and used for all kinds of marketing misdemeanours. The Minutemen, however, seemed to have no idea what to do with Eusebio, especially as he was by now pretty much hobbled thanks to several knee operations. The team's PR director, Fred Clashman, said that Eusebio's signing had not triggered a surge in season ticket sales, but added, 'I'm getting crap from up top because I'm supposedly not pushing Eusebio. He's been profiled in the paper, but I'm thinking about getting him caught in a Playboy club or something. People want a human personality. He hasn't really caught on.'[2]

Prior to the game at Nickerson Field, the out-of-training Pelé had played one hastily arranged, and televised, exhibition game on Randalls Island against Dallas (he duly scored in a 2–2 draw), and one home game against Toronto (a 2–0 win in front of 22,000). Eusebio had played one away game for Boston, a 4–1 defeat at Rochester, in front of what had been Rochester's lowest gate of the season (just above 4,000). It's impossible to say whether it was Pelé alone that brought so many to the game that night, or the belated realization among the local Portuguese community that one of their national heroes was in town for the medium term at least. But come they did, prompting the *Boston Globe* to write the next day: 'For a league that prides itself on being professional, it was a hopelessly amateur display of planning and crowd control.'[3]

The home team must have partly intuited the possibility of a large turnout, because they had talked about moving the game to Schaefer Stadium, or to Boston College's Alumni Stadium, where they had played the previous season. The *Globe* wrote that both options proved 'impractical', while another press report a few days earlier had said that extra seating would be brought in to raise the capacity to 16,000, but it didn't happen. A short *United Press International* report printed in the *Globe* on the day of the game said that 15,000 fans were expected. Ticket prices were upped to a flat $5 (a raise of a couple of bucks), with Minutemen owner John Sterge claiming that the price increase was out of his control because Pelé's contract with the League was a joint venture. 'When Pelé used to come here with Santos,' he pointed out, 'the prices were generally $8 or $10, and that was before inflation.'[4]

The higher prices in no way put people off coming. Two hours before kick-off, there was no parking within half a mile of the stadium, and the *Globe* reported that 'the stands were jammed after seven o'clock' (kick off was at 8pm). To add to the chaos, at one point several thousand fans were locked out of the stadium when firemen had to put out a smoking gas canister beneath the stands. After the game started, the crowd spilled over the small wall separating the stands from the field, and from then on it was six deep, according to both the *Globe* and eyewitness reports. 'They clustered around the goals and sprawled on the netting,' wrote the paper. The NASL was having its Wembley 1923 moment, and crowd estimates varied from 18,000 to 25,000 for a ground barely fit to cope with half that number.

The Cosmos' Joey Fink was playing that night and remembers the game well. The Eusebio–Pelé confrontation 'was billed as a pretty big rivalry,' he says. 'The stadium was a college field with a low seating capacity, but the Boston owners realized there was a chance to make money, and I think they oversold it. There was a ring of people around the field. Eusebio was playing with a very severe knee injury. I believe he scored a goal, and after he scored a goal a number of people ran on to the field and hugged him, and eventually they got him off. Then the same happened with Pelé, and it was quite a trouble restoring order. Pelé didn't finish that game. It was kind of the most chaotic game, there was no crowd control whatsoever.'[5]

Fink doesn't recall personally being scared by the crowd. 'Back then you didn't think of being harmed,' he says. 'You just thought of it as over-exuberance, or passion from all the foreigners that were there – there were a lot of Portuguese, Italians. I think the number of Americans there was very low at that time for games like these.'[6]

The reaction of the Cosmos to the incident, and the immediate press coverage, painted a more dramatic picture. Very few events in the game itself were recorded, because the field invasion took priority in terms of news, and there was in any case only a limited amount of space given to soccer reports at the time. To place things in chronological order, there were no goals until Eusebio scored from a free kick with twelve minutes to play, prompting the first mob, but this was nothing compared with the reaction to Pelé's subsequently disallowed equalizer a minute after play resumed. 'What resulted last night was a chaotic and nearly tragic nightmare that never would have happened anywhere the game of soccer is taken seriously,' wrote the *Boston Globe*'s John Powers in his match report. The excess fans 'turned Nickerson Field into a shoving, marginally controlled maelstrom, and ruined what could have been a wondrous piece of nostalgia.' Fortunately, Pelé's personal bodyguard Pedro Garay ran on to the field and reached him just a few seconds after the crowd. 'I threw my body over him,' said Garay. 'He told me he was hurt and wanted a stretcher. I think we were lucky he wasn't hurt worse than he was.'[7] Before boarding the plane the next day, Pelé said, 'I was shaken up and scared.' Cosmos GM Clive Toye claimed that Eusebio told him, 'I thought they were going to kill Pelé. I feared for his life and mine.'

Powers, writing for the *Globe,* described the riot – which

saw Pelé stretchered off, a fifteen-minute break in play, and then Eusebio leaving the game a few minutes later – as 'a macabre climax to a game that at once offered more and less than anyone had dared expect.' He also wrote that the anticipated confrontation between the two players 'never really came off. Age has transformed them from deities to choreographers. They prowl the midfield now, pointing and directing, teaching and cajoling.'[8] This seems to be a poetic way of saying that they were past it, but it's a touching, generous analysis of the roles they had joined the NASL to play in their twilight years. Regardless of their waning pace, they had both managed to place themselves at the centre of the drama, and that was something the Cosmos were keen to spin out over the following days by appealing against the result and making demands for better security. Boston had gone on to win the game 2–1 in sudden-death over-time (a fifteen-minute period to decide drawn games that had been introduced at the start of the 1975 season) after Mark Liveric had levelled for the Cosmos with two minutes left, and then Wolfgang Sühnholz scored the 'golden goal' winner after 100 minutes. Powers concluded his report regretfully. 'It might have been magic, had the Minutemen and the NASL known precisely what they had on their hands. As it was, we are fortunate that it was less than manslaughter.'[9]

Clive Toye says now that he doesn't even remember the game, or that the Cosmos appealed to the League to have the result overturned. The day after the game, though, he thundered, 'Unless our security demands are met, I will not allow Pelé to play again.' The *New York Times* reported that the player's shorts, shirt and shoe had been ripped, and that he suffered a pulled knee muscle and a sprained ankle. 'We were very lucky,' Toye elaborated. 'When the crowd started mobbing him, he kept his leg flexed. If he had kept it stiff, he would have broken it. And there was no police to protect him.'[10] The Minutemen, wrote the *Times*, 'had assured the Cosmos they would have at least 200 policemen at the game. Toye said he had counted only fourteen Boston policemen and eight Boston University guards at Nickerson Field.' Cosmos vice-president Rafael de la Sierra went to the nearest police station at half-time to ask for help and was told, 'Soccer attracts only 2,000.' Still, if the League wasn't ready for Eusebio versus Pelé, why should the local cops have had any idea about the importance or popularity of two mere soccer players who were coming to town?

A later account of the pitch invasion in Chuck Cascio's book *Soccer USA* paints a slightly less dramatic picture, backing up Joey Fink's recollections: 'By most accounts, including Pelé's,' wrote Cascio, 'the crowd was not hostile. It had reacted more out of a swelling admiration for Pelé's excellent sense of drama. Pelé was soon covered by admiring fans who may have been souvenir hunters, but who were nevertheless inflicting pain as they grabbed, wrenched, twisted and clawed for a memento.' Pelé himself joked about the incident a few weeks later at a press conference in Washington DC prior to a game at the Diplomats. 'I don't see violence,' he said, when quizzed about the Boston riot. 'People treat me nicely all over the world. The only problem is when fans want to take my clothing off.'[11]

Boston's Fred Clashman was dubious about the Cosmos' post-game outrage. 'We got hate mail over the Pelé game,' he said. 'New York overplayed things and loved every minute of it. Toye loved every minute of publicity he got from the Pelé injury. Toye complained about inadequate security protection, but he had hot property getting mobbed, and he loved it.'[12] The League nonetheless upheld the Cosmos' appeal and the rematch was set for later in the season. Did the Boston Minutemen care? It's unlikely that they offered any fans their money back for the annulled game, or free tickets for the rescheduled game, and already in July they began to run adverts in the *Boston Globe* touting the rematch between the two men.

In between, the Minutemen came to Randalls Island, still the Cosmos' home ground in 1975, for the return game, but this was also an anti-climax. Although the Cosmos won 3–1 and Pelé assisted on the third goal in what one match report called 'the best play of the night' ('With his back to goal, [he] spun and flicked a pretty pass' to Johnny Kerr, who scored), the same report said that Pelé, 'like the rest of the Cosmos, tired from the stretch of four games in a week, walked through most of the game, only occasionally turning on some magic'.[13] Worse still, Eusebio had limped off injured after 23 minutes. The crowd was just over 18,000, around 4,000 short of the stadium's capacity, so the Pelé–Eusebio billing had failed to lure as many fans as it maybe should have. Strangely, the official match programme (*Kick* magazine – a generic, League-wide publication with only the centre pages tailored for specific games) featured on its cover two shots of goalkeeper Bob Rigby, who at that time was a Philadelphia player. Rigby was featured inside, along with the Minutemen's goalkeeper and future Cosmos player Shep Messing, and their striker Ade Coker, but there was no mention of Eusebio at all except in the team line-up. Perhaps it was ignorance, or maybe the perceived wisdom at the NASL was that Eusebio was past it, and in any case, we have Pelé, so we don't need to waste any energy talking up a player who, seemingly, did not boast the same image or pulling power.

The replayed game in August at Nickerson Field in the end drew just 4,445 fans, because Pelé and Eusebio were both out injured. Boston won 5–0, but neither side made the playoffs. The following season, Hubert Vogelsinger – under pressure from the financially strapped team owners – traded Eusebio to Toronto in a move that barely registered. The focus was all on New York. Now that Pelé had the chance to direct the Cosmos from the centre of the field for a whole season, surely he would bring the team their second championship, to follow the one they had won with little glory or acclaim in 1972's short, fourteen-game season. It was assumed that there would be few other teams able to compete, especially when they signed the charismatic and consistent Italian-Welsh striker Giorgio Chinaglia, by way of Swansea and Naples – the controversial, loud-mouthed but utterly brilliant player destined to become the League's all-time top scorer. For the sake of their investment, the League hoped for nothing less than the 'right' 1976 Soccer Bowl final to crown its season and garner the maximum amount of media coverage: 'The Cosmos versus A.N. Other.'

Pelé and his Toye boy

The story of Pelé's signing by the Cosmos has been much told. To briefly recap, the team's general manager Clive Toye chased Pelé around the globe, wooing him like a wealthy but slightly bloated, face-hairy bachelor besotted with the world's most longed-for, albeit ageing, movie star. The star toyed with Toye, the former *Daily Express* journalist (think a bit-part extra who's just inherited a fortune and is now trying to seduce Sophia Loren), perhaps sensing that the more he played along, the less likely that Toye would be to give in, and the higher that the offers would go. The Cosmos, on their side, sensed that signing Pelé would Change Everything, and that was why Warner Brothers thrust a cheque book into Toye's intrepid fist. From Frankfurt to Rio, Brussels to Rome, the assiduous Toye stalked down luxury hotel corridors for four years, searching for yet another audience with the Brazilian, travelling 75,000 miles in the process, and no doubt heavily expending the cheery charm that had got him to New York in the first place.

Was he never discouraged? 'You know what Winston Churchill said?' he asks rhetorically. '"Never give in, never give in, never give in." I just wanted to do it.' Though he admits that 'sometimes I came back from a trip and thought to myself, bloody hell, Toye, what are you doing? I remember the time where I was nearly at the end of my tether in Brussels and Pelé wrote on a piece of notepaper in the hotel "Pelé's last offer." So I said to him, "At least sign the bloody thing." And then in Rome two weeks later he says, "Clive, my English is not good?" and I'm saying, "No no, your English is getting better all the time." And he said, "No, I said to you in Brussels, \$3 million for two years. And here you are offering me [the same] money for three years."'[14] Why the player signed at all was the topic of plentiful speculation, and once the announcement was made, there was prolific PR spiel about how he was going to be the saviour of US soccer. That was the deal, and he was very good at holding up that end of the bargain. Yet the figures making him the highest-paid sportsman in the world were not only what gave the NASL worldwide publicity, they were surely the only reason – given the years of haggling – that Pelé rescinded his decision to retire from the game one year before.

US Secretary of State Henry Kissinger, a self-proclaimed soccer fan, did his bit to help bring Pelé to the US by sending him a telegram: 'Should you decide to sign a contract, I am sure your stay in the United States will substantially contribute to closer ties between Brazil and the United States in the field of sports.'[15] Brazil's Foreign Minister Antonio Azeredo da Silveira weighed in too, urging him to go and play in the US. No political sketch writer would have been unkind enough to observe that the two men were using Pelé for their own ends in seeking some kind of commercial or geo-political pact in a murky but mutually advantageous way. Kissinger continued to associate himself with the NASL for as long as it was a popular vehicle to skim off some of the game's transient glamour, but disappeared from view as his own career sank into disgrace following the carpet-bombing of Cambodia that he ordered, and after the League itself stopped attracting celebrity hangers-on from parallel branches of the entertainment industry.

For his fellow Cosmos players, signing Pelé meant that they now suddenly travelled in style, and stayed at the best hotels. Joey Fink says, 'the first third of that [1975] season we were still staying in budget hotels, then all of a sudden travel was on a first-class basis – Hyatt Hotels and so forth.' It also meant 'a complete change of culture in our style of play and training. With Gordon [Bradley] we did a lot of running and sprinting before Pelé came, but afterwards everything changed to more like a samba rhythm, with abdominal exercises, and all of that sprinting went out of the window in favour of a Brazilian style of training.' The year before, in 1974, he remembers playing a 4 July game at home to the Washington

Diplomats in 100-degree heat. 'We looked at the stands and counted about 150 people, half of them friends and relatives and girlfriends [the official gate was 1,301, but it's possible the actual attendance was closer to Fink's estimate]. One year later in that same stadium, Pelé's first game against Toronto was an absolute sell-out, with a couple of thousand looking down from the bridge over the stadium.' Playing for the Cosmos was suddenly 'fun. As a young American soccer player, to be on the same field as Pelé, it was a great time.'[16]

Amid the League's now frenzied coverage, there were some sceptics, and not just among established sports journalists who viewed soccer as invasive at best, downright subversive at worst. 'I was sort of dubious about the whole thing,' admits Paul Gardner. 'He got a tremendous amount of publicity, not because he was a good player but because he was the highest-paid soccer player in the world.' A lot of the journalists sent to cover the signing had no clue about either the player or the game. 'It could be really irritating of course,' he says. '"I thought he played for Santos, not Brazil", that kind of thing. By the time he came here ... he was still capable of doing a few nice things, but he wasn't capable of dazzling football and goalscoring anymore.' He sees parallels between Pelé's signing and the LA Galaxy's coup in landing David Beckham to play in Major League Soccer in 2007. 'It was difficult for him and the Cosmos and the NASL to maintain that hype – to me it was not unlike the Beckham situation, because he wasn't producing. Is soccer a sport that lends itself to that? You're going to bring in one player and he's going to dribble through everyone in every game and score goals like crazy, and overhead kicks? I think that's what people were assuming. I remember a friend of mine saying he took his daughter out there one night to see Pelé in a very ordinary game, and at half-time she said to him, "That guy, the number 10? Is he the best player in the world?" And he said yes, and she said, "Are you sure?" You could watch whole games like that where you wouldn't really see much.'

Gardner doesn't think that Pelé much changed the sport in the US, 'but then I don't think Beckham did either. But people who made those decisions and spent that money are not going to tell you that. Because if they do tell you that, they're saying that they wasted their money.'[17]

Eusebio's last stand

In the early years of the NASL, many teams tried an 'ethnic' approach to signing players. In 1968, for example, the Chicago Mustangs signed three players from Poland with the aim of wooing the local Polish population. Such policies met with limited success, if any, when the teams or the players were not especially good, and the demographic was limited to soccer-friendly pockets of the local area, none of whom were neces-sarily guaranteed to come along just to sing for and support their blood brothers. Gradually this idea was discredited, and the NASL developed more ambitious goals aimed at spread-ing the game to everyone. Cosmos president Ahmet Ertegun, however, expressed an already long outmoded view in the late 1970s when he said that while he was all for 'foreign stars', he thought that 'the teams in LA and Dallas are crazy not to have some Mexican players. Washington should have some more blacks or Africans. Minnesota should get some Scandinavian players.'[18] Either he was trying to sabotage the rest of the League by leading them down a path already proven to be a dead end, or he was remembering the success of Toronto in 1976.

As mentioned earlier, Toronto picked up and dusted off the limping Eusebio before the 1976 season after he was sold by a Boston team headed for extinction thanks to the imminent bankruptcy of owner John Sterge, director of a stock company called An-Car Oil that went bust after defrauding investors (some of whose money reportedly ended up bankrolling the Minutemen).[19] Toronto's full name was, awkwardly, the Toronto Metros-Croatia. In their previous participation as the Toronto Metros they had, like many, run into financial problems and sought new investors, and were taken over by a group of local Croat businessmen who'd been running Toronto Croatia, a very successful team in the ethnically oriented Canadian National Soccer League (CNSL). Although the NASL frowned upon such a narrowly focused name, there was in fact nothing they could do about it. Toronto itself enjoyed a downtown construction boom in the 1970s, in contrast to many North American cities where inner city areas were being abandoned in favour of commerce in the suburbs. The well-run, immigrant-friendly but conservative city had not been overly affected by the cultural turns of the late 1960s, however – the city's annual gay pride parade on Halloween was regularly pelted with eggs and could only take place under police protection.

The city's multi-ethnic make-up was reflected in the Toronto clubs that played in the CNSL, comprised of Italian, Portuguese, Hungarian, Serbian and Croatian teams. 'These ethnic groups were very proud,' recalls former Toronto defender Bob Iarusci – a rugged but skilful full-back who went on to enjoy a long and storied NASL career at both the

Cosmos and the Washington Diplomats. 'To distinguish themselves in the community they used their soccer teams, and so the standard of soccer in Toronto at this time was very, very strong.' Iarusci himself joined the Metros from a National Soccer League team called Toronto Italia. Such local teams were 'well followed. You have to appreciate that the media at the time wasn't too kind to the sport. So we had a strong following from the ethnic communities.'[20]

There were also several imported Croatians, including defender Damir Šutevski, who came over to Canada from what was then Yugoslavia at the age of nineteen to play for Toronto with two other young players, all unable to speak English. The other two soon went home, but he stayed, being well looked after as he came to terms with a new environment several thousand miles away from home. 'In terms of adapting to the playing style, it wasn't really Yugoslavs *per se*,' he says. 'It was mainly Croats and Macedonians, and the rest were from Europe, so it was more an ethnic Croatian team. Probably six or seven starters would be Croatians and the rest other nationalities. That was okay, as Croatians rank pretty well in the soccer world, so the contours of the game didn't really change that much [for me]. In terms of our short passing, that was how we played, with the occasional long ball. That was our style of play.'[21]

Italian-Canadian midfielder Carmine Marcantonio, another product of the strong local ethnic league, says that 'Pelé and the League were trying to market the NASL in North America, and here you have this team in Toronto with an ethnic name. So it was a bit of a love-hate relationship within the League, but the Croatians are very proud people – they wanted the name added to the Metros name. Originally it was just the Metros, but there wasn't much of a following just as a Canadian outfit; they were struggling. So that was why they merged with the Croatian semi-pro team, because they had a good following, and it was an opportunity for the Croatian team to play in a professional league.'[22]

They brought over several top Croatian players, like veteran Dinamo Zagreb defender Filip Blašković and promising young striker Ivan Lukačević, and, on top of that, Eusebio. 'He had one knee that looked like Mount Everest,' says Marcantonio. 'He was limping almost in one leg, but still you could sense the greatness of the player. We became a great team because of the Croatian players, and we had the German Wolfgang Sühnholz who came mid-season, a former Bayern Munich player, and then we had some young players locally like myself and Bob Iarusci.'[23] Iarusci concurs that the team was 'incredibly talented'. While he understands that the League wasn't delighted with the ethnic name, 'we were very proud of our team and of the group we had. Our GM that year was a genius to put together that team. He went to Croatia and picked up a lot of players. That said, we had Eusebio up front and the Brazilian Ivair Ferreira, who in the 60s was called the Prince of Brazil because the King was already Pelé. We had some terrific players to learn from.'

As at Boston, Eusebio was at the centre of the team's tactics. 'It was a team effort but he was our fulcrum,' says Iarusci. 'He played behind our two strikers, and when he collected the ball things happened. He was so brilliant in terms of decision-making and understanding the space he was given. Both of his knees were in terrible shape. It was funny, when he walked he really hobbled, but when he was on the field he picked up speed and it was almost as if the knees realized that they could hurt later, but not at that moment. He did some wonderful things even at the ripe age of 35, and without him we wouldn't have won.'[24] Šutevski also recalls Eusebio's ability despite a 'shattered knee, it was really in bad shape. Before each game he'd have to submerge his knee in a bucket of ice in order to play, and he barely trained between games. I guess compared to Europe it must still have been a secondary kind of play to him. A lot of the goals were from free kicks; he had an incredible shot. He was like a little kid: he wanted to be participating in every attack we had, and he would ask for the ball in every attack.'[25]

Toronto started the 76 season well, winning eight of their first ten matches, and Eusebio, who missed the first two games, scored six in six appearances. There followed a mid-season, seven-game slump when the team won only on penalty kicks (three times – through this season, drawn games were decided on penalties if no one scored during sudden-death extra time), and failed to score in open play for all seven games – a highly unusual sequence for the high-scoring NASL. After that seventh game, the Yugoslav coach Ivan Marković was sacked, but it wasn't just because his team had lost its scoring touch. It was because of Eusebio.

The two men had already fallen out at training, with Eusebio resenting that Marković would come in to the dressing room and tell him what boots to wear. 'Marković was a genius, but geniuses are sometimes like fools,' says Marcantonio. 'He lived for the game, and he was a Croatian guy who grew up coaching Hajduk Split, then Marseille and the Yugoslav youth national teams. He was a genius and he could teach us young guys even how to tie our shoes. He had his own bag of cleats and would say, "Today it's a bit dry, you need this type of cleats." He'd bring that bag to the game and tell us what we should be wearing. But imagine you're Eusebio and you have this guy telling you what kind of cleats you should be wearing – they almost came to blows about it. Eusebio is telling the coach he uses his own shoes – "I cannot play with gummi-shoes on a wet field" – and there'd be this flash between greatness in the coach and greatness in the payer. You don't tell Eusebio, at 34, what kind of shoes he's going to wear. And so then there was a struggle between Eusebio and the coach and that affected our game.'

Marković, both Marcantonio and Šutevski testify, was good with young players like themselves, but tended to treat *all* players as though they were youths, including Eusebio. There was another dispute in San Antonio when Marković refused to let Eusebio take free kicks and penalties, despite a somewhat impressive career record from dead balls. Then, says Iarusci, recalling that seventh scoreless game, 'We were playing the Cosmos at Varsity Stadium. It had just received a new pitch in time for the 1976 Montreal Olympics, and the soccer was in Toronto. It was like Wembley Stadium that day, the Cosmos came into town for their only visit with Pelé and Chinaglia, and Eusebio wanted to play badly. But Marković had him on his shit list because they had had an argument a fortnight before during a friendly game against Glasgow Rangers, so Marković was punishing Eusebio. Eusebio went to the team president with his bank book and said, "Here's all the money I have in my bank account that you guys gave me, but I must play this game." The president said he couldn't go against the coach.'[26]

Marcantonio says the team ownership was split down the middle on whether to side with Eusebio or Marković in their running dispute. 'The team was struggling,' he concedes, 'and this clash was going on between Eusebio and Marković, but then there was this game against the Cosmos in early July. Marković said Eusebio was not going to play and kicked him out of the team. So it came to this game and the future of both depended on the outcome of this game. If we won, then Marković would stay and Eusebio would leave. If we lost, Marković would be gone and Eusebio would stay. We lost 3–0. I remember just before kick-off, Eusebio came into the dressing room and started throwing money around saying, "Here's all the money I have, take it, but I must play this game", because of his rivalry with Pelé. He almost came begging to play, but Marković wanted none of it. So we lost 3–0 and he was gone the next day.'[27]

Marković's compatriot Domagoj Kapetanović took over, and his first move was to install Eusebio as captain, 'and we started winning', Iarusci says. Marcantonio adds that Kapetanović 'basically handed him the team to run on the field'. Success didn't come immediately, though – of Kapetanović's first four games, two were wins on penalty kicks, and the other two were losses. Only after signing Wolfgang Sühnholz from Boston did the Metros win their last four regular-season games and scrape into the playoffs, with Eusebio on another scoring streak – he hit nine goals in five games, including a four-goal haul against Boston in a 6–2 hiding, though the ailing Minutemen had by now sold their best players and were fielding part-timers as they headed for bankruptcy. 'We had this easy feeling about ourselves because we were on a roll going into the playoffs,' says Iarusci, 'and we'd also signed Sühnholz. He was a tremendous midfielder who grew up in the Bayern Munich system, but he'd suffered a terrible knee injury when he was young, and the club locked him in with the other under-used players and he got frustrated and came to North America. He'd played with Eusebio in Boston, so Eusebio got the GM to get him in and he became the final piece of the puzzle that took us over the top.'[28]

'A bunch of hobos at the Soccer Bowl'

The playoffs were single-game knockout ties at this stage of the League's evolution. In the first game, Toronto beat the Rochester Lancers 2–1 at home. Aside from the 12,000-plus that came for the Cosmos game, it was their best gate of the season at a modest 6,852. After this, though, all their games were on the road due to their low League standing. For the quarter-final, they flew to the Chicago Sting – a Brit-centric team coached by Manchester United legend Bill Foulkes – without their regular goalkeeper Paolo Cimpiel, who hadn't realized that there would be playoffs at the end of the season. When he found out, he asked for more money and was refused, so he left the team. 'His back-up,' says Iarusci, 'was Željko Bilecki, who had hardly played that year, but he took over. So we went to Chicago and it ended in a 2–2 tie, and the artificial turf there was just horrible, but we ended up winning on penalty shots, and Bilecki made two big saves on penalties.'[29]

The semi-final was a trip to the reigning champions, the Tampa Bay Rowdies, who had won the 1975 championship in their very first year, and had become the most talked-about team of the season alongside Pelé's New York Cosmos, whom they had just eliminated 3–1 in their own quarter-final before almost 37,000 home fans. With their soaring gates, their superstar signings like Rodney Marsh, and a marketing campaign that was going from strength to strength, this was the franchise of both the present and the future as far as the League was concerned. The Rowdies–Cosmos game should have been its showpiece final, starring two exciting, well-supported clubs on the rise. Clive Toye partly blamed himself for voting the Rowdies into the same division as the Cosmos in a League meeting, because he didn't think they'd do so well two years running – this ensured they'd meet in the quarter-finals at the latest. As it was, the League would just have to be content with only one of its big name teams at the Soccer Bowl, with another upstart team, the Minnesota Kicks, as the hoped-for opponent.

The Rowdies were 'slated for the final', says Iarusci. 'We were there in front of nearly 40,000 people and we played one of the best games we ever played. They had the PR guy announcing that a lucky winner was going to go with the team [the Rowdies] for the final in Seattle, and they were still making that announcement with ten minutes to go.' By that time, Toronto had won the game. They opened the scoring with a superb goal from Eusebio, who looked far from immobile – he passed the ball from central midfield out to Ivair Ferreira on the right, then sprinted in to the penalty area to emphatically head home the Brazilian's cross. Austrian-Polish midfielder Tadeusz Polak added a second, and that's the way it stayed. Šutevski says, 'That year nobody paid us any attention, and it wasn't until we made it all the way to the final that they woke up.'[30]

The result was unexpected even for Toronto. Indeed, many of the players hadn't realized that if they won in Tampa, they would be flying straight to the final, being played on neutral ground in Seattle against Minnesota. 'They hadn't even brought a change of clothes,' says Iarusci, clearly relishing the memory. 'One guy only had a pair of sandals because they told him he was going to go to the beach. At the pre-Soccer Bowl awards banquet we looked like a bunch of hobos that had just got off the last cross-country freight train. And the whole Minnesota team was in tuxedos, and we looked like the raga-muffin group.' Marcantonio agrees that it was 'quite a scene. Talk about an embarrassment to the League.'[31]

'We took the wives and girlfriends [to Florida],' says Šutevski, 'hoping to take the time after the Tampa game for a vacation. But once we beat Tampa we knew that we were going to win the title. Team morale was so high, to lose the game would have been unheard of. We knew once we'd made it all the way to the final that we were going to win it, it was just a question of what the final score would be. We beat Minnesota 3-0 and we totally demolished them.'

Iarusci's view is similar: 'We destroyed them. Eusebio scored on a dead ball that went off Alan Merrick's chest and into the top corner. We were so superior to them; Sühnholz was MVP*, but honestly the ball was on a string that day. We had a little winger, Ivan Grnja [another late-season signing from Croatia]; he just created havoc on the wing. We didn't have speed on both wings, but eventually that day we did because he'd just go from the left side to the right side – he was amazing.'[32] 'The Prince', Ivair Ferreira, scored the second, and the victory was sealed, appropriately, by a Yugoslav, the striker Lukačević.

English striker Alan Willey, who was playing for the Kicks

---

* MVP – Most Valuable Player. In the UK, Man of the Match, but also used to denote League MVP for Player of the Season.

that day, has no quibbles with the score. 'We'd beaten them pretty comfortably during the regular season,' he says. 'We were playing well. Not only ourselves but the rest of the League was probably expecting us to win it, but when you show up you've got to play your game. But we didn't play well, and we had no excuses. It wasn't like "we should have won, we could have won, we outplayed them". They outplayed us.'

If the League was underwhelmed by the Toronto victory, there wasn't much of a reaction in Toronto either, what with the game being so far away and the players heading off on holiday straight afterwards. 'We were on the front page of the *Toronto Star* the next day, and the mayor actually broke session to recognize our group,' says Iarusci. 'We didn't get the type of coverage we should have, but at that point I think we did okay, to be quite honest.'[33] Šutevski says the team got better recognition decades later when they were invited back to the city to commemorate the victory. 'At the time the game wasn't established enough in Canada that you would get any national attention. We stayed in Seattle for a day [to celebrate], and then we went our own way with our wives and girlfriends.'[34]

Carmine Marcantonio lauds the Metros-Croatia as 'the best team I ever played for out of all the ten years I played in the League. We were kind of the bad boys of the League, definitely, because of the Croatian name, for example. But the Croatian group didn't care. A lot of the Croatians played in the Yugoslav league at the time – they were top-notch players, so it wasn't really a fluke. We gelled as a team, we played very entertaining football.'[35]

Unlike many around them, Toronto kept a team going until the League's demise in 1984, and were losing finalists in the last two years. By 1979, however, they'd moved with the trend for conventional, storm-and-strength associated monikers and became the Toronto Blizzard after the ownership moved out of Croatian hands. Eusebio hobbled on to play one more season, in Las Vegas of all places, after his final senior triumph with Toronto. In the meantime, numerous new – though not always younger – world stars were beginning to flock to the burgeoning NASL.

Season-by-season overview

1972

Still eight teams, but a shortened season of fourteen games to save cash. Washington moved to Florida and became the Miami Gatos. No, not the 'Gators (which they have in Florida), but the *Gatos*, Spanish for cats (which, it must be supposed, they also have in Florida). The **New York Cosmos** moved out of Yankee Stadium to Hofstra Stadium on Long Island, and beat the St Louis Stars there in the single-game championship final, 2–1, in front of 6,102 fans. Their Bermudan striker Randy Horton was the League's top scorer (nine goals), and League gates edged up to an average of almost 5,000.

Fun facts: Montreal fielded a young Scotsman, Graeme Souness. An experimental 35-yard offside line was introduced (see Chapter 7).

1973

One addition, the **Philadelphia Atoms**, and two name changes: the Atlanta Chiefs became the Apollos, while the Miami Gatos gave up the Spanish feline moniker and became the more combative Toros (bulls) instead. Neither new identity helped, as both finished bottom of their respective three-team conferences, but the Atoms – with six US players as regular starters – lifted the championship trophy in their first season by beating the Tornado in Dallas, 2–0, with almost 19,000 there to see it. Philly's two Southport loanee strikers, Jim Fryatt and Andy Provan, had to miss the final due to the start of the English season, having scored the bulk of the team's goals. US defender Bill Straub started as a forward instead for Philly, making his debut for the club, and scoring one of the goals.

Fun facts: More encouraging crowd news – average gates were almost up to 6,000. The League had its first household name US soccer star – Kyle Rote Junior of the Dallas Tornado was the namesake son of a famous American football player with the New York Giants. Rote Jr was the League's top scorer.* He was also the three-time winner of the popular 70s TV series *Superstars*, in which athletes from different sports competed against each other in multiple disciplines.

---

* With ten goals and ten assists – the NASL consistently took both statistics into account when compiling its scoring charts, using a points system whereby a goal was worth two points, an assist one point.

3   Leaving old Europe behind

> 'Over here sportsmen are treated like Gods.
> Athletes get respect. Everything is done for them.
> Here they're 10 feet tall. I'd like that for myself
> and my team-mates. People here are so excitable.
> They go wild for sports and I love it. I'm moti-
> vated by the spectators. The bigger the crowd, the
> better I play.'[1]
>
> —Former Norwich City and New England
> Tea Men goalkeeper Kevin Keelan

Although films, books, music and memories have a habit
of painting past eras as either much better or much worse
than they really were, there is little doubt that in the 1970s
the United States was a more glamorous and opulent place
to live than Great Britain, with its endless strikes, shutdowns,
power cuts and three-day weeks. This was certainly the case
for soccer players following the money and the trend to spend
their summers on a Californian beach with a cheerleader while
rubbing shoulders with Pelé and Cruyff at the weekend. That,
of course, is a parody of life in the NASL, and while it contains
a streak of truth, it was not just the dollar that brought some
of the world's most daring players – and many more besides
– to play in the USA.

There was a sense among many players of escaping grim
times, not just in the stultified culture of domestic football,
but in terms of the British social climate (not to mention its

actual climate), with its lingering Victorian judgments and the cowering and kowtowing to the chinless but still lofty and exclusive aristocracy. The convivial American stereotype of the grey British weather dogged by fog and rain was (and is) largely accurate, especially considering that soccer was not a summer sport in Europe. Games were played in the cold and the wet, on pitches which by December at the latest had turned to mud down the middle, where most English teams now liked to play the ball. Crowds were plummeting thanks to widespread hooliganism, and fans were treated by police and administrators like herds of potentially seditious cattle – escorted by law enforcement from station to stadium, then fenced in behind barbed-wire barriers in shoddy, outdated grounds that had seen the barest of maintenance and virtually no development since before the Second World War. The ugly culture of violence spawned in the late 1960s seemed to spread like a schoolyard craze across Britain, pervading the game at every level. 'If I was the average family man I wouldn't even consider going to a soccer match in England,' said Seattle's English striker Roger Davies, who won the League's MVP award in 1980 for his 27 goals. 'It used to be a great day out for the family. But not any more.'[2] It eventually took three major stadium tragedies in the mid- to late-1980s (Bradford, Heysel and Hillsborough) to prompt a rethink about more humane ways to watch Britain's most popular sport.

Things weren't much better on the field of play. With a few exceptions – Holland at international level during the 1974 and 1978 World Cups, and Ajax (early 70s) and Liverpool (late 70s) at club level in domestic and European competition – tactics were geared towards getting the right outcome, at almost any cost, and to hell with style or beauty. Flamboyance was going out of fashion because it didn't get results. And so play-ers like Frank Worthington and Rodney Marsh were lured by America's promise to start afresh and rethink the game before it killed itself with off-field unrest and on-field nihilism. At the game's pinnacle, Argentina's 1978 world crown was sullied by the team's support from a murderous military dictatorship, and suspicions that the 6–0 final group game win over Peru – which took the Argentinians to the final against Holland – had been a fix. West Germany were the 1980 European champions, and Italy were crowned in 1982 as the World Cup winners, but few now care to remember how they did it. The teams that played the best soccer (Holland in 1978, Brazil in 1982) did not end up winning. This merely encouraged those who said that the game's beauty took second place to tactical acuity, defence, discipline, and the art of clinical victory by a solitary goal.

Meanwhile, British players were flocking to the US to see for themselves what this 'special relationship' was really all about. Like most people who come to the US and take a good look around, they discovered that the snobbery and conde-scension that British people have historically displayed in the face of America's perceived global gluttony was based on ignorance. That is, the loudest anti-Americans in Europe are usually the ones that have never been there. US citizens, by contrast, have such a fond image of quaint old Europe that they have always seemed to take even the bluntest of insults about their endless imperialist ambitions with a dose of good humour. This is maybe because they know, deep down, that all stereotypes are untrue, and can be broken down with a smile and some basic human contact. British footballers arriving in the US in the 1970s discovered much the same. What they had seen on *Starsky & Hutch* at 9pm on a Saturday night, just before

Match of the Day, or on *Dallas* on a Thursday evening just after *Top of the Pops*, bore no resemblance to the landscape and the people they experienced when they landed on the far side of the Atlantic. If they bumped into a cop, it was likely they'd be let off for drunk-driving when the officer found out they were a star player on that new local soccer team that had just come to town. If they were met at the airport by a Texan in a Stetson, they were probably more charmed by his hospitality than disgusted by his craven lust for oil, power and boundless wealth.

Marilyn Monroe vs Ukrainian tractor girl

The British soccer journalist Paul Gardner, who came to the US in the 1950s, makes a sound case for the attractions – both real and imagined – that were offered by Britain's close ally in both world wars. 'When you lived in England or elsewhere,' he says, 'the whole idea of modernity was always with an American flavour, and the idea of progress in those countries was to be like the Americans. To grow up during the war in England when we had nothing in terms of glamour – you'd go to the movies and see these huge great cars and marvellous suits: that was what life was going to be like. So if there was such a thing we understood as progress, it meant to be like the Americans. How could it be any different? What was the alternative? Soviet Russia?

'By 1946, we knew what a hell-hole Soviet Russia was. They didn't stand a chance. You had glistening, shiny Hollywood with glamorous guys and girls, and what was the Soviet Union offering? The five-year plan? Forget it. I think it was that the Americans were the first country to have nationwide prosperity in a way we never even dreamed of in England. We had the working class without much money and they were going to stay there. The Americans – that was all we had to look at. And there was nothing wrong with it – we wanted those things, those cars, and clothes and canned goods. Those who knew better, that this wasn't the whole story of America by any means, weren't going to get anywhere telling us that we should be looking at women driving tractors across fields in the Ukraine.'

Gardner says that he was 'very left wing at that time [post-WW2], so the only thing we advocated that was American was jazz, real black American jazz, because the blacks were put down by the American establishment. But when your parents were suddenly starting to earn more than before and you became more affluent, what were you going to do – send off a cheque to Russia?'[3]

This would especially apply to soccer players, not often known for their political engagement, and is backed by the story of how soccer slumped in communist East Germany in the early 1950s. The president of the country's Soccer Department, former Leipzig defender Fritz Gödicke, pinpointed the lack of discipline among the country's players and a failure to achieve good results on the field as a consequence of political immaturity, and too much 'capitalist ideology' on the part of coaches and club administrators. He ordered a tripartite policy to get things back on track: no tolerance of bourgeois behaviour; the implementation of criticism and self-criticism; and the compulsory study of Marxism-Leninism. The result, wrote German political scientist Hanns Leske, was that 'more than a few coaches and players realized that a sensible approach to work under such oppressive conditions was no longer possible, and they moved to the West.'[4] Needless to say, there are few post-war stories of ideologically driven player migration to the Communist bloc, while in the NASL era, the only semi-open, quasi-capitalist Communist regime – in what was then Tito's Yugoslavia – allowed countless players to come over to the US and bank some extra money, while earning some hard currency in loan fees for their clubs.

So America, for better or worse, was still the land of promise and prosperity. Many young British players, though, had no clue about the geography of the United States. 'I thought it was the San Francisco Earthquakes. I didn't know it was San Jose until I read it on me jersey,' said Newcastle United's Derek Craig after signing for San Jose in 1975.[5] Middlesbrough's Alan Willey came to the Minnesota Kicks in 1976 and admits, 'I'd no idea where Minnesota was, I just remember getting out of the airport and the cars were massive and the freeways were huge, but I didn't know what to expect. It was a real culture shock. I lived in a place called Houghton-le-Spring, half an hour from Middlesbrough, and that was the furthest away I'd ever been from home – into Middlesbrough; and here I was abroad living with a crowd of blokes.'[6]

Alan Birchenall of Leicester City remembers being whisked from the plane to the soccer field, where he was expected to take part in a trial game after flying all the way from the UK to San Jose, California. 'It was 1977,' Birchenall says. 'The owner was Milan Mandarić, and I'd never met him, and I didn't realize he'd set up a practice match for me at Los Gatos College for when I arrived. I'd flown for twelve hours from Heathrow and had a few beers on the flight, so I was in no condition for a match and I was half cut. So I couldn't run, and because I couldn't run I hit this ball from 35 yards and it screamed into the net, and I remember one of the English boys, Laurie

Calloway, said to me, "That'll keep you here." I said I was signing a contract that evening, but he said, "That means nothing
here" – some lads had come over the previous week and signed
a contract, but they were rubbish and were out on the next
plane home. Whereas I'd had a few beers and just hit a shot
because I couldn't run; but Laurie was right, it set me up.'[7]

His former Leicester teammate Frank Worthington was
greeted with a little more panache in Philadelphia, where the
team had been taken over by a panoply of rock 'n' roll personalities. The flamboyant striker arrived at the airport to find
co-owner and Rolling Stones manager Peter Rudge 'waiting for
me in a huge stretch limo with smoked glass windows – a bit
of a step-up from the on-loan Lada I'd left with the keys in the
ignition on a double yellow line back at Manchester Airport.'
Rudge presented him with a limited edition 'Taking Care of
Business' necklace 'which Elvis had made in 14-carat gold for
all his male friends. It was in the shape of the thunderflash
Elvis used as signature and, knowing I was a big fan, Rudgie
had got Elvis' dad Vernon to secure one for me.'[8]

While being treated like a rock star represents the top end
of the VIP treatment scale, it was not untypical: Rodney Marsh
was flown to California in Elton John's private jet while being
wooed by Los Angeles.* But even in the League's pre-Pelé days,
the journeymen players recruited from the lower English divisions were not left to fend for themselves. Wages were higher,
while decent apartments and loaned cars were part of the deal
as a matter of course. 'The wages were better when I came from
Scotland,' says Derek Spalding, who arrived from Hibernian
to play for the Chicago Sting in 1978. 'Here [in the US] it was

---

* See Chapter 4.

around $25,000 per year when I came over, and maybe I was on £100 a week at Hibs.'[9]

Canadian Bob Lenarduzzi went over to England as a fifteen-year-old to play for Reading in the Third and Fourth Division in the early 1970s, but came back to his home town of Vancouver when he was nineteen, in 1974. 'I think in Reading I was making £10 a week, but here I was making $500 a month, which for me was a lot of money when I was nineteen – significantly more money than I was making at Reading.'[10] Steve David, a Trinidadian forward, had the chance to make the grade at Leicester City in 1974, but opted for Miami instead: 'When I came to the NASL they paid me $200 a game and $150 a goal and $100 per assist, compared to England where they gave me maybe $20 a week or something. And I know that the better players, like Peter Shilton and those guys, I think they were making maybe $200–$400 a week, so it wasn't very encouraging. For my first season in Miami [in 1974] I did well, and went up to around $25,000 for the year, which made me one of the highest paid players on the team.'[11]

'Kissing in public – I liked that'

While cash was a factor, opportunity and a nose for adventure were just as important. Scottish defender Charlie Mitchell was one of the early pioneers, moving to Rochester from St Mirren in 1970 after a chance conversation at the shipyards between his dad and the father of another player, Johnny Kerr, who'd gone over to play there from Partick Thistle. Kerr's father suggested that Mitchell should give it a try too. 'I thought that sounded like a plan,' says Mitchell, 'and it was good to have someone there already. I was just going to go over for one year, make some money, and come back over. But after a year, you were already a big star in a small pond; they looked after us well, the training facilities were great. To go back to St Mirren with the muddy training gear, [where] you had to fight like a bastard to get into the team. I was only nineteen or twenty at the time and was enjoying life in the US and being popular there, so I decided to stay.'[12]

In its early years, the NASL had consciously targeted lower-level players at 'clubs in financial trouble' in Britain and Europe purely for economic reasons – they were the cheapest professionals around, together with reserves and youth team players from top flight teams, and could be taken on loan at no great expense.[13] The lower European clubs were pleased at the extra income for otherwise idle players, who would also benefit from the playing experience. The League, meanwhile, could be seen to be recruiting actual professional players, and planned to pay them no less than $7,000 per year,[14] which was very good money for that level of play, at that time (the late 1960s).

The players themselves discovered that in places like Rochester, as Mitchell points out, you could attain a certain level of local celebrity, and that being recognized as a soccer player was a pleasant experience, unlike in Scotland, where 'if you made one mistake then the crowd would boo you and be right on your back. In Rochester if you made a mistake, there weren't too many people who knew you'd made a mistake, so you could just get on with it and enjoy your game. Back home there was a lot more pressure, first to get in the team and stay in the team, and second, as a local boy, you had people in the crowd saying, "Ach, I played against him at school and I was better than him", or, "I played against him and he was nae good".'[15] San Jose's English defender Laurie Calloway said,

'Here the players are appreciated. In England, the attitude is that we are overpaid and underworked, and we get a lot of abuse.'[16] Former Everton and Scotland midfielder Jimmy Gabriel, who came to the Seattle Sounders in 1974, calls the fans there 'magnificent. It wasn't like back in England when the fans have paid their money, and if you play well they cheer for you, but if not then they get upset and they walk out before the end. They [Seattle fans] would get behind you 100 per cent the whole of the game, whether you won or lost.'[17]

Like Calloway and Gabriel, many British players came to the US and felt the love of the people who greeted them. In turn, they fell in love with the country and its space and its beaches, its possibilities, its openness. They escaped the claustrophobia of a socially conservative society where the lingering mores of a country still largely run by former Etonians and Oxbridge cliques continued to influence the way that young men were expected to behave. Even when you arrived in a city striven with riots, as Manchester City's Roy Cheetham did when he went to play for Detroit in 1968, you were unlikely to be too affected by them. The country and its cities are so vast that the focused sportsman can remain untouched by, for example, civil unrest, and lose himself in his own narrow, fitness- and ball-oriented world. 'My initial thought,' said Cheetham, 'was "What have I done!" I'd left a championship-seeking side for a riot-torn city. Despite that, I loved the two years there and it was all a great experience. The razzmatazz was all different from Manchester – we had names on our shirts and each player was announced individually. I know that's all normal now, but back then it felt more like showbiz. The team would be made up of about seven or eight different nationalities, and away games were like going on a long holiday.'[18] 'I fell in love with America and the Americans,' said the Washington Diplomats' Scottish defender Jim Steele. 'I found things were a little more free and easy over here and I fell right into the lifestyle. In England nobody touches another person on the street, but I saw Americans hugging and kissing in public, and I liked that.'[19]

Two players from Northern Ireland were especially grateful to escape a country occupied by British troops while in the throes of an oppressive and deadly civil conflict. 'It is so free and easy here. It's fabulous,' said forward Tony Armstrong, who had signed with the San Diego Sockers in 1979. In Northern Ireland, he said, 'so many lives have been destroyed and the people know nothing but trouble all their days. It is like wearing a leaden overcoat all the time. The army can stop you on the street for anything. The soldiers can make you spread-eagle against the wall and search you. They give you a number and take your picture and you feel so indignant.'[20] Two years later, his compatriot Martin Donnelly wound up in the same coastal Californian city. 'I sit here in San Diego,' he said, 'where the sun shines ... and sometimes I feel very bad.' The player reflected on how close he came to joining the Irish Republican Army, which he called 'our only form of protection'. He added, 'I'd love to go home. But once you've tasted the freedom you have in this country, it's hard. My children have the right to grow up away from gunfire and street fights. Here everyone is a friend.'[21]

Woosnam as Jehovah's Witness

The League's enthusiastic commissioner, Phil Woosnam, evangelized tirelessly throughout the 1970s about the attractiveness of the NASL, and how it would become the future of sport in the US and a major player on the international soccer scene. Early in 1979, at a point where the League had expanded to 24 teams and crowds were almost at their peak in the post-Pelé boom, he noted that the League was now getting respect from the media in the form of positive coverage both at home and abroad, and he wondered what was catching the imagination of people overseas. 'Why do they now believe in our future as much as we do, bearing in mind that we still have a long way to go and obstacles to overcome?' he mused. He willingly answered his own question: 'It appears to be that they are totally impressed with the quality of our major stadia, by the superb half-time entertainment provided by the best groups in the country, with the enormous interest shown by the whole family which also means high female attendance at games, by the social atmosphere, by the tailgating, and the pleasure on the faces of fans in casual attire. Also they see the sport being played under summer conditions as opposed to the wintry elements that are often a part of the soccer scene elsewhere in the world.'[22] If that sounds like a press release, or one of those Jehovah's Witness pamphlets depicting heaven as a place where pretty white children cavort with tame tigers, then that was part of Woosnam's self-prescribed job description. Relentlessly, he could be prompted to list the positives, while paying lip service to the work that still needed to be done as a mild concession that yes, the League still had *some* way to go before global domination.

Much of the British coverage of the League was sceptical, however. One pertinent piece, written by the *Daily Express* journalist Roy Collins for London-based *Soccer Monthly*, juxtaposed the brave new US world of spacious, sparkling stadiums and leggy cheerleaders with the ramshackle grounds, 'lack of amenities, negative soccer and the increasing hooligan problem' in the UK, conditions that American sport fans 'simply wouldn't put up with'. Yet despite being able to enjoy soccer in safety, from a seat, and with the family, soccer in the US was, Collins continued, 'handled just as any other marketable commodity, like corn flakes or soap powder. You package it, you advertise it and aim it at the consumer group most likely to buy it – normally young, successful professional people and their kids.' An English fan going to his or her first NASL game 'would find some of the gimmickry distasteful, unnecessary, or both'. Collins also quotes the Vancouver Whitecaps' English coach Tony Waiters as saying, 'Hooliganism is strangling the game in Britain. Decent fans are scared to go to the grounds any more. No one has to worry about that here.' Yet although he tries to strike a balance between the US and British approaches, the tabloid journalist in Collins can't help playing up to the prejudices of his British readership. 'The problem in America is that the fans are invariably too passive,' he concludes. 'The passion of the game has been lost under all that blatant commercialism. You can hire the sexiest cheerleaders in the world and the reaction won't match the spontaneous roar of the Kop. The Yanks, as usual, tend to overdo it. There are cannons and fireworks when the home team scores, organs, trumpets, even bongo drums accompanying their every attack.'[23]

How many games did Collins watch from the stands rather than the press box for us to take this as an accurate reflection of US soccer crowds? Dick Cecil, the vice-president of the Atlanta Chiefs in the League's formative years, remembers that Atlanta crowds 'got' the game of soccer early on, and that it wasn't merely a case of passionless punters reacting to the exhortations of the public tannoy. While on an exploratory trip in the late 60s with Phil Woosnam to watch a Tottenham versus Manchester United game at White Hart Lane, Cecil found himself 'leaning forward, and all of a sudden I'm kicking the seat in front of me. You either get it or you don't. It's a very, very emotional game, horribly so. A lot of frustrations, near misses. I didn't understand the game, but I understood the *emotion* of the game, and that's what caught me, and that's what caught a lot of people here too.' He cites a game between the Chiefs and St Louis in the 1967 season, with the Chiefs 3–0 down and reduced to nine men (and they had a third player red-carded in injury time): 'We came back and almost tied the game, getting it to 3–2. I'll never forget Peter McParland – it was a very dirty game, and Peter goes over to one of their players [who was down injured] and grabs him by the foot and just starts dragging him off the field so we could keep the play going. The referee sent Peter out. There were these nice suburban mothers standing on the seats screaming at the referee, and I was just dumbfounded at the emotion that was coming out; these very reserved southern women, they just lost it. And as I said, anything that can create that kind of emotion has got a place in our society.'[24]

There was also an intense rivalry in the Pacific North West from the mid-70s onwards between Seattle, Vancouver and Portland, who all became well supported teams. Their fans were geographically positioned for that rarity in US sports – mass migrations of away supporters. Seattle's Jimmy Gabriel likens the healthy regional rivalry to the Merseyside derby, a game he appeared in multiple times during his seven-year spell at Everton in the 1960s. 'When Everton and Liverpool played each other it was a huge game because of the atmosphere,' he says, 'but they never fought with one another because they were all from Liverpool, they were cheering for their team. The Pacific North West rivalries were all like that.' The Washington Diplomats' Northern Irish goalkeeper Bill Irwin called the NASL crowds 'very vocal and very enthusiastic.'[25]

There's no doubt that some of the passions displayed in NASL stadiums were synthetic compared to English support, with its century-long foundation of deeply engrained memories, rivalries and prejudices passed down from one generation to another, and its firm place as part of both communal and personal identity. That depth of support, however, had metamorphosed into something that was threatening its own existence, with gangs of young men staking claims to their terraces as territory, only to be yielded after a violent fight with no rules of etiquette – knives, darts, stones and bricks were just as valid in the fight as bare-knuckle fists, and heavy boots to kick a rival fan when he was down. This no more reflected a passion for soccer than cheering teams of choreographed dancing girls and cheap hot dog promotions. The players, meanwhile, kept a low profile when Britain's stadiums turned into heavily policed, segregated battlegrounds. They ran from the field at the final whistle to evade a random idiot who might jump out of the crowd swinging his fist. As Charlie Mitchell pointed out, contact with the public tended to be abusive and unpleasant. It's little wonder that so many European players found that in the US they had the time and space to relax, and that mixing with normal people was not only tolerable, but a way to expand your personal horizons and career possibilities.

This is America. It's okay to talk

> 'Every time I get the ball the commentator goes
> crazy and calls me Trevor Francis Superstar. I was
> interviewed by a woman journalist soon after I
> got here and one of the first things she wanted
> to know was how long I'd been a superstar. I said
> "about three days".'
>
> —Trevor Francis, who played two seasons, 1978
> and 1979, with the Detroit Express.[26]

British players, by dint of a common language, found themselves thrown under the media spotlights, whether they liked
it or not. That was the flip side to being unrecognized in public. Some were reluctant to express themselves, unused back
home to muttering anything more than a bland expression of
delight or disappointment to the local newspaper hack waiting outside the dressing room or lurking in the car park for a
crafty exclusive. Many of these habitually inarticulate young
men found that, once in the United States, they had to get
used to the idea of talking, and in the end this was no bad
thing. Whether it was standing in front of schoolkids explaining the very basic structure and laws of the game, publicizing
forthcoming fixtures on local radio, or playing up to the crowd
at the behest of a mascot with a microphone, reticent British
men with no media training were thrust into unfamiliar roles
promoting their chosen sport.

'I embraced it because I'm a bit of a showman,' says Leicester
City's current club ambassador Alan Birchenall, who played
for San Jose in 1977 and Memphis the year after. 'I've put on
all kinds of stuff at Leicester. I've always had something on at

half-time, which I link back to my days in San Jose. You'd run out and the PA would announce, "sixteen-year veteran of the English First Division, Alan Birchenballs". They never got my name right: I used to laugh about it. And I had the honour of singing the US national anthem at a couple of games.' He says that he was one of the first ex-players to come back from the US and start a job like the one he still holds 33 years later. 'The American experience definitely had a big influence on that. Not the football, because I was coming to the end of my career.'[27]

David Chadwick, a former Southampton and Middles-brough winger who came to Dallas from England in 1974, remembers that a lot of players were still part-time and held other jobs, leaving those players on full-time contracts to conduct camps and tour schools in the afternoons. 'It was there in our contracts that we had to do two appearances [a week],' he says. 'Some sort of clinic or school assembly or speech at a rotary club to promote the game. People who knew me when I was younger said that I was a very quiet guy – I think America changed me for the better, I became much more confident and outgoing, I was forced to think about the game. You're trying to teach someone who's never played soccer before and doesn't even know the rules, and so it was a continuing education to get people to the game and understand the game. Some people hated it, but I loved meeting people and doing the clinics.'[28] Without being forced to address large groups of people, Chadwick doubts that he would have gone on to a long and successful coaching career.

Former West Bromwich Albion defender Alan Merrick came to the Minnesota Kicks in 1976 after a decade at the Midlands club, and also thrived in his new environment. 'I became captain and spokesman for the club, so I was involved in many of the community and corporate outings that were needed to expose the Minnesota people to the game,' he says. 'And I was something of a front man for the club, which I really enjoyed. I wasn't too gregarious before that, but I became more accustomed to that responsibility. And I really enjoyed that, it helped me grow as a person.'[29] Terry Garbett, another ex-Middlesbrough man, moved to the New York Cosmos at the age of 32, and really enjoyed doing the soccer clinics because 'it helped me to talk better, to be a public person, and I needed that because I have ambitions to stay in the game.'[30]

Promising Oldham striker Carl Valentine moved to the Vancouver Whitecaps in his early twenties and said, 'I have never regretted the decision. It helped me to mature, not only as a player. For once I had to stand on my own two feet and make my own decisions.'[31] This again ties in with the idea of escape, and of re-forging your personal identity by moving to a new environment where few or no people know you. The Swiss author Max Frisch explored this in his 1954 novel *I'm Not Stiller*, where the protagonist walks away unannounced from his sterile, constricting existence in the close, oppressive landscape of Switzerland and forges a new life for himself in the United States as Mr White – the blank name denoting a new start and a flight from the existential straitjacket that his narrow social circle had strapped around him. Fiction, of course, presents an extreme example to illustrate a point – few of the players who boarded a plane would have consciously thought of themselves as a Mr White. Yet so many were driven by a sense of the adventurous and the yet-to-be discovered, and finished by embracing the opportunity. Even for established stars, the change of environment allowed them to escape from the restrictions that fame had placed on their lives.

'One of the reasons I came to America was that I didn't think I could live up to the standards I had set back home,' said Gordon Banks, shortly after joining the Fort Lauderdale Strikers in the late 1970s. 'If I can't live up to it, people here won't be saying, I remember him when. This takes a lot of weight off your shoulders. I won't miss the finger-pointing kind of thing. I wasn't the kind of person who liked it anyway.'[32] Franz Beckenbauer was more explicit. 'Everybody likes to be famous,' he conceded. 'But it is an enjoyable difference here [in New York]. In Munich when I went out at night I could read in the paper the next day every place I had been, who I went with, what I ate. Photographers and journalists followed me everywhere. I had a big house surrounded by a big wall. After a game I went home, locked the gate and shut out the world. In the US I can go unrecognized. I have a private life. I had none in Germany.'

The German press, he said, only aimed to 'tear you down. Here I have found the press to be friends.' [33] His compatriot Karl-Heinz Granitza, a prolific striker with the Chicago Sting who became one of the League's leading all-time scorers, agreed. 'I like Berlin and I liked my club [Hertha],' he said. 'It's a beautiful city and I have good friends there. The problem in the Bundesliga is that maybe one game you may score two goals, and everyone likes you ... especially the press. Then maybe the next time you don't play so good and suddenly you're a nothing player.'[34]

Former Manchester United goalkeeper Alex Stepney came to Dallas in 1979 and enjoyed the simple pleasure of a trip to the amusement park with his family. Back home, he said, you 'couldn't go out for a quiet drink or dinner. There was always someone who knew who you were, and it became a bit of a bind. People were quite ruthless. When my wife and kids were here, we went to Six Flags, and it was absolutely fabulous. No one knew us. We wouldn't do things like that in England.'[35]

A trip to Six Flags amusement park was *absolutely fabulous*. The kind of activity most average parents dread for weeks and then endure for a long and expensive day was, for Stepney, a wonderfully mundane trip free of some knucklehead following him around and shouting out 'Fuck Man United!'. Peter Osgood, upon arriving in Philadelphia in 1978, was also enjoying the lack of on-street recognition. 'It's nice and easy at the moment,' he said. 'Nice and quiet. You don't get too many people bugging me. I'm enjoying the obscurity. It's a much more quiet, much more relaxed life. But one day, I hope to walk through Philadelphia and be recognized.'[36] Ex-Coventry forward Alan Green was happy to return full-time to the Washington Diplomats after a loan spell, despite a very English penchant for watching Benny Hill over a cup of afternoon tea. 'One of the big reasons,' he said, 'was that when I came here I had a lot more confidence in my ability. I'm the type of player who needs a pat on the back, but in England you make one mistake and 25,000 fans get down on you.'[37]

Bermudan striker Clyde Best – one of Britain's first black soccer players in the late 1960s and early 1970s – left West Ham United for the Tampa Bay Rowdies in 1975 because of the naked racism in England at the time, both on and off the field. Even though he made almost 200 league appearances for the Hammers, and was eventually accepted by the home support, 'I began to think, why should I go out there and perform when I have to put up with that sort of stuff? There were problems with the amount of abuse I was taking and I decided I didn't have to put up with it. Things weren't going too good for me. Those problems were affecting me so I said, "I'm getting out".' Rather than point fingers at the English, and without explicitly mentioning that the abuse was racial, Best generously called it 'a situation that is all over the world. No matter where you go, you can't find a place where that sort of thing doesn't exist.'[38] In the US, though, such abuse was presumably less prevalent, given that he spent the final decade of his career there. Steve David, by contrast, said that Leicester City, during his trial period there in the early 70s, 'definitely' tried to integrate him – it was the cold weather, lack of friends and the promise of better wages that drove him away, although he never faced any hostile crowds like Best as he didn't play first-team soccer.[39]

'You can keep your limos and your showmen'

Lest this all seem like an over-idealized picture of the North American Soccer League's lure, there were dissenters. Everton's Welsh defender Terry Darracott came to play for the Tulsa Roughnecks in 1979, and although the team's nickname certainly corresponded to his style of play, the League apparently did not. 'I can't tell you how good it is to be home, there's no place like it,' he said with undisguised relief. 'You don't realize what a wonderful game we have until you've spent time in the States.' The perks of a large, rent-free apartment and a limousine were all very well, but, 'I couldn't come to terms with playing for fun. Their game isn't real. I play to win, I'll always be like that. For all the good things they made available, they couldn't come up with competitive football at the highest level. The American scene is for showmen. I'm not that, never will be. It's tailor-made for the Marshs, Tuearts and Worthingtons of this world.'[40]

Despite enjoying huge success with the New York Cosmos, where he played alongside both Pelé and Carlos Alberto, Steve Hunt declared upon returning home that 'British is best'. He contradicted Darracott by declaring that the US game was 'physical' – game recordings certainly back him up on this, although at the same time the preponderance of artificial playing surfaces meant fewer sliding tackles and 'over the top' challenges. Hunt went on to profess that he was annoyed by the lack of understanding among fans of the laws of the game, and also complained about the hard plastic pitches and the long distances on away travel. 'Away trips are the worst part of American football,' he said. 'You could often be away from home for up to five days. My first experience of an away trip was to Las Vegas. We spent ten days there playing two fixtures. But I had only been married a couple of months and [my wife] Sue was on her own in New York. She didn't know anybody.'[41]

Even the League's advocates concede that the travel and the variable, rarely satisfactory playing surfaces were two of the most challenging aspects of US soccer. 'We'd go to Seattle and play Vancouver the next day to save on expenses,' says David Chadwick, 'so that was hard. I don't think that was great for the game. You'd have jetlag, and be playing sometimes on different surfaces.' Depending on the field, he says, you had to adapt your style of play. On the Astroturf in Texas Stadium 'you'd be playing the ball to feet instead of in front of your teammate. But then you'd go to San Jose, a very small and narrow field, a football-type field, or to San Antonio, where there was a long jump pit partly on the field, and you're running up the wing and there was suddenly sand under your feet. Or you'd be running on the baseball diamond at places like Atlanta. You always took your cleats, and your Astroturf shoes – Sambas. Very rarely you'd wear a studded boot, because the surfaces were usually too hard.'[42]

Dennis Tueart, the England international who moved from Manchester City to the Cosmos in 1978, said that he missed the English atmosphere, despite the large numbers that the Cosmos attracted. 'We're luckier with crowds at the Cosmos than anywhere else in the States, but it's not the same as having an English crowd behind you,' he said. Worse, though, were the pitches. 'The thing I really miss about England is the grass. You get a better bounce on the Astroturf, and you're not as likely to get ankle injuries because you can wear training shoes on it. But if you try an English slide tackle, you can end up with burn marks up your leg.' The amount of travelling was 'unbelievable. And we're on the coast, so if we play in Los Angeles, it's 3,000 miles.'[43]

It was not just the travel that took its toll, but the tight schedule too. The NASL had always been squeezed in, as much as possible, to fit with the European summer break so that US clubs could take as many loan players as possible. By the late 70s, both the NASL (wanting to extend its tight season) and the English Football League (sick of exhausted players playing twelve months a year) were finding the loan situation unsatisfactory, so both acted to make sure more players made full-time transfer moves to the US (and back). 'The schedule is one of the things that makes this league the toughest in the world,' said Eddie Firmani, coach of the Cosmos when the extended time span for the season was announced for the 1979 season. 'We have to play eleven games in 33 days. This is murderous for the players. This is soccer, not baseball where they can play every day.' His winger Steve Hunt added, 'I lose six pounds a game. I can't put it back on when I have another game two days later.'[44]

The heat, the tiredness from too many games, and the bone-hard nature of the playing surfaces were all factors in the quality of soccer played in the NASL. There were more decisive forces, though, that dictated the League's *style*. Clearly, to appeal to the nascent, native soccer audience, goals and entertainment were needed. Yet with such an abundance of European, and especially British, players in the League, was there anything to silence critics unfavourably comparing many NASL teams with the blood-and-thunder, kick-and-rush tactics characteristic of the English Second Division and below?

English crudity vs Latin finesse

'Most of the British players were going out there doing clinics, and I was the director of coaching, so myself and a few Brits would take the South Americans along to the clinics so that they could do all the tricks and juggling while we would do all the talking.'

—Charlie Mitchell of the Rochester Lancers[45]

As the above quote illustrates, there was far more to the NASL than just Brits. Both the Caribbean and Anglophone Africa provided numerous players, again by dint of the common language needed to explain and spread the game. Yugoslavs (cheap) and northern Europeans (available in summer, and usually able to speak English) also came in large numbers. There were, of course, the token US players – much discussed in terms of the game's future, but under-used in practice. And finally, South and Central Americans, because you needed players with technical ability who could actually play the game rather than just run through it. In the case of the Rochester Lancers, Mitchell points up how this was an ideal mix. The South Americans demonstrated what the Brits could only explain.

How did this translate into an actual style of play on the field, at a time when there were still very distinctive differences from continent to continent, and even country to country? Up to and including the 1970s, players still largely remained in their domestic leagues, with the exception of a few noted South Americans moving to the big-name clubs of Spain or Italy. Pelé stayed at Santos his entire career until he retired, then came to New York, and even that was seen as exceptional – or as a betrayal – by many Brazilians. The North American Soccer League was the first truly mobile league, where every team was enhanced, or burdened, by its multinational nature. It was a proving ground for the idea of sport without borders that was finally realized by the English Premier League in the post-Bosman era, and an early experiment in the trials of mixing several ethnic backgrounds, mostly young men with extremely high opinions of themselves. In addition, coaches came from a cross-section of countries, and even two coaches from England could wildly disagree on the correct approach to the game, either at home or in America. Add to that the vastly differing pay scales – both across and within clubs – and you have a recipe for dissension, unrest and dressing-room rebellion.

The New York Cosmos won the Soccer Bowl in 1977, Pelé's final year in the League, but they didn't have a smooth year until the latter part of the season. Journalist Ike Kuhns looked back at some of the problems at the end of that season. 'The polyglot of styles clashed,' he wrote. 'The English resented the lack of defence from the South Americans and called the finesse game the Latins played "gutless". In turn, the South Americans sneered at the "crude", rough English and were appalled by the English players' penchant for beer and lack of dedication to training. [Giorgio] Chinaglia brooded about being ignored by team-mates who came back with the nickname "Italian Statue" in reference to Giorgio's defensive skills.'[46] The American defender Bobby Smith went public with his complaints about the divided atmosphere among the players – world superstars in one corner, the English in another, and the Americans excluded entirely – and was dropped for his troubles until a new coach, Eddie Firmani (coming from Tampa), let him back in. The following year, though, he was still fuming about what he saw as the poor treatment of American players in the League. 'Who's looking out for the Americans in the NASL?' he demanded to know. 'The owners? They can't get their faces out of the trough long enough to be moral. The coaches? They're so scared of losing games they won't take a chance on us. The foreign players? With a few exceptions like Chinaglia and Rodney Marsh, who will help out an American? The old guys who were over the hill in Europe or South America are too insecure with their own starting positions here. As a result, we're getting the shaft right here in our own country. We're the window dressing. They keep telling us to wait, to take our time. Well, we've heard those lyrics and we want it now.'[47]

The Cosmos' opponents in that year's championship game, the 1977 Soccer Bowl, were the Seattle Sounders, whose coach Jimmy Gabriel concedes that the meeting of multifarious nationalities in the NASL led to a 'mishmash' of styles. He wrestled with the dilemma facing most coaches in the League: how to be entertaining, but get results too. 'I didn't want to have a team that just went out there and kicked the ball and chased after it,' he says. 'You know, defences sitting back and booting it up the park and hoping for the odd goal. I wanted my team to control the game, to pass and move – the teams that I played for played like that, and I tried to put that into our play.' In fact, although they lost 2–1 to the Cosmos in what was Pelé's final competitive game, the Sounders easily matched the Cosmos in what Gabriel calls 'a great game. It was end to end, the fans loved it, and they [the Cosmos] won – it was meant to be. He [Pelé] was a great player. We certainly tried to mess it up: we hit the post and crossbar, we gave them a real good game. I was really pleased at the way the team played. We didn't have the kind of money that New York had, but we showed that if you work with a good team of players and get that rhythm, you can also get all the way to the final.'[48]

The Three Interpretations of Peter Osgood

Gabriel also admits that the NASL was an attractive place for a lot of older professionals because, like himself, they were looking for a path into coaching, and wanted to enjoy the last few years of their career enjoying themselves while still looking like stars. The perception that too many old pros were coming to the NASL was an image the League never managed to shake off, although it was arguably an unfair stereotype. Let's take Peter Osgood as an example, and interpret his NASL career from three different angles.

The First Interpretation of Peter Osgood comes from the player himself. The former Chelsea and Southampton striker came to the Philadelphia Fury in 1978, part of a team launched with rock star panache by, among others, Rick Wakeman, Peter Frampton and Paul Simon, and which boasted Alan Ball and Johnny Giles in its playing ranks. Aged 30, Osgood left England disillusioned with its tax laws and because, he said, he wasn't excited by English football any more. Young players were being forced to play too defensively and 'goal artists' such as himself, Rodney Marsh and George Best had suffered through a time when play was becoming more negative. He declared that the NASL was improving precisely because there were now fewer loan players coming from Europe, and so 'the full-time players are putting their heart and soul into it because they want to be successful'. Osgood was happy to help promote the game and be touted as a superstar, and surmised, 'What it all boils down to is they build me up, and I've just got to perform on the field and do it.' He promised Philly's fans a side they would be proud of, 'a soccer side that will be entertaining, and players who will do their darndest* to get soccer going in Philadelphia.'[49]

The Second Interpretation comes from a teammate, the Scotsman Tony Glavin, who came to the Fury from Queen's Park on the advice of his older brother, Celtic's Ronnie. Glavin refutes the idea that the likes of Giles and Osgood were old pros cashing in at the end of their careers. 'Giles was 38 and I was nineteen,' he says. 'I remember my brother telling me

---

* Those who doubt that Osgood would have said the word 'darndest' do not give him credit for quickly adapting to the local slang. Or perhaps what he really said was translated into family-friendly American.

before I went over that I needed to talk to the experienced players, and he mentioned Giles by name. I asked him if I knew him, and he said, "No, just trust me, go speak to him if you need anything." He maybe wasn't in his prime, but the value he brought to the team and to players like myself ... you can't put a figure on help like that. Peter was also at the end of his career and only scored one goal for the Fury, but he could do great things to help young players. And Giles would put his arm around your shoulder and talk you through things when you were down. It helped in so many ways, developing the game in this country. Look at the number of players who stayed in this country after things went downhill – that speaks volumes and tells you those players didn't just come for a pay cheque, they were here for the game itself.'[50]

The Third Interpretation comes from the sidelines. As Glavin notes, Osgood scored just once in 22 games in 1978, although he did register eight assists. For a player still in his prime, this was unimpressive compared with other British forwards that season – Mike Flanagan scored 30 goals, Trevor Francis 22, Kevin Hector 21 and Rodney Marsh, more of a midfielder, notched eighteen. Paul Gardner cites Osgood as the 'classic example' of the NASL throwing good money at bad players. 'He never did a fucking thing, he just wasn't that good,' he says. 'You know that the English overrate their players anyway. The reason the Brits of course were imported and became popular was simply the language. You want to sell the sport, you want to have players with personality who can go on TV and mix with the local populace, you've got to have them speak the language. There was a logic involved to the whole thing, but it was unfortunate because it meant bringing in a certain brand of soccer, and that meant certain attitudes that came along with it. Just take a look at British soccer ... the sad thing was they were playing dull, outdated soccer, and by that time, by 1975, I'd spent a lot of time in Brazil and talking to Brazilians and Italians and Argentines here in New York, and I had a much wider understanding of the game and a broader appreciation of the different styles.'[51] American players coming out of college in the 1970s didn't help matters, he adds, because 'the college game ... was adapted to a sort of Brit, blood-and-thunder-type game. It was leaving out the artistic elements.'

Many agreed with this at the time. 'The game in England now is based on the physical aspects only,' said Frank Worthington, another Philadelphia recruit who was effectively Osgood's 'superstar' replacement in 1979. 'No skill. No techniques. Mostly it's how fast you can run. Skills are ignored. I found more use of skills over here and I like that. The game is going backwards over there and that is criminal. There is more free expression over here.'[52]

Writers who came to the US were often surprised at what they saw. 'To anyone who has not seen the NASL game, the competitiveness comes as a jolting shock,' journalist Rob Hughes wrote in the book he co-authored with Trevor Francis. 'American soccer was reputed to have all the cut and thrust of kindergarten. Not so. There is not the rapport, the interplay of emotions that would pass between an English crowd of 20,565 and the players, but the breakneck speed, the physical endeavour and tight, defensive discipline are familiar enough.'[53] Dennis Tueart said, perhaps somewhat defensively, towards the end of his first season, 'It's no holiday over here. I'll tell you, the quality of play here has definitely surprised me. It really has.'[54]

The style of play you saw, though, largely depended on which team you watched, and who was the coach. There was an unwritten brief from the League to play attacking soccer, and to provide goals and entertainment. Yet you couldn't have commissioner Phil Woosnam standing behind the coach's bench telling Gordon Jago to throw more men forward. Furthermore, different coaches held different philosophies on what constituted positive soccer. 'I am not interested in the destroying factor of the game,' said New England Tea Men coach Noel Cantwell, despite having no fewer than eleven English nationals in his small squad of nineteen for the 1978 season. 'I am not interested in people that kick each other and the violence of the game. I want it to be presented as a spectacle. I want it to be entertaining. I say at almost every Tea Men meeting that we are an open theatre and we've got to present the show. And if the show isn't good, the public won't come back. I don't put restrictions on players. I believe in players expressing themselves.'[55] He was true to his word that season, with the Tea Men at one point going on a seven-game winning run. They scored 27 goals in the process, including six against San Diego and five each against San Jose, Minnesota and the California Surf.

The former QPR and Millwall manager Gordon Jago, who spent four years coaching the Tampa Bay Rowdies, also declared that he only enjoyed 'entertaining, attractive soccer. I promise to give our fans what I want when I watch soccer ... the thing that makes soccer a special sport ... that burst of something special and unexpected springing from intelligent, calculating teamwork.'[56] Note that final qualifier, though – entertainment's all very well, but you can't have eleven jugglers on the field. Still, in 1978 Jago's Tampa team scored one more

goal than Cantwell's New England, and further nurtured the
Rowdies' reputation as a good team to watch by making it all
the way to the Soccer Bowl.

Orient's Derek Possee came to the US in 1978 at the age
of 32 to join the Vancouver Whitecaps 'and their new coach
Tony Waiters – a fierce proponent of attacking soccer'.[57]
By the time he'd been in the US for a year, though, Waiters
decided, 'It's not razzmatazz and hoop-la that we want here.
What we're looking for is complete professionalism – both
on and off the field.'[58] His successful 1979 squad of twenty
consisted of twelve English players, six Canadians, a Scot and
a Zimbabwean (Bruce Grobbelaar). His squad lacked diver-
sity not because other players 'were from a country other than
England, but because I had not been able to properly gauge
their ability to fit into our way of doing things. In England I
know the kind of player I want. I know all about him. His playing qualities – good and bad, his characteristics, his lifestyle,
his hopes and ambitions, and most of all his ability to fit into
the Whitecaps community.' His team scored an average of just
over 1.8 goals per game on their way to the title – respectable,
but not stunning. To put that in context, they netted 54 goals
in 30 regular-season games. The Cosmos – the Royal Standard
of the NASL and its entertainment philosophy – scored 84
goals in the same time span.

It's hard to say objectively, though, which was the better club. The teams met four times that season, plus a 'mini-
game', and the Whitecaps won the first three. In the regular
season, they beat the Cosmos 4–1 at home in front of their biggest crowd so far that season, over 32,000. In New York, they
became the only team to beat the Cosmos at Giants Stadium
all season in open play (Seattle beat them via the shootout),

and here the bad blood started – the game was stopped due to a mass confrontation when Vancouver's Scottish winger Willie Johnston (sent home from the Argentina World Cup the year before after failing a drugs test) collided with the Cosmos' Andranik Eskandarian – the Iranian defender who had put through his own net to give Scotland their sole goal in a dreadful 1–1 performance at that same competition. The pair started fighting, both benches joined in, and at the end of a fourteen-minute stoppage, Johnston and Eskandarian were both ejected by English referee Keith Styles, as were Giorgio Chinaglia and Vancouver's John Craven. The long-since-retired Pelé, who had been sitting on the Cosmos bench, was 'escorted from the field', according to an Associated Press report, while Chinaglia's agent, Peppe Pinton, was arrested at half-time for trying to enter the officials' locker room.

The team officials hardly did their best to help the atmosphere. 'What we saw tonight was disgraceful,' said the Cosmos' technical director (effectively their coach at the time) Julio Mazzei. Yet he wasn't talking about his own players, who had merely been defending themselves: 'I'm sick and tired of having teams coming here trying to kill our players. I applaud my players for fighting for the team and we will not accept the poor job done by the referee.' Tony Waiters countered that 'Carlos Alberto started the whole thing by kicking our player. We weren't going to lie down. I think the Cosmos felt kind of sore about losing to us in Vancouver and they didn't take kindly to losing to their country cousins twice.'[59] Oh, Vancouver won the game 4–2.

That the Cosmos were poor losers was already common knowledge, not just a rumour. In the first leg of the playoff semi-final in Vancouver, this time in front of almost 33,000 fans, the Whitecaps won again, 2-0, on goals by Trevor Whymark and Johnston. The Cosmos complained bitterly that Whymark had been offside, but the replays are inconclusive – if he was, it was a very close call. With a few seconds left, Eskandarian took out Vancouver's Kevin Hector with a horrible, premeditated challenge and was ordered off. Then in the tunnel following the game, Carlos Alberto, in the words of the League's PR director Jim Trecker, 'threw his shirt at, verbally abused and spat upon game officials'.[60] The League banned him for the rest of the season and fined him heavily. The Cosmos moaned and threatened legal action (a favourite ploy), but the League stood firm. This meant that both he and Eskandarian missed the return leg at the Meadowlands.

So, the scene was set for the comparison between the supposedly physical English approach of the Whitecaps, and the apparently sophisticated, trans-continental style of the Cosmos. It wasn't that simple, however. The Cosmos welcomed back into their team the Dutch duo of Wim Rijsbergen and Johan Neeskens, who had both missed the first leg, and who were both extremely robust players, the hard men in the Dutch national team who allowed the soccer players around them to flourish (though Neeskens was not at all short on skill himself). And so the game proved only that generalized talk of style was often meaningless when applied to the NASL. The Cosmos committed twenty fouls as against thirteen by Vancouver. They played a prettier game, but only by a slight technical margin thanks to the finesse of Franz Beckenbauer and the sublime Yugoslav playmaker Vladislav Bogićević, who'd come to the Cosmos at the age of 27 after several successful years at Red Star Belgrade, and after playing for Yugoslavia at the 1974

World Cup.* There was very little to choose between the two teams in terms of either overall skill or chances created, with the game pretty much end to end throughout. Vancouver passed the ball along the ground almost as often as the home team, with the Englishman Alan Ball as their creative fulcrum, while the Cosmos were not averse to playing the long ball every now and then. And why not? It's not against the rules, and a perfect long pass is just as much a part of the game's beauty as a seven-man move. In fact such a pass, played out from the back by Brazilian Nelsi Morais, put the Angolan-Portuguese Seninho free on the right, and his deft left-footed pass after taking the ball down was converted by Welsh-Italian-American Chinaglia for his second goal of the night just before half-time to put New York 2–1 ahead (Whitecaps defender John Craven had earlier cancelled out Chinaglia's first). Johnston equalized a few minutes before the end to make the final score 2–2, which under any more sensible system would have put Vancouver through to the final. However, the NASL eschewed the idea of draws in any shape or form, and so the game went to fifteen minutes of sudden-death over-time, which brought no more goals, followed by a New York win in the shootout. At least there was no fighting this time.

This now meant that the overall two-legged tie was level at one game each, necessitating a 30-minute mini-game with new line-ups, but no sudden death. There were no legitimate goals, but another incident did nothing to dispel the Cosmos' reputation as a conglomerate of whiners. Vancouver's Carl Valentine, at the start of the second 'mini-half', cut inside the Cosmos

---

* Established Yugoslav players could only leave the communist country aged 28, but 'Bogi' made it out a few months early.

defence and cracked off a shot that hit the underside of the
bar, appeared to bounce behind the line, then came back into
play, where Beckenbauer headed it out over the bar. Initially,
the referee and linesmen appeared to award a goal, and that
sent the Cosmos players into overdrive. Several of them, led
by Beckenbauer and Chinaglia, ran over to the linesman, surrounded him and started screaming in his face. The linesman
was eventually shielded by a police officer. After another long
delay, during which the referee and the linesman held a long
talk, the goal was annulled. The message was relayed to the
ABC television team that the linesman had not been 100 per
cent sure it was a goal, and had never given it in the first place,
though the horde of bug-eyed Cosmos players maybe helped
place a little doubt in his mind. The TV replays of the shot
are not absolutely conclusive, though if the linesman wasn't
100 per cent sure, he must have been at least 95 per cent certain it was a goal. Justice prevailed in the end – in the second
shootout of the night, the Whitecaps won and went forward
to the Soccer Bowl, which they also won in the same stadium
the following weekend, beating the Tampa Bay Rowdies 2–1
with a Whymark brace.

What does this tell us about the style of the NASL? Only
that style also includes character, and characters are multi-
faceted mixtures of good and evil. The Cosmos played the best
attacking soccer in the League, of that there's little dispute, but
they were the rich and arrogant sons of bitches that everyone
else came to dislike at best and set out to kick off the park at
worst. Did the Cosmos invite this attitude because they were
so good? It's more likely that the other teams' periodically
negative reaction was provoked by the New Yorkers' unstinting will to win at any cost, even if that meant pressuring the

game officials and the League at every opportunity, while publicly proclaiming how everyone was against them. It's the hallmark of a 'great' club, and a short jump of the imagination from the Cosmos to the modern mega-brands of Manchester, Munich and Madrid. No one likes us (apart from our millions of revenue-generating fans worldwide), but we don't care, because despite constantly playing the role of the victim, we're rich and win everything anyway.

Benched Americans still lacking 'pizzazz'

Around the time that the Whitecaps and all their Englishmen were lifting that 1979 trophy, a few young Americans were nonetheless complaining loudly about the English style of coaching. The Tulsa Roughnecks' Billy Gazonas, who had been the 1977 College Player of the Year, said, 'The English coaches like a long-passing, hard-running game, but the better soccer colleges here teach us the short-pass, field-working style. So they don't understand us, and we don't want to play their way.' (In response, his English coach Alan Hinton said, 'The Americans are just going to have to play the English style. After all, we control the sport here, don't we?') Rick Davis, a nineteen-year-old US prospect who had performed really well for the Cosmos in 1979, said, 'They tell you that just practicing with Beckenbauer and Chinaglia and the others will make you a better player, but it won't. The trick is to get a starting slot and hang on. I played centre forward all my life, but here I'm a midfielder, and I'm glad I can start.'[61]

Fellow American Tim Twellman says that after joining the Minnesota Kicks as a forward in 1977, and playing well up front in pre-season, he received a 'rude awakening' when forwards Ron Futcher and Alan Willey arrived from England and walked straight into the team. 'It took me quite some time to get comfortable with it,' he concedes. 'And when I did, I knew that I wasn't going to be playing as a forward. And unlike some other American players, I was willing to play anywhere. If they said, Tim, can you play right back, centre back, midfield? I would say sure. Some American players didn't and they were sent home. I was willing to do whatever was required of me, and it paid off.' At that time, there was only a minimum of two US players required on the field, and one of those was usually a goalkeeper – a strong position for US players because of the handling sports like basketball and American football they played from a young age. 'So you were fighting for a [single] spot just among the American players,' Twellman says. 'Often you were more concerned what American players they were bringing in and whether they were better than you.'[62] He ended up making his career at first as a midfielder, and then as a defender.

Joey Fink remembers that 'a lot of the coaches were still predominantly English and didn't have confidence in US players. [Cosmos coach] Gordon Bradley had a high regard for anyone playing in England, and a player might arrive on Wednesday afternoon and go straight into the team that evening. A lot of the foreign players and coaches had no confidence in US players and that created a little bit of a rift.' He's grateful, however, that this taught him 'pretty much the foundation of my whole life – that there's always someone coming to challenge you for your job, and you have to have the confidence to fight off those challenges.'[63]

Imported players could also find the regime of an English coach challenging. Steve David from Trinidad – who had won the League's coveted Most Valuable Player award in 1975 with Miami – was traded from LA to Detroit during the 1978 season, and couldn't stomach the tactics of coach Ken Furphy. He describes Detroit as 'a very, very English team, and the style was not the style that I liked. I had to do a lot of work deep, coming back, chasing people back, which I hated doing, so I had to expend so much energy defending that up front my energy was done. You had to be exceptionally fit.' Rather than play a style he hated, he asked for a transfer, but was refused it and so then just didn't bother turning up at the airport for an away game in San Diego. 'They called me and said, "Where are you?" And I said, "I'm at home, I'm not going. I told you guys I want out."' The team relented and traded him to the California Surf. 'Which was fine with me,' he says. 'I came from [a team in] California and I went back to California.'[64] This outcome seems appropriate – nothing could be more starkly juxtaposed than the laid-back vibe of California and the harried, hustling English way of playing soccer. However, players coming from English soccer, as we've already heard, found the US game much less frenetic, even under an English coach. Alan Willey says the NASL style was 'a little more laid back. In England it was 100 miles per hour. In England it's more stressful – as soon as you get the ball the crowd's on your back to get it upfield and score.'[65]

When Frank Worthington moved to the Tampa Bay Rowdies in 1981, he was seen as a replacement for the hugely popular Rodney Marsh, in the same way as he'd been seen as compensation for the failure of Peter Osgood in Philadelphia two years earlier. An interviewer compared him with Marsh, and Worthington agreed that the now-retired Marsh and himself were 'alike in most aspects. I would say he was more of an

out and out individual than me. I am more of a front player.'
Marsh, he said, was 'theatre'. Was Worthington there to bring
back the pizzazz to Tampa, he was asked.

'Pizzazz, eh? That's what you call it? Okay. If I can add –
what is it, pizzazz? – so much the better.'[66]

That the NASL was still relying on maturing pros with
'character' to bring in the fans is a reflection of its failure to
imprint itself permanently on the US sporting map, and to
develop its native talent quickly enough to tap into the deep
and easily accessible mine of homeland patriotism. However,
that the League still existed at all, and that it had attained such
(albeit transient) levels of national popularity, was in large
measure due to the 'pizzazz' of players like Marsh and George
Best. They found the US an ideal platform to explore the free-
doms denied them on the muddy fields of the English Football
League, where they had been too often the victims of hatchet
men roaming under the orders of conservative, entertainment-
killing coaches who lived for results alone.

4 Marsh and Best: Entertaining the USA

'There are very few people in soccer with the
sort of ability Marsh has. You usually find with
this sort of player a mental approach that is
different. You have to accept them the way they
are. Only a fool would try to submerge those
assets.'

—Gordon Jago, coach of
the Tampa Bay Rowdies[1]

Rodney Marsh stopped the game, although referee Peter
Johnson hadn't blown his whistle. The Tampa Bay Rowdies
midfielder fell to his knees, stretched out his arms and gestured at the ball in his possession. *Come and get it*, he was saying to the New York Cosmos, a team that was losing 4–0, and
whose pivotal player, Pelé, was not having his greatest day.
Come on, come and get it – I know you can't, but try anyway.

It was the 1976 season, and the first visit by the Cosmos
to the upstart Tampa Bay Rowdies since Pelé's signing the
previous year. The New York team, fresh off the plane from
an exhibition game in the Dominican Republic, looked dis-
tinctly out of sorts, playing in front of a national TV audience and a regular-season League record crowd of over 42,000.
They finished exhausted, outplayed, and soundly beaten by five
goals to one. The talking point of the game was not, however,
the exemplary hat-trick that Derek Smethurst put past New
York's hapless second-choice goalkeeper Kurt Kuykendall. It

was Marsh, down on his knees, taunting a team that featured the greatest player of all time.

The Englishman, playing his first NASL season, opened up and flaunted a full bag of tricks that day. There were cheeky back-heel passes, nonchalant dummies, and a flawless back-heeled lob over his own head down the left wing that saw him breeze past a floundering opponent. On another occasion he effortlessly robbed an oncoming Cosmos player of the ball, then passed it forward down the line to a teammate, all the while holding his left boot, lost in action moments before. Marsh fully exploited the vast space in midfield that the Cosmos and the 35-yard offside line (see chapter 7 for more on this NASL innovation) permitted him, prompting CBS's co-commentator Paul Gardner to say at the end of the afternoon, 'Marsh has overshadowed Pelé, no doubt about it.' When he left the field shortly before the end of the game, he received a standing ovation.

There was more to it than Marsh simply having a stellar game against a great opponent. No, this was personal and Marsh made sure everyone from the Cosmos, to the crowd, to the television audience knew it. When Marsh went down on his knees and teased the ineffective Cosmos, he outraged the Brazilian too.

The Cosmos' Northern Irish midfielder Dave Clements was marking Marsh. Well, it's more accurate to say Clements – the sort of fading, 30-something journeyman commonly signed by NASL teams prior to Pelé's arrival – chased him as Marsh ran with the ball. Watching footage from the game, as you see Clements try to tap Marsh's ankles from behind, you think of Marsh as the cruel dad shielding the ball from his four-year-old at the park, teaching him the tough way that neither life nor football is an easy game, son. Eventually, Clements half-tackled him, but Marsh still managed to retain the ball as he ran back towards his own goal, now inside his own half ('I elbowed him in the face to get away from him,' says Marsh[2]). He turned, Clements was now ten yards away, so this was the moment when Marsh knelt down and gestured, inviting Clements to come and fetch the object he desired, but had no chance of obtaining. Then Marsh stood up again and made another back-heel pass without even glancing to check if it had reached his own player. It had.

At this point, Clements charged into Marsh and knocked him over. Watching the game now, you expect a straight red card for violent conduct. Meanwhile, Giorgio Chinaglia, having a stinker all afternoon, came over and grabbed Marsh by the arm. Pelé applauded Marsh sarcastically and tweaked his ear, then applauded him again, and also grabbed his arm. The whole time, Marsh did not react, did not even look a Cosmos player in the eye. Johnson had by now blown his whistle. He talked to Marsh, and gave a free kick against him for unsportsmanlike conduct. Clements escaped any kind of punishment or lecture.

'Rodney had a certain arrogance about him,' says Rowdies teammate Joey Fink. 'He was a great player, but he had an arrogance about him that affected the team a little bit, not in a negative way, but he carried himself a little bit above [the others].' Fink contrasted that with Pelé, who 'was one of the guys, he never had any kind of attitude that he was better than anyone else'.[3]

Yet on this day, Pelé was second best. Marsh showed him no respect at all, and that was clearly crossing a line for his fellow pros. For a whole year, the Cosmos had been the League's

115

publicity flagship, but in a short second Marsh had pricked their balloon and shown them what he thought of all that. *We're 4–0 up and you can't even get the ball off me.* This is the player originally introduced by the Tampa Bay owner at his first press conference as 'the white Pelé'. Marsh corrected him. 'No, Pelé is known as the black Rodney Marsh,' he said. He explained in his autobiography, *Priceless*, 'I meant it as a joke, but if you don't believe in yourself, who else is going to believe in you?' At the same time, Marsh later learnt from Pelé's teammate Rildo that when the Cosmos played the Rowdies the following year, Pelé told the dressing room: 'Tampa are a good team. They have one player in particular to watch out for. His name is Rodney Marsh. He wears the number 10. He is English but he plays like a Brazilian.'[4] That, says Marsh now, 'was one of the biggest compliments anyone ever paid me.'[5]

Englishmen who play like Brazilians are a rarity, never faring particularly well in their home country. Fans may love flair players, but managers tend to dispense with them the moment that the need for results overtakes any notion of delighting spectators. The 70s became the era of the flair player, but a lot of them had trouble sticking with clubs. There's always that nagging feeling as a manager or a coach that, when faced with individual footballing genius, you have the choice of letting it speak on the field while risking your tactics and team, or suppressing it for the mundane but more virtuous goals of the collective.

Players with character on the field, by no coincidence, tended to be highly individualistic off the field as well. This became problematic in a team game in the post-war austerity era, especially when professionals started to earn decent amounts of money in the late 1960s. As discussed in chapter three, managers were still old-school disciplinarians from a generation when young men obeyed their seniors, or their officers. How would we have beaten the Nazis if mere foot soldiers had broken rank? Did anybody sitting in a bunker waiting for the bombs to stop falling on 1940s Britain envision a future that looked remotely like the 1970s? So when long-haired, free-living, free-drinking, freestyle dribbling players like Marsh and George Best came along, the British game was ill-equipped to deal with them. Marsh was a player who had no problem saying what was on his mind. Best didn't care about disappearing for days and missing a training session or three. They were working-class boys who were adored by masses of people, getting handsomely paid for what they could do extremely well, and they saw no reason why they had to answer to anybody.

It's too easy, though in some measure it's true, to say that Marsh and Best thrived in the NASL because they were allowed the freedom to express themselves. Both players had problems with their teams in Manchester, and both suffered the same trouble in the US – Marsh fell out with his coaches, and Best fell out with his teams over absenteeism and alcohol. Marsh left Manchester City because, in his words, 'I had an enormous confrontation with then [City] manager Tony Book and the chairman Peter Swales over the philosophy of football. We argued and argued, and eventually they said, "We can't see us going forward with you as our captain on the field of play, so we're going to put you on the transfer list."'[6] He toyed with the idea of going to play for Anderlecht in Belgium, but then his agent Ken Adam said that Elton John was buying into the LA Aztecs, and wanted to make Best and Marsh his marquee signings. While he was out taking a look at LA and watching the singer in concert, all on Elton's dime, Tampa Bay – a place he couldn't find on the map – asked him to come and take a look at Florida. The minute he stepped off the plane, he felt that this was the right place. 'I've always looked back on that and said it was intangible,' says Marsh. 'I just felt it was the right thing to do. I've no idea why. It was not dissimilar to David Beckham leaving European football and suddenly going to Los Angeles when everyone said he'll never go, and he suddenly did.'[7]

Marsh doesn't pretend that he was heading out on a self-declared mission to grow the game in the States. By default, that's what every pro who came from Europe was going to end up doing anyway, whether they liked it or not. The training clinics in local schools, the radio interviews with football-blind reporters, and interminable publicity sessions signing autographs for fans were not optional. In fact, Marsh says, 'My decision was made purely for me. It was a selfish decision. I wanted to do something massively different in football.' Happily, the clinics and the publicity work suited Marsh right from the start. 'The fact we were going out to teach young ten-year-old kids how to play while playing for the first team, we were teaching the gospel of soccer.'[8] Perhaps, this was where Marsh enjoyed the novelty of being loved by both the fans and the press, rather than being alternately lauded and vilified as he was in England.

It's a paradox that the maverick player, who thrives on his sense of rebellion and being a significantly better player than the water-carriers, the workhorses and the henchmen, also wants to be accepted. Marsh claims that the only manager 'who understood me' was Queens Park Rangers manager Alec Stock, who signed him from Fulham. 'I had a problem with all the Fulham managers,' says Marsh. 'Alec Stock said,

"Rodney, go out and play, play your own way, and we'll adjust around you." If you ask any of the QPR players from that era, we developed a pattern of play that was so progressive, it was like the teams of today. We played one up front, four at the back and four in midfield, and Rodney Marsh. I could do whatever I wanted to do, and play wherever I wanted to, and the team adjusted around me. I felt loved and felt that was how I should have been treated.' He lauds 'seven glorious years at QPR', where he scored 44 goals in his first season (1966–67), won the League Cup and the Third Division championship, and the following season a second successive promotion that took QPR to the top flight.

In the NASL, though, Marsh faced the old problem of how to fit in – even though it's obvious watching the Cosmos footage that, if given free rein, Marsh could control a team of variable quality like a puppeteer pulling at multiple strings with his eyes half-closed, all the while moving at a pace suited to the heat. Yet his coach at Tampa, Eddie Firmani, didn't like Marsh. At first he made Marsh his team captain, but that only lasted three games before the Englishman stepped down. There was talk that players resented him wearing the captain's armband so soon after his arrival, and that they were peeved he might displace the excellent Clyde Best from the team, although as it turned out both players were starters for most of the season. The real reason seems to be that Marsh was completely unsuited to being the coach's interpreter on the field. Marsh's approach to the game was spontaneous and flamboyant. If there was a 90-minute game plan, he wouldn't be following it for more than ten. There's barely a coach or manager alive who is happy to see his team captain adopt that kind of approach, in any sport.

After Marsh's first year, Firmani told Tampa that either Marsh went or he did, and here's another difference between the NASL and the English league. When he feuded with Manchester City, Marsh ended up on the transfer list. He may have cost City £200,000 (a massive fee in 1972), but in England no single player could ever be seen to look like he was bigger than the club, or undermining the manager's authority. Chairman Peter Swales was not going to throw out Tony Book over the football philosophy of a player (though Swales wasn't shy of throwing out managers for other reasons, like not winning enough games). Things were different at Tampa Bay, with owner Beau Rodgers telling Firmani to grin and bear it. Marsh's arrival had led to bigger crowds, after all. 'Firmani didn't want me [in 1977],' says Marsh. 'He felt that I was disruptive, but the owner wanted me because the crowds came in, our crowds went up from 7,000 to 20,000 after about the first year, and we were winning and getting massive amounts of publicity. Firmani didn't want me at the start of that second year, but the owner did, so Firmani had to accept that. But as soon as he could he went off to New York.'

Marsh stayed, the coach left. Two years later, in 1979, Marsh said that Firmani had told him 'in no uncertain terms' that he wanted his star player to run harder and pace himself less. 'There are some ways of getting the best out of soccer players,' Marsh said. 'Some, you can bawl them out. Others, you have to say sweet things in their ear and throw them candy.'[9]

That's a nice idea, that a good manager will keep his maverick sweet with regular doses of candy. At the same time, in a team game, it might just be the 'disruptive' factor that Marsh alludes to above. Most cosseted professional sportsmen are in some respects little more advanced than young boys. Their innate sense of justice, coupled with an even more intrinsic sense of self, says that if they see one boy getting candy, they'll want some too. *Why does he get special treatment? Because he does a bloody pirouette on the ball and makes the fans go 'Whoo!'? And here I am running up and down the field for 90 minutes, covering my mark, getting my tackles in, closing down the space. Mr Consistency, that's what they call me, but do I get any bloody candy?* That's the problem with having been a Dave Clements. It could be that the only reason anyone remembers you was because they saw you body-check Rodney Marsh that time he got down on his knees in front of you and said, *Hey kid, here's the ball. Want to have another try?*

Accept George, love George, stay off George's case

'I hate being told what to do,' George Best said in 1978 while still with the first of his three NASL teams, the LA Aztecs. 'I always did.'[10] Like Marsh, though, Best could get away with rebellion in the States because the prestige he carried as a superstar outweighed the authority of a coach.

He almost became the Cosmos' first marquee signing, a few months before Pelé. 'I tried to sign George Best and I went to Old Trafford and did a deal to sign him,' says Clive Toye. 'George was in his not well-behaved times, and after we did the deal we couldn't find him; we looked for him in every pub and bar, but I ended up catching a plane and came back and later he signed for LA. The next time I saw him, after we'd signed Pelé, we were in Arizona for a pre-season exhibition game and the teams were lined up for the national anthems, and I went up and put my arms around him and said, "So that's where you got to, you bastard". And he just said, "Oh, hi there Clive."

121

You couldn't dislike George, you really couldn't, [he was] a charmer. I would have signed George and then gone after Pelé and said, "I've got George Best, now I want you".'[11]

The story of George Best at the New York Cosmos would no doubt be worth a book of its own, had it happened. However, he later told the *St Petersburg Times* that he didn't sign for the Cosmos because 'they wanted to run my life from the time I got up in the morning (normally close to noon) to the time I went to bed (often close to dawn).'[12] Instead it was the Aztecs in 1976, where his coach Terry Fisher tolerated, or was told to tolerate, Best missing practice. In 1978 the Aztecs were sold to new owners who weren't so lax. When Best missed training twice in two days he was benched. Professing himself 'unhappy', Best met the new owners, who duly listened to his advice on signing new players, then duly ignored it. When he missed training a third time, the club president Larry Friend suspended him, and when the Aztecs won their next two games without him they decided that Best was more trouble than he was worth.

Like Marsh, Best did not hang around where he felt unloved. 'The president and I didn't get on,' he said in late 1978. 'A change was inevitable and as he owned the club, it was me who left.'[13] He moved to Fort Lauderdale, away from a city where he'd taken to the beach and owned his own bar, a place where he could unwind (or get hammered) in relative anonymity. He tells the story of his departure in more detail in his autobiography, *Blessed*: 'His [Friend's] feeling was that the way to bring the fans to the games was to tap into the Latin character of the city by signing Mexican players. That would have been okay if they had signed some good ones, but the players the club brought in were hopeless.' Following that,

Best lapsed into 'the now familiar pattern of drinking to forget the football and managing it so well that I even forgot to turn up for training. Then the club would suspend me, I would promise that it wouldn't happen again, and a few days later we would start the cycle all over again.'

Best was another player who clearly felt that the team should be built around him, with the players of his choice. When that didn't happen, he'd miss training and misbehave. Articles in the US soccer press followed a similar pattern to Best's drinking – they appeared regularly, with Best pledging that the worst times were in the past and that he was ready to give his all for the team. 'George Best: My Wild Days Are Over' was the headline on a 1979 article in *Soccer Digest*. Best claimed in the piece that he had become more 'health conscious' (not a bad idea for a professional player, even if 32 was somewhat late), and wanted to stay involved with the game once he'd quit. 'Like this morning, when we had no training because of the rain,' he said. 'A few years ago I'd just lay around or go to the bar somewhere if that happened. Now I'm disappointed not to train. I used to feel it wasn't important if I missed a day. But I'm turning 33 this season and I feel in terrific condition. I'm not ready to lay down and die.'

When he played, he often *was* in terrific condition. Fort Lauderdale thrived upon Best's signing, winning eleven out of his first thirteen games. Best scored twice in a 5–3 win over the Cosmos. Goalkeeper Arnie Mausser testifies that Best 'trained pretty hard, and put in a lot of effort.'[14] Other opponents and teammates during Best's NASL career sing nothing but praise, both for his play and his quiet, friendly personality. 'The best player ever was George Best,' says Alan Merrick. 'He was by far the best player. I played with him for half a season at San Jose and he was phenomenal.'[15] Says Carmine Marcantonio, 'Best could turn it on, there was nobody like him.'[16] Trinidadian striker Steve David formed successful scoring partnerships with Best at two different clubs, LA and San Jose. 'George was such an intelligent player and I learned what he wanted me to do very quickly,' he says. 'Every time George got the ball I knew where he wanted me to be, so I ended up with a lot of goals. It was great, I got to play my game and be free and do what I could do best. George was a great teammate on and off the field.'[17]

Yet although Best's overall statistics in the NASL are impressive, there was never quite the form to sustain a run that would bring his team a title. Much as Best genuinely hated to lose, off-pitch factors always ended up overriding that desire for success. At Fort Lauderdale there was another coaching problem, this time with Ron Newman, although Newman tried his utmost to minimize conflict. Before Best's alcoholism kicked back in, Best was sober and obviously still passionate about his game, as illustrated by an incident during the 1979 season's home opener against New England. 'You know how hot it gets in Fort Lauderdale, especially playing in the afternoon,' says Newman, 'and we used to have to play in the afternoon a lot because of television. So we're playing and George was having a good game but he was slowing down pretty rapidly, and then started to kick back at young players who were taking the ball off him.' Best had suffered a lot of suspensions while at LA, and Newman wanted to avoid the Irishman getting any cards. 'So he's getting redder and redder in the face, so I thought Christ, if he gets sent off now we're in the shit. So I take him off to do him a favour. And George comes off, he starts pulling at his shirt, and I was already thinking he was going to throw it at me. He's walking along the touchline and I know what he's going to do. He throws it at my head, and I knocked it down nonchalantly and kept on giving instructions to the team. We won the game but on my way out the media was all over me. "What are you going to do about that?" Me: "About what?" "About Georgie Best – you took him off and he threw his shirt at you." Me: "Everybody wants one of George's shirts, I'm no different. George knows that I wanted one of his shirts. I'm going to take it home and frame it and put it over my fireplace." I made a big joke about it. I saved George's hide, because he was in big trouble.'[18]

Yet he couldn't win Best's respect. 'I throw a fit when I get taken out,' said Best after the game (his replacement Nico Bodonczy had scored the second goal in a 2-0 win). 'If he [Newman] thinks this is the best line-up then he can start them again next week.'[19] During the same season, Newman substituted Ray Hudson and David Irving during an away game at the Cosmos, with Fort Lauderdale 2-0 up and with 20 minutes to play. They went on to lose the game 3-2, and Best 'lost the plot completely' as Newman went around the dressing room, as Best tells it, 'saying "well done" to all the players. "What do you mean, well done?" I said. "We've just lost 3-2 because you took two of our best players off and put on a couple of kids." "Well, it's no disgrace to lose here," he said. I tore off my shirt and threw it at him. "I'm starting to get really pissed off," I said, "do you know that?" I said the same in the local newspaper, which probably wasn't a great career move. But after Newman suspended me for failing to turn up for training, the paper ran a poll asking whether the Strikers should get rid of me or Newman. They voted for Newman to go but he still had the owner's backing, so in July I walked out.'[20]

Throwing shirts, drinking, missing training, and walking out on clubs were repeat events in Best's career wherever he played – Manchester United, Fulham, Hibernian, LA and Fort Lauderdale. As with Marsh they raise the question of how to manage a maverick. Was Best badly handled, or was he unmanageable? Maybe in the modern era a manager like Alex Ferguson might have been able to get the best out of Best if he'd mentored him from an early age, and a resourceful club with a full array of counselling services would nowadays surely offer a more enlightened approach to such a talent, if only to protect their investment. On the other hand, it's hard to imagine Ferguson tolerating even one shirt thrown in his direction by a player, let alone two.

Then there's Marsh, suffering a nervous breakdown in 1975 and spending eighteen months drinking a bottle of vodka every day, who describes the latter-day big club atmosphere as similar to what he experienced in the 70s. 'I talk to people today still directly connected with teams,' he says, 'and they tell me it's not too different. You've got players today that are gambling fortunes. I've been told that players at the top of their careers are out drinking five nights a week and are still playing in the Premier League at the top of their game.' He cites Stan Collymore and Paul Gascoigne as more recent examples of class players who weren't treated, for depression and alcoholism respectively, 'so it's an ongoing situation in football. Yes, 30 years ago it was there, but it's still there today.'

Marsh says that when he played 'it was "get your boots on and get on with it". And you had to fend for yourself.' He recalls talking to football writer Jeff Powell, when he was still with QPR, and telling him 'that the psychology of sport is far deeper than anyone can understand. Now, every team has a psychologist and counsellors. We look at depression and drinking and gambling – we need to look at those things, and it's right to help the players.'[21]

As a fan, you feel deprived when you look back at the careers of Best and Marsh and wonder what might have been if they'd been treated differently, or if they had treated themselves differently. Perhaps an England team built around the talents of Marsh might have qualified for the 1974 and the 1978 World Cups. A George Best who had looked after himself might have made the Northern Ireland roster for the 1982 World Cup, where his countrymen astonished the hosts Spain by beating them 1–0. There had even been talk until quite close to the tournament about Best, who would have been 36, making the squad. Best himself regretted not ever having been able to play at this level, but tended to wonder what 'it would have been like to play for a strong World Cup team'.[22] In other words, not a Northern Ireland team, but a team that would have played around him, no doubt with a manager that would have loved him. Seeing Best and Marsh in a league with players who really did make their marks at the World Cup – Pelé, Beckenbauer, Cruyff, Eusebio and Gerd Müller – only accentuates the holes in their overall careers.

Yet this is being greedy, and not only fails to appreciate what they did for the game – both in Europe and in America – but also fails to appreciate the nature of their genius in the era they performed. As Marsh says, the handling of players with personal problems was founded on 'ignorance', and in such a climate players of their character and calibre were only going to thrive to a limited extent – in flashes, with peaks of perfection, and troughs of despair coupled with predictable walkouts. To expect them to display the consistency of the midfield drones and the journeyman central defenders would be like asking for Christmas every day, and possibly just as dull.

In a way this boils down to the essence of what makes football special – the relative rarity of its outstanding moments, the value of its goals. It's why a 1–0 win can be just as thrilling as a 5–4 win, and may in many respects be more memorable. A player like Best did not dribble past five players and score every time he received the ball. Maybe some days he was too hung-over to even see it properly. In the end, we have to be grateful that he was there at all, and that in between the times when he let himself and his teams and his fans down (as one of his managers conceivably lectured him), he dazzled in a way that made him the perfect player for the NASL. He was a harbinger of the unexpected, a creative original who, whenever he'd had enough, did what most humans would love to do when they're pissed off with their boss. He stood up, said, 'Fuck this', and walked out to the nearest bar.

Young lion, blond mane

> 'Just like a rock performer, my soccer is an exten-
> sion of myself. My primary concern is the fans.
> It's no good entertaining the fans and not win-
> ning. Worse, you can't win without entertaining.'
> —Rodney Marsh, 1979[23]

This is a far more insightful, intelligent quote about the nature of football than the overused, misunderstood Bill Shankly quote about football being more important than life and death.* It's worth breaking the quote down sentence by

---

* In this writer's view, Shankly was being mischievously ironic.

sentence, because it covers all the important areas of being a professional sportsman, as well as explaining the psychology of the exhibitionist that every player should aspire to be. Because if players are not out there on the field to impress the people watching, what are they doing there at all?

Sentence one: 'Just like a rock performer, my soccer is an extension of myself.' In that 1976 'stuffing' (Marsh's noun) of the Cosmos, the player had his socks around his ankles, his hair long and wavy around his shoulders, and a silver medallion conspicuously dangling outside the front of his shirt. 'The young lion with the blond mane,' is how the television commentator Mario Machado described him during the live broadcast. Marsh was dressed for his role. At that time the laws of the game allowed you to play without shin-pads, and jewellery was not considered a health and safety risk. The lack of shin protection was quite courageous on Marsh's part. In the same game, his teammate Derek Smethurst had also opted for no shin-pads, and in the second half went down clutching his lower leg after a heavy foul from Cosmos defender Keith Eddy. Marsh himself received plenty of attention from opponents eager to let him know what they thought of his fancy-Dan footwork. It was a calculated risk. In the end, the rock performer image was more important than protecting himself from potential injury.

George Best was famously known as 'El Beatle' in the sixties, christened thus by Benfica fans after he starred in Manchester United's 5–1 away win in the 1966 European Cup quarter-final. Best's hair was soon longer than that of his contemporaries, and his good looks and stylish clothing perfectly reflected the way he played the game. For both players, football really was an extension of their characters and

129

the way they lived their lives – colourful, vibrant, lively, always looking to make things happen. 'I've never been one to curl up with a good book and stay home,' said Best in 1978, looking back on his career to that point. 'Maybe I should have, but it seemed boring to me. I had to be moving all the time. I had to be where the action was. And if there was no action there, I'd create it.'[24] Not curling up to read a book was as much a part of his make-up as not making the easy back pass to safety rather than going on a run. Rock performers are not shy, retiring types. At the risk of flogging an obvious point, they are on stage for a reason. They want to entertain, and in return they will soak up your adulation.

Sentence two of Marsh's quote: 'My primary concern is the fans.' Woe to the rock or football performer who does not understand this. The media may scavenge for details of your lifestyle and condemn your satanic immorality. Your managers will try to keep you on a tight rein and control the way you perform. Your owners – be they a football club or a record label – may encourage you to cultivate an image, but they'll always have their limits, and they'll never love you as more than a commercial proposition. Your fans, though, pay to see you, and in this way they show you what they want to see – the way you entertain them. Managers, hacks, chairmen, and even some players for decades saw the fans as little more than an inconvenience. Sure, we'll let them pay their way into the stadium, but we will regard them with contempt as a potentially out-of-control mass prone to violence and periodically making unreasonable demands for big signings and better results.

In the NASL, players like Marsh represented a revolutionary realization of what football needed more than anything – its audience. At a time when leagues in Europe were suffering year after year of depressingly downward crowd figures, the USA showed a new understanding of the seemingly blatant truism that without any fans, there would be no game. There would be no one to entertain. Which brings to mind Prime Minister Margaret Thatcher's suggestion to football journalists after the Hillsborough disaster in 1989 that perhaps it would be better to play all games behind closed doors. Even the generally right-wing reporters who usually advocated public floggings for football hooligans were quick to point out to her that, without a crowd, there would be little point in playing the games at all, and the idea was given no further mileage. So no matter how much the crowd is feared or despised, even the wary establishment reluctantly acknowledges that it has to exist.

Let's take sentences three and four together. 'It's no good entertaining the fans and not winning. Worse, you can't win without entertaining.' The third sentence is great. It acknowledges that, in spite of all the insolent back-heels and crowd-wooing flicks and feints, Marsh is a professional who desires to win. On the other hand, he's toeing the line with the sort of sentiment his managers would approve of, only to undermine it all with the fourth sentence, which almost slaps back down the preceding words. You have to win, but not any old way. Not by *catenaccio*. Not by foul play and negative tactics and a lucky breakaway goal in the last minute, or by hanging on for the 0–0 draw and taking the game on penalty kicks. *You can't win without entertaining.* What would be the point? It would be like wolfing down fine Belgian chocolates without giving them the chance to touch your taste buds. It would be like going to the Grand Canyon wearing a blindfold. It would be like going to a rock concert wearing industrial earplugs that blocked out

131

all the music. If you're not going to entertain while trying to win, don't bother at all.

Asked about this quote now, Marsh says, 'I always wanted to entertain, and so did George, and so did many others. Frank Worthington, Alan Hudson, Alan Ball, Peter Osgood – once I'd made the break [to play in the NASL] many other players wanted to come over as well, and there were some world-class players in that league. But ... there were some very violent games in that league in those days. Pelé was the top player in the world, we all know that, and at that time he was still a magnificent player. Teams would put a young US player on him to mark him out the game. There was one game in Miami when he launched into this guy [in retaliation], and the ref was saying, "I can't send Pelé off, he's the greatest player in the world". That was the idiosyncratic way the League had evolved.'[25]

So it's false to idealize the NASL as a league where players only wanted to entertain, but correct to laud it as a league which at the very least offered the football field as a platform for the game's more eye-catching performers. It's also certainly true that after the mid-70s, teams in the NASL wanted to win in style. The Cosmos were famously booed off the field for only winning 1–0 against the Philadelphia Fury during the 1978 season.* This was one of the stories that made it back to the UK at the time, and was further material to denigrate the American way of approaching soccer. How can you boo a team that wins? Yet watching the English Premier League over

---

* 'Cosmos Booed in 1–0 Triumph' ran the paradoxical headline in the *New York Times* (12/6/78). 'Our fans proved today that they are the greatest,' said a sarky Steve Hunt. A week later the crowd was up by 5,000 to almost 48,000 for a game against the Diplomats. The Cosmos won 6–1.

the past decade, even watching on television you can sense the *ennui* when one of the Champions League regulars are only 1-0 up against a lowly team that has come to defend and limit the damage. The game is in its late stages and people are leaving early to beat the rush for the car park. No one boos at the end, but few will stay around to applaud the players off after such a routine win.* The expectation now of teams like Chelsea, Arsenal, Manchester City and Manchester United is that they should tear teams apart and the goals should flow. A 1-0 win over Fulham or West Ham is analysed critically as either an off day, or a sign that something is wrong with the team.

Topping the flair play league

Just as the rock performer wishes to be centre stage, all of the time (even a drum solo is just a breathing space as we wait for the singer to take a drink, recover, and come back to the microphone even bigger and brasher than before), so the flair player always wants the ball, and the home fans always want him to have the ball. They are here to see things happen, and the flair player is, most likely, the man who will get things going with a shimmy, a dribble, a feint, an unexpected shot or an audacious pass. Or maybe, like Marsh against the Cosmos, he will merely play keep-ball. Marsh did this too during an indoor game (the NASL had started an indoor league in 1975 to generate cash and keep its players occupied year round) against Dallas in early 1978. The Rowdies were 7-3 up with five minutes to go

---

* The Germans have a great word for this – *Pflichtsieg* – which is hard to translate well, but it means 'duty win'. It's not meant as much of a compliment.

when Marsh began playing keep-away and taunting his opponents to try and take the ball off him. 'He has a world of talent but I wouldn't have that bleeping bleep on my team,' said Dallas coach Al Miller. 'He's a bleep.'[26] The Rowdies coach at the time, Gordon Jago, said, 'If Rodney Marsh can give me 85 hard minutes out there, he can have the other five.' After all, if the game's won, and there are only five minutes to go, why not find new ways to entertain the fans?

It seems odd that this behaviour would inspire such vitriol and anger in his fellow pros – remember the reactions of Pelé, Clements and Chinaglia in the Rowdies–Cosmos game. Sure, it's breaking an unwritten code between professionals about not humiliating a fellow player. Does a fan give a rat's arse about any such code, written or not? Of course they don't. More to the point, what if there are players out there who deserve to be humiliated, who need to be taught that a fundamental skill in football is to be able to hold on to the ball?

In the English game, the problem ever since the end of the Second World War has been an inability to do just that. An over-emphasis on fitness and speed at the expense of technical basics were pinpointed by Willi Meisl in his 1955 book *Soccer Revolution* as the bane of English football, and the reason they had twice been so heavily defeated by Hungary (3–6 in 1953, 7–1 the following year), and had failed at the 1954 World Cup. Almost 60 years later, the same failings were on show in the 2012 European Championship quarter-final game against Italy, where England could not get out of their own half because they could not keep possession. They somehow held on for a 0–0 draw and could have won the game on penalties, which would have been a perfect example of a win without entertaining. How the England team could have used a player like Rodney Marsh on so many occasions, to hold on to the ball, to caress it, to shield it, to slow the game down for a few seconds and wait for teammates to find better spaces to receive his pass. Marsh was capped just nine times by the England team. Alan Hudson, another gifted English midfielder out of time and in the wrong country, represented his country just twice. Hudson, whose speciality was possession, joined the Seattle Sounders in 1979 and called it 'the best experience of my life so far'.[27] Former Sounders general manager John Best says, 'He'd never give the ball away. When you have a talent like his, you can do whatever you want with the ball'[28]

George Best was another player who was notoriously difficult to get the ball off. Asked to name his most difficult opponents in the NASL, long-serving Canadian left-back Bruce Wilson – who played eleven seasons in the League, including one at the Cosmos – named Portland's Willie Anderson ('he absolutely took me to the cleaners the first couple of times I played against him') and George Best, whom he describes as 'incredible. You're looking at a small guy, but he could dribble, he could shoot, he could pass; he could kick you – he had no problem with that. Don't forget this was a summer league and these games were played when it was so darned hot. I remember going to LA and it must have been 90 degrees, and I was thinking, he can't be that fit, he won't be running around. But he'd nutmeg you, run around you. You go into a tackle on him, he's not shirking away, he's coming back at you.'[29]

Nonetheless, for all their influence, neither Marsh nor Best won a title in the North American Soccer League. Their statistics are both impressive and consistent, aside from two unsettled seasons for Best in 1978 and 1979. Best twice came close to a championship game – first with LA in 1977, where they

lost to Seattle in the Conference championships, the last hur-
dle before the Soccer Bowl. Then again with Fort Lauderdale
in 1978, when he joined the team at the tail end of the season,
but they lost to the Rowdies at the same stage – thanks to
Rodney Marsh. Marsh and Best had both scored in the game's
first leg in Fort Lauderdale, a 3–2 win for the Strikers. Tampa
won the return, 3–1, but there was no overall aggregate score
– under NASL rules, this merely meant the tie was tied at one
game each, as we saw in the last chapter with the Cosmos–
Whitecaps 1979 semi-final. A 30-minute mini-game produced
no goals, and so with the rain tipping down and the field a
British-style mud pool, the farcical shootouts began, with
players from both teams getting the ball stuck in the mire
before they could get their shots off within the required five
seconds. Marsh stepped up to take the final attempt with the
scores at 1–1. 'The Rowdies crowd of 37,000,' wrote the *Evening
Independent*'s Bob Chick, 'must believe their hero knows all
about walking and shooting on water.' Marsh scored 'on a
field that looked like a marsh – a tract of low, wet, soft land,
a swamp.'[30] The Rowdies were in the Soccer Bowl, to face the
New York Cosmos just four days later.

Despite having played through the semi-finals until the
heroic last kick in the deluge, Marsh had to withdraw from the
final through injury thanks to the lingering effects of a challenge he'd suffered during the playoffs from Fort Lauderdale's
English defender Maurice Whittle, the former Oldham stalwart. By this time the rivalry with the Cosmos had turned into
a genuine fight, not just a manufactured marketing tool for
the League. In 1976, the Rowdies had knocked the Cosmos out
of the playoffs, and in 1977 the Cosmos returned the favour.
Regular-season games between the two were highly anticipated,

highly attended, and they rarely disappointed. When the Rowdies went up to New York in 1976 after the 5–1 game in Tampa, the Cosmos players were talking advance trash. 'Come and see me on July 14,' Giorgio Chinaglia had told the *New York Times* after the first game. Asked about Marsh's keep-away in the 5–1 game, Dave Clements said, 'That's Mr Marsh. But he will come to New York, won't he? We'll show them who they really are when they come to New York.'[31] The game was no anti-climax – the Cosmos won 5–4, Pelé scoring twice after the Rowdies had taken a 3–1 lead. According to Marsh, Pelé took him out with a 'scything tackle' that led to a fifteen-man brawl.[32] Two years later, in 1978, here they were meeting in the Soccer Bowl, and Marsh withdrew from the game because of an infected left shin.

Some Tampa fans scapegoated him for the 3–1 loss, and players muttered about his sudden absence. Marsh was certain that he had made the right decision for the team – if you are unfit, then you do not play, especially in such an important game. 'Two writers told me I should have started the match and then come out,' he said. 'They said that's the American way. That might have made me look good, but it would have been an embarrassment to the Rowdies.'[33] Considering the delight he took in beating the Cosmos in previous games, it hardly seems likely that he would have pulled back from such a huge game without a legitimate reason.

He also confessed that the 'bad publicity' around his non-appearance, as well as remarks in the press from star signing Mirandinha that he and Marsh couldn't play on the same team (the Brazilian only managed two goals to Marsh's 21 that season, and was gone in early 1979), sent him into 'a bit of depression. I was drinking a few beers, eating lots of stupid food. I was really upset by what went down.' So he called his wife and children back from home in the UK, where he'd sent them two years before, went on a diet 'only eating pure health foods', and took 'no drink at all, apart from champagne and white wine' (well, they hardly count, do they?). He focused on his family and charity fundraisers and claimed, 'I've graduated. That [old] lifestyle, in my opinion, is the lifestyle of an immature person.'[34]

That all presumably helped Marsh refocus on reaching another Soccer Bowl, and in 1979 the Rowdies made it again, without encountering the Cosmos in the playoffs. Their opponents at Soccer Bowl were Vancouver,* and it was Marsh's final game as a professional. His coach was Gordon Jago, a man whom Marsh had stated earlier that year 'knows how to handle me'. Jago himself said that 'only a fool would try to submerge someone with Marsh's assets.'[35] If Marsh paused for breath, it was not that he was lazy, but because he was pacing himself. As Marsh said, 'That's my style of play. That is the reason I will win games in the last few minutes, where other players are flagging. What I do in the first minute of a game, I will do in the last.'

All of which makes it hard to explain why Jago substituted Marsh with eleven minutes of the game remaining, and Tampa Bay 2–1 down.

As Marsh tells it now: 'He [Jago] said, "Sorry Rodney, we needed a little more pace up front." I said, "Fuck me Gordon, you've known me 20 years and now ten minutes before the end of my career you've decided I'm too slow." I went and sat at the

---

* Who'd memorably beaten the Cosmos in the semi-final – see Chapter 3.

end of the bench and the *ABC* reporter Verne Lundquist came up and said, "Why have you been subbed?" And I said, "That fucking arsehole down there fucking beep beep beep", live on television. I know why he took me off. At the end of the games that season, we were so successful, and the media would come up to me and ask why did you make that change etc. So they were coming to me and they wouldn't go to Gordon. And they kept coming to me for quotes about the team, being captain, and Gordon got the hump about that. Later in life, someone told me, "Gordon was making a statement." I can't say who.'[36]

Marsh traces Jago's possible resentment back to one of the semi-final games against San Diego when he and Steve Wegerle had worked out a free-kick routine: 'I looked to the right, he ran over the ball as though we didn't know what we were doing, then looking the other way I'd pass him the ball and he'd cross it, or whatever. And in the semi-final he scored, but everyone thought it was a muck-up; only Steve and I knew. After the game he [Jago] got the hump because I said, "We couldn't tell Gordon about it, otherwise he'd have changed it."'[37]

Converting a redneck city to soccer

Best scored over 50 goals in the NASL, and registered countless assists, but he was never at a team long enough to make an impression like Marsh did at Tampa Bay, and his bursts of brilliance were alternated with slumps in form. In 1976 he scored a hat-trick for the LA Aztecs as they beat Boston 8–0. The Aztecs then lost their next five games, including a 6–2 defeat in Minnesota. These anomalous, lopsided scorelines were one of the League's quirks, and reflect quite accurately the pattern of Best's US career. That year, though, he was LA's top scorer with fifteen goals, and was voted by the other NASL players as runner-up for the League's MVP Award. The winner was Pelé. 'I should have been first, but I knew who would get it,' Best said the following year. 'He [Pelé] is the only guy who gets an assist on a throw-in.'[38] Best's form in 1977 was equally as impressive, although he dropped back into more of a play-making role and formed the League's most dangerous striking partnership with the aforementioned Steve David. Many of David's League top-scoring 26 goals resulted from Best's eighteen assists. His two following years – first in LA and then in Fort Lauderdale – were, however, marked by serial absences, fines and mediocre form.

Ultimately, though, it's far more important that Best and Marsh played, and largely played very well, in the NASL. Fans and players alike remember them far more than they remember who won the Soccer Bowl in any given year, particularly up to the mid-70s. Their influence was huge. 'It was an honour to be on the field with a player like that,' says Bruce Wilson of Best.[39] Joey Fink recalls his time at Tampa with Rodney Marsh and says, 'I enjoyed playing with him, I kind of looked up to him. One year he didn't go back to England at the end of the season, and we went to the practice field every day and worked on finishing – very basic stuff, drilling the ball and bending the ball in several different ways. I'd never been coached like that before as a forward player and it was very special. He had that ability to make a second seem like a minute just before shooting. A lot of the time as a forward you panic, but he did these drills that taught us not to panic, and I learnt more from him than I learnt from any other coach, even though he wasn't the actual coach.'

Marsh, understates Fink, 'was a little controversial, no question, and in the US they built him up with a little bit of a reputation and he lived up to it, but it sold a lot of tickets. Tampa Bay was a redneck city back in the 70s, and they didn't have a lot of idea about soccer, but they built up the team with a first-class owner.'[40] Within two years of starting up in 1975 with four-figure gates, the Rowdies would regularly bring in crowds well over 20,000, and twice that number if the Cosmos were in town.

Regardless of trophies won, when the foreign stars with a reputation were on the field, more people came to watch. It was that simple. And when 45,000 people were coming to watch a soccer game in a 'redneck' town the size of Tampa* with a large military population from the nearby MacDill Air Force Base, people with money to invest in sport sat up and started to pay attention.

Best goal ever? 'A step up to soccer heaven'

Best showed what he was still capable of even at the age of 35 in a game for the San Jose Earthquakes against the Fort Lauderdale Strikers on 22 July 1981. On the television broadcast, the co-commentator observes that there are 'more people than I expected here tonight.' Indeed you wouldn't expect as many as 11,629 San Jose fans (around their average that season) given that Best's team had lost its previous eight games, including a 7–0 shellacking at the California Surf. Fort Lauderdale, meanwhile, were looking strong, having won seven of *their* previous eight games. San Jose still had a theoretical

---

* Tampa's population in the 1970s was around 280,000.

outside chance of making the playoffs, which was always a possibility if you could put together a sudden streak at the end of the season.

This was Best's final NASL season, and he was effectively at the end of his playing career, in a quasi-meaningless game, kicking off at the height of the Californian summer during daylight hours. Yet he still cared about the team, and about winning. Two weeks earlier, after a 4–1 loss at Fort Lauderdale, Best had railed to the press, 'I know what some of these players are getting paid and I can get better players for that money. We've tried all combinations. I was thinking of taking the team on tour but I couldn't do that. I'd embarrass myself. I don't mean to hurt the team with my criticism. I'm trying to benefit everyone concerned.'[41] Another report from that year cited Best's anger at the team's form and the way that the Quakes were being run: 'It's been better than last year,' he said, 'but is that enough encouragement? To me it's not. I don't want to be just a little better than last year. I want to be ten times better.' His coach Jimmy Gabriel sympathized: 'George's passing this season has just been fantastic. I've never coached a team with so many good scoring chances that we've missed. Maybe 85 per cent of those chances were created by George.'[42]

Fort Lauderdale may not have been the strongest team he ever faced, but they were a consistent side boasting a solid line-up. Yet this was a game dominated by Best and, ultimately, won by him after his team slipped into a two-goal deficit. He played as a free-roving midfielder, quite deep, not quite a central playmaker. In the early stages of the game he looked to make something happen whenever he got the ball, always searching for the pass into space and the free player running into that space. On free kicks out wide he looked for the accurate pass or cross, rather than aimlessly floating it in and hoping someone would get a head on it. There was also poor communication with his fellow players. As József Horváth shaped up to take a direct free kick in front of the Strikers' goal, Best stepped ahead of him and took a quick one instead. As the ball hit the wall, Horváth shook his head in exasperation. Clearly that wasn't one they'd worked on in practice.

Chirpy Geordie Ray Hudson – the diminutive but skilful former Newcastle United midfielder who played seven solid seasons for the Strikers – put his team 1–0 up after playing a nice one-two with Branko Segota and finishing with a cheeky clip from his inner-heel past Phil Parkes. In the second half, Best took a yellow card for dissent after complaining about a perceived foul let go by referee Ian Foote, whom the commentator observes is 'letting the game flow' (in other words, he's giving us* fuck all). A possibly offside Bernd Hölzenbein then made it 2–0 from a quick free kick while Best and the Quakes were still arguing with the ref about the call. And then it happened.

San Jose's Anglo-American Gary Etherington takes up the story. 'I ended up as an overlapping full-back for the Quakes, probably the best position I ever played,' he says, 'with George Best playing me 50-yard passes to my feet, and then I'd put crosses in.' Does he recall the goal? 'I got the assist, mate!' he

---

* If the partisan phrasing of this 'translation' seems curious, it's because TV commentators were, thanks to the nature of the locally negotiated TV deals, mostly cheerleaders for the home team – they commentated the same team every week, and were very close to those clubs almost by necessity. It's much the same in Major League Soccer today, and can make for a challenging listen if you're a neutral or a fan of the opponent.

says. 'It was from the kick-off, and it was all because Bestie was pissed off at the referee. They'd got a free kick and ended up scoring from it, and Bestie was jawing at him before the restart. They restarted, the ball came wide to me, I kind of faked and knocked it back in there, and from there on he took the whole team on. As I pass the ball I'm just standing there 30 yards out watching the whole thing and thinking, *This is ridiculous!*'[43]

Best took eight touches to beat three men in a narrow space, mainly inside the Fort Lauderdale penalty area, to score the goal. 'That's the greatest soccer goal I've ever seen. Outstanding! They'll give him the goal and they'll give him three assists,' shouted the co-commentator (neglecting poor Etherington). 'You see from the video,' says Etherington, 'when he's walking back to the centre circle he's still angry and says to the ref, "I told you so!" It was incredible.'

Best was then lucky not to get sent off, but as Marsh observed earlier about Pelé, the NASL's superstars largely got away with being red-carded 'for the good of the game' (an unwritten League rule). First he picked up the ball and slammed it into the ground after a foul on him was called back – he wanted the advantage. A clear yellow card for dissent, but it wasn't given. Then he harshly fouled Steve Ralbovsky, also worth a second yellow to add to the one he got earlier. Best stayed on the field. And he was covering that field as the play went backwards and forwards, with chance after chance for both teams, showing remarkable energy for a man of his age, in a hot climate, especially considering how many times he used to skip training. 'This is the kind of soccer fans love to see – end-to-end action,' gushed the commentator. 'Never a dull moment in this second half.'

As the game approached its close, Best hit the crossbar

with a corner kick (having scored from one directly a few games previously against the Jacksonville Tea Men). He then initiated and finished the scrambled equalizer with less than two minutes left. Finally, in the first period of sudden-death extra time, Best made the winner with a run, a shimmy to the right and then to the left past Jon Pot, then put in a shot that was saved but not held. Mustava Hukić scored the rebound. The Quakes' Joe Silveira said afterwards that Best came into the game with a sore toe but 'decided to give it a go'. He commended Best for running all over the park the whole game. So he not only ran for more than 90 minutes at the age of 35 in extremely hot conditions, he was carrying an injury too. Best also later wrote that he was nursing an injury to his right knee throughout the season.

His coach that day, Jimmy Gabriel, remembers the game well. Best, he says, had 'the attitude of a normal player, but he was a genius. He was just one of the players, he never walked in and said *I'm George Best, I'm the king of it all*. Unfortunately for him we didn't have a strong enough team to take what he had and turn it into something fantastic, and one player can't win it all for you.' Against Fort Lauderdale, though, that's exactly what Best did. 'He woke up,' says Gabriel. 'It was like he took a step up to soccer heaven. I felt like, *George, Why don't you do that every game?* It was in him, that's what he could have done. That wasn't the only time he did stuff like that, he could be fantastic. But with a stronger team around him he would have been magnificent almost every game. He had it in him to be like that.'[44]

This game not only shows Best's inarguable genius, it's also a somewhat melancholy viewing experience. It makes the viewer think of the lost years in his late 20s, when Best should have been at his peak, but retired after walking out on Manchester United and headed to the pub, lured out again two years later by Los Angeles. He is clearly a class above all the players around him. It's wonderful to watch, and almost frightening to see the ease with which he runs the game – a player at the fag-end of a partially thwarted career, in the final stages of a season in a league starting clearly to show the first signs of over-indulgence, running up and down and caring so much about beating the Fort Lauderdale Strikers. And then there was that goal too, which Best called 'one of the best I've ever scored'. Although it had no effect on San Jose's season (they won only two more games that season, both of them without Best in the line-up), 'it meant everything to me in terms of personal pride'.[45]

'I hear people say [Ryan] Giggs and [Eric] Cantona are better than George Best,' says Rodney Marsh. 'That is complete and utter tosh. George Best was the greatest player in the world for a short period of time; for two or three seasons, he was untouchable.' He thinks that it's ridiculous to talk about Best in terms of what might have been. 'I would never write that,' he states with some emotion. 'It doesn't do service to one of the greatest players ever.'[46]

5

Gimmicks, girls and teenage kicks: Selling soccer to the US public

'While [Alan] Willey was scoring three goals in the Kicks' 4–1 victory over the Earthquakes, hundreds danced, passed Frisbees and made passes at each other. The dancers, drinkers, Frisbee throwers were oblivious to the soccer being played inside the stadium. To them, summer had arrived. The soccer? Maybe next week. "Last time I went in and I wished I had stayed out here," said nineteen-year-old Scott Matson of Mound. "It's cheaper just to stay here and have a party".'

—Columnist Doug Grow describes
a typical scene at a Minnesota Kicks home game
outside the Metropolitan Stadium
in Bloomington, 1979.[1]

For young people in the Upper Midwest twin cities area of Minneapolis and St Paul in the late 1970s, the soccer game was the place to go if you wanted to get high, get drunk and get off with someone. It wasn't really planned that way, even though when the team arrived in the city in 1976 after failing in Colorado they hired an advertising agency that decided to target the young demographic. A peculiar set of circumstances turned the parking lots outside the 49,000-capacity Metropolitan Stadium ('the Met') in Bloomington, a town fifteen minutes south of the Minneapolis city border, into

147

a bacchanalian celebration of all the things that youths the world over will do if given the time, the space and the tacit permission. One local writer, Jon Bream, said the parties had the feel of Woodstock, but that, by comparison, 'rock has lost much of its counter-cultural spirit. There was a certain tribal spirit that brought the people together. It was a force greater than the music or adulation for a particular performer or band.' Only at the Grateful Dead did you still see that spirit, but at the Kicks, 'the Woodstock generation and their younger bothers and sisters stand around in the Met Stadium parking lot sharing bread, a bottle of wine and a joint just like those hippies did at the Woodstock festival. Some people urinate in public because the lines at the portable toilets are too long – just as they did at Woodstock. They toss frisbees and frolic in the sun.'[2]

The usual American word for such activities is 'tailgating', which just means picnicking quite elaborately in the car park outside a sports stadium before a game. The Kicks' fans were into much more than tame tailgating, though. Tailgating was what the older fans of the Minnesota Vikings football team did in winter, at the same stadium. This was a summer celebration, with fewer clothes and inhibitions, and a lot more recreational drug taking, and was always going to be more lively than the mere setting up of a portable grill to make burgers and hot dogs with a couple of cold beers to wash them down. Essentially, these were unregulated raves, but without the dance music and the mass dancing. There had been nothing like it before in American sport, and nothing since. It was why, as the Kicks' former goalkeeper and coach Geoff Barnett puts it, there developed 'an absolute love affair' between the team and its fans.[3]

The Kicks had moved to Minnesota from Denver, Colorado, as a failed franchise – a two-year team whose home crowds had dropped to below 3,000. The Denver Dynamos' dilemma had typified the problems facing many professional US soccer teams in the mid-70s. In their first season, Denver played in the massive Mile High Stadium, at that time a 63,000-seat venue that always sold out for Denver Broncos games in the NFL. Predictably, there was no atmosphere at the poorly attended soccer games in such a giant arena, and rents were too high, so for their second season they moved to Jefferson County Stadium in the Denver suburb of Lakewood. Teams in the suburbs, though, could easily get forgotten, especially if they lost far more games than they won. Despite some flashes of brilliance from the South Africans Ace Ntsoelengoe and Kaizer Motaung, and a rare home-grown goalscorer in Mike Flater, the Dynamos fizzled out long before the season's end and were bought by new owners in Minnesota. Retail entrepreneur Jack Crocker had been visiting a friend in Portland, Oregon, who was a co-founder of the NASL's Timbers. Crocker went to a game and was fired up by the 30,000 crowd, so he came back to Minneapolis and persuaded a group of associates in the food industry to join him in bringing the Dynamos to the twin cities.

There was direct major league competition from the Minnesota Vikings (NFL) and the Minnesota Twins (baseball), both of whom also used the Met. Nowadays the stadium's former site is covered by the Mall of America, a gargantuan multi-floor shopping complex where it's easier to get lost than it is to find something you want to buy. This serves, incidentally, as a blunt reminder of the puny role that sentimentality plays in the face of business when it comes to preserving historic

sporting landmarks in the US. There's a metal plaque somewhere in the mall commemorating where the home plate was
between 1956 and 1981, but that's it.*

Crocker and his partners employed an advertising agency
called Chuck Rohr Associates, and the account landed on the
desk of a reluctant Jim Moore, who knew nothing about the
game, but who knew about targeting youth. If you get young
people first, the older generations will follow, 'but if you do
it the other way round, it won't work. Look at music, clothes,
hair styles, even some major social issues.' Using radio ads,
they hit their target market. 'We didn't talk down to them,'
said Moore. 'We didn't get into any of the currently popular
slang. We just tried to inform them in a straightforward, honest way.'[4]

The chief key to bringing in young people (or indeed any
people during the recession-hit 70s) was to make it a cheap
trip. The Kicks offered free parking at the stadium, another
rarity in the US, where steep parking fees were, and still are,
considered an important part of match-day income. The Kicks
took a $114,000 loss on the parking, which it had to pay to the
stadium authority that owned the Met. Then it offered tickets starting as low as $2.50, a pittance at the time compared
with a stadium rock concert or a Vikings game. In that first
summer of 1976, wrote local soccer writer Allan Holbert, the
fans 'strolled round the stadium before and after the games
kissing and holding hands. Tailoring the traditional tailgate
party to their own tastes and budgets, they drank a little beer

---

* The Met was replaced by the ultra-modern Metrodome in the early
1980s, a roofed-in venue that itself is now on the way out – the Twins
baseball team moved out in 2009, and the NFL's Vikings will have built
a new stadium on the site by 2016.

and smoked a little grass. They were pretty people and Kicks games quickly became The Place to go for class girl-watching. The "Soccer Foxes", as some of their t-shirts described them, bore out the Tampa Bay discovery that the game would attract more females than other spectator sports.'5 It should be noted that this was in the relatively permissive 70s, when the majority of teenagers' lives were largely unregulated by their parents, and before the stricter drink-driving laws of the late 70s and early 80s were introduced and enforced.

How much influence did the game itself have on attracting young fans? Initially, very little, according to Alan Merrick, who went on to become the team captain and a hugely popular player at the Kicks. The police, he says, ultimately became 'part of our posse. People would come in their old VW vans and they'd bring absolutely everything, including tables. It wasn't tailgating – it was almost like fine dining, with huge barbecue grills and chandeliers on tables. It became a four-to-five hour event for them; they'd keep going after the game. There were some real party-goers – a lot of younger people would come in with a cool-box in their boot.'6

As the owners were involved in the food retail business they translated their business practices in the food industry to selling tickets for soccer. 'They were used to aiming for low margins, low mark-ups,' says Merrick, 'and their philosophy was they wanted lots of fans to come in, so they'd sell cheap ticket packages for people on a tight budget. Nobody had marketed that kind of sporting event to this demographic before. The NFL had never done anything like that, the baseball team wasn't doing particularly well at that time, the hockey team was average as well. So this soccer team came into town and they marketed it really well. They made this advertising poster that said "Minnesota Joins The World", with a globe and a soccer ball, like soccer was going to put Minnesota on the map.'[7]

The marketing campaign was backed up by the players conducting what had by now become the usual tour of soccer clinics and training sessions at local schools and community centres. By the time of the first home game against San Jose on 9 May 1976, the Kicks had already lost twice on the road and, says Merrick, 'they were expecting maybe eight or nine thousand'. It was also Mother's Day, and the team offered a free rose to all attending mothers. In the end, they had to delay the start of the game twice to allow all the fans into the stadium 'because there were so many still outside buying tickets. It was at least half an hour, maybe even 40 minutes, then Jack Crocker lost patience and said, "Let them all in, it was our fault because we didn't prepare properly".' The official gate was 17,054, but that didn't include 3,000 fans the team let in for free. When it was announced that fans were being let in for nothing, those who'd already paid to come in to the stadium actually cheered at the generous gesture. 'Next day's paper touted our unbelievable PR job,' says Merrick. '"This team just opens the doors and lets people in." That was a marketing coup in itself; that was unheard of, the idea of letting people in for free. That ingratiated the entire operation, and we won the game as well, so we were up and running. In general it was a very professional operation – we had good players, good management, and a very professional front office.'

That was just the start. Although crowds dipped a little for the next three home games, to between 9,000–14,000, the visit of the Cosmos in early June, combined with the fact that the Kicks had won all of their first four home games, saw a gate of over 46,000. This was no flash in the pan. Attendances pushed up gradually over the course of the season into the 20,000-plus range, then 30,000-plus, and finally, for the last regular home game of the season – a 6–2 hammering of LA – to more than 42,000, helped by a McDonald's promotion where you could redeem your ticket stub for a Big Mac. 'I think they had 35,000 redemptions,' recalls Geoff Barnett, 'and you couldn't move in McDonald's that night for fans getting their free burgers.'[8] The playoffs yielded yet more healthy attendances – over 41,000 for the victory over Seattle, and a sell-out crowd of 49,452 for the 3–1 win over San Jose that took them to the Soccer Bowl. Mostly, the Kicks won, while scoring lots of goals. English strikers Alan Willey and Ron Futcher finished with 35 goals between them.

Alan Willey thinks that winning was primarily the key factor to the Kicks' quick success. 'I know the Vikings had been in Super Bowls, but they weren't that great at the time,' he says. 'The baseball team too. We started winning right off the bat; word got around.' Then of course, 'the big thing back then was the pre-game tailgating. The parking lot would open at 4pm, we'd come in at 5–5.30 for a 7 o'clock kick-off, and the place would be packed with people barbecuing.' Willey, still a Minnesota resident today, says that many people now miss tailgating at the Vikings' games. It won't return until the new stadium is built in 2016.

'Sometimes we'd go around in golf carts talking to people,' he says, 'and I don't think any other sportsmen were doing that, going out and winning over the fans. And along with taking the game out to schools, that was all new at that time for professional athletes – to be coming out and talking to fans, engaging with people. And we'd get changed after games, have a couple of drinks, then come out and the parking lot was still full of people.'[9] Tim Twellman, who joined the team in its second year in 1977, was unprepared for a phenomenon he describes as 'amazing. The first time I ever went to a home game my wife and I were stuck in traffic and wondering what the hell it was. We had no idea it was because of the game. The parking lot was absolutely packed two hours before the game. It was definitely a party atmosphere, and that was what made the game day special.'[10]

Going to the Kicks had suddenly become, especially for young people, the thing to do, but the game itself played its part. 'Early on,' says Willey, 'when the game started there were some people inside the stadium but not a whole lot, so the security people started going around the parking lot and ushered fans into the stadium. People were enjoying themselves in the parking lot so much that they forgot about the game. Once we started winning games and people got the hang of what was going on, then people were in there at the start.'[11]

As the quote on page 147 shows, though, for a certain section of the crowd the soccer was not their priority. Then again, the drinking culture wasn't to everybody's taste. In 1979 the club started to receive complaints about rowdy, unregulated behaviour in the car park. In August, a police-man was mugged by five young fans trying to bring drink into the stadium, while one businessman wrote to the club bemoaning 'the foulest language imaginable', and saying 'we just can't subject business guests to such an abusive environ-ment'. Another correspondent, Ronald Grant, declared him-self a fan 'since the team came to Minnesota', but wrote to the team in 1980 saying he wouldn't be bringing his children to games any more, because 'the combination of incredible sums of alcohol, mass profanity, various degrees of sexual activity ... were more than enough to detract substantially from the play on the field.'[12] In 1979, the team had started to charge $2 for parking, and upped ticket prices by a buck each in every category, and immediately gates started to fall – in 1979 the average gate was down from almost 31,000 the previous year to 24,600. In 1980, law enforcement in the stadium car park was bolstered, but this led to a strained, less carefree atmosphere, as well as a further drop in crowds to an average of just over 18,000.

Kicks were playing tremendously under the coaching nous of former Manchester United and Leeds midfielder Freddie Goodwin. After making Soccer Bowl in their opening year (see chapter 2), they knocked out tough competition in the form of Seattle, Portland and Vancouver to win the Western Division title in both 1976 and 1977, a feat they matched in the following two years when moved to the more geographically pertinent Central Division.* They made the playoffs in each of their six years of existence. The team's highlight videos from the late 70s show perennially packed stands and a raucous, joyful, nigh-on fanatical crowd urging the team forward. An attacking triumvirate of Willey, Ron Futcher and Ace Ntsoelengoe – all three are in the top eight of all-time NASL scorers – ensured that the Kicks were prolific entertainers, while developing a testy rivalry with the Tulsa Roughnecks (a 1978 start-up team more closely examined in chapter six). Futcher,

---

* You may have intuited by now that the NASL's baffling divisional and playoff format changed almost yearly, thanks to the fluctuating number of teams, and too much tinkering on the League's part.

described fondly by Geoff Barnett as 'a moaning bastard',* was instrumental in helping the Kicks beat Tulsa 3–1 in the first round of the 1978 playoffs. 'It was vintage Futcher,' wrote the *Minneapolis Star*. 'He was tough on defence, dribbled down-field like a midfielder, and used his striker's head as a hammer to propel shots towards the Tulsa net.' Ntsoelengoe was celebrated by his teammates after the game for chinning Tulsa's English midfielder Brian Smith. His punishment? A yellow card. 'I punched him out,' said the South African. 'Smith was calling me names – dirty, filthy names. I can't repeat them. He did the same thing at Tulsa. So I popped him.'[13]

That was that. No week-long enquiries as to who said what. One swift blow, and you like to think that Brian Smith never insulted another player again. Meanwhile, the culture of the Kicks was spreading around the League.

Marketing prayers answered – a Pelé hat-trick on Father's Day

Tailgating had also led to soaring crowds in New York by the 1977 season. The Cosmos had played Pelé's first two seasons on Randall's Island (1975) and in Yankee Stadium (1976), but the following year moved out to East Rutherford in New Jersey, to the massive new Meadowlands arena, also known as Giants Stadium in recognition of its NFL tenant, the New York Giants. True, Pelé and the enhanced roster that now featured Franz Beckenbauer were pulling in ever more people

---

* Barnett: 'When I was coach in 1981 I once fined him $1,000 for getting sent off and he moaned like hell. I told him that if he scored against Washington in the next game I'd waive the fine. He scored a bloody hat-trick.' (Author interview)

in 1976, but it wasn't until the move out of the city that they were able to come close to filling the stadium. 'Suddenly, overnight, the Cosmos were getting 60,000 or 70,000,' remembers journalist Paul Gardner. 'It couldn't have been just because of Pelé. Why didn't it happen at Yankee Stadium? It wasn't going to happen at Randall's Island, that's for sure [the Cosmos' Downing Stadium home on Randall's Island was notoriously down at heel, and hard to reach]. What led to that? I haven't seen any explanation at all. It wasn't that they were suddenly playing more interesting soccer; that came later. In terms of celebrity names, the only one they had [apart from Pelé] was Beckenbauer. I'm perfectly amenable to the idea that it was all down to Pelé, but I don't quite see how that could be. Were the Yankees and Mets dull that year? Was it the new stadium? I honestly don't know. You'd have to talk to the sociologists about what was going on in this city at that time.'[14]

In fact there was a Father's Day game on 19 June 1977, when all the stars aligned. The idea of a picnic on a summer's day outside the new stadium to help appreciate the qualities of good ole pop was an attractive one. The opponents were the by-now-hated rivals of Tampa Bay. And, to help make the record attendance of 62,394 think about coming back again, the Cosmos won 3–1, and Pelé scored a hat-trick. The first goal was thumped in from around the penalty spot from a cross from Nelsi Morais, the second was a direct free-kick, and the third was a feeble shot, possibly intended as a pass, that confused the Rowdies' English keeper Paul Hammond, who obligingly fumbled the ball over the line. The quote-friendly Brazilian duly dedicated his hat-trick to all the fathers in attendance.[15]

'Word got around very quickly, that's clear,' says Gardner. 'It's quite possible the move to New Jersey made a big difference. There were fans who didn't like coming in to the city – people are very strange about coming in to the city. You've got the [MLS] Red Bulls now sitting out in New Jersey, and they won't draw anybody from Long Island because they've got to come through the city via the Bronx Expressway and they just won't do it. Just like no one would go from New Jersey out to the first Cosmos stadium on Long Island*.'[16] The *New York Times* that same month addressed the issue in a piece headlined 'The Cosmos Phenomenon'. 'The chemistry is obvious,' wrote Dave Anderson. 'Take the charisma of Pelé, add the cool of Franz Beckenbauer, mix in the charm of a division-leading team and pour them all into Giants Stadium out there in the Meadowlands with its cozy seating and vast parking lots. Tailgates in those parking lots have helped to create a pro-football atmosphere.'[17] A Cosmos' press release couldn't have expressed it better. An actual tailgater, a liquor store owner from Wallington, New Jersey, named Edward Jakubiec, organized tailgates to Cosmos games with up to 100 of his customers, mostly second- or third-generation Poles who didn't watch soccer live 'but had it in their blood anyway', according to Jakubiec. 'We consider the Cosmos New Jersey's team. They're right in our back yard and it's a lot of fun rooting for them. Once the people saw the game, that the Cosmos were winners, they wanted to come back.' He won the first official Cosmos tailgating contest by serving up Chinaglia spaghetti, Pelé paella, and Beckenbauer *wurst*.[18]

Tailgating, it seems, was becoming part of a gastro-cultural

---

* The peripatetic Cosmos played at the following stadiums: Yankee Stadium in the Bronx (1971); Hofstra Stadium on Long Island (1972–73); Downing Stadium on Randalls Island (1974–75); Yankee Stadium in the Bronx (1976); Giants Stadium in Meadowlands, New Jersey (1977–84).

fan movement elsewhere in soccer. The game was now becoming so American, wrote the journalist Hank Gola in 1978, that 'Mom is bringing her apple pie to the game, packing hamburgers and hot dogs and flipping down the back door of the family station wagon'.[19] The Tampa Bay Rowdies, the Fort Lauderdale Strikers and the San Jose Earthquakes all followed the Kicks and the Cosmos in turning games into an extended day out. They made it an 'event', to use the modern PR parlance. In Britain at the time, there was no such thing associated with soccer, because tailgating was something that posh, wealthy English people did out of hampers in the back of their Range Rovers at rugby games at Twickenham for England internationals, or at Royal Ascot for the horse racing, or for the Oxford–Cambridge boat race. The only drinking before British soccer involved several pints of beer at the pub before the game, and (until it was banned in the 1980s) several more inside the stadium. Food was fish and chips hurriedly snarfed down on the street, or some approximation of a re-heated hamburger either from a dubious truck outside the ground or a tin wagon on wheels at the top of the terrace. The food culture of British soccer was an ongoing joke, and a reflection of the way that fans were poorly treated in every respect. Food inside grounds was so bad that it later became the subject of cult nostalgia, and a certain pride among fans at having shovelled so much shoddy or downright dangerous fodder down their throats. English grounds especially (Scotland was partially redeemed by a fairly palatable, spicy beef pie) held to the philosophy that the fans were probably drunk in any case, so it was best to provide them with the absolute minimum of taste and quality in exchange for an extortionate amount dictated by their monopoly status. This kind of anti-entrepreneurial spirit for decades pervaded most forms of commerce in Britain, and is partly why the 1970s are remembered by those who were there with both a sickly smile and a slight shudder.

Which isn't to say that things were perfect in the US, however much game day for the fans involved what, to the rest of the soccer world, was the alien idea of relaxation and having a good time. As mentioned above, the casual party atmosphere at Minnesota repelled some businessmen and families from coming to the Met. Outside of the Kicks, though, unpleasant incidents were usually one-offs. If there is ever crowd trouble at US sporting events, it almost always involves a spontaneous, small-scale, on-the-spot conflagration that's the result of a carelessly slung insult at an opposing fan's team, or a physical collision caused by too much alcohol. Geography dictated that crowds of away fans were almost non-existent, and it rarely, if ever, occurred to anyone to attack a fellow human being for wearing the opposing team's colours. More than likely you'd be offered a burger and a beer to make you feel welcome in the host city. In the Pacific North West, where – as mentioned earlier – the proximity of Portland, Seattle and Vancouver allowed away fans to travel in numbers amid the fostering of a healthy rivalry, there was little question of violence.

At the Meadowlands Stadium in New Jersey there was a 'park atmosphere. It's really nice to be out there on the day of the game,' according to the Cosmos' 'head of tailgating' Tom Werblin (it's unclear whether or not this was an actual position within the Cosmos organization, but it's not implausible). He added, 'We're in the entertainment field. And fans are going to enjoy it more when they help make their own fun. Tailgating is the family sport, a summer happening, and the thing to do.' A Fort Lauderdale Strikers front office staff member, Steve

Rankin, said that in the absence of marketable big-name players, the team decided 'to capitalize on a fun, festive atmosphere and make the game a complete social event for the fans.' Once they'd established tailgating through radio ads and got people to start turning up early with their cool boxes and picnic baskets, they cultivated it with competitions and free beer. 'It got so that any function involving the Strikers ended up being a tailgating party. The team's winning ways helped. We wrapped up the Eastern Division on a three-game western road swing [in 1977] and, when we got back, there were 1,500 to 2,000 people tailgating at the airport. It couldn't have worked any better. We got people to the game without handing out masses of tickets and it got to the point where, if we had an 8pm game, the lot would be full by 6.30.'

Werblin's point that fans liked to be encouraged to make their own fun may have been accurate, but that was only true for the time spent outside the stadium. Once fans were in, they were at the mercy of whatever gimmicks the marketing staff had come up with in the previous week's brainstorming sessions. That was their job, after all. No one was going to sit back and claim that, like in the rest of the world, this game was going to sell itself.

Harleys, mock funerals and ducks behind the goal

'English football is a grey game played on a grey day before grey people. American soccer is a colourful game played on a sunny day before colourful people.'
—Rodney Marsh, about to board the plane for the US and turn his back on the English game, 1976.

Marsh's most famous quote with respect to the differences between US and English soccer cannot be sourced, but it's not something that Marsh denies having said. Even if it was refined retrospectively (and Marsh once recorded it several times over, with differing emphases, for the benefit of an archival sound website) it contains a core of truth. The quote doesn't necessarily take into account that English football to some extent gloried in its greyness. Being a fan was a duty, an endurance and a badge of honour. You kept going to games *in spite of* all the hardships, discomfort and disappointment. For a bright spark like Marsh, that wasn't good enough. He wanted to go where the game was presented with a smile.

That meant a large helping of corn and cheese on top of the presentation. Geoff Barnett always remembers the San Diego Chicken, inside of which was a man called Ted Giannoulas who hired himself out to any sports team who'd pay him $5,000 plus expenses. 'In one game when I was coach [at Minnesota], our left-back David Stride had kicked one of the opposition players, and he went down clutching his leg. The chicken had this move whereby he'd do a pirouette and then flop over playing dead with legs in the air. After this foul, the chicken ran on to the field and did this move right next to the player that Stride had fouled, implying that the player wasn't injured. The referee goes nuts and comes over to me, as I was the coach, shouting, "Get that fucking chicken off the field!"' Former Everton defender Pat Howard remembered thinking during his debut with the Portland Timbers, away at San Diego in 1978, 'What have I got meself in for? What kind of football is this? I mean, there were blinking cavalry charges up the wings, ducks behind the goal, firecrackers going off ... I felt it was a bit stupid.'[20]

David Chadwick, while assistant manager to Ron Newman at Fort Lauderdale in 1977, remembers the 'interesting' promotions the team staged, and that 'to be honest, the players hated it, but we'd have to do it, even players like Gordon Banks.' They were, he says, just a bunch of solid pros who got on with it and realized that entering the field of play 'on some sort of vehicle' every home game was part of their job. 'We rode in on Harley-Davidson motorcycles, on the back with a driver, in our kit and boots,' says Chadwick, 'and we never knew when we arrived how we would be entering the stadium. We came on in London double-decker buses, we came in on horses, every week it was like, oh my gosh, what are we going to come in on this week?' Ron Newman staged a mock funeral in reaction to negative media coverage after the team had lost three home games in a row. 'So we get out there and there are all these hearses and funeral music. They wheel this coffin out on the field, the fans are going crazy. They lift the lid of this coffin and out pops Ron and shouts, "We're not dead yet!" It was entertainment, people loved that stuff.'

The San Jose Earthquakes were earlier pioneers of the gimmick, and Serbian computer parts entrepreneur Milan Mandarić – later the controversial owner of Portsmouth, Leicester City and Sheffield Wednesday in the UK – started selling out the team's 18,000-seater Spartan Stadium within months of the club's 1974 kick-off in the NASL. His general manager Dick Berg had worked doing promotion for teams in both the NFL (San Francisco 49ers) and the NBA (Seattle Super-Sonics). His promotions included Miss Legs Night, Blind Date Night, Record Scramble Night, and Money Scramble Night. (It's diverting to briefly wonder how any of these events would have gone down at, say, Millwall vs Portsmouth in 1974.)

'We want the people to come out and try soccer, and to have fun while they're doing it,' said Berg. 'There is no reason why they can't enjoy a good game and have a couple of laughs at the same time. I think we've shown in San Jose and Dallas that you can create a family-fun atmosphere around the game.'[21]

In a book-long account of the San Jose Quakes' 1975 season, written with the co-operation of the team, Richard Lyttle describes how a hired super-fan, Krazy George, was used to whip up the crowd.* At the season's opening game, he came out in a vintage car, following the team's cheerleaders, the Shakers (the team names for cheerleaders were not imbued with sexual subtlety, as we will learn), who themselves had come out on a fire truck. In future games, Krazy George made his entrance on a camel, in a helicopter, on a hang glider, on a trick bicycle, and in a police car. He 'assisted' in a half-time lacrosse game between two local teams, but was also reactive to the play on the field. The home game with Portland turned nasty when the Quakes' English defender Derek Craig chinned his compatriot on the opposing team, Graham Day. While Day lay unconscious, Krazy George incited fans from the roof above the Timbers bench to boo and start throwing objects, prompting Portland coach Vic Crowe to ask for police protection. In another home game, near the end of the season against LA, the score stood at 1–1 after 90 minutes and was about to go into extra time. Krazy George 'once again above the visitors' bench, showered beer on the Los Angeles players as they tried to catch their breath. The fans cheered and hooted.

---

* By 1978 Krazy George was making $14,000 a year hiring himself out to various sports teams as an inciter of crowds. (*Soccer Monthly*, US edition, August 1978)

They loved it.' After the Quakes won 2–1, LA lodged a formal protest with the League, claiming that Krazy George's antics had 'interfered with [the] team's preparations for overtime.' Commissioner Phil Woosnam considered the protest, but 'in due time denied it'.[22]

Still, the team was aware that the gimmickry might start to grate with fans in the end, and toned it down once the crowds proved to be loyal. 'There was an interesting phenomenon here,' said the team's PR director Tom Mertens. 'As the fans became more interested and aware of the game, they wanted to see less of the peripheral activity. They want us to keep it lively, without being overbearing.' In the end, San Jose refrained from overdoing its on-field promotions and, like so many other teams who'd managed to woo a base of core fans, sent its players out into the community to perform at the obligatory soccer clinics and fulfil speaking engagements.[23]

Other teams were splendidly, or disastrously, inventive with gimmicks. At Tampa Bay, crowd numbers were healthy but season ticket sales were low because buying a season ticket was too great a financial commitment for their mainly middle-class* fan base. Therefore, constant promotions were needed to lure fans back and keep the team in the public eye. The Rowdies were famous for leading the League in team-related freebies – tote bags, team photos, trips to the Soccer Bowl, discount tickets. Every now and then, though, an idea would bomb, like telling fans to bring a radio to a particular game so that everyone could tune in to a rendition of the Rowdies' theme tune at half-time (nobody bothered). However, a

---

* In terms of income, it should be noted that in the US 'middle class' equates roughly to 'lower middle class to working class' in the UK.

Musical Instrument Night – where fans got in for a discount if they brought along something to blow, pluck or strum in an impromptu half-time parade – was a huge and noisy success. One writer described the Rowdies' home games as borrowing 'the best elements of a picnic, a church revival, an amusement park and a mass sing-along.'[24]

'We were all part of it [the promotional push],' says Joey Fink, who played for Tampa in the team's prime years (1976 to 1978), after leaving the Cosmos. 'The marketing campaign was the catalyst to paying attention to your fans, saluting your fans, and before that in pro sports there was a little bit of aloofness; you didn't go into the stands and sign autographs for an hour. That transferred to the NFL and eventually to Europe.' Everything about the Rowdies' set-up placed it perfectly to be a successful team, he says. 'It was a great group of guys in a great stadium, great marketing, in a team that was a winner. The social life was great, the first time I ever saw a soccer team with cheerleaders, the Wowdies. The Cosmos followed that later. We were young, single guys, sort of "celebrities" as there was no other pro sports team in town, so after the game you'd go out and party a little bit – we all had a lot of good times, a lot of girlfriends back in those days.'[25]

Sex on the sidelines – Shakers, Poppers and Honey Dips

Few UK media reports on the NASL in the second half of the 1970s could make it through their opening paragraphs without mentioning the cheerleaders, usually in the same sentence as the word 'razzmatazz'. Although cheerleaders were only one part of the sideshow, to the British mind they typified the

American approach to sport. They were a distraction from the serious business on the field, and a crass illustration of how the Yanks didn't understand soccer, and didn't take it seriously. A row of leggy dancing girls with pearly white teeth certainly ran head first into the European stereotype of American girls as smiling paragons of health and sunshine – all very lovely, and worthy of a laddish 'Phwoooargh!', but surely they were just an interference? Their place on the sidelines of an American Football game, however, is as much a part of that sport as fantastically priced hot dogs and stoppages for advertising breaks. What at first seems an absurd irrelevance soon becomes just another part of the whole circus, blending into the maelstrom of coaches, referees and touchline reporters that populate the vast technical area.

It was logical that the NASL would follow the NFL and also make cheerleaders a part of their promotional repertoire. NBC reporter Jim Collis said, 'I'm a soccer fan and I'd love to see every stadium packed to capacity. If it's sex that helps sell the game then the NASL is going the right route.'[26] Not too much sex, however. 'If a girl appeared in Playboy, she would immediately be fired,' warned Diane Gilmour, the director of the Cosmos Girls. Their choreographer Ed Brazo tried to paint the phenomenon with a superior lacquer. 'Soccer is a sport that requires an artist to play the way it should be played,' he said, perhaps while draped across a chaise longue and smoking a cheroot. 'The function of the girls is to provide another means to convey that art. They are actually working with the guys on the field.'[27] That's right – Beckenbauer, Pelé and Chinaglia doubtless spent entire practice sessions synchronizing their moves to match the rhythm of the high kicks and the pumping pom-poms. For them, a goal would only count if its execution was timed to finish at the same climactic moment as a shout of 'Goooooooo Cosmos!' Or perhaps not.

Although Pelé appeared on the selection panel one year to choose the next generation of Cosmos Girls, his view of their role was more traditional. 'During the game,' he said, 'cheerleaders are not good. It's bad when you miss a beautiful goal to see a beautiful girl. You can see the girls any time.'[28]

Cheerleaders had the advantage of costing the clubs very little – most of the women were volunteers, although the Cosmos Girls earned $15 per game. They were also high-profile employees. Many teams used them to staff locations like information booths and press boxes, and to appear at all kinds of promotional events. There was mostly no need to pay them because the position was in very high demand. In Memphis, 70 cheerleader applicants were narrowed down to a team of 23. The Oakland Stompers chose 30 girls out of 130 applicants, and in Tampa Bay 30 women made the cut from the 200 who'd applied. In New York in 1979, over 200 hopefuls enjoyed the honour of parading themselves before a panel that included Pelé and Warner Brothers president Ahmet Ertegun. Thirty-two were chosen. Sixteen cheerleaders would form a greeting tunnel prior to the game, and all 32 would perform a choreographed half-time show. Gilmour complained that at the previous year's auditions they'd seen too many girls looking to further their modelling careers and get exposure. 'This year,' she said, 'we're looking for the all-American girl types – someone with a cheerleading or dance background who isn't so career-oriented. It would be foolish for me to say looks aren't important.'[29]

The Cosmos Girls at least escaped the suggestive and at times borderline pornographic labels that most of the troupes were given. The Shakers and the Wowdies we've already mentioned. Oakland's featured women were the Corkpoppers, and the Fort Lauderdale Strikers' cheerleaders were the Striker Psychers – both names evoking the image of a drooling male fan staring at a young woman in a short skirt or hot pants. The California Surf's 'Surf Breakers' appears to have been an innocuous enough name, but the Washington Diplomats, known as the Dips for short, saw nothing wrong in calling their cheerleaders the Honey Dips. One journalist breathlessly reported how Fort Lauderdale did everything possible to ensure that 'they have pretty people on the sideline'. The chosen women had to enter a beauty pageant and wear a bathing suit. 'They are hostesses, do promotions at shopping malls, and do charity work. They even paid their own way to support the team in Vegas.'[30]

Another excited account, this one about the women who made up the Memphis Vogues, explained that 'this high-kicking bunch of good-looking gals takes to the field with pom poms and hot pants and encourage team players and fans alike at all Rogues home games.'[31] The piece tells how the Rogues put out radio ads for 'the prettiest girls in the mid-South', and quoted the team's PR director, Rudi Schiffer, as saying, 'Hey, these gals will make you forget the Dallas Cowgirls. We've got the best-looking girls in the city and the best choreographer too.' The rewards for giving their free labour and being handled with the lazy sexism of the 70s were t-shirts, season tickets, and their official Vogue outfits.

What kind of girl wanted to be a cheerleader? The Memphis Vogues were aged 18–27, some were married, but most were single working girls or students. One report described the NASL cheerleaders overall as coming from 'all walks of life.

You'll find models, school teachers, students, sales clerks, mothers, aspiring actresses, in addition to soccer fanatics.'[32] At San Jose, cheerleader Nancy McDonald, who also worked in the team's front office, said that they practised routines twice a week, appeared at promotional events, and met visiting teams at the airport. 'I love it, but I guess it's lucky that I have a lot of energy,' she said. The fourteen unpaid Shakers of 1975 were chosen from 'one hundred applicants for looks, personality, and dancing ability'. McDonald, a divorcee, said, 'There's not as much dating with players as you might think. Right now, just one player is dating a Shaker. I just think it's a bad policy, and besides, they're not my type.'[33] An unnamed woman NASL executive admitted to one reporter that, after her team formed a cheerleader troupe, she thought the team would be labelled sexist by women's rights organizations. 'But when we formed our own group I talked to all the girls,' she said. 'They convinced me otherwise. They felt they were doing an important job not only for the team but for the community. Also, they felt it was a way to work into different professions. Some of them have gone into public relations work because of their exposure to working for teams.'[34]

Fast forward to 1992, when Sky Sports first started broadcasting Premier League games on Monday evenings under the banner (stolen word for word from the NFL) of Monday Night Football. One of their new features in an attempt to glam up the game were pre-match cheerleaders. What may or may not have worked in enhancing the fan experience on a balmy evening in Florida and California did not translate well to a cold January night at Loftus Road. English crowds were as nonplussed at the sight of dancing girls as snobby Euro-hacks travelling to the US had been in the 1970s, and the concept was dropped, although a handful of English clubs still occasionally put on a cheerleader show. In current Major League Soccer, cheerleaders are a rarity. It could be that the now more sophisticated US soccer fans prefer their match-day experience to be based more on the European model. Or perhaps there's now a cheerleaders' union, and they asked for a fair wage.

More (or less) gimmicks

Let's enjoy a quick rundown of some other strange and imaginative ways that teams tried to alert the US public to the existence of soccer.

The Rochester Lancers once invited the actress Gina Lollobrigida to attend a game. According to writer Chuck Cascio, 'she accepted and the club promoted Gina from various angles. The result was roughly the same average-sized crowd [of around 5,000], and a lot of people wondering just what the hell Gina Lollobrigida had to do with soccer in Rochester.'[35]

In Toronto in the early 70s, the team once offered a free dollar to the first 1,000 kids showing up if they cheered loudly for the home team. There is no record of how this was monitored, or if any overly taciturn youths had to hand their cash back on the way out of the stadium. A later franchise in Toronto staged armadillo races, a must-see if you've ever looked at a fez* of armadillos and wondered which one would be the fastest.

Goalkeeper Arnie Mausser remembers playing for the Colorado Caribous, a team that lasted only one year, but which is arguably one of the League's most famous – in the internet

---

* Yes, this really is the collective noun for armadillos.

age at least – for their shirts that featured an actual fringe of tasselled leather across the chest. The Caribous are a shoo-in to be included high up on the list in any soccer webzine's standard feature about the *50 All-Time Craziest Football Shirts!* 'We used to have people poke fun at us because of the tassels,' Mausser concedes. 'We also had these big five-gallon cowboy hats we had to wear on the plane for road trips.' Presumably the cowboy demographic wasn't impressed because, as Mausser describes it, 'we played in the gigantic Mile High Stadium with just a few thousand people, and a lot of the time it looked like there was no one there.'[36]

The Washington Diplomats hit a scoring slump in the middle of the 1977 season and brought in a 'witch doctor' at a home game to put a spell on their opponents. The witch doctor was given a name – Chief Diplascore. It is perhaps imposs-ible to fathom at this remove in time how many thousands of extra fans this brought to the match in question. You only need to imagine the conversations in the bars and the barber shops of Washington DC at the time. 'Hey, I hear the city's soccer team are getting a witch doctor in for this Saturday's game.' 'Wow, soccer sounds like a swell sport – count me in.' As the team's general manager John Carbray acknowledged at the time, many potential fans didn't even know how to find DC's Robert F. Kennedy Stadium, opened sixteen years earlier. 'Next year [1978], every piece of material we print is going to have a map showing people how to get here,' said Carbray. The team also gave away thousands of free tickets, and he admitted that their average home gate of 13,000 for 1977 included only around 7,000 people who'd actually paid to get in. 'I know we could probably take a hard line on our tickets and have 5,000 people in here every night and tell everyone that's our paid attendance. But what's the point? If people come to a game free maybe they'll have a good time and pay their way in next time. Our first job is to get the people out here.'[37] The perils of too many giveaways, however, are obvious. If fans get in for free once, there's no guarantee at all that they will want to pay money next time, especially if giveaways are so abundant. The San Diego Jaws failed in 1976 when they flooded the market with free tickets and the team lost credibility because its product was devalued. There's always the sense in an advanced capitalist society that, while people may pounce on anything that's free, they also like to pay for the perception of value. If a ticket costs them money, then they might believe that what they're about to see is worth the cash they've paid (although this tends to break down if, like the Jaws, you lose ten of your first fourteen games and feature players with names like Archie Roboostoff).

The Seattle Sounders started playing in the NASL in 1974 and, under a mainly British team coached by John Best, built up a solid fan base year by year until they were pulling above 25,000 per home game by the end of the 1976 season. 'By playing aggressive soccer in a small, but close to full, stadium the feeling of excitement is multiplied,' wrote Chuck Cascio in 1975.[38] They didn't rely on big-name signings, unless you count a 35-year-old Geoff Hurst a full decade after his World Cup final hat-trick, but as well as playing attacking soccer they tried to appeal to a wide fan base. 'We've tried to make fans part of the team,' said marketing chief Brian Runnels. 'We've had the players enter through the stands passing out flowers to the women. We've had "guess-the-goal" contests. We opened practice to the public, and more than 10,000 kids showed up. If you try just to appeal to one group – whether its kids, adults, women or ethnics – you're cutting down on your potential audience. If you have a million people in your area, you have to try to appeal to a million people.'[39] Something about this approach may have stuck in Seattle for the long term – in the 2013 Major League Soccer season almost 40 years later, the Sounders topped the League's attendance table with an average of just above 43,000 per game, over 21,000 more than the second-placed team, the LA Galaxy. 'A guy named Hal Childs was the PR director,' says John Best of the NASL-era Sounders. 'He had worked in pro sports – basketball and baseball – for many years and he knew everybody in the sports media world, and he was a smart guy. And so we set out to do it, had a great time doing it, worked our butts off. I was out all the time, almost every night, and we'd basically tell everyone the story about soccer, tell them to come out and give it a try.'[40]

In the end, it was only the game itself that was going to keep people coming back. You can only let off Fourth of July fireworks once a year. You can only hire so many elephants or Bengal tigers (San Jose again) before you run out of novel but sufficiently tame zoo animals to surprise the crowd. Eventually, Krazy George and the San Diego Chicken might become nothing more than pains in the ass. Even the most devoted fan may not want yet another poster or scarf or pencil sharpener with the team's logo on, especially if that logo represents a team that's not scoring goals. 'Management can have a fire engine on the field before the game, release 1,000 balloons, light 50,000 candles, have the fans burn down the stadium for all I care,' said Eddie Firmani in 1981, by which time he was coaching the Montreal Manic. 'But when it comes to who plays inside left and inside right, that's my decision.'[41] Firmani had been managing teams in the NASL for seven years at its most highly sold franchises – Tampa Bay and the Cosmos – and the quote betrays a slight tetchiness at the lingering presence of gimmickry. *Don't bother me with that crap any more*, the down-to-earth South African is saying. *Let's get on with the bloody game.*

Sex and naughty boys: 'I ain't driving a fucking Chevette'

Long before Ruud Gullit tried to sell the idea of being a manager who advocated 'sexy football' (he failed, several times over, including at the LA Galaxy), the NASL was pushing the supposedly sexy side of soccer, and not just through its lasciviously labelled cheerleaders. 'The soccer player has more sex appeal than the others,' claimed commissioner Phil Woosnam, referring to other species of sportsmen. 'First, they are normal-sized people without major ego problems. Second, they are dressed more scantily. In football and hockey you don't know what's under all that bulky equipment they wear.'[42] While baseball players, it goes without saying, are generally overweight, chew gum, spit buckets, and look like sex would be the last thing they'd want to do on a list topped in block capitals with the words BAR BRAWL. The 'normal' build of a soccer player was part of the game's push to paint itself as a democratic sport playable by anyone, of any height or shape. You didn't need to be seven feet tall, like a basketball player, or boast a neck the width of a redwood. These regular soccer Joes were just the kind of guys that might ask you out to the diner for a Coca-cola and a hot dog. Indeed, the NASL's audience was almost half female.

'You know they chose Trevor [Francis] as the second sexiest athlete in Detroit last year?' said a girl named only as Sharon, a medical student at Michigan University working at the Detroit Express as summer intern in 1979, the second year of Francis's two-year stay in the League. 'Look, I'm not a groupie or anything, but gosh, NASL is so exciting partly because you see real men – human beings of human size performing out there. I mean, look at Trevor. He's not a blown up 180–200lb freak or anything. He's not a giant, just a human guy playing with a lot of skill and emotion. I love it, and I play it too. Lots of women do.'[43] Dallas general manager Dick Berg also claimed that 'normal folks can identify with soccer stars. You don't have to be 7' 3" or weigh 230 pounds to play it. And 49% of our paying customers are female. I don't think a sport will make it again if women don't like it.'[44]

Juxtaposed with this image of the nice, handsome lad with just an average body was the attempt by certain clubs to garner publicity from the bad behaviour of players with a noisome reputation. You may recall the earlier quote from Boston's PR director Fred Clashman about wanting Eusebio to get caught in a Playboy club. Clashman's counterparts at other teams found such wishes were realized when certain rowdy players arrived from England with a party tag attached. When former Newcastle United striker Paul Cannell came to the Washington Diplomats and dropped his shorts to the referee after being given a yellow card against the Tulsa Roughnecks, Washington's GM John Carbray said the publicity generated 'was worth hundreds of thousands of dollars; far more than would normally have been created by newspaper, radio and TV ads. It had lifted soccer onto the sports pages of every newspaper around the country.'[45] This, at least, was according to the possibly overstated retrospective claims of Cannell himself, whose reputation as a party-goer in DC's

Georgetown district was seemingly not discouraged by the team. Although Cannell was fined two weeks' wages and suspended by the League for mooning the ref, Nike was impressed enough to sponsor his footwear, as long as he wore boots as white as the cocaine he confesses to regularly snorting while he played in the NASL, along with the frequent ingesting of Quaaludes. When he moved to the Memphis Rogues, a club PR representative took him out on the town 'to live up to my image in Memphis, to be what they had bought, a player with a bad guy reputation!'[46] His antics included getting arrested at a Who concert with a teammate while off his head on coke, and getting stopped while drunk by the cops despite being on a driving ban from DC (he had a Tennessee licence, so they didn't know). The police realized that they were Rogues players and that they were only two miles from Cannell's home, so obligingly escorted them to safety 'with sirens wailing and lights flashing'.

Geoff Barnett only half-jokingly describes the social atmosphere in Minneapolis as 'scary', but quickly qualifies that by adding, 'It was great! Around the airport and in Bloomington, that whole area was called the Bloomington Strip, it's where all the night clubs were – it's where we hung out and the Vikings hung out. I met my wife on the Strip, we've been married 32 years. They fell all over you because of your accent. It went two ways – they liked us, and we liked the way they treated us, we were very approachable.' Before meeting his wife, Barnett was forced to act when the Kicks told the players that under a new sponsorship deal they would all be driving Chevrolet Chevettes – a car, it's been unkindly said, that might have been designed in eastern Europe. 'Light blue, little tin boxes,' the goalkeeper recalls. 'I say to Tommy [Scallen, Kicks' president], "I ain't driving a fucking Chevette." He says, "Why not?" I said, "I'm single, I play for the Minnesota Kicks, I'm kind of a star around here. You think I'm driving around the city in a fucking Chevette, what are the women going to think? My contract says if I don't drive the car provided, you have to give me a certain amount of money to compensate." I called my attorney, and five minutes later I get a call back telling me to go and see a guy called Kjell Bergh, a Volvo dealer down in Minneapolis. I go down and see Kjell and 20 minutes later I'm driving a Volvo.' Didn't the other players notice? 'Yes,' says Barnett. 'And did I care? No.'[47]

'My long hair and English accent were looked upon as exotic,' wrote Frank Worthington in his autobiography, 'and I became quite the celebrity around the [Tampa] Bay area with all the benefits that entails. I was having a great time. Legend has it that before I arrived the Rowdies were just called Tampa Bay. Apocryphal, perhaps, although we did work hard at living up to the name.' Worthington admitted that getting drunk, and then driving home and crashing into a central reservation after falling asleep at the wheel was, to use his description, 'unprofessional'.[48]

Showmanship indeed had its limits. Alan Birchenall says that while at San Jose he was 'a bigger hit in the tailgating parties after the game, singing with the band they had, than I was playing. I think that upset the owner Milan Mandarić. There was one game when we were playing against Las Vegas and Eusebio tackled me, a bad tackle, and I went down. I'm writhing, and all the beer cans start getting thrown on to the pitch. Eusebio was helping me up, and it got a bit nasty, so to defuse the situation I picked up an empty beer can, pretended to drink it, then wobbled around a bit to pretend I was drunk. The crowd started laughing, but unfortunately Mr Mandarić didn't see the funny side and said, "I bought you to be a damned footballer, not a circus clown".'

Birchenall, though, disputes any perception that he wasn't taking the game seriously. And talking to Paul Cannell in person, he comes across as a far more earnest thinker about, and participant in, the game than he does in his book of party tales and its selling point of himself as a wild man. 'I was more of a social secretary, and I think that's what upset the owners,' says Birchenall. 'My motto is: Win, lose or draw, don't be a bore. Play with a smile on your face. I played here [at Leicester City] for fourteen years and I can't ever remember coming off the pitch without having a smile and a laugh. I just carried that on in America, and it was looked upon like I wasn't taking it seriously, like I'd come over for a jolly, but I hadn't. I'd come over to work and enjoy it.'[49]

Superstars

Sex, mammals from the jungle, and public drunkenness aside, the NASL's most notorious asset during the second half of its existence was its fixation upon superstars. After Pelé, most teams wanted at least one. The Cosmos wanted several, and only pushed Johan Cruyff – who had appeared for them in exhibition matches – towards LA because they realized the need to spread the talent around a little bit in order to prevent their complete dominance. The accepted wisdom was that big names sold seats, or at least they did in the short to medium term until the novelty of seeing a particular player wore off. Soccer, as we've seen, does not by its more nuanced nature necessarily lend itself to the idea of the star performer, who might be marked out of the game, or even kicked out of it. The star performer might lose his temper and be red-carded. The star performer might miss the easiest chance in the world in a way that a talented basketball player would never miss a slam-dunk opportunity. Soccer stars can compile great highlight packages to make them look like world-beaters when a given player's best career moments – spectacular as they are – could encompass no more than a few minutes from a decade of play.

Still, teams in the NASL were looking to Europe for already established talent, and they started to pay heavy money for the best or most recognizable names. When Trevor Francis came to Detroit he was at the peak of his gifts, and his two loan spells at the club were sandwiched around his £1 million move from Birmingham City to Nottingham Forest in 1979. Detroit was partly owned by Jimmy Hill, whose company had made a stack of cash as 'soccer advisors' to Saudi Arabia. As a TV pundit, Coventry City chairman Hill was forever harping on about the need to change the game's laws, and clearly saw America as both a proving ground for the game's future, and another wealthy country where he could make further profits from the game. As director of the Express, he instigated the Francis move, which netted the player an estimated £100,000 in his first year at the club, and two to three times that in his second year. Francis rewarded his club with lots of goals – 22 in 1978 and sixteen during a half-season in 1979, right after he'd scored the winning goal for Forest in the European Cup final (Francis, intuiting the possible disapproval of Forest manager Brian Clough, had it written into his contract when he moved from Birmingham that he could return for one more season in Detroit). Watching footage of a 1978 playoff game at the Fort Lauderdale Strikers, where he scores twice in a 3–4 defeat, he is so clearly the best player on the field that it's almost embarrassing.

The downside for Francis was that his fat salary included around £70,000 for media duties, and his highly spun role as the club's superstar. 'The publicity is embarrassing,' said the modest, low-key Francis. 'When we played in Memphis it was as if *I* rather than Detroit was playing the whole Memphis team. It was advertised in the town that the $2 million soccer star was "leading" Detroit. Well, I told them, I don't lead, in England it's a captain who leads. But they said, "You are the franchise". It's really embarrassing, but I had to go along with it.'[50] He put an average of 5,000 extra spectators per game on the home gate, but according to the team's executive director Roger Faulkner, 'in cost terms we have not even cut even on Trevor – although he created an identity here, a base on which to build.'[51] On away trips, the player would be sent ahead by hours or days to conduct interviews with local media. When he had to cancel going to a Kinks concert because the team had sprung a social event on him – an 'exclusive banquet' for 100 people who'd paid $70 a head for an autographed print of 'Night Game at the Silverdome' (the home stadium of the Express later used in the 1994 World Cup) – he told Rob Hughes, 'I hate being anywhere where I'm the centre of attraction. I'm like a prize poodle on show for the evening, rented out for two hours by Detroit Express. It's not something I want to do, but it's part of my job.' The team's PR director Steve Unger said, 'the club needs to work Trevor this way. It's put the whole of its investment money over two years into him, so he's got to be up front the whole time.'[52]

At Fort Lauderdale, manager Ron Newman encouraged team owner Joe Robbie to follow the superstar policy. In the team's first two years – 1977 and 1978 – it relied on Gordon Banks as its big name, and he appears in every advert imaginable, right down to an air-conditioning unit, next to which he duly stands with a game smile. Good as he was, though, Banks had only one eye and was almost 40 years old. 'We need players you can talk about,' Newman says he told Robbie. 'You couldn't talk about players that came out of college, you had to go for big names. I had the smallest bloody budget in the whole League.'[53] And so in 1979 he was given more money and the Strikers signed the Peruvian Teofilo Cubillas and the World Cup-winning German striker Gerd Müller. The two men instantly gelled, setting each other up for multiple goals – the German was top scorer that season with nineteen, while Cubillas scored sixteen, and the Fort Lauderdale crowds increased from an average of 10,500 in 1978 to almost 14,000. 'When Pelé came and all the other stars followed we loved it because it was changing the League,' says Steve David, 'and I was very much more comfortable playing in LA with George Best and those guys [compared with a no-star team in Miami]. And the other teams started trying to sign stars too, so that was great. We thought the League was here to stay.'[54]

There was a paradox in all this talk about superstars, and it wasn't just the fact that in soccer a superstar cannot perform to the same spectacular levels every time he gets the ball. The idea of the superstar was in direct contradiction to the selling of players as the normal, regular guys who weren't the physical freaks of basketball and American football, or the thugs of the ice hockey rink hidden by equipment, or the fat, chugging, lesser athletes of the baseball field. 'I hope the sport stays on a human scale like this,' said Dallas manager Al Miller in 1977. 'We need heroes, not gods.'[55] It was a thin line between the two. American soccer's way of keeping its superstars as heroes, not gods, was to drop them in the middle of a public that was sometimes adoring, but often more curious than it was fanatical. And when a foreign superstar only came by for the summer, or even half of a summer, before heading back to his real job, it was hard to cultivate the image of someone devoted to a city and its fans, no matter how enthusiastically he waved, or how hard he talked up the game on television and radio.

So, it was still down to the action on the field. Once you strip away the marketing and look at some of the League's most outstanding games, it's still just possible that it was the attacking approach to the game itself that made soccer so popular for a few glorious years in the late 1970s. Al Miller again: 'The most successful teams at the gate are usually the high-scoring, offensive sides. We don't want what happened to English soccer to happen here, where not losing becomes so important that all you do is go for the tie on the road, and play so defensively at home that fans go to sleep.'[56] There was absolutely no shame in a big score.

Minnesota Kicks 9 New York Cosmos 2, 14 August 1978

In the 1978 playoff quarter-finals, the two best-supported teams in the NASL met over two legs. A reminder of the rules at this point – there was no aggregate score, so if the teams won a single game each, then a further mini-game was used to decide the winner. If that game was tied, it went to a shootout. The two teams had met once only in the regular season, a 4–2 away win for the Cosmos in front of 46,370. Almost 46,000 turned up for the first-leg rematch in Bloomington's Metropolitan

Stadium, and the Cosmos, featuring Franz Beckenbauer, Carlos Alberto, Giorgio Chinaglia, Dennis Tueart and the mercurial Vladislav Bogićević, fully expected to win. They had lost just twice over 90 minutes the whole season, and had scored 88 goals in 30 games – 20 more than the second highest total.

A Cosmos defeat would have been a surprise. A 9–2 mauling was almost as unthinkable as the USA's 1–0 defeat of England at the 1950 World Cup, or Atlanta's triumphs over Manchester City. Unfortunately, there was a newspaper strike in New York at the time, so no ticker-reading flunkey could see the scoreline, assume it was a mistake and print it as Kicks 0 Cosmos 2, or Kicks 9 Cosmos 12. The Cosmos' official team video for the 1978 season shows the goals very quickly, with a kind of Benny Hill blooper soundtrack as accompaniment. This was an aberration, a freak result. There was no reason or explanation, as such.

'We were so dominant,' says Kicks' defender Alan Merrick. 'Nobody came to that stadium with a chance. We had a mindset that we took care of business there. I think that was spurred by the spectacular group of fans.'[57] Tim Twellman, who came on as a substitute for the Kicks that night, says the game had a slightly surreal air: 'My main memory is that it just didn't seem real. Once things got out of hand, [Cosmos] players just quit playing. I think it was just one of those weird things that happened. Everyone was kind of looking at each other and going, *Really? Another goal?*'[58] Alan Willey scored five goals for the Kicks that night, and says, 'Obviously when you score five goals it's not something to be taken lightly, but everything seemed to go right for me that night.'[59] Indeed, the highlights show that, Chinaglia-like, he was often in the right place at the right time. Solid finishes from good build-ups, but nothing spectacular. It really does look as though the entire Cosmos team is standing back and inviting the Kicks to score at will. 'We might as well have pulled our whole team off the field and let the Kicks fire away at our goalie,' said Cosmos coach Eddie Firmani after the game.[60]

Cosmos defender Bob Iarusci was dropped for the game and still says he has 'no idea why, but I think Firmani for some reason thought away from home that the match-up on my side would be dangerous for me. They had Ace Ntsoelengoe on the left side and he was a very fast, tricky guy; he was terrific, and I think Firmani took Werner Roth and put him back in the middle. That atmosphere for the play-off game was unbeliev-able. We got skewered early in the game and then the whole thing collapsed.' Afterwards in the changing room, 'Giorgio's every second word was a swear word, I remember that. He took a couple of guys to task. When we won we all loved each other, but when we lost, batten down the hatches, right? Carlos [Alberto] was shaking his head because there were so many holes in the team, midfielders weren't coming back, there were mismatches in the mark-ups.'[61] Alan Willey says that during the game, 'Chinaglia, you could see him barking at all his people. We scored early on, their keeper got hurt and there was all kinds of arguing going on among their players. The goalkeeper Jack Brand came on for the guy who got hurt, Erol Yasin, and everything we put on goal we scored.' Chinaglia told reporters after the game, 'We were betrayed by the attitude of our own players. Every so often you have to shed the cloak of a superstar and go to work. We never did tonight, but we'll have to on Wednesday night [for the second game].'[62]

The Cosmos took the defeat very seriously, and not just the players. Iarusci recalls how before the return leg two days later, Warner Communications president Steve Ross, who was effectively the Cosmos' boss, paid the team a visit. 'He came to Giants Stadium in his helicopter and made it clear that we couldn't do that to him, how he'd been embarrassed, and that the people he'd been bragging to about the Cosmos for business reasons weren't impressed by results like that.' Merrick remembers the pressure that the Cosmos came under after the first game. 'They had a lot on the line in terms of their credibility as a playing group,' he says. 'They were under a lot of pressure to produce unbelievable performances to get the tie back, and they came through.' With two goals apiece from Chinaglia and Tueart, they won the return game 4–0 in front of a 60,199 crowd, taking the tie to a sudden-death, half-hour mini-game.

During the mini-game, recalls Alan Willey, 'we had a break down the right, a cross to the far post, Ron Futcher headed it across to me, and I headed it to the top corner. And somehow Jack Brand made this save, an incredible save, and I think that's the only save he made across the three games. If there's one moment I could have back again it would be that header – if that had gone in, we'd have beaten New York in New York, which would have been huge at the time.' Instead, the game went to a shootout, which was decided with each team taking five attempts, followed by sudden death. The Kicks led 2–1 after their five kicks, and the Cosmos needed to equalize with their final attempt to stay in the game. Carlos Alberto, who had never taken part in a shootout, stepped up.

Iarusci, recalled to the Cosmos' defence after the first-leg 9–2 debacle, remembers how Alberto 'flipped it up in the air off his knee and over the keeper's head and then into the goal. No one had seen that kind of shootout goal before.' Alberto said merely, 'They pay me to be cool.'[63] The crowd went nuts, and after Merrick missed for the Kicks, Beckenbauer converted to win the overall tie for the Cosmos, who went on to beat Portland in the semi-finals and Tampa Bay in the final, 3–1. 'Heartbreaking,' says Merrick. Yet a typically NASL outcome – a team could lose 9–2, and still progress. However skewed that seems, it meant that the game was exciting right down to the very last kick.

Bitter at Sweet – the rapid decline of the Kicks

What the League giveth, the League taketh away. Hardly had the Minnesota Kicks soared to the Soccer Bowl, several divisional titles, and the second-top slot in the attendance charts behind the Cosmos than they were gone.

The demise was quick, but it was hastened by a change in ownership. At the end of the 1980 season, with crowds waning (although still 4,000 above the NASL average, at just over 18,000 per game), Jack Crocker and his ownership group put the team up for sale after making a loss that year of around half a million dollars. During the 1980 season they had reinstated free parking, but according to Minnesota historian Timothy Grundmeier the 'old problems' of underage drinking, exploding fireworks and people not attending the actual game returned, and so later that season parking fees were brought back, 'and crowd sizes began to decline', many put off by the subsequent extra security mentioned earlier.[64] In the first round of the playoffs, the Kicks lost 1–0 at home to Dallas in front of 17,461, over 10,000 below the equivalent playoff game one year before.

The new owner came from England, a former Notts

County vice-chairman called Ralph Sweet, a man of average appearance and an educated accent whom Barnett estimates to have been around 60 years old at the time. Sweet claimed to have unlimited wealth 'from land deals and automobile dealerships that thrilled the imagination of us boobs who bought his stories', as one journalist put it after the team went bankrupt within a year.[65] However, 'there was a big belief that he wasn't the guy with the money,' says Geoff Barnett, and Alan Merrick agrees, although Sweet had reportedly bought the team together with two Irish real estate executives. 'He was a front man, a puppet,' says Merrick. One of the reasons they give, strangely enough, was his car. 'You see, the club had got him this Ford Thunderbird,' says Barnett. 'He was too excited about this Thunderbird. If you've got that kind of money he was claiming, a 1981 Thunderbird isn't going to excite you that much.'

Sweet had close ties to Notts County chairman, Labour MP for Nottingham East and Football League chairman Jack Dunnett, who'd periodically come over to visit and watch games with a man called Dudley Sanger. 'Ralph Sweet was kind of like a front man for the real owner,' says the Kicks' PR officer at the time, Dave Ferroni. That owner was widely presumed to be Dunnett, but both Sweet and Dunnett denied this, even though the MP had been present at all the negotiations to buy the Kicks.[66] Ferroni describes Sweet as 'a watch dog [as in, minding the team for its real owner] – he was very friendly and cordial with the media, and was loved by a lot of people. He talked like he had a lot of money. He fabricated a lot, there's no question about that. He would say one thing one day and something else the next. I could sense at the beginning something wasn't right. I'm not really sure why they bought the Kicks. Why did they want to invest in US soccer? There had to be an ulterior motive.'[67]

During the 1981 season, the Kicks continued to win, crowds continued to fall, and Sweet cut the team's front office staff in half to save money. The whole year, he quibbled about costs, and that moving to the new Metrodome stadium the following year would double the team's rent compared to what they were paying at the Metropolitan. One writer sat by Sweet and Dunnett (over visiting again, though of course he had no financial interest in the team ...) at a home game against Tulsa, and watched as the apparent owner winced at a wrongly ignited firework – the Kicks would light a firework after every goal, but in this case the rocket went off after former Liverpool forward Steve Heighway had a goal ruled out for offside. 'Not now, you bloody fool,' said Sweet, before complaining that 'last month I paid $1,600 for fireworks. I could be spending that money on a player. I'm stuck with the fireworks for the rest of the year.'[68] And yet he had also boasted to journalists, 'I could afford to lose a million dollars for 20 years.'[69]

In an interview with the *Minneapolis Star*, the paper's assistant sports editor Dick Pufall quizzes Sweet on his motives for buying the team. Sweet insists that, 'I didn't come here to make money, if that's what you think.' Pufall says that surely he didn't come to lose money either. 'Yes, I came here to lose money,' insists Sweet, claiming that is 'the British attitude'. Pufall replies, 'That's interesting. Shocking, in fact.' Sweet argues back that it isn't. How does he survive? Sweet laughs and says, 'I have money elsewhere. I'm here partly for fun, and I'm here for the love of the game. It's as simple as that. It might sound a bit wishy-washy to you, but it's quite true.' Pufall says this sounds refreshingly different, but 'maybe a little hard to believe'.[70]

Alan Willey, who had been among the League's leading scorers for four consecutive years, was sold during the 1981 season, and suspects that it was down to the team's financial troubles. 'The [previous] owners were good but decided to get out one day,' he says. 'Ralph Sweet took over, I don't know if he was the owner or the front guy for some people. Anyway, they weren't spending the same kind of money that they were before, and in July they traded me to Montreal. That was Minnesota's last season, in 1981 [under the Kicks name]. The atmosphere wasn't the same. I never wanted to leave Minnesota, but at the time they thought they could get some money for me. They maybe knew the team was going to fold at the end of the year, so why not sell one of our best players and get some money for him?'[71]

'After the [1981] season we were told by Ralph Sweet that everything's great,' remembers Tim Twellman. 'Go off on your holidays! So we went to visit family in St Louis, and when we came home the team had folded. That was a little hairy. I was fortunate enough to get a transfer to Tulsa.' The fragility of life as a soccer player in the NASL was demonstrated by what happened next. 'When I was brought to Tulsa I thought I was going to be in for a long time. So during my first season I went in with them and talked about my contract and renewing it. I drove home, and when I arrived my wife told me, "You've just been traded to Chicago."' He laughs. 'I thought the talk had gone well, but I guess it didn't.'[72]

Barnett, who had been appointed coach midway through the season after Sweet and Freddie Goodwin fell out, was on a scouting trip in Europe when he was summoned to Sweet's home in a Hampshire village south-west of London. He'd just been to Sweden to take possession of a brand new Volvo, courtesy of the Kicks, and then picked up his girlfriend from the airport. 'We went to see Ralph,' says Barnett, 'and he makes me a cup of tea, and then he goes, "I've got some bad news for you, Geoffrey. We're folding the team." And I said, "What the fuck am I doing over here scouting for players, getting this new car?" And he just says, "That's the way it is. It's done."' Ferroni heard while on holiday in Italy. Back in Minnesota, some local businessmen were keen to put together a new ownership group but couldn't get enough backing. The team ended up at the local bankruptcy court, fighting for a stay of execution and hoping to survive on the two letters of credit for a total of $650,000 that Sweet's ownership group had posted with the NASL. These letters of credit – posted as a guarantee to supposedly ensure that clubs operated responsibly – were now to keep the team afloat through 1982 until new ownership was found. However, an advertising agency, MR Bolin, was owed $110,000 by the Kicks and filed an injunction that prevented the League from using the letters of credit. The Kicks' president Tom Scallen had also tried to get the League to activate the letters of credit in order to compensate staff and players who'd gone unpaid for several weeks, but the League had refused, still hoping to find new owners.[73]

It turned out that the Kicks' money in 1981 had all come from Switzerland, via that haven of financial transparency, Lichtenstein. The two letters of credit, as well as a further $700,000 line of credit to the team for the 1981 season, had been arranged through the aforementioned Dudley Sanger, the London representative of Établissement Oberberg in Lichtenstein. According to a case brought by Oberberg before the US Bankruptcy Court in 1985, the lines of credit had been guaranteed by the Swiss Bank Corporation, 'rather than Oberberg itself because the parties were concerned that Oberberg's credit did not have the international recognition of the Swiss Bank.'[74] As Joe Soucheray wrote in the *Star*, 'Nobody in this town can be sure if Ralph Sweet was ever the principal owner of the Minnesota Kicks, as he privately claimed, or if he was acting on behalf of silent partners back home, as he conveniently mentioned in public.'[75] Equally, nobody can be sure what his motivations were, or those of his silent partners.

At this remove in time it barely matters either way, other than as another illustration of how dubious ownership and poor management could quickly run a decent team into the ground. Barnett says, 'There was a feeling throughout the League that if the Kicks can't make it, with their average crowds, then who the hell *can* make it?' Sweet, whom Barnett says is no longer alive, claimed at the time that the club had lost $1 million during the 1981 season, and that it was $500,000 in debt. On the day that the club was closed in November 1981, staff were left unpaid and players, who hadn't been paid for several weeks, were released as free agents. 'After eleven years at Anfield, where everything was so stable, being in a situation where the wages don't arrive takes some getting used to,' said Steve Heighway just before the club was finally wound up. 'It is a real problem for my family, who really love the life out here. My house will be completed in a fortnight, but I can't get the mortgage money. Still, I am better off than some of the lads, who literally can't afford petrol to put in their cars. A few of them organized a garage sale recently to raise money to live on.'[76] Scallen pronounced himself 'bitter' at

Sweet. 'A sports franchise isn't a shoe franchise,' he said. 'Ralph did an injustice by putting us in these straits.'[77]

'That was the demise of the Kicks, and that's what led to the demise of the League,' claims Merrick. 'For a lot of the ownership groups, when they saw that the Kicks were gone, that was like a free-fall for the League. Joe Robbie brought his Fort Lauderdale team up to Minnesota [in 1984] because he was looking to tap into that fan base, but the stadium was gone and they were in the Metrodome stadium downtown,' which had limited parking and thus limited scope for tailgating. 'The complexion of the franchise had changed dramatically, and we couldn't get the extra fans back into the stadium.'[78] The city's final NASL game, played as the Minnesota Strikers in 1984, was a 4–0 defeat at home to the San Diego Sockers. Crowd: 8,989.

Season-by-season overview

1974

Bam! The NASL exploded from nine to fifteen teams. Atlanta and Montreal quit, but Baltimore, Boston, LA, Washington and Vancouver came back for more, and Denver, Seattle and San Jose lined up as League virgins. Franchise cost: sources on this are conflicted – one puts it at $75,000, another at $250,000. Either way, it was going up, and would continue to do so.

John Best, who'd been playing in the League from the very start, says that during the quiet years the standard was not as high as in 1968, when there had still been a lot of cash around, but that the NASL had 'maintained a presence, and that was very important. The whole sport at a professional level was taking a big, deep breath to get more oxygen, and we turned it around. 74 was the major turnaround point.'[79]

Crowds were approaching a comparatively respectable average of 8,000, while players who would turn into quality League stalwarts were joining, such as Nigerian striker Ade Coker (Boston) and Trinidadian forward Steve David (Miami). David's team and the **LA Aztecs** drew the final 3–3 in front of 15,507 in Miami's Orange Bowl, but LA took the game on penalty kicks.

Fun facts: the Cosmos moved again, to Downing Stadium on Randalls Island, an absolute shithole venue in an utterly inaccessible location, but which is now hallowed ground for US soccer history buffs (see next chapter). You have to make a pilgrimage just to understand how desolate the place is.

Half-time

It's halfway through the book, so get yourself a hot dog, a Bud Light, and sit back to enjoy some light entertainment. Pop-up cheerleaders and effervescent, non life-threatening indoor fireworks were too expensive, so here are some lists instead.

Top 10 scorers in the NASL

1. Giorgio Chinaglia: 193 goals (213 games)
2. Alan Willey: 129 (238)
3. Karl-Heinz Granitza: 128 (199)
4. Ron Futcher: 119 (201)
5. Paul Child 102 (241)
6. Illja Mitić: 101 (166)
7. Steve David: 100 (175)
8. Ace Ntsoelengoe: 87 (244)
9. Mike Stojanović: 83 (179)
10. Alan Green: 82 (138)

Top 10 creators (assists)

1. Vladislav Bogićević: 147 assists (203 games)
2. Karl-Heinz Granitza: 101 (199)
3. Ray Hudson: 99 (197)
4. Steve Wegerle: 88 (196)
5. Ace Ntsoelengoe: 82 (244)
6. Giorgio Chinaglia: 81 (213)
7. David Bradford: 80 (197)
8. Jean Willrich: 78 (192)
9. Jorgen Kristensen: 73 (130)
10. David Byrne, Julie Veee and John Bain: tied on 68 (132, 166 and 191 games respectively)

The author's ten greatest NASL players:

1. ***Giorgio Chinaglia*** – few people in the NASL remember Chinaglia with a great deal of warmth, and he was playing with a world-class team to assist him. Yet he scored when it mattered (in four Soccer Bowls, and in multiple playoff games), and he scored often, no matter whether he was linking with Pelé or Bogićević. The archetypal anti-hero, a comic strip striker who could pull off spectacular overhead kicks as well as two-yard tap-ins.

2. ***Karl-Heinz Granitza*** – Chicago's left-footed cannon was about as popular as Chinaglia due to his, ahem, strong personality, but he was out there to win games and score goals, not make friends. Like Chinaglia, a merciless finisher, but a forward who made the right runs and wasn't shy of passing to teammates in a better position to score. Teamed up with playmaker and fellow German Arno Steffenhagen – no slouch himself with 60 goals and 43 assists.

3. ***Ace Ntsoelengoe*** – power, speed and cool made the South African midfielder the creative fulcrum of all the NASL clubs he played for (Miami, Denver, Minnesota and Toronto). 'He saw the game in slow motion,' says teammate Alan Willey. 'He could see everything around him. He probably assisted on 90 per cent of my goals.'

4. ***Vladislav Bogićević*** – the Yugoslav paired up with Chinaglia for the NASL's most unstoppable combination. A playmaker who worked very hard at making the game look effortless.

5. ***George Best*** – 'The best player ever was George Best, he was by far the best [in the NASL],' says defender Alan Merrick, who played alongside him at San Jose. With 54 goals and 54 assists, Best won the respect (and often the affection) of almost everyone he met or played against in the US.

6. ***Bob Lenarduzzi*** – the kind of consistent North American player the League needed in duplicate, Lenarduzzi was a solid but attacking defender who stayed with one club for eleven seasons, scoring 31 goals and tallying 57 assists in 288 games for the Vancouver Whitecaps.

7. ***Rodney Marsh*** – brought the requisite panache, flair, cheek, audacity and charm to the League.

8. ***Pelé*** – his presence, personality and marketability alone would be enough for him to make the top ten, although he's only equal 92nd with Johan Cruyff on the all-time NASL scoring list (taking into account both goals and assists).

9. ***Carlos Metidieri*** – the closest that the NASL had to a superstar in the pre-Pelé era, this Brazilian striker was outstanding for the unsung and mainly unloved Rochester Lancers from 1970 to 1973, sandwiched between spells in LA and Boston. He led the League in scoring in 1970 and 1971, winning the League's MVP award both years too.

10. ***Phil Parkes*** – not just included as a token stopper, but because goalkeepers had to go an extra mile to stand out in the attack-oriented NASL. The former Wolves player enjoyed excellent spells with both Vancouver and Chicago, and while at the Whitecaps topped the keeper stats in 1978 and 1979 – in both these seasons he was the League's only goalkeeper to concede an average of less than one goal per game.

League's Most Valuable Players (Player of the Year)

1968 – John Kowalik (*Chicago Mustangs*)
1969 – Cirilo 'Pepe' Fernandez (*Kansas City Spurs*)
1970 – Carlos Metidieri (*Rochester Lancers*)
1971 – Carlos Metidieri (*Rochester Lancers*)

1972 – Randy Horton (*New York Cosmos*)
1973 – Warren Archibald (*Miami Toros*)
1974 – Peter Silvester (*Baltimore Comets*)
1975 – Steve David (*Miami Toros*)
1976 – Pelé (*New York Cosmos*)
1977 – Franz Beckenbauer (*New York Cosmos*)
1978 – Mike Flanagan (*New England Tea Men*)
1979 – Johan Cruyff (*LA Aztecs*)
1980 – Roger Davies (*Seattle Sounders*)
1981 – Giorgio Chinaglia (*New York Cosmos*)
1982 – Peter Ward (*Seattle Sounders*)
1983 – Roberto Cabanas (*New York Cosmos*)
1984 – Slaviša Žungul (*Golden Bay Earthquakes*)

20 odd names in the NASL:

Billy Woof (*Vancouver*)
Jon Pot (*Fort Lauderdale*)
Archie Roboostoff (*San Jose, San Diego, Portland, Oakland*)
Wilberforce Mfum (*Baltimore, New York*)
Barry Salvage (*St Louis*)
Les Parodi (*Seattle*)
Jesus Tartilan (*Cleveland*)
Harold Heck (*San Diego*)
Benny Dargle (*Detroit, DC, Seattle*)
Paul Coffee (*Chicago*)
Gerald Lightowler (*LA*)
Djoko Koković (*Philadelphia*)
Howie Charbonneau (*Houston*)
Slaviša Žungul (*Golden Bay*)
Richard Chinapoo (*New York*)
Julie Veee (*LA, San Jose, San Diego*)*

---

* a strange Anglicization of his Hungarian name, Gyula Visnyei

Delices Chardin (*New York*)

Bertus Hoogerman (*Pittsburgh, Kansas City*)

Geoff Crudgington (*Toronto*)

Kenny Killingsworth (*Dallas*)

Ten young and future famous players to knock the claim that all the NASL's foreign players were aging lags:

Peter Beardsley (*Vancouver*, came to the NASL aged 20)

Hugo Sanchez (*San Diego*, 20)

Steve Hunt (*New York*, 20)

Peter Withe (*Portland*, 23)

Roberto Cabanas (*New York*, 19)

Gordon Hill (*Chicago*, 21)

Brian Talbot (*Toronto*, 17)

Graeme Souness (*Montreal*, 19)

Mark Hateley (*Detroit*, 18)

Trevor Francis (*Detroit*, 24)

Ten players who should have played in the NASL:

Kevin Keegan – Keegan was in talks with the Washington Diplomats at one point, but a deal could not be reached. That is, they didn't offer him enough cash.

Günther Netzer – an egotistical individualist, and a sublime play-maker who loved cash, fast cars and women, so he would have fit right in.

Zico – never quite 'the new Pelé' as billed, but he would have been the perfect choice to take over when his compatriot retired.

Mario Kempes – the 1978 World Cup's top scorer and one outstanding performer would have been a fit for the Cosmos, if Giorgio Chinaglia had ever allowed them to sign another star forward.

Tibor Nyilasi – the last great Hungarian player was scoring non-stop for Ferencvaros throughout the late 70s and early 80s while at his peak. He deserved a little limelight and hard currency.

Claudio Gentile – the hated Italian hatchet man could have toughened up the young US players and effortlessly played the role of villain to the crowd.

Ferenc Puskás – true, he was 40 years old when the League kicked off in 1967, one year after he retired, and he did coach the Vancouver Whitecaps in 1968, but he could probably have squeezed in another season or two and helped it off to a better start.

Didier Six – there were very few French players in the NASL, but this swift and breathtaking, old-fashioned winger travelled well to clubs in Germany, England and Turkey, so he might as well have tried the US.

Allan Simonsen – the prolific Danish striker opted for Borussia Mönchengladbach and Barcelona instead. His loss.

Paul Breitner – the German midfielder, as a Maoist, probably disapproved of the US.

Five NASL players who scored winning goals in the FA Cup final

1. Charlie George, Minnesota (1971 for Arsenal vs Liverpool)
2. Alan Taylor, Vancouver (1975 for West Ham United vs Fulham)
3. Bobby Stokes, Washington (1976 for Southampton vs Manchester United)
4. Roger Osborne, Detroit (1978 for Ipswich Town vs Arsenal)
5. Ricardo Villa, Fort Lauderdale (1981 for Tottenham Hotspur vs Manchester City)

Ten European defeats to NASL teams

Home teams listed first. After Atlanta's double defeat of Manchester City in 1968, the NASL teams' record against top-class European opposition makes for painful reading until the mid-70s. After that, when clubs from across the water were beaten they always accepted it in a sporting manner by blaming either the heat, the artificial pitch, or the fact that they were out of shape, out of season, and tired of touring (or all those reasons together). When European teams lost to NASL sides at home, they were of course too busy focusing on an important upcoming league game, or resting all their top players.

Atlanta Chiefs 3 Manchester City 2 (15/6/68) See Chapter 1

Toronto Metros 3 Torpedo Moscow 1 (22/8/73) Reports are scarce – some sources say the result was only a 2–1 win. Former Northern Ireland international Terry Harkin scored at least once, a fact that the world needs to know.

Vancouver Whitecaps 4 Borussia Mönchengladbach 3 (27/7/76) The German giants were in the midst of a three-year reign as Bundesliga champions, and gamely threw themselves into this entertaining encounter. They were felled by an unlikely hat-trick from Canadian forward Buzz Parsons, who otherwise scored only four goals all year for the Whitecaps.

Paris St Germain 1 LA Aztecs 2 (18/9/79) Johan Cruyff led the moody but free-scoring 1979 Aztecs team to victory at the Parc des Princes.

Seattle Sounders 2 Celtic 1 (14/7/81) Almost 21,000 saw Alan Hudson set up Jeff Bourne for two goals in this Trans-Atlantic Challenge Cup tie. 'You know they probably sit around in England

and laugh at us,' said Hudson, 'but we beat the British.'[1] The Sounders went on to win the tournament.

Vancouver Whitecaps 3 Manchester United 1 (18/5/82) In something called the Euro-Pac Tournament that also featured Seattle and Hajduk Split, the Whitecaps 'ran rough-shod' over United, according to the commentator on a very brief highlights clip featuring three beautifully taken goals. United lost 3–0 to Seattle on the same trip.

Toronto Blizzard 1 Juventus 0 (30/5/82) Most of the 35,000-plus fans were local Italians cheering for the visitors, who'd sent mostly second-choice players. The Blizzard showed the locals what they were missing by dominating the game and winning it with a second-half goal by Scottish forward Duncan Davidson.

New York Cosmos 7 SV Hamburg 2 (15/6/83) Cosmos trounced the newly crowned European and Bundesliga champions, who weren't pleased. See Chapter 10.

New York Cosmos 5 Barcelona 3 (28/5/84) In the last of the Trans-Atlantic Challenge Cup's five tournaments, the last of the Cosmos stars – Johan Neeskens, Paraguayan Roberto Cabanas, and Vladislav Bogićević – all scored against a Barcelona team built around Diego Maradona in his prime.

Tampa Bay Rowdies 3 VfB Stuttgart 2 (6/6/84) – a good result on the surface, but in fact it was a shootout win over the German champions, and the actual game result was a 2–2 draw. The 6,000-plus gate was a sure sign that things were going downhill at the once-vibrant club, despite coach Rodney Marsh's claim that it was 'a magnificent victory'. Stuttgart coach Helmut Benthaus had the standard excuses at the ready: 'I think our team had difficulty with the climate and temperature.'[2] What did he expect, a Swabian snowstorm?

Ten NASL team owners (sample season: 1978)

1. *Elizabeth Robbie*. The hugely popular sole owner of the **Fort Lauderdale Strikers** was a mother of eleven and the wife of Miami Dolphins owner Joe Robbie (a wealthy attorney).

2. *James William Guercio*. The part owner of the **Colorado Caribous** and full owner of the Caribou Ranch, a recording studio built in a converted barn in the Rocky Mountains near Colorado. Elton John, Supertramp, War, Chicago and Earth, Wind & Fire all recorded there.

3. *Herbert Capozzi*. The founder of the **Vancouver Whitecaps** was the son of Italian immigrants and a former Canadian football player. Described as 'a dominating influence on the business life of Vancouver'.[3] Still revered by Whitecaps fans.

4. *The People*. The **Portland Timbers** were a rarity in US sport, owned 100 per cent by local citizens who had invested in the team.

5. *George Strawbridge*. The **Tampa Bay Rowdies** owner was once a professor of history at Widener University, Pennsylvania, but coming from a family with a large share in Campbell's Soup was of more help in allowing him to invest in sports teams. He also part-owned the Buffalo Sabres ice hockey team and the racehorse Secretariat.

6. *Milan Mandarić*. A name that may cause fear and loathing among fans of Portsmouth, Leicester City and Sheffield Wednesday, the Serbian-born Mandarić originally bought **San Jose**, then sold out to take over the **Oakland Stompers** instead.

7. *Warner Communications*. Took over the **Cosmos** and ran it with an iota of extravagance, appropriately allocating the

huge annual losses to the vast media empire's comics book division.

8. ***World Sports Academy***. Jimmy Hill's company that had made a stack of money showing the Saudis how to play soccer owned the **Detroit Express**. It didn't end well (see Chapter 8).

9. ***Rick Wakeman, Paul Simon, Peter Frampton***. This trio would probably have been better off collaborating on an MOR folk-prog rock double live concept album than sinking their cash into the **Philadelphia Fury**. The team lasted three royalty-sapping years (see Chapter 9).

10. ***Alan Rothenberg***. The big-shot lawyer was one of three men behind the **LA Aztecs**, and was later in charge of the hugely successful soccer tournament at the 1984 LA Olympics. That in turn eased his election to president of the US Soccer Federation, where he oversaw both the 1994 World Cup and the birth of Major League Soccer.

The author's top ten NASL games

1. ***New York Cosmos 2 Seattle Sounders 1*** *(28/8/77)*. One of the most entertaining cup finals ever played, in any competition, this game produced non-stop, end-to-end action with over 50 attempts on goal. Fittingly, it was Pelé's final competitive game, played in Portland in front of a capacity 35,000 crowd (seats had been added to meet demand), and the only thing missing from the script was for the Cosmos number 10 to score the winning goal. Steve Hunt put the Cosmos ahead after stealing the ball from the feet of Sounders' keeper Tony Chursky. English striker Tommy Ord equalized a few minutes later, finishing a fine, five-man move after Franz Beckenbauer lost possession (a goal missed by TV viewers because of an ad break). Then, after dozens of near-misses, woodwork

shots and excellent goalkeeping from both Chursky and Shep Messing, Chinaglia headed the winner from a cross by Hunt, voted MVP by the assembled soccer hacks. Some lenient refereeing allowed Seattle's Mike England to stay on the field and several other players to escape deserved yellow cards. It didn't matter: the fans were enthralled from first kick to last.

2. *Minnesota Kicks 9 New York Cosmos 2 (14/8/78)*. The one night when the Cosmos were both annihilated and humiliated, though striker Alan Willey – who scored five – reckoned he'd had better games. The Cosmos were bollocked by Warners management and bounced back to take the second leg 4–0, then the overall tie on a shootout following a goalless mini-game (see Chapter 5).

3. *New York Cosmos 8 Fort Lauderdale 3 (14/8/77)*. Exactly one year earlier, the League's flagship game – a packed stadium of over 77,000 watching lots of goals and superstars. As good as it got.

4. *Toronto Blizzard 2 Chicago Sting 3 (3/10/84)*. The League's final ever game is a forgotten classic. Commissioner Howard Samuels had abolished the single-game Soccer Bowl for a three-game series. Having won the first game of the 84 Soccer Bowl, the Sting took a two-goal lead, but Toronto clawed it back late to 2–2. Paul Simanton then bagged an even later, deflected winner for Chicago, and in the final action of the League's history, their Mozambique goalkeeper Victor Nogueria pulled off a stunning one-handed save to win the title.

5. *Chicago Sting 5 New York Cosmos 5 (28/6/81)*. The official score is 6–5 to the Sting as they won the ensuing shootout on

an afternoon of non-stop scoring and stirring Cosmos come-backs, including the equalizing goal with 42 seconds left.

6. ***Fort Lauderdale Strikers 3 Seattle Sounders 4*** *(8/8/82)*. In the playoff semi-finals, Seattle had already lost the first game at home, 0–2. After a goalless first half Fort Lauderdale were leading 3–2 and within a minute of making Soccer Bowl when Seattle's Roger Davies headed his second goal of the night, and only his third of the season, to take the game to extra time. Wolves legend Kenny Hibbitt scored the sudden-death winner for the Sounders with a diving header, meaning a third game back in Seattle. Hibbitt scored the winner there too, taking Seattle through, where they lost to the Cosmos.

7. ***New York Cosmos 2 Vancouver Whitecaps 2*** *(1/8/79)*. A game as legendary for its longevity as its substance (see Chapter 3). Officially, the Cosmos won this second playoff semi-final encounter 3–2 after extra-time and a shootout. As the Whitecaps had won the first game 2–0, the tie was now level at one game apiece. So the two teams then played a goalless 30-minute mini-game, which was then followed by the second shootout of the night. The Whitecaps prevailed, and became champions a week later.

8. ***New York Cosmos 5 Tampa Bay Rowdies 4*** *(14/7/76)*. Grudge match rerun after the Rowdies had won the League's breakout game 5–1 the previous month (see Chapter 4). Pelé scored a brace but Tampa later knocked the Cosmos out of the playoffs. Years of variously classy and feisty encounters were to come.

9. ***Miami Toros 3 LA Aztecs 3*** *(25/8/74 – Aztecs won on penalties)*. The TV broadcast of the 1974 Soccer Bowl, transmitted live to

the rest of the country, was blacked out locally, but still only 15,500 showed up to the 80,000-seater Orange Bowl. The no-shows missed a see-saw thriller, with Miami taking a 3–2 lead with three minutes left, only for US-Scot Doug McMillan to equalize a minute later. LA scored all five of their penalty kicks to take the title.

10. ***New York Cosmos 3 Chicago Sting 4*** *(31/5/82).* The climactic game of the 1982 Trans-Atlantic Challenge Cup (so technically not an NASL game, but still a competitive title match between two NASL teams) saw the Sting take the title in Giants Stadium, despite a Cosmos hat-trick for Chinaglia. Chicago held a 3–1 half-time lead thanks to a goal from Karl-Heinz Granitza and a brace from his link man and compatriot Arno Steffenhagen. Chinaglia levelled the game with two penalties, but Gordon Hill scored the winner with two minutes left. Winners' prize money: $20,000.

NASL soundtrack

Steely Dan – 'Glamour Profession' (1980). A song set in LA around 70s drug dealers apparently mixing with basketball and American football stars, and equating the two vocations. See popular stories about the Cosmos and Paul Cannell.

Chris Bell – 'I am the Cosmos' (1978). Bell joins the centurion of artists in the 70s who rhymed the word 'phone' with 'alone', but more importantly, he likens himself both to the cosmos, and to the wind. Blowing strong one day, gone the next ...

Talking Heads – 'Cities' (1979). David Byrne wants to find a city to live in. He was obviously looking through the eyes of an immigrant NASL player searching for a team, any team, in the early to mid-70s.

David Bowie – 'Young Americans' (1975). Bowie's youthful Americans ask if they've lived their first 20 years just to have to spend the next 50 dying. Perhaps this was why the NASL imploded at seventeen – die young, stay pretty. Life will never be this much fun again.

Supertramp – 'Breakfast In America' (1979). Hairy Brits who'd crossed over from prog rock to commercial superstars but who, quite frankly, were not the best-looking bunch of lads, wistfully compare their ordinary girlfriends to the image they have of girls in California. Without wanting to labour the point, this is really about playing for the San Diego Jaws and the San Jose Quakes instead of Swindon Town and Barnsley.

Electric Light Orchestra – 'Wild West Hero' (1977). Jeff Lynne remains a loyal Birmingham City fan, but that didn't stop him constructing heroic fancies about being a politically correct cowboy who was the friend of Native Americans, while riding around doing the right thing, when asked. Another example of the hold that US movies had on the British imagination.

T Rex – 'Cadillac' (1972). Marc Bolan loves his baby, yeah, and wants to buy her a Cadillac. All young English lads wanted to do the same in the glam rock era.

Tom Waits – 'Better Off Without A Wife' (1975). Waits desperately wanted Franz Beckenbauer to come and play in the NASL, so wrote this song in the knowledge that the Kaiser was having domestic problems and needed a fresh start. The promise of being able to howl at the midnight moon and not get up until noon eventually lured the German World Cup winner to Manhattan.

Elvis Costello – 'Crawling to the USA' (1979). Although he quite understandably didn't want to go to Chelsea, Costello was one in an eventual long and tedious line of new wave singers decrying the

US as imperialists etc. In this song everyone's down on their knees in front of the US except for the Russians and the Chinese. The song was just too early for the Iranian Revolution, which would have made his rhyme a lot more problematic.

Lou Reed – 'Temporary Thing' (1976). Reed was not one of the New York celebrities posing alongside Mick Jagger and Muhammad Ali at the Cosmos' home games. He knew already in 1976 that the NASL was just a transient entity.

Blondie – 'Detroit 442' (1978). Some claim that this song is about riding around in an Oldsmobile 442 with Iggy Pop, but in fact it was Deborah Harry's barely coded tactical advice to Detroit Express coach Ken Furphy to play four in midfield and two men up front when the team kicked off that year. Harry's musically articulated guidance took the Express to the playoffs, but they were eliminated by the Fort Lauderdale Strikers (who were being secretly coached by Patti Smith when she sang *Break it Up*).

The Love Twins – 'Miami Heatwave' (1979). Just because this song was part of a concept album centred on a gay love affair in multiple US locations doesn't mean it's not also about the tough summer playing conditions in Florida in the mid-70s, with 90 minutes of ultra-sweaty, full-on, man-to-man contact followed by a decadent night on the dance floor.

Donny Hathaway – 'Love, Love, Love' (1973). Pelé took Hathaway's song and turned it into his speech at his farewell game between the Cosmos and Santos on 1 October 1977 at Giants Stadium. 'And I want to ask you,' he said to the 75,000-plus fans before the game, 'because I believe love is the most important thing in the world that we can take in life: people, say with me three times, *love, love, love*.' And they did. Now wipe away those tears and let's get on with the second half.

A local Atlanta cartoonist was in bullish mood after the Chiefs beat English champions Manchester City in 1968.

Pelé and George Best were the first two big-name players targeted by the NASL as it jumped on the fast-track to international recognition.

Boston Globe via Getty Images

While Pelé grabbed the headlines, the less heralded and partly hobbling Eusebio stole in to win an unlikely NASL championship with Toronto in 1976.

'You don't tell Eusebio what kind of shoes he's going to wear.' Toronto coach Ivan Markovic (left) was one of several NASL coaches who had problems dealing with star names.

Jeff Goode/GetStock.com

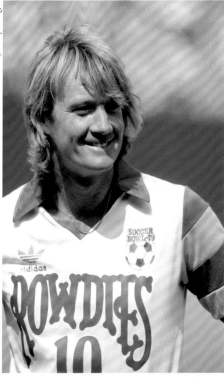

'Just like a rock performer, my soccer is an extension of myself.' The flamboyant Rodney Marsh of the Tampa Bay Rowdies.

George Best and Los Angeles Aztecs part-owner Elton John, seen here in LA in 1976, personified the thin dividing line between soccer and rock-star lifestyles.

The imperious Franz Beckenbauer was another global icon who brought notoriety and attention to the League and his team, the New York Cosmos.

The hard-fought rivalry between the Minnesota Kicks and the aptly named Tulsa Roughnecks proved that it wasn't all glamour and cheerleaders in the NASL.

While the Cosmos, the Rowdies and the Kicks pulled in impressive crowds, lesser teams struggled to fill large stadiums, as seen here during the New England Tea Men versus Philadelphia Fury, June 1978.

AP Photo/Dave Tennenbaum

'Get that fucking chicken off the field!' Gimmickry like the San Diego Chicken would entertain fans, up to a point. Referees were less keen on the interference.

Miles Nadal/Action Photographics

Johan Cruyff of the Washington Diplomats looks nonplussed at being welcomed on to the field of play by pom-pom shaking cheerleaders.

Peter Robinson/EMPICS Sport

'The North American Soccer League will be the world's No. 1 soccer league.' The brilliant, industrious, innovative and perhaps fatally optimistic NASL commissioner, Phil Woosnam.

AP Photo/CRP

Broadcaster Jimmy Hill invested in the Detroit Express and lured over Trevor Francis as his star signing. The Express went bust, as did Hill's next team in Washington DC.

Bob Thomas/Getty Images

A convivial meeting with President Ronald Reagan did little to help Team America, a curious attempt to supplant the US national team in the NASL. They lasted just one season, in 1983.

Pelé and, behind him, the NASL's all-time leading scorer Giorgio Chinaglia, at the head of the Cosmos lineup. With them, the League flourished. Without them, it might have survived.

Yes front man Rick Wakeman, seen here disguised as a referee, invested in the Philadelphia Fury, lost a ton of money, but professed he had fun doing so.

6 Brilliant mistakes: Quicksilver teams in Vegas and Honolulu

'Las Vegas is the only place I know where money
really talks – it says, "Goodbye".'
—Frank Sinatra as Joe E. Lewis
in *The Joker is Wild* (1957)

Part of the delight in looking back at the North American
Soccer League is the constant surprise factor. You can cast an
eye at the English Football League in the 1976–77 season and
say, 'Oh, that was the year Liverpool won the title again, and
Workington dropped out of professional soccer.' You can scan
the NASL tables and exclaim, 'They put teams in Hawaii and
Las Vegas! What the hell were they thinking? How did that
even work?'

In truth, it didn't. Just as the League was embarking on a
significant surge in attracting fans, media attention and world
superstars, the patterns of its future decay were being sketched
by hurriedly trying to locate soccer in the unlikeliest of places.
Islands and desert cities, for example, where it is very, very
hot. The lack of any history or culture of soccer in Hawaii
and Vegas was not necessarily reason enough in itself to stop
them hosting an NASL franchise. After all, there were numerous other similar cities such as Tampa and Minneapolis/St
Paul which were proving that Americans could take to the
sport very quickly. There were, however, plenty of other reasons that should have alerted the League to the overreaching

ambition of making a number of teams from the East Coast, for example, fly to the middle of the Pacific Ocean for a single League game. It would be like trying to establish a county cricket team on the Shetland Isles, or a professional croquet league in the mountain villages of Moldova's Trans-Dnestr region. Or, come to think of it, in Hawaii or Vegas.

'We have reached the point where we can and must be selective in the granting of new franchises,' said League Commissioner Phil Woosnam in late 1976 upon announcing the move of the San Diego Jaws to become the Las Vegas Quicksilvers, and the likely move to Hawaii of the San Antonio Thunder – a team of mainly Scotsmen and Americans who had struggled for two years in southern Texas in front of crowds of between 3,000 and 6,000. Furthermore, he stressed, 'it will have to be the right sort of ownership in the right sort of markets.'[1] If only Woosnam had listened to his own advice. The respective ownerships no doubt had the best of intentions, and in both Vegas and Hawaii they put in plenty of money and enthusiasm, at least to start with. The players, though, remember two things about Las Vegas and Hawaii – the unbearable heat, and the good time that most of them had when they came to town.

'That was one trip I didn't want to miss,' says Alan Birchenall of San Jose's away game in Hawaii. 'Hawaii had a lot of West Ham players, and those lads had had the pick of teams to join, so surprise, guess where they ended up. I remember walking out [on to the pitch] and it was absolutely boiling. It was shimmering, it was that hot. We got the game out the way and then ... we went out there for about four or five days. Wherever you went in the NASL there were always English players and they'd look after you. Because of the travelling distances you rarely went just for the game, and the host team always laid on a bit of a party – it was absolutely fantastic.'[2] Birchenall doesn't mention the score, but San Jose lost 3–1 in front of fewer than 3,000 fans.

Alan Willey also enjoyed a long stay in Honolulu when he flew there with the Minnesota Kicks. 'When we played in Hawaii, we travelled on from a Sunday game in LA,' he recalls. 'We travelled right after the game and didn't play until Wednesday. So we walked down to the beach with our shirts off for 20 minutes, came back, and then next morning you woke up with blisters on your shoulders from sunburn. [English defender] Steve Litt dug his feet into the sand, and when he pulled them out they were all swollen and he had to have injections so that he could play the game. His feet looked like potatoes.' Still, 'it was fun, and not many people can say they played soccer in Hawaii. Almost everywhere you went there was some kind of party put on by the home team for the visiting team.'[3] The Vancouver Whitecaps' Bob Lenarduzzi confirms that 'the game in Hawaii was almost a side-affair compared with the idea of taking a trip out there.'[4]

Alan Merrick, the Kicks' former West Bromwich Albion defender, says that it was 'stinking hot, ridiculously warm, I don't think I left the hotel. We'd been in the game about 30 minutes and I realized something was wrong with my right foot, but I was in the middle of playing so I couldn't look down. In fact the field was so hot that the shoes I had, a pair of Adidas World Cup rubber-soled shoes, had disintegrated because the glue had melted – that's how hot those places were, because the exact same thing happened in Las Vegas. Just going over there, it was exciting to go to Hawaii, but the conditions were extreme. We were just waiting to see all of the beaches, but it was so hot you couldn't go anywhere, and you suffer from heat exhaustion so you concentrate on keeping up with your fluids.'

Merrick is more generous than most when it comes to retrospectively assessing the wisdom of Team Hawaii's existence. 'Of course the NASL made mistakes,' he says, 'but if someone has the wherewithal to start a franchise there you've got to give them the opportunity. They were looking to develop and they needed the extra teams to make the League function, so if someone comes forward then you let them try it.' It was just that 'Hawaii was an experiment that failed.'[5] Don Droege, a US defender who travelled to Hawaii with the Rochester Lancers, is more damning. 'It took you forever to get over there,' he says. 'You played one game, and then you had to come back again. Whoever came up with that idea, it really needed rethinking. It was crazy. I remember playing in this massive stadium and we're being announced as we come out on the field and there were probably more players than there were people in the stands.'

Not only did the Lancers get hammered 4–1 in front of a paltry crowd of less than 2,000 in the spanking new 50,000-capacity Aloha Stadium – part of the reason Hawaii wanted an NASL team was to have an additional occupant inside their expensive but sparsely used new venue* – but the Lancers' Yugoslav coach Dragan Popović forbade his players from going to the beach. 'The thing about Popović,' says

---

* Principal tenants the Hawaii Warriors – the University of Hawaii's gridiron team – only had, and still have, around a half-dozen home games per season.

Droege, '[is] he was a different breed. He would fine you if you got a suntan, and he wouldn't let you do a lot of things. We did do it, obviously. We weren't allowed to go on the beach, but it was done.'[6]

One of the larger crowds that Team Hawaii attracted was for the visit of George Best and the LA Aztecs, but Best's strike partner Steve David did not enjoy the trip. 'Hawaii was a very tough place to play,' he says. 'I didn't like it very much because of the partying and everything – I did take my game very seriously, and what I did or wouldn't do. As a matter of fact in Hawaii, somebody – I can't tell you who – put something in my drink. I got back to LA a day later, missing the flight with a couple of my teammates, which I was very upset about. I woke up with this strange feeling. I don't blame anybody, but I was very upset with the coach and these guys just leaving me and not protecting me.'[7] David says that he normally remembers all his games, especially ones where he scored, but because he thinks his drink was probably spiked at half-time, he has no recollection of the freaky 5–6 defeat, or the fact that he scored two goals in front of just over 6,000 people.

Team Hawaii belonged to Ward Lay, a member of the family that owned Lay's potato chips. Lay had moved the franchise from San Antonio because of the low crowds, and brought in as coach the well-travelled Austrian Hubert Vogelsinger – the man who had sent (or had been forced to send) Eusebio from New England to become a title winner in Toronto. Scottish defender Charlie Mitchell, who'd failed to land much playing time the season before with New York Cosmos, was one of Vogelsinger's new signings in Hawaii. 'I was disappointed not to be in the Cosmos team,' says Mitchell. 'I was 28 and wanted to play. So [Cosmos coach] Gordon Bradley came to myself and Brian Tinnion and asked us if we wanted to go to Hawaii and play.' Mitchell laughs at the memory. 'So we looked at each other and both said, "Well, I imagine so." They offered me the same contract I'd been on in New York, with an apartment and a car, so it was a no-brainer.'

Mitchell says that Lay was very involved with the team and came over to watch quite a few games. Vogelsinger had connections with West Ham United at the time and had brought in Tommy Taylor, Pat Holland, Keith Robson and Keith Coleman on loan from the London club, 'so we had a good squad. It was first class all the way there too, the facilities were terrific.' Unfortunately, says Mitchell, 'it just didn't work. About halfway through the season Vogelsinger wasn't in favour with the ownership, so they came to me with around ten games left – I was 29 – and asked me to coach for the rest of the season. So I said to Ward Lay, "If I can get a vote of confidence from the players, I'll take them for the rest of the season." And his reply was: "We don't ask the players, we tell the players."'

Hawaii 'was a good experience', Mitchell insists, 'but there weren't enough supporters. You had a college soccer team there, but among the Hawaiians, there just wasn't enough interest and they couldn't cover the expenses and were obviously losing money – the way they were keeping us in our salaries and all the other perks.' The players did the 'whole dog and pony show' in terms of clinics and community outreach, but the heat and the travel – for both visiting teams and Team Hawaii itself – were constantly a problem. 'It was just too far away. We would go over to the mainland and play two, three or four games at a stretch.'

In their single season, Hawaii did once manage to attract

a five-figure crowd – almost 13,000 came for the second home game of the season against the Cosmos, a 2–1 loss. 'When New York came we had a big reception because of Pelé, I remember that,' says Mitchell. In general, 'a lot of the players knew each other from playing together around the League. Some of the players would meet ex-teammates at the airport and take them to the local pub. A lot of the British players came from a social background anyway. There was a social environment in Hawaii, especially after the games. I remember taking my old teammates from Rochester out, mainly just to show off how good we had it there.' Ultimately, though, 'it was expensive bringing a party of 25 for several nights.' The team won just eleven of its 26 games, and six of those were shootout victories. 'They'd poured enough money into it and so they wanted to move it to another franchise,' says Mitchell. 'Nobody went anywhere without Phil Woosnam's approval.'[8]

Owner Ward Lay blamed the team's failure on the high expenses, and the lack of any local ownership coming through to help him out, leaving him 100 per cent responsible for the team. 'It cost us a fortune to travel,' he said. Aloha Stadium was too far out of town, out near Pearl Harbour, and even laying on buses for the fans didn't work. 'We tried different promotions, but that didn't work. The team never did very well at home, either. I believe the players were so disappointed when they saw the home crowd, they played poorly at home. It is tough to come home and play before an empty, lonely place.'[9]

So just one year after crossing the Pacific Ocean from San Antonio the team was off again, this time to the almost equally improbable destination of Tulsa, Oklahoma. More of that later, because first we must take a trip to Vegas.

North of Paradise Valley

From a writer's point of view, naming the NASL's team in Las Vegas the Quicksilvers seems almost too good to be true. The unpredictable, mercurial league that had tried its hand at steady growth now found itself eager to grab every opportunity to expand while the going was hot. In the early 1970s, the NASL was like a steady married man who'd settled down with a frumpy but reliable girl following a turbulent youth filled with heady heartbreak. Then, all of a sudden, the steady married man went on a trip to, let's say, Vegas, and was reminded of how exciting things used to be. The married man forgot about all the accumulated stability he had worked so hard to build back in his home town, and found himself gambling inadvisable sums in a casino, while drinking reckless amounts of alcohol. There were strippers sitting on his lap, and all kinds of temptations and distractions that came with the strippers. Sure, it was just a brief fling, and all details would stay within Vegas, but once Mr Steady had renewed his taste for the high life, would the lapse into decadence become a pattern that would usher in eventual divorce and ruination?

Like Hawaii, the Las Vegas Quicksilvers didn't have a bad team – the by-now-standard mixture of Brits, Germans, Yugoslavs and statutory North Americans. They also had Eusebio, in his final season in the top flight, one year after winning the NASL title with Toronto, although his knackered knees rendered him even less mobile than the year before. To try and get the new franchises off to a running start, early games against the Cosmos were scheduled. As we have seen, Hawaii's second home game was to host New

York, but Las Vegas were granted the opener. It was Pelé and Eusebio's final face-off, and Vegas goalkeeper Alan Mayer recalls it well.

Mayer had been the team's goalkeeper at its previous home in San Diego, having moved there with the whole franchise from Baltimore, and was becoming used to the fits and starts of a career in the League. He found out the team was moving to Vegas while he was on tour with the US national team in South America, after calling home to speak to his wife. 'She said, "Oh my gosh, the team was just sold to Las Vegas and we have to move out there, and we have to move right away." I was on a six-week sojourn with the national team, and she had to pack everything up and move us to a new apartment, so when I came back I went to Las Vegas. The other players on the US team were just like, "Well, that's the way it is", but you could tell it got them thinking about what their team was doing. I'm sure they were thinking, *I hope my club's solid*. No one came up and said they were sorry to hear I was going to Vegas, because it was starting to become part of the game. In fact I just felt fortunate that I'd been chosen to stay on the roster, because when you make a move from one city to another, they don't take all the players, maybe six or seven.'[10]

The Quicksilvers were owned by Ken Keegan, a car dealership owner, and Mayer says 'we saw him now and again. As a business person, I don't know whether or not he did a good job, all I wanted to do was play.' When Keegan took the team to Vegas, 'they welcomed us tremendously. That was the first time I was starting to think this was professionalism. They sent two players in advance and we started doing season-ticket sales, door to door to all the businesses in the city. That turned out to be a great experience, because I went into sales myself when soccer was over, and I developed that knack in Vegas trying to sell a sport not many people had heard of. People had heard about the team coming to town, but we were fighting for the entertainment buck there. We started off the season with a bang, and I remember some crowds being seven to twelve thousand.'

In truth, most gates were in the 5,000–9,000 range, averaging 7,092 over the season, but the opener against the Cosmos brought in just under 12,000, the team's only five-figure crowd. 'It was one of the highlights of my career,' says Mayer, who played in the NASL for eight seasons. 'There was a lot of to-do about that game. They made a big deal about Pelé vs Eusebio. I was your token American. It was my first time at a big-time event, but it worked out very well. We had a big crowd; we ended up winning the game – Chinaglia had a bunch of opportunities, but we went ahead through a long shot and won the game 1–0. Winning that game gave us a lot of credibility, and for a couple of months we were on a high and were well received throughout the community. We were wined and dined, we could go to see any shows we wanted, and we got shown up to the front seats.' The three-paragraph Associated Press report on the game describes Mayer as having made 'nine saves, including several diving ones'.[11]

Again, visiting players to Vegas remember the heat. LA's Steve David, five days after having his drink spiked in Hawaii, stepped out into the Nevada sun and remembers 'it felt like I was in the back of an exhaust that was just blowing hot air; it was so hot, it was like a hundred and something degrees.' David scored in a 3–2 win for the Aztecs, but more detailed memories are 'lost, gone, I guess because of the festivities'.[12]

The heat 'was actually terrible', admits the Quicksilvers' Mayer, even though he played in it every week. 'We would come in, and even as a goalkeeper, the bottoms of my feet were absolutely burning. You'd come in to the locker room and dunk your feet, with your shoes still on, straight into a bucket of cold water. At that time they didn't have all the protective wear that keepers have today. So if you slid on Astroturf you got burnt, and you got burnt pretty well. The burns you got, I can still feel them today, they were atrocious.' He says that the heat was probably an advantage for the home team, not only because they were more accustomed to it, but because so many visiting teams partook in David's 'festivities'. Mayer says 'a lot of teams came to Vegas and they wanted to go out on the town, so if they didn't have the discipline to refrain from that, then we were at an advantage there as well. A lot of people used it probably as a little party time during the season. In that heat you didn't want to play with a hangover, but I guarantee you that several players did. There were still a lot of loan players at that time, and a lot of them came with the attitude, *Let's go to America and have a good time.*'[13]

For those players who were living full time in Vegas the temptations were there too, and Mayer thinks that caused the team's collapse from the middle of the season onwards. 'I think the living style had something to do with the slump,' he says, after the team went from winning nine of their first twelve games to then losing twelve out of the final fourteen. 'I don't want to name names. I went off to play with the national team, got a concussion and then an injury mid-season. Everything had been working together nicely, but then it started to fall apart a little bit. It was probably a bit down to injuries, and some of it was down to partying.' Mayer himself took his game 'very, very seriously, and I didn't get involved heavily in the social end of it, I was always concentrated on the next game. Years later, I found out that several people on that team had a pretty good time there. Let's put it this way, they had a great time, and they probably paid a little bit for it too.'

The Quicksilvers featured 'several characters', says Mayer. 'We had a lot of English players, but the biggest character was Trevor Hockey. We called him the Wolf Man – he had a big beard, and he was a funny, fun-loving person, a really nice guy, worked very hard at practice, he was a hard-nosed player, but he could laugh too. He'd kick anything that moved, wild hair flying everywhere, always joking. We had Wolfgang Sühnholz, a really good player, then three Portuguese players who liked to go out and have a good time in the casinos and all that.' Once the slump set in, the team fired English coach Derek Trevis, and replaced him with another Englishman, Jim Fryatt. It made no difference – Las Vegas finished bottom of the Southern Division of the Pacific Conference, three points below Team Hawaii. That meant neither side made the playoffs.

The Quicksilvers played an English style 'incorporating the more skilful players into the team,' Mayer recalls. 'It worked pretty well in the beginning, but towards the end it didn't. Derek Trevis was fired in the middle of the season. In my opinion it was unjustified. He worked hard, he took no prisoners, but he was fair and let you know where you stood.' Neither his replacement, Fryatt, nor Eusebio could turn things around – in fact, the Portuguese was benched for the final few games of the season. 'He could still strike a ball,' says Mayer. 'You should have seen his knees after all those operations, it was ugly. He was such a wonderful person, but he couldn't keep up with the running, especially in the heat we had there. But if there was a free kick 35 yards out, it would be coming in hard and bending. That was mainly what he did. He didn't train a whole lot, but he still had those spurts of brilliance.'

Another Quicksilvers player who doesn't appear in the record books was porn star Marilyn Chambers, who had been the pure white advertising face in Ivory Soap commercials. After the ads failed to launch her acting career, Chambers opted for the lead role in *The Devil in Miss Jones*, one of the porn films that, along with *Deep Throat*, ushered sexually explicit cinema into the mainstream during the increasingly blasé 1970s. Chambers suited up to play in a celebrity all-star game initiated by the team's general manager Marvin Milkes, but it turned out that the numerous celebrities in Vegas didn't want to be seen humiliating themselves on a soccer field in 100-degree heat. Chambers was, in fact, one of two celebrities in a game filled with what the team's PR representative Jerry Kissell described as 'wanna-be lounge performers'.[14] The other 'celebrity' was Foster Brooks. Yes, you can google him, and discover that he was 'an actor and comedian most famous for his portrayal of a lovable drunken man'. A porn actress and a lovable lush – a celebrity match made in Las Vegas, on a very hot soccer field.

With promotional savvy like that, it's little wonder that the team was sold at the end of the 1977 season, owing a five-figure rental sum on Las Vegas Stadium. Vancouver's Bob Lenarduzzi, the current president of the Vancouver Whitecaps in Major League Soccer, says that 'there was no way that city was going to support a franchise. I don't know what check-points there were to owning a team compared with MLS now.'

In early 2014, those checkpoints were on show as Las Vegas put forward plans, unapproved as this book went to press, for a new 24,000-seat soccer stadium downtown at Symphony Park. Las Vegas mayor Carolyn Goodman called the plans 'really, really exciting', while Major League Soccer held initial talks with the stadium's developers. Unlike the NASL, though, MLS can afford to be choosy, and few can choose to afford it. A new franchise fee had risen to around $70 million by the time that the Orlando Soccer Club successfully bid in late 2013 to start a new team in Disney World's home town for the 2015 season. On top of that, you have to finance and build a new soccer-dedicated stadium in a geographically viable part of town. Teams now have to be built to last, with a solid fiscal footing, and the carefully researched guarantee of a fan base. The new Las Vegas developers estimate that the total investment needed for an MLS team in Vegas – including the franchise fee and stadium construction – would be around $300 million.[15]

Today's sober and sensible planning are no doubt fitting for a league so keen to avoid the errors and excesses of its predecessor. At the same time, the carefully honed rows of projected figures outlining a stable future for teams like Orlando are as off-putting as the dull, dark blue suits of the businessmen who present them with such bland assurance. Maybe it's a mistake to romanticize the potato chip millionaire and the car dealership owner who dared to try soccer in Hawaii and Vegas at a time when the risks heavily outweighed the rationale, and when the myopic hope that soccer in the desert heat would be a long-term proposition trumped the head-shaking naysayers. Ward Lay died in 2011, and Ken Keegan has disappeared off the electronic radar of modern times, but they deserve an A for audacity.

Roughnecks, rough as heck

> 'Here, when things don't go well, they criticize. I
> am glad they criticize and tell me what they think
> is wrong. It shows me they are interested in the
> team. It shows they care.'
> —Tulsa Roughnecks coach Alan Hinton[16]

Team Hawaii became the Tulsa Roughnecks, owned by the
Rainbow Baking Company, although Ward Lay still had a
stake. What had been for one year a mid-Pacific surf team playing in a location close to paradise, had now become a Midwest
outfit with a name suggesting drunken brawls on Saturday
night while the saloon doors swung, shots rang out, and nervous horses shuffled and whinnied in distress. This team would
be tough enough to tame the local bison and then ride on their
backs into the stadium just in time for kick-off. At least, that
was presumably the implication of the new name.

Few of Team Hawaii's players carried their surfboards
across the ocean and into the Oklahoma heartland. One
player, to be precise – Charlie Mitchell, the coach who'd
taken over from Vogelsinger in Honolulu, and who came to
Tulsa as assistant to the new boss, Manchester United legend and Munich survivor Bill Foulkes. The usual recruiting
grounds provided the rest of the players – nine Englishmen
formed the bulk of the roster over the 1978 season; the rest
were Welsh, Irish, Scottish and North Americans, plus a Greek
and a West German. Late in the season there was a rush of
budget Yugoslavs. There were no major names, at least not in
the NASL meaning of the word. One of the players' main tasks
was again to sell the professional game from scratch, although

youth soccer was expanding in the state, and had been one of the positives that prompted the NASL to try a team in Tulsa.

Ultimately, the Roughnecks were a qualified success. They lasted several years longer than Team Hawaii and became, under controversial circumstances, the NASL champions in 1983. They also went bust in doing so, limping on for one more year after a public appeal for funds via a radio station – instigated by their now loyal fans – had allowed them to pay players and staff. The ownership changed hands twice, but nothing could stem the losses. The Roughnecks did, however, attract decent crowds even while they were losing money, and although they never sold out Skelly Stadium – the 40,000-capacity football venue where they played – they posted average crowds of around 15,000. Down the years, their fate was closely linked with their general manager Noel Lemon, a man with an opinion on most matters, and rarely shy of expressing it.

The Northern Ireland native, who'd played soccer for Glentoran before coming to the US to play semi-pro, knew how to garner news coverage with attention-catching quotes. His most famous line, delivered in 1980, was a variation on Millwall fans' proud claim that 'No one likes us, we don't care'. Lemon's version was: 'We've only been in the League two and a half years and already half the teams hate us. Give me another two years and we'll have them all.'[17] He made great play out of the fact that Tulsa was the smallest city in the League, and consequently cultivated the role of the scrappy underdog to go with the redneck name. Even if the team had been able to afford superstars, they probably wouldn't have come to Tulsa, and who knows if Tulsa would even have wanted them. The city wasn't for everyone. 'Somehow I got to Tulsa,' says Don Droege, speaking on how his career had progressed by 1982. 'I played at Scully Stadium, an Astroturf field. I made it halfway through the season; I didn't like Tulsa much, and they traded me to Tampa.'[18]

Being traded away from Tulsa was not unusual, and that was at the behest of Lemon. 'Bill [Foulkes] brought in a bunch of great players,' says Charlie Mitchell, but Foulkes and Lemon 'continuously argued' about who to bring in. 'It's a long roster for that year, and it was like a revolving door – some players would be in and out in just a few weeks. So they fired Bill Foulkes, which I thought was a diabolical decision. It was strictly personalities, it wasn't based on credibility or knowledge; I was flabbergasted. Noel Lemon made a contact with some Yugoslavian agent, so we ended up with a bunch of Yugoslavian players.' When Foulkes left, Mitchell resigned as assistant coach and stayed purely as a player, while the German defender Alex Skotarek took over coaching duties. Having taken over from Vogelsinger in Hawaii the previous year, 'I didn't want to get the reputation as an assistant coach taking over every time.' The team won half of its 30 games, but fell to Minnesota in the first round of the playoffs.

Lemon, says Mitchell, was 'a great marketing guy, a genius', who landed several sponsorships for the team. 'But he got himself involved in the day-to-day running of the team, and team selection, and that should never have happened. That's why I asked to be transferred at the end of the year.'

So for the 1979 season, Mitchell left for Toronto and former Derby County midfielder Alan Hinton took charge at Tulsa. The previous season, he had set a League record for assists, totalling an impressive 30 in 29 appearances for the Vancouver Whitecaps. By the time he left Tulsa after just one season, however, he had failed to impress Noel Lemon: 'We gave up 44 goals in 1978. When Alan Hinton came here he said one of the first things he was going to do was change that. And he did. We gave up 54 goals that year [1979].'[19] Lemon was no more impressed with another former Derby forward who turned out for Tulsa that year, Roger Davies. 'When he left here,' said Lemon, 'I was going to send [him] a bill for our training table. He wore out the one we had here. Every time I went into the locker room he was on the training table ... He's a baby.'[20] In spite of all this, the Roughnecks had a good year in 1979 – this time they beat the Minnesota Kicks in the first round of the playoffs, then hammered the Cosmos 3–0 in the first leg of the quarter-final, at home in front of 26,000, with the 'baby' Roger Davies scoring twice. They went down 3–0 in the return leg and then lost the mini-game. That wasn't good enough for Lemon. Hinton was gone, and in his place for the 1980 season Charlie Mitchell returned. Given Lemon's reputation and his reasons for having left a year before, it seems like a bold move.

'Alan Hinton didn't have a good experience in Tulsa,' Mitchell confirms, 'and I knew what I was walking into at Tulsa with Noel Lemon. But I just loved it in Tulsa, it was a great all-American support, I wanted to come back, I liked the town. In New York someone would say to you, "Hey, I want to invite you to dinner", and then you'd never hear from them again. In Tulsa, when they invited you to dinner they actually called you and really did invite you to dinner. I liked the weather and the people, it was more of a family atmosphere.'

Knowing how much Lemon liked to be part of running the team, Mitchell made a deal with the GM that he, as coach, would be 100 per cent in charge of the players, and that Lemon would be in charge of paying them. 'It started off perfect,' he says. 'We preserved the nucleus of the team that Alan Hinton left and it worked well the first season. I signed Johannes Edvaldsson from Celtic, Alan Dugdale, Alan Woodward from Sheffield United – he's still here in Tulsa; Viv Busby, who went back to England and started coaching; Barry Walsh from QPR – we had a good team; I really enjoyed the coaching there. It was a good year, we beat the Cosmos at home, and we had a good bunch of guys.' Again, the Roughnecks faced the Cosmos in the playoffs, but went down 3–1 at home in the first leg, with a crowd around 2,000 lower than the previous year, at 24,000. They were then mauled 8–1 in New York – more significantly, that 40,000 crowd in Giants Stadium was 36,000 below the number that had come to watch the same match-up one year earlier in 1979.

Unlike Hinton, Mitchell was retained, but in his second year, 1981, things began to fall apart. 'Halfway through the second season we lost to Minnesota. He [Lemon] told me I'd picked the wrong team. I said, "Well, you can stick it", and he said, "*You* can stick it", and I lost the battle. I was hoping the ownership would stick by me, but unfortunately they stuck by Noel.' Lemon wanted to bring in new players, and Mitchell wanted to work with what they already had. Although the team had won half and lost half of their games by the time he was fired, more than half of the defeats were through shootouts or sudden-death extra time. 'You need time to get a formation going,' says Mitchell, echoing the words of so many coaches and managers sacked by owners impatient for results. 'You can't just keep chopping and changing the players around all the time. There's no magic formula, as any coach will tell you. I was all for keeping the squad together. We had some great players – we had Duncan Mackenzie on that team – and I wanted to give them some time.'

Mitchell adds with genuine humility, 'If Noel Lemon felt

that he was big enough to fire Bill Foulkes, then he was quite welcome to fire Charlie Mitchell, because I was not in the same class as Bill Foulkes.'

Mitchell stayed in Tulsa 'and opened up a pub'. Noel Lemon, who died in 2012, wasn't exactly barred, but 'I don't think he wanted to come in,' says Mitchell. 'We didn't have a good relationship. We bumped into each other a few times over the following years and all was forgiven; we were all grown men and we moved on. I was still quite a young man at the time, and maybe I should have listened more too.'[21]

No Futcher

In the middle of the 1981 season, Mitchell's replacement was his former assistant Terry Hennessey, an ex-Welsh international with a long career at Derby, Forest and Birmingham. The playoffs followed a familiar course for Tulsa – defeat to Minnesota the first year, defeat to New York the next. In 1983, with the League down to twelve teams, Hennessey took Tulsa all the way to the final after disposing of Fort Lauderdale and Montreal. Chief among the goalscorers was Ron Futcher, who had been so prolific alongside Alan Willey at the by now defunct Minnesota Kicks. Loaned out to the NASL from the age of 20 by Luton Town and Manchester City, the prolific Futcher scored twice in the 3–0 home win in a best-of-three series against Montreal to secure a place at the 1983 Soccer Bowl in Vancouver against the Toronto Blizzard.* The only

---

* By 1983 there were twelve teams in three separate divisions of four. Eight teams made the playoffs for best-of-three quarter- and semi-finals, followed by a single-game Soccer Bowl at a neutral venue for the championship.

problem was that he also picked up a red card and was automatically suspended for the final.

Noel Lemon was no longer Tulsa GM by this point, but the team still retained his feisty spirit and let the NASL headquarters know that the Roughnecks would not show for the final unless Futcher was allowed to play. The League's director of operations, Ted Howard, would not submit to such blackmail. Commissioner Howard Samuels, who'd taken over from Phil Woosnam the year before, was more open to persuasion. He overruled Howard 'in the interests of the sport and the game tomorrow'.[22] Futcher, after all, had been a remarkable success in the League, and was one of the few young players from Europe who'd stayed the course, while scoring goals wherever he went. At spells with Minnesota, Portland and Tulsa, he ended up scoring 119 times in total, fourth on the NASL all-time list of scorers.

That Tulsa were hated around the League was more than just Noel Lemon's rhetoric. 'They aren't the prettiest players, and they're not the big names,' said coach Terry Hennessey before the final. 'We're the smallest city in the League and have a reputation for rough play, but we kept on working and it's paid off with a chance for the title.'[23] The large crowd of 60,000 in neutral Vancouver got behind Tulsa as Toronto had eliminated the Whitecaps from the playoffs. The Roughnecks dominated much of the game, where they 'established a good rhythm and attacked with purpose, allowing Toronto to control play only sporadically in the first half,' according to the *New York Times* match report.[24] Ten minutes into the second half, Yugoslav-American Njego Pesa scored from a direct free kick just outside the penalty area, then six minutes later Tulsa increased their lead. Barry Wallace took a corner kick, Toronto

231

goalkeeper Jan Moller was slow to the ball after it was touched on by Canadian defender Terry Moore, and Ron Futcher ('Who else?' you can imagine a TV commentator exclaiming) nipped in to score with his left knee.

'Everyone said we didn't have any quality players,' Hennessey crowed afterwards, still relishing the team's underdog status. 'I've made mistakes with some players, but this bunch was prepared to go out, work hard and do the job.' The team referred to themselves mockingly as 'a bunch of rejects'.[25] It's also a reflection of where the League stood in terms of its quality and style. A bunch of rejects, mainly no-name British and North American players, had won the title, pretty much bringing the League back around to where it had been a decade earlier. Hennessey claimed at the team's homecoming celebration, where 1,000 fans and a marching band came out to greet them, that 'all over the world, the Tulsa Roughnecks will be remembered as the guys who won the 1983 Soccer Bowl'.[26] Presumably, the champagne in Tulsa was very good. No one was mentioning Ron Futcher's reprieve, but the ruling still rankles with at least one former Toronto player.

'That was probably the biggest defeat I've ever suffered, because we were favourites,' says defender Bruce Wilson, who'd been with Toronto since 1981. 'They'd come in [to Vancouver] on the Thursday night for the Sunday game after a tough playoff series, and we'd been there a week waiting to see who we were playing, and we ended up losing 2–0. Futcher got a red card in the final play-off game. Which of course everyone in the world, media and clubs and everyone, they understand the rule – you're out of the final. Guess what? For the good of the game, the commissioner said we're going to let Futcher play in the final. As players we thought, *This is* *bush league*.* We're sending a message to the rest of the world – the guy gets a red card and should be out of the next game, possibly two or even three games. But no, we're letting Ron Futcher play in the final. Guess who scores one of the two goals? The media jumped all over it, before the game, during the game and after the game.'[27]

Former Cosmos GM Clive Toye was by this time running Toronto and, says Wilson, 'met the team before and said we didn't want to make a big thing out of it. We didn't care if he played or not, it was just the nature of the decision in a professional league that's being watched, *somewhat*, around the world.' Wilson believes such a ruling reinforced the prejudice outside of North America that the NASL played fast and loose with the game's laws and 'showed an American weirdo idea of rules. It was such a ridiculous decision that we did not deal with it as players at all.'

Tulsa's goalkeeper that day, the US international Winston DuBose, sees it differently. Another convert to life in Oklahoma, he says that 'Tulsa suited me down to the ground.' The team had a great following, and was 'a very English and Irish-oriented team – we had some very good players. Some skill players, but very workmanlike. Going to Tulsa, after six months I'd adjusted and really fell in love with it – a really great city and a nice community to live in.' Noel Lemon, he says, 'believed in the American goalkeeper concept' – namely that the position of goalkeeper was an exceptionally strong one for American players. Does he feel, nonetheless, that the 1983 title is a tainted one?

---

* Standard North American sports insult meaning 'the lowest level of amateurism'; or, Sunday League, pub league.

'I don't think it was tainted at all,' he says, 'but you're asking the wrong person. Our best XI played against their best XI. Was Ron a big part of our team? Absolutely, he was critical. I think we were all grateful that the commissioner saw to it that one of our best players was allowed to go ahead and play in the final. I think they [Toronto] had Roberto Bettega, so it would have been like them not having him play. It was at least a final where you couldn't say, well, if we would have had this, if we would have had that. On the other hand, if he'd turned around and said, rules are rules, Futcher can't play, then we wouldn't have had a leg to stand on.' Told of Wilson's lingering resentment, DuBose laughs and says, 'He wouldn't be saying that if they'd won. Jimmy Nicholl was another good player they had, they had a decent team.'

In his book *A Kick in the Grass*, Toye in fact pinpoints Nicholl and one other player's late night out on the eve of the final as being just as much to blame for the defeat as Futcher's inclusion for Tulsa.[28] 'You might want to ask Jimmy about that,' says DuBose, 'but at the end of the day I think the right team won.'[29]

To the outside world, it was of little importance whether or not Tulsa or Toronto were the North American Soccer League champions. The League was not only diminishing in terms of its team numbers and the calibre of its top players, but it was already becoming a more distant, fading star in the galaxy of world soccer. Who beyond North America even remembered that Tulsa and Toronto had soccer teams? In this context, it's perhaps understandable that Samuels made his decision to allow Futcher to play 'in the interests of the sport and the game tomorrow'. On the one hand, he was playing fast and loose with the League's credibility by breaking its own rules, and the generally accepted international laws of the game. On the other hand, he was probably taking a gamble that, in the wider soccer community, no one was paying the League that much attention. It was, therefore, more important to have one of its few remaining star names (and even then, good as he was, Futcher was hardly Cruyff or Müller) playing in the game than not.

Except that Samuels was damned either way. If Futcher contributed nothing to the game, then all the commissioner had done was to make the League look amateur. If Futcher scored and Toronto won, as they did, then the League looked like it had manipulated the outcome, and for what? Was Futcher's goal going to be shown on sports highlight reels that would attract new investors to the NASL? Frankly, no. Samuels's forecast that this would be in the interests of 'the League tomorrow', however, was more pertinent than he could have known. A desperately unprofessional ruling that pandered to the fits and threats of a Wild West franchise and its bolshie advocate spoke volumes about the state of the NASL in its twilight years.

Yet the North American Soccer League had a tradition of making its own rules, and that had not always necessarily been a bad thing. In many respects, they foreshadowed soccer's future legislative path – although, fortunately, ignoring red card suspensions wasn't one of them. From the start, this put them on a collision course with FIFA, and an analysis of the League is not complete without examining the troubled relationship between the game's profoundly conservative world governing body and the cocky, nouveau riche upstarts from the vast and wealthy North American continent who wanted to do things their own special way.

Season-by-season overview

1975

Another significant expansion as confidence in soccer blossomed, with five new teams added to bring the total to twenty. Chicago returned, while Portland, Tampa Bay, Hartford (the preposterously named Bi-Centennials) and San Antonio made their NASL starts. Two newcomers, Tampa Bay and Portland, made it all the way to the final (for the first time marketed as 'Soccer Bowl', played to a sell-out crowd in San Jose), with the **Rowdies** winning 2–0 – the third successive expansion team to lift the trophy. South African Derek Smethurst, who'd failed to do much with either Chelsea or Millwall, led the front line with 21 goals, supported by ex-Hammer Clyde Best.

Fun facts: Philadelphia's Chris Bahr, son of Walter who'd played in the 1950 US World Cup team that beat England 1–0, was voted the League's Rookie of the Year, then promptly left the NASL to become a place kicker with the Cincinnati Bengals in the NFL. Miami's Steve David was top scorer and League MVP with 23 goals. Didn't that make him a better player than Pelé? David recalls how the following year, when he was selected to play alongside the Brazilian for Team America in the Bicentennial Cup against Italy, England and Brazil, a reporter asked him how he felt playing alongside the great man. David replied: 'You should have asked the question the other way around because I'm the League MVP. You should go and ask Pelé how it feels playing with Steve David.'[30]

7   The NASL vs FIFA and the world

> 'Dealing with FIFA and the way we've been treated
> has made me nostalgic for the Middle East.'
> —Henry Kissinger, former US Secretary of State
> and part of the United States bidding committee
> that failed to land hosting rights for
> the 1986 World Cup.

FIFA president Sir Stanley Rous was not amused. In fact he was mad as hell, and seemingly on the point of shutting down US soccer for good and casting it into the sporting wilderness. It was just before Christmas, 1967, and the three warring factions of the American game had come all the way to Zürich in the hope that Sir Stanley – the normally reserved and extremely conservative Englishman who'd been FIFA president since 1961 – could bestow upon them the peace, harmony and goodwill of the festive season. Instead of seeking compromise, however, they had continued to fight, in FIFA headquarters, right before the president's very jaded eyes.

According to the verbose Ken Macker, the commissioner of the 'outlaw' National Professional Soccer League (NPSL), the meeting was full of 'threats and counter-threats and the epidemic of equivocation. Sir Stanley, heatedly, angrily and with considerable asperity toward us, repeatedly threatened to bolt the meeting.' Rous was finally persuaded to stay. 'We were convinced that his withdrawal would have doomed our efforts, and all professional soccer in the US would have been imperilled had he departed from the room.'[1]

This illustrates the troubled start to the NASL's relationship with FIFA, and it didn't much improve over the next seventeen years. Even though, by the time of this meeting on 16 December 1967, the 'outlaw' NPSL (not FIFA-approved) and the 'rent-a-team' United Soccer Association, or USA (FIFA-approved), had already agreed to merge after just one unsuccessful year of them both going it alone, there were still some legal issues to resolve. The main issue does not seem, with the benefit of hindsight, to be at all insurmountable, but this apparently *was* the case, and so the two leagues, along with representatives from US soccer's governing body, the United States Soccer Football Association (USSFA)*, flew all the way to Zürich for an audience with an understandably apoplectic Rous.

Macker's typed account, sent to all NPSL team directors upon his return, is the only narrative that we have of this rambunctious meeting. The issue, as mentioned, was quite straightforward. NPSL players had been blacklisted by the USSFA and several other leagues, including the English FA, for playing in the 'outlaw' league. The NPSL wanted the ban on their players to be lifted in view of the coming merger. In return, it would drop its own legal action against the USSFA under the Sherman Antitrust Act.[†] By now, though, the dispute had become personal. Judging from the tone of the meeting as described by Macker, it was clear that the USSFA officials despised everyone involved with running the 'outlaw' league,

---

* A recap: the USSFA became the USSF in 1974.
† See Chapter 1.

and were livid that their attempts to grind that league into extinction had failed. The ill-feeling was quite mutual. Stuck in between was the 'rent-a-team' USA league, still indebted to the USSFA for its recognition as the official league a year earlier, but needing to work with its new partner too. The simple issue on the table was trumped by the grievances that all involved with the US game had been bottling up over the previous two years.

In Zürich, wrote Macker, the USSFA and the USA 'seemed [too] preoccupied with acrimony, complaints, allegations, mistrust and a "wronged woman" attitude, to appreciate their own serious jeopardy.' This 'posture of hostility and estrangement', he continued, showed in the USSFA's complaints that the two leagues continually ignored the governing body, treated it with 'something akin to contempt', and saw it 'only as a convenient rubber stamp'.[2] Although at this point in its history, it seems that being a convenient rubber stamp pretty much describes the limits of the US soccer's governing body's capabilities.

Sir Stanley's patience with the quibbling factions eroded further when the two leagues together left the room to draw up a draft letter of reconciliation, then came back in and proceeded to argue about its contents in front of Rous. 'Sir Stanley obviously was in contemplation of tearing the sheet into small bits and burying them in the nearest snowdrift,' wrote Macker, who according to Atlanta Chiefs chief executive Dick Cecil was not, in real life, a particularly funny or jovial man, in spite of his sardonic prose. All sides took a five-hour recess for dinner, during which Macker and his colleagues drew up another letter outlining their case. Macker conceded in his report that it was 'verbiage', and that when he read it out loud, Rous was only half listening and just became more confused than before.

'Much to our consternation,' Macker continued, 'Sir Stanley reacted convulsively, his face reddening, disdaining a *sotto voce* tone, showing a set of mannerisms, while altogether unexpected, that reinforced our earlier analysis that he might well come to the meeting prepared to cast us all in the role of schismatics, proclaiming an excommunication for us as certain as anything within the scope of the Holy Mother Church. I mentally began packing my baggage.' It seems that 'verbiage' really was Macker's strong point. Fortunately, the NPSL's attorney, a Mr Bower (no first name given), intervened and explained the NPSL position to Rous in plain English. The mood changed. 'Suddenly, Sir Stanley became aware of the import of what I had said and he promptly softened his demeanour, and, although I suspected it might have been a trick of the poor lighting in the room, I imagined the beginning of a conciliatory smile.'

The USSFA representatives continued to complain, but now the 'outlaw' NPSL suddenly had Rous on its side. Macker told USSFA committee member Jack Flamhaft that 'I was sick and tired of his obstructionist conduct the past several months'. A series of letters between the two bodies during 1967 testifies to this reproach – the USSFA were masters at stalling, obfuscation and procrastination. Rous had in fact upbraided them for exactly this at the start of the meeting, calling them organizationally weak. Now the FIFA president, perhaps ready for bed (the meeting had not resumed after the long recess until 9.30pm), declared to the NPSL that, 'You will see that your faith in my good offices will stand the NPSL in excellent stead.'

In short, the NPSL got what they wanted – the ban on their players was lifted, and they only had to agreed to suspend their lawsuit, not drop it (though they did shortly afterwards). 'Whether or not saving soccer in the US was a Pyrrhic victory, or a genuine accomplishment,' Macker wrote, 'we concluded the meeting by hosting refreshments, during which we were regaled by Sir Stanley out of his storehouse of mild jokes.' He doesn't say whether any of those jokes included one about the three warring parties of US soccer who flew all the way to Switzerland to patch up their differences with the help of a crusty old Englishman, and even then they almost failed.

Flattery may well have played an important role in saving the day. Macker's report includes the letter of 'verbiage' he read out to Rous, and one sentence in particular would have left Rous in no doubt of its meaning. 'I have been impressed,' Macker had written, 'by your zeal, your leadership and your character which is wholly consistent with the title of "sir" which your name bears.' You can never overdo flattery when it comes to a knight of Her Majesty's realm. Whether this was egregious smarm, or a shaft of nicely disguised sarcasm, it worked. A FIFA employee, a Mr Courte, told Macker the next day that 'our attitude had saved all US soccer from being separated from its brethren in the rest of the world. He left me convinced that Sir Stanley was now our staunch colleague and advocate, although, in truth, I did not gain the impression that Sir Stanley, from his lofty heights, regards many as his equal among equals.' Indeed, it seems unlikely anyone at FIFA was left with a favourable impression of US soccer after this internal fight was played out in Sir Stanley's presence.

The peace, like Christmas, was only temporary. Macker's time as one of the NASL's co-commissioners lasted only another year, and Phil Woosnam, the man who replaced both Macker and his counterpart at USA, Dick Walsh, had brand new ideas about soccer in the USA. Although the NASL was now fully sanctioned by the USSFA, and by proxy FIFA, the relationship staled at the barely cordial stage as the upstart league sought to meddle with the conservative game's sacred laws. The debate over the wisdom and advisability of changing the points system and the offside law, as well as the abolition of drawn games, frames its own set of on-running, contentious debates throughout the League's short history. Woosnam's ideas were radical, but not as radical as the conservatives abroad at the time would have had you believe. He adjusted the game, rather than altering it, and many of his innovations were later at least partially adopted as the global standard. They also cut once more to the heart of sport's very existence and the overriding question of its purpose: are professional games played primarily to be won at any cost, or to entertain the fans who pay to watch them?

What is the point of points?

The NPSL's new points system in 1967 originated from Atlanta, where Dick Cecil and Phil Woosnam had worked on a new scoring system before the NPSL even kicked a ball. At that time, the world standard was two points for a win, one for a draw. The NPSL awarded six points for a win, three for a draw, and a bonus point for each goal scored, up to three. So a team could take a maximum of nine points from one game if it won and scored three goals. A team 3–0 down would still have the incentive to go forward.

Woosnam, says Cecil, was 'a hard-headed man. A tough

negotiator, and very focused on the League. One of the things we were concerned about was the 0-0 problem. At that time it wasn't going to endear us to the American public. So Phil and I worked probably six months developing the new scoring system, and finally sold it to the League. I don't think it failed. I think it's been tweaked.'[3] In 1967, of course, the year before the merger and the start of the NASL, 'being an outlaw league we could do what we wanted. It came out of Phil's head, and he always played it against me, and we ended up arguing about it for hours, we tweaked it, and finally we got something I could accept.'

The FIFA-sanctioned USA league and its rented teams had in 1967, needless to say, played under the international system. When the merger happened, the new NASL opted to retain the 'outlaw' scoring system. By 1970, this system was coming under fire. The Washington Darts' General Manager Norman Sutherland called it 'overly complex', while Atlanta's coach Vic Rouse complained that 'last year Kansas City won the championship, although we won more games.'[4] True, under the international system, Atlanta (who had won eleven, drawn three and lost twice) would have finished the season with 25 points. The Kansas City Spurs (W10, D4, L2) would have tallied 24 points and come second. In the NASL, however, Kansas City had scored 53 goals to Atlanta's 46 across sixteen games, so the Spurs finished one point ahead of the Chiefs, 110 to 109. As there were only five teams in the League, there had been no championship game that year, so in a way Woosnam's system worked – the more attack-minded team won the title by scoring a healthy average of more than three goals per game.

It's perhaps only natural that Rouse would bemoan a system that didn't work in his favour, and it's unlikely that he would have complained if the situation had been reversed. Yet the League stuck with its system more or less throughout its life. In 1974, it took a step towards abolishing drawn games – they were decided by penalty kicks, with the winners getting four points rather than six (three for the tied win, plus a bonus point for the 'goal' awarded for winning on penalty kicks), and the losers got nothing besides points accrued for goals scored during the game. In 1975, draws were decided by the first goal in a fifteen-minute period of sudden-death extra time, with six points for a win, and again nothing for the loser bar points for goals scored. If the game was still tied after extra time, though, it was back to penalty kicks. This only lasted for two years. In 1977, the penalty kicks were replaced by the infamous 35-yard shootouts – more on those to follow.

If you were to now test yourself on the contents of the last paragraph, it's doubtful you would score very highly at the first attempt. In that sense, criticism that the system was too complex is valid, if seen from the viewpoint of the casual fan. In hindsight, though, most of those involved with the NASL have nothing but praise for the incentive to score more goals. Bruce Wilson, who played in the NASL from 1974 to 1984, says that the League's philosophy towards encouraging attacking play 'changed dramatically' once the big world names started coming to the US. 'Management and coaches were told, "We want to entertain, that's what this game's all about, hence the rules. But we don't want to win 1–0, we want to win 3–0, because there's three extra points in every game." That's what I liked about it, it was an attacking style rewarding teams that went out to score goals. A lot of people criticized our points structure, saying it was too complicated, but when you looked at it, it made a lot of sense – it made for attacking soccer.'[5]

Minnesota Kicks' Alan Merrick calls the system 'exceptionally innovative', because 'the team that scored the most still won, but you'd have losing teams still going for more goals at the end of the game.' He points out that under the conventional scoring system 'you see so many games where the last 20 minutes, nobody goes forward. I think the experiment in the US would be almost the template for re-enacting it.'[6]

The system that Atlanta coach Vic Rouse had lamented in 1970 worked to the reformed team's favour in 1981 under coach David Chadwick. He says that the points system was all just part of the hoopla and 'it attracted attacking soccer'. When he played for various English league clubs, 'sometimes we went to play an away game and were told to bunker in behind the ball and break away and score a goal. Well, who wants to come and watch that? But the NASL forced you to attack because at the end of the day it was the points, not the win–loss column, that got you to the top. At Atlanta [in the 1981 season] we had a worse win–loss record than the [Fort Lauderdale] Strikers, but we had more points and beat them to the division title. When you went on the road there was no point in defending – say you lost 3–2, you got two points for those goals and that meant a lot to us. So everywhere you went teams wanted to get forward. The League wanted you to come to the game. They didn't want to see ten guys behind the ball. At times of course there was a 1–0 game, but that was a big deal.'[7]

In fact there are few dissenters on the subject of the points system. Even veteran journalist Paul Gardner, who says he disliked most of the NASL's innovations on rules, calls the points system 'extremely good. It doesn't change the rules at all, but teams went after goals because an extra point can help even if you're losing 10–0. But the Euro-snobs were saying, "Oh, but the fans will get so confused, six points for a win", but that was the fall-back position – that the Americans were so fucking stupid they couldn't understand anything like that.'[8]

The points system was also the cause of some bizarre scores. Near the end of the 1979 season, the Seattle Sounders beat Edmonton 9–0, then just one week later managed to lose 7–1 at Los Angeles. 'It was my fault,' confesses their coach at the time, Jimmy Gabriel. 'In LA, I was trying to get us into the playoffs.' He worked out that a goal would gain them a point, and then a win back at home in their final game against Vancouver, if they scored three goals, should be enough to get them into the playoffs. 'So I said go out and get the goal, so they did – they went all out to get the goal. It didn't matter how many goals we had against us, we just needed to get that goal, and then beat Vancouver to get into the playoffs, but we didn't do that.' The LA crowd that day surely appreciated his approach, though.

Beating the offside trap

One of the rumours that did the rounds in the 70s was that 'the Yanks want to abolish the offside law'. This was another supposed example of how the Americans wanted to mutilate and destroy our game, and although it was mooted by a couple of teams at the League's inception, it was voted down by those who had a vague clue about soccer and its place in the world. However, anyone who recalls the offside trap of the 1970s and 1980s in European soccer might grant the idea of even discussing a change to the offside law a little sympathy. For the benefit of those who weren't there, or who have shut out the memory, lines of defenders would step forward at the apposite moment with their arms simultaneously raised in appeal, usually catching an opponent clear through on goal, but yards offside. This could happen time and time again, and would prompt much agonizing among television pundits about what to do. The answer, as always from the European game, was nothing. On the other hand, it was of course a wonderful sight when one or more of the defenders got his timing wrong, the linesman kept his flag down, and all of a sudden the forward was through on goal with only the keeper to beat. If the forward scored, the defenders would jaw at the linesman as if he had personally advised them to step up like line dancers and ignore the ball in favour of a negative, under-handed tactic which had never been envisioned when a more Corinthian generation had devised the law as a way of avoiding goal-hangers.

For the unique case of the NASL, though, a modification was in order. In the middle of the 1972 season FIFA allowed the NASL to experiment with an offside line in line with the penalty area, but it was a fiasco – defenders played so deep that play became entrenched in the penalty area and goals per game actually decreased. It was brought upfield to become a 35-yard line for the 1973 season. Long-serving NASL coach Ron Newman explains that one of the reasons the offside line was introduced 'was mainly down to the fact that we kept playing in high school arenas and they were so long and narrow. You were fitting a soccer field inside a running track, and it was hard in this country, because the running track was a different shape here – more narrow, and you'd get things like a long jump pit down the edge of the field and you had to cover it up.'[9] With the game already constricted by narrow pitches, having the offside line on halfway squeezed play still further. Despite its introduction being designed to fit the unique case of US soccer, Newman believes 'without question' that a 35-yard offside line would have worked for the rest of the world.

Phil Woosnam explained the rationale when FIFA, after a year of deliberation, finally gave the League the go-ahead to try the experiment. 'By opening up the play with this change in the offside law, we feel that spectators will be treated to a more exciting and enjoyable brand of soccer,' he said. 'The entire world of soccer recognizes that changes in the laws that produce greater goal-scoring opportunities must be considered. It is our belief, shared by many European officials, that the ultimate answer is to make a change in the offside rule and the size of the goal.'[10] Some years later, he explained to *Observer* journalist Hugh McIlvanney another reason for the offside line: 'An increasing influence of coaches and players from England in North America was resulting in an increase in the use of offside tactics, congestion of players in midfield and tight marking of skilful players by extremely physical defenders.'[11]

Making the goals bigger was another idea thrown around that might have helped gain the NASL the reputation as a gunslinger who was happy to ride roughshod over the game's traditions. Of course that idea was irrefutably crass, but Woosnam was a canny operator. There's every likelihood he threw that in so FIFA would have something to reject while approving the trial of the offside line. Meanwhile, the new offside line – which simply meant that attacking players could only be offside in the final 35 yards of the field – was rarely unpopular, and it's clear from watching NASL games during the 1970s how much more time the players had on the ball in midfield. They were significantly less harried into making mistakes or hoofing the ball upfield for safety's sake. Woosnam claimed the League's coaches viewed the line as having more advantages than disadvantages by a ratio of 2:1.

'I think there is an NASL style, and the 35-yard line has a lot to do with it,' said Washington Diplomats' coach Gordon Bradley five years after it was introduced. 'There is more room to play. It's a good idea. The fans want action. They don't want to see slow play. They want to watch the ball in the attacking area. We are using mostly imported players here and they are playing better over here than they did at home. Why? Well, they have a better opportunity to exhibit their skills because the game is not as fast.'[12]

Few disagree with that assessment, and again many will recall the scrappy, packed midfields of Europe, where all twenty outfield players could be confined to a 25-yard stretch of the field, usually somewhere in the middle, and seconds prior to another offside call when anyone dared to play the ball forward. The US law, though, says Alan Merrick, 'gave the midfielders more space to be creative. You get more action around the goalmouth – what could be wrong with that? You still have offside, and you have linesmen more likely to be able to cope with the rule.'[13] Chicago Sting coach Malcolm Musgrove said the US modification made it 'a harder game to defend. The defence can't push forwards up to the midfield line and force an offside. The offside is not as much a defensive threat and weapon. We are creating an entertainment medium for the fan here.' He did point out, though, that the different bonus system played a role as well in prompting players to be more positive. Whereas in England players could double their salaries for winning and drawing, in the US players only made more cash when they reached the playoffs.[14]

Frank Worthington was another English import who loved the line, and who contrasted it favourably with the game as played in its homeland. 'Week in, week out, I watch defences charge up to the halfway line to catch players offside, or see a linesman give a marginal decision, and it fills me with dismay,' he wrote as late as 1994. 'It stifles the game and kills the spectacle for fans who are, after all, paying good money to be entertained. The 35-yard line ... stretches the game and thus provides an environment where skill and creativity can flourish.'[15] David Chadwick says the rule 'helped a lot of people'. When he coached Gerd Müller at Fort Lauderdale, 'he could ride that 35-yard line. You know in England and other parts of the world it was like a minefield in there [the middle of the field], and people were getting kicked – here it gave everyone more chance to set up the plays until you got into the attacking third.'[16] Defenders were not really opposed either. South African Webster Lichada at Atlanta said, 'I don't mind it at all. I think it's worth taking the risk, if it prevents a negative attitude, and it's also good for the fans.'[17]

Trevor Francis was one of the few players with anything to say against the rule, but even then his dissent was courteous. The offside line 'probably makes my life a little tougher because you find the midfield men are a long way back from you. Back home you'd be looking for them to push up and support you but here, most of the movement up front is between the strikers themselves. Even so, I like the idea.'[18] In fact Rob Hughes, in his 1980 book on Francis, observed while watching the player in the US that the 35-yard line 'is tailored to the Francis gifts of extraordinarily quick turn, of pace and dynamic shot'.[19]

Although the overwhelming consensus is that, for the NASL at that time, the 35-yard line was A Good Thing, the once prevalent discussions about reforming the offside law have now all but dissipated. Tactics have evolved, and the Neanderthal offside trap is no longer such an insidious encroachment on the game. Forwards and their coaches, quite simply, evolved their style so as to render the offside trap largely ineffective. Much as romantics lament the huge amounts of money that now affect the top of the game, this is one area where the increased emphasis on professionalism born of higher wages has led to greater speed and fitness at the top level. Timing a run into space behind the defender has become an art to be applauded, even though it means the linesman's job in making the correct call has become one of the most challenging aspects of refereeing.* It's still a frustrating law for both fans and players, but nowadays is seen less as a necessary evil, and more as an accepted institution that can provide its own measure of delight – either in beating it with a nippy run, or in the immense relief that comes when your team has conceded a goal, the opposition is already celebrating, and then you look over at that beautiful, lovely assistant referee (as we will eventually all end up calling them) and see that he or she has raised their flag and cancelled out the momentary joy of the triumphalist.

FIFA never took a liking to the 35-yard line, and was aggrieved that the NASL had, by 1981, continued with the experiment for two years longer than authorized. The two

---

* Try it sometime – you will never scream at a linesman again.

sides continued to argue the issue until FIFA threatened to de-recognize the NASL and return it to the 'outlaw' wilderness. The USSF, spineless as ever, did little to defend the League's position – in fact its president Gene Edwards was openly hostile to his country's principal league. 'The NASL has been bending the rules for years,' he said at the start of the 1981 season. 'They will not suffer one iota because of the abolition of the 35-yard rule. If they want brighter soccer, maybe they should buy better players.'[20] The NASL caved in, promising to revert to the international norm by the 1982 season, but was allowed to keep it in 1981 for one final year.

Its abolition didn't noticeably stem the number of goals in the League, but 1982 was considered a particularly dire season. 'More NASL teams than ever before seem to be playing a negative brand of soccer, which is driving the fans away in their thousands,' wrote Colin Jose in summing up the season for *World Soccer*. The fans, he continued, 'are being bored to death in their seats. To succeed, soccer in North America must first of all entertain, and the entertainment value I have seen this year has been almost non-existent.' He wrote that in one particularly bad game between the Toronto Blizzard and the Jacksonville Tea Men, played in high winds on an artificial pitch, there were often twenty players 'crowded between what used to be the 35-yard lines, with both goalkeepers punting the ball well into their opponent's half, a tactic which produced a string of offside calls.'[21]

The following year, though, Jose had changed his tune. 1983, he said, 'could well go down as the best season in the history of the League' due to a concentration of better players into fewer teams.[22] He makes no mention of negative tactics or bored fans. Allowing for the generalizations to which we journalists, for our sins, all succumb, it could well have been a case of the League taking a year to adapt to the abolition of the 35-yard line. It's not a change that anyone lobbies for these days, even if it was deemed to have been a wholesale success in its NASL heyday. Perhaps there's something to be said for FIFA's unwitting approach – leave a bad law alone for long enough, and eventually, through a process of evolution, it will take care of itself.

Shootouts in the Wild West

> 'It doesn't matter if the shootout isn't popular in Europe. If it gets people excited here, it's bloody good. I like shootouts, simply because the attitude is to go forward and get the game won. Go forward and make an exciting game of it.'
> —Don Megson, Portland Timbers coach[23]

Let's rewind a couple of pages and recall the thrill of the attacker beating the offside trap and suddenly finding himself through on goal: one-on-one with the keeper, and there's no one else involved in the play because the rangy defenders were too slow. Is there any extended open-play moment in soccer as exciting as this? Welcome to the shootout, used by the NASL from 1977 onwards in place of penalty kicks to decide drawn games, provided that neither team had won during sudden death extra time.

'A lot of the purists around the world go, "What the hell is that bullshit?"' says Bruce Wilson. 'But as a player, when you're in Dallas and it's 110 degrees on artificial turf, and it's 0–0, and no one's running much, but at the end of the game you've got five players on each team running on the goalkeeper – that added excitement.'[24]

Starting from the 35-yard line, a player would have five seconds to shoot from the whistle, while the goalkeeper could come off his line, but couldn't handle outside the penalty area. Converting required speed, accuracy and composure, a far more challenging assignment for the outfield player than the penalty kick. True, spot-kicks are tense, but the expectation is always that the kicker will score, and that the goalkeeper has a minority chance. In the shootout, the goalkeeper was on a roughly equal footing with the attacker. Who could possibly be against an innovation that levelled the playing field and made the challenge much more egalitarian? Compared with the 35-yard line, however, the issue is more divisive among its former participants, even in the goalkeeping fraternity.

Goalkeeper Winston DuBose, who won fourteen US caps, represents the expected view for his field position. 'I loved it,' he says of the shootout. 'I loved that kind of finality of it, that you walked off with one winning team and one losing team. It was nail-biting, but fortunately for me that was something I really enjoyed doing.' He says that FIFA is 'in the dark ages' for not having replaced penalty kicks with the shootout for deciding games, and that the only reason they opposed the shootout back in the 1970s was because 'they wanted to whip America into line with the rest of the world. This is the most popular sport in the world, but they're so reluctant to change that it's ridiculous.' The shootout, he adds, is 'unbelievably exciting. Can you imagine Lionel Messi against Tim Howard, or something like that? It would be unbelievable to see that, fantastic. FIFA's extremely reluctant to change and it's crazy.'[25]

His national team goalkeeping colleague Alan Mayer (six caps) also 'loved them, absolutely loved them. Penalty kicks,' he says, 'you should score 80 per cent plus of the time. The shooter has an unfair advantage, but in a shootout I think the goalkeeper has the advantage and should save six or seven out of ten shootouts. I liked it because a one-on-one situation was perfect for my skills. I was fast and aggressive and I didn't mind contact at all.' Shootouts were a true indicator of a player's skill, be they attacker or goalkeeper, and of course 'as a goalkeeper, you always came out as a hero, and you had more chance of helping your team win.'[26]

The much-travelled Arnie Mausser, another US goalkeeping stalwart with 35 caps, was less keen. He didn't really relish the chance to be the hero because 'you had enough times during the game when you could do that.' He actually preferred penalty kicks, even though he concedes that penalties are a 'crazy' method to decide a game. Instead, says Mausser, the NASL should have played much more extra time to decide games, as they did in the League's early days – but that policy was scrapped after a 1971 playoff game between Dallas and Rochester lasted 176 minutes.* Mausser says he doesn't think 'too many keepers want to do shootouts if they have to. With a 50-50 chance of winning/losing, then maybe you're looking at it a little apprehensively. A lot of times coaches would sub in specialist shootout keepers just before the end, so that was kind of a crazy situation, like sending in a pinch hitter in baseball.' On the other hand (presumably now that he doesn't

---

* A sudden-death golden goal ended the tie and both sets of players collapsed to the ground in relief, as though they were all suffering sudden death.

have to face them), he reckons 'they would help the modern game immensely'.[27]

Alan Merrick was another opponent of the shootouts. 'I'd never seen them before,' he says. 'It was like they were introduced from [ice] hockey. It was an aberration from another sport they were bringing in.' Although, in fact, during the 1970s National Hockey League regular-season games that finished level at full-time remained as draws.

At the time of their introduction in the NASL, few players were opposed to the shootouts. Johan Cruyff declared imperiously, 'I would suggest that the rest of the world follow the lead of the NASL and replace penalties with the shootout when a game is tied after regulation and overtime. With penalties you've always got problems about whether the goalkeeper moved. You don't get this with the shootout.'[28]

This was an excellent point, albeit one rarely cited when promoting the shootout. Goalkeepers moving off their lines too soon at penalty kicks is certainly one of the least enforced laws of the game. The reasons are possibly twofold. First, the odds are so stacked against the goalkeeper on a penalty kick that most referees don't begrudge them a little movement to give themselves a slightly better chance of stopping the ball. Only a really blatant infringement tends to get penalized. And second, if penalty kicks were retaken every time the goalkeeper moved prematurely and the penalty was missed, the entire penalty-taking process would likely last longer than that Dallas–Rochester game.

'The game isn't for the owners or the coaches or the players,' said Minnesota Kicks coach Freddie Goodwin, defending the shootout. 'It's for the fans, but some European teams have forgotten that.' Dallas Tornado publicity director Paul

Ridings recalled an away game in 1977 in Hawaii that went to a shootout after a 2–2 draw. During the game, 'the fans sat on their hands until the shootout, and then you couldn't hear yourself talk, and there were only about 3,000 there.' To him, the shootout was 'more of a contest and the fans feel it's more of a challenge. We lost it once at home and it's not much fun, but winning against Portland in the last game of the year was unreal. The fans were going crazy.' The Tampa Bay Rowdies actively promoted the shootout in radio adverts as a way of attracting more fans. At San Jose, PR director Jim Parker said that during the shootouts 'as each player got ready for his shot last year [1977] there was pandemonium.'[29]

The shootout was 'magical', says Ron Newman. 'I remember going back to England to watch Southampton against Tottenham and it was a bloody awful game. And at the end of the game it was 0–0 and a shootout would have saved the day.'[30] Rodney Marsh is still convinced it would improve the world game when knockout matches are tied. 'I've said this for 35 years,' he says. 'FIFA should adopt the 35-yard-line shootout. Penalties are not conducive to skill, players just stepping up and smashing the ball at the goal until somebody misses. It's far better to have players dribble up from 35 yards and shoot – that is skill. It's fantastic to watch.'[31]

Washington Diplomats coach Gordon Bradley was sceptical about claims that the shootout helped attract more fans to soccer. 'I don't think the tie-breaker or the 35-yard line have helped the game reach the point it's now at in America,' he said. 'It's exciting, and I guess we're in the entertainment business, but in American football it's a tie after the 15 minutes and in [ice] hockey it's a tie. I'm really not keen on it. I don't think Americans have to have a result. It's good quality soccer and high quality players that have put 77,000 people in New York. We did not promote the 35-yard line or the tie-breaker, did we?' Nonetheless, he still preferred the shootout over penalty kicks, if there absolutely had to be a tie-breaker, because 'it is more difficult, more exciting'.[32]

Bradley's claim that Americans are quite capable of coping with the idea of a drawn game is worth looking at in more detail. As he points out, the tie was a possible outcome in both American football (it still is – though it's a rarity) and ice hockey (no longer – now there's, guess what, a shootout to decide games tied after over-time). Baseball plays on and – like the infamous Dallas–Rochester NASL epic – can run into the small hours before a dwindling crowd if neither side can score, but play they will until somebody does. The NASL's successor, Major League Soccer, which started play in 1996, staged shootouts for drawn games to begin with, but abolished them after three years under pressure from both FIFA and fans who now wanted US soccer to conform to the international game. They were becoming soccer connoisseurs, not whooping, razzmatazz-loving dupes who could only be drawn back to the stadium by bells and whistles. MLS persevered for a few more years with a sudden-death, ten-minute period of extra time. However, if no one scored after those ten minutes, the game was a draw. No one died. No fans suffered psychological scars following a 0–0, 1–1 or 2–2 game. The ten-minute extra-time period was axed. The game survives.

The idea that Americans could not cope with drawn games likely came from PR directors at clubs looking to jazz up their sport and pack more fans in. The yearning for an outcome and a climactic winning score was understandable from their point of view, even if the reasoning behind it ('Americans don't like draws') was unfounded. Journalists then bought in to the original myth spread by PR directors, and stuck with it. Americans just won't accept drawn games! It's endured longer than the laughable theory that soccer is a communist game.* Maybe the latter theory in itself was based on a hatred for the concept of a draw. That two competing sides would end up equal. Americans won't stand for that, because in capitalism, there are only losers and winners. Rich and poor, it's how the system works. As though all soccer games in the Soviet Union had to end as draws.

If you set a 90-minute period for a game between two sides, and at the end of that period neither side has outscored the other, is that not a fair result? If you were not good enough to win, but not bad enough to lose, surely an egalitarian splitting of the points is the best possible outcome. What kind of human being is seriously ill-equipped to deal with that idea? Upon examination, of course, the 'Americans hate draws' theory is flam. It's no more true than the 'Americans hate equality' theory. It's hard to disagree with Gordon Bradley that this was nothing but a side issue.

There was a counter-story from the Bundesliga in late 2005 when a group of seven Tibetan monks attended their first ever soccer game, a 0–0 draw between VfL Wolfsburg and Schalke 04. The monks were by no means unhappy with the scoreline, in fact one of them politely explained that 0–0 was the ideal outcome. 'As a Buddhist I'm very happy with the result,' said Lama Lobsang Tashi. 'A draw means the golden medium. It's

---

* A genuine accusation levelled by the significant clutch of anti-soccer US sportswriters since the 1970s, now finally dying and diminishing. This book grants them no platform.

the best possible result for both teams. There is no disappointment and no success. 0–0 is the path of peace.'[33]

You maybe wouldn't go that far if you were a Tottenham Hotspur supporter watching your team play Arsenal (or, to be frank, any supporter watching any team, anywhere), but it's the extreme antithesis of the stereotypical, media-generated American war cry of, 'How can you have a game that ends 0–0, goddammit?' A draw is just the happy medium between joy and despair, and there have been plenty of exciting drawn games thanks to last-gasp equalizers or a sharing of two, four, six or more goals. If the NASL scrapped drawn games in the mid-1970s to bring in higher crowds and make the games more climactic, however artificial that now seems, it was an entirely understandable move. However, it had little to do with what made the NASL suddenly popular, nor what led to its demise.

For a final word to counter all this talk of post-game excitement, here's journalist Paul Gardner, an unequivocal opponent of the shootout because 'it favours goalkeepers and I think goalkeepers are a fucking nuisance. They're not soccer players. It put the goalkeeper more in the centre of things – it's a win-win situation for them, they're either going to be a hero, or there's a goal' that they're not blamed for. Gardner's not interested in the notion that the fan was king in the NASL, and that their entertainment was the primary concern. 'The shootout was an add-on,' he says, 'and by adding frilly bits to it before the game, marching bands at half-time, the elephant and so on, no one's going to mistake those for soccer involvement, that's clearly showbiz.' Shootouts, though, 'began to be considered part of soccer, and most Americans would think that's the way soccer's played. If it got to the point where people were saying they liked soccer because of the shootout, and it did somehow feel that's what was happening, then I have a big problem with it, because I think if they make this thing successful it's because of the wrong thing, and they're selling it at the expense of the real thing.'

Gardner concedes that the shootout did not alter how you played the actual game, but he still felt 'that it was an intrusion of a showbiz mentality. The entertainment should be what happens during that 90 minutes.'[34]

NASL: the league of the future

It's true that changes to the laws of the game need to be very well considered, but it doesn't mean they shouldn't happen at all. In the 1950s, the National Basketball Association realized that teams who were leading could make the game very dull just by keeping possession and not attempting to score. It introduced the 24-second rule, dictating that teams had to attempt to score a basket within that time or cede possession. The result was an upsurge in scoring and spectator interest, and the rule was adopted worldwide. Here are four more areas where the NASL met resistance, but was spot on in terms of foreseeing where the game was heading.

Names and numbers on shirts. It was the Cosmos who were the first to come up with the idea of putting players' names on shirts, according to Rodney Marsh, but the idea itself came from baseball, and had also been picked up by American football. The reason was simple – so that fans could better identify the players, and then identify *with* them. 'I came back [to England] in 1976 and said they've got to put the names on

261

shirts,' says Marsh, 'and they laughed at me. Players could go out and sign their own shirt, but they all laughed at me.'[35] Squad numbers were allocated to players for the same reason, while Europe stuck to a strict 1–11 numbering system for several more years (an aspect of soccer still recalled fondly by purists not keen to see players with numbers like '88' on their backs). With the advent of larger squads and constantly revolving line-ups at the top end of the game, and lower league clubs relying on a huge turnover of loan players to get by, squad numbers have become a permanent reality, providing a simpler way of identifying a player from a squad of 40 or so players. In the club shop, meanwhile, players' numbers have become irrevocably, and lucratively, linked with their names (think Beckham 23, or CR7), just as Marsh predicted.

Another logical idea, yet to fully have its day except at international level, was to put the number on the front of the shirt as well as the back, an innovation that Paul Gardner strongly supports. 'That was a huge help to journalists and commentators, and to referees, and to fans,' he says. 'I was doing TV work for a number of years, and the difference was enormous, everyone said it was a great idea. If you bring it up with people here [in MLS] they start talking about how the sponsors wouldn't like it, and Adidas wouldn't like it, and there's no room for it. I did manage to persuade FIFA to do it – that was entirely due to me because I kept on at them.'[36]

Substitutes. In 1981, when FIFA was pressurizing the NASL to drop its offside line, it also ordered them to desist from having three substitutes and revert to the international norm of two. It's unclear, with hindsight, quite how it took soccer so long to come around to the idea of using subs. It was almost a century before the game allowed even one, and permitting three by the late 1970s was no doubt deemed a concession bordering on excess. How dared the NASL allow a gargantuan trio of bench players? Three, however, is of course the number allowed under the laws of today.

Back passes. In 1984, its final year, the NASL was scorned for sending League officials to every game who were charged with monitoring the number of unnecessary back passes. At this time, goalkeepers could still pick up back passes with their hands, and it was a tedious trick for wasting time, roundly booed by all fans. So the League decided to fine clubs who took advantage of the rule too often. 'The only effect was to again make the League a laughing stock among knowledge-able soccer observers,' wrote one journalist a couple of years later in analysing why the League had failed.[37] Less than a decade later, FIFA outlawed goalkeepers from handling back passes.

Women. The NASL was the first league to turn soccer away from its entrenchment as a male-only sporting pastime. Fat credit here to Phil Woosnam, who recognized that, given the right atmosphere, women would come to watch soccer, and that there was absolutely no reason why they couldn't play it too. 'Tradition has a great place in sports and life,' Woosnam conceded, 'but it mustn't restrict you from going forward according to the demands of society. I'm thinking here of the interest of women in soccer, for example. Soccer in the rest of the world is still regarded as a blue-collar male adult sport. It's a very chauvinistic situation, whereas here, soccer has become very much a family sport. We have a 40 per cent female attendance at games.'[38] In 2004, the Disney Channel broadcast a fictitious kids' series called *Phil of the Future*. It wasn't about Woosnam, but it could have been.

The development may not have been entirely intentional – it just so happened that soccer appealed to a lot of women as a spectator sport compared with the more brutal offerings such as ice hockey and American football, or the macho gum-chewers dragging their porcine bodies around a dusty baseball diamond. There was also a huge rise in the number of girls and young women playing the game. It was cheap, and required no special abilities, and the NASL also happened to coincide with the 1972 Title IX Act that legislated gender equality in education. High schools and colleges began offering soccer programmes as one of the easier ways to achieve this now legally required equality.

When the League realized that almost half of its fans were female, it celebrated the fact and used it as a selling point to bring in a family audience. As early as the late 1960s, when players went out to preach soccer at their endless clinics, girls as much as boys were starting from scratch – there was no tradition of male domination in the sport to hold them back. The global spread of women's football was born and nurtured in 1970s America, and a first generation of women players later pushed the reluctant US Soccer Federation into financing a women's national team in 1985. Now there is a sixteen-team Women's World Cup where the quality of sportsmanship and the commitment to open, attacking soccer make for a conspicuous counterpoint to the men's tournament. When Mia Hamm and Julie Foudy were inducted into the US Soccer Hall of Fame in Oneonta, NY, in 2007, grown women and men in their hundreds listened to the two women tell stories of how they had struggled for recognition and won, and few present kept their eyes dry.

Future imperfect

In other areas, there was some muddled thinking. However, it should be noted that, although some radical but nutty ideas were discussed, they were never put into action. In Europe during the 1970s, these ideas were often the ones cited most to perpetuate the fear that the Americans were going to ruin the game.

Bigger goals and goalposts. Prior to the 1981 season, with gates starting to fall following the late 1970s boom, the NASL considered an even more complicated points-scoring system (you are being spared the details), and the idea of bigger goals and bigger goalposts. The *New York Times* quoted Minnesota Kicks president Freddie Goodwin as saying that the League 'would consider such proposals as widening the goal by two feet; shortening the game from 90 minutes to 70 minutes but with timeouts; making the posts and crossbar 16" wide, and making back passes to the goalkeeper illegal. The aim of widening the goal would be to get more scoring. Timeouts would accommodate television. The reason for seeking wider goal posts and crossbars is to create more rebounds, and elimination of back passes would serve to avoid delaying tactics used by a team that is leading.'[39] As discussed above, only the back pass rule out of this sorry selection makes any sense.

Abolish offside. This was often mentioned in Europe as something the Americans supposedly wanted to do. Was the idea ever seriously entertained? Yes, according to Paul Gardner, though less by the League and more by team owners who 'all wanted bigger goals, to abolish offside'. Such measures, though, were not feasible because the League 'realized FIFA wouldn't put up with more radical changes to the game. That led to much criticism on the part of the owners, none of whom were used to being told what to do or how to run their businesses by a bunch of starched shirts in fucking Switzerland of all places.'[40] In fact, the NASL's Strategic Plan for the future, covering 1978–87 and adopted in October 1977, sombrely notes that 'FIFA inhibits the ability to make unilateral rule changes no matter how desirable from a marketing perspective.' The Plan rather prosaically focuses on marketing strategies, development of US soccer, and the necessity of sensible financial planning for NASL franchises – there are no proposals to further alter the game's laws.[41]

Ban goalkeepers, allow waist-high tackles, change the ball's shape from round to oval, and make charging legal. Just kidding. These ideas were not discussed (as far as we know).

Showing FIFA the finger

At certain times, in exasperation, owners or journalists would trenchantly call for a renunciation of FIFA and holler for a return to 'outlaw' status. These businessmen, as Gardner observes, were not accustomed to being accountable to unelected law-makers in faraway mountain countries. They could not see the need for FIFA if all that it did was obstruct them from taking the game in what they believed to be a progressive direction. They didn't understand the consequences, in either the short or the long term, of cutting ties with FIFA. Still, they must have released some anger at telling FIFA to basically go fuck itself. They are not the only ones in soccer's history who've felt like some cathartic emoting in Zürich's general direction.

By 1983, with the League losing teams, and teams losing fans and money,* the president of the San Diego Sockers, Jack Daley – who'd been involved with various League teams for almost a decade – declared that 'Our product has to be improved. The outdoor game in America has to be overhauled, which means going back to the 35-yard line and three-substitute rule.' He claimed that the NASL had its best days in the late 70s when 'we weren't afraid to experiment with the game, but now the NASL is back into a shell.' He said he didn't care they had to become an outlaw league to survive because, 'If we go broke, FIFA won't hold a tag-day sale for us.'

In that last point, at least, he was right. At the same time, he was clutching at straws. Clive Toye, at this point general manager of the Toronto Blizzard, offered a sober rebuttal. 'Nobody has convinced me that any tinkering with the rules will in fact improve the product,' said Toye. 'It will get better only with more quality players, coaches, and the growth of the North American players. Our club wishes to operate under FIFA. If nothing else, there are practical economic reasons, such as the ability to bring in top international players for our team, plus clubs to play against, and a chance to compete for the World Cup.'[42]

---

* See Chapter 10.

In 1981, just after FIFA had ordered the League to rescind the 35-yard offside line, San Jose Quakes owner Milan Mandarić had said that he would 'vote for a 100 per cent pull-out from FIFA. I think most owners would agree with me.' In a bullish piece written for the *San Jose Mercury*, hack Dan Hruby pronounced, 'It's time to tell FIFA to take a hike.' FIFA, he went on, 'has shown an abysmal ignorance of the American sports scene. The furious war for the fans' dollars in the US outdoes anything else seen in the world. Nowhere else has soccer had to come from so far back.' Never mind getting barred from international competition, at least the NASL could buy any players it wanted without paying a transfer fee. Except that those players would be banned and blacklisted, just like those NPSL players back in 1967. Still, Hruby concluded, 'The US should go it alone. If soccer fails to survive here, it won't make any difference what FIFA wanted. Will it?'[43]

Again, for every one of these bellicose calls for the NASL to arm itself and head for the hills, there was a sardonic response. A young David Wangerin, who a quarter of a century later authored the US soccer history book *Soccer in a Football World*, wrote in a reader's letter responding to Hruby's article: 'If one wants nothing but immediate success in American soccer, at the expense of all time-tested rules, why not play with more than one ball, let the players play naked, and let the fans take turns goalkeeping? Oh, how everyone would love soccer then!'[44]

FIFA had its own passive-aggressive ways of snubbing US soccer. In the programme to the 1979 Soccer Bowl, commissioner Phil Woosnam welcomes Dr Henry Kissinger to the game, as well as English FA president and secretary Sir Harold Thompson, and his sidekick Ted Croker, 'who have been instrumental in assisting the growth of our League'. FIFA officials, though, had to decline because 'regretfully' they were at the Under-19 World Cup in Japan.[45] All of FIFA was in Japan, presumably, for the entire duration of that important tournament. Not a single one could tear himself away to come and be a guest at the NASL's championship game. That's not just a snub, that's a big chocolate Swiss finger right back at you, America.

The USSF vs NASL: still fighting after all these years

> 'FIFA is run a bit like a country club. They have to get to know you before you're accepted. If you're going to join a club, you abide by the club's rules. When you become president, you can change them. But you don't change them by standing outside the door, kicking at it, then spitting in the eye of the man who opens it.'
> —Clive Toye on the USA's failed bid to win hosting rights to the 1986 World Cup[46]

The feuds at the League's birth and the subsequent years of debate over the extent to which the NASL could tamper with soccer's apparently sacred laws are useful background to consider when looking at the United States' bid to host the 1986 World Cup. Colombia had originally been awarded the competition back in the 1970s, it being South America's turn to host after Spain '82. Prior to the Spanish tournament, however, FIFA had finally begun to realize just how much cash could be generated by a tournament watched on television by almost the entire world, and had increased the number of countries at the finals to 24. Increasing the number of World Cup participants had also been the crux of João Havelange's successful bid to oust Sir Stanley Rous as FIFA President in 1974, in the light of justified complaints from the African and Asian confederations that they were severely under-represented at the finals. Unfortunately, 24 teams were too many for a country like Colombia, which was also suffering from internal political unrest and an overly ambitious stadium-building programme that was well behind schedule. So Colombia pulled out, and the two main candidates to replace it were Mexico and the US. Brazil had shown an interest, but quickly withdrew, while Canada also made a bid as an also-ran that no one took seriously for a second.

The main argument both for and against Mexico was the same – it had hosted the tournament as recently as 1970. In terms of rotational fairness, Mexico was clearly jumping the queue. At the same time, and given that Colombia pulled out less than four years prior to the tournament, it was a plus to have so recently hosted the World Cup. It showed the Mexicans could do it. They had, after all, transmitted games in colour and by satellite around the world in 1970. Everyone had thrilling memories of the magnificent Brazilian team and exciting games such as West Germany's comeback from 2–0 down to beat England in the quarter-final, as well as the Germans' subsequent 4–3 defeat to Italy in the semi.*

The United States argued that as a fledgling soccer nation it deserved to be given a chance, for the good of developing

---

* Although the tournament's reputation as one of attacking brilliance is something of a myth – there were only six more goals scored in 1970 than were scored in 1966 in England, generally considered a dull World Cup.

interest in the game in a still largely soccer-sceptical nation. Or, put another way, hosting the 1986 World Cup might save the NASL, which by the time of the US bid in 1983 was in serious decline – down to twelve teams from 24 just three years earlier. The infrastructure was in place already, because the US boasted a raft of spacious, modern and superior American football and baseball stadiums across the country, most of which could be adapted to soccer without too much trouble. The USSF put together a strong campaigning team that included Pelé, Franz Beckenbauer and the former Secretary of State Henry Kissinger, who had been the chairman of the NASL Board of Governors since 1977. *World Soccer* magazine referred to its 'brilliantly presented dossier of the American World Cup dream'.[47] The US team predicted a potential minimum income of $360 million, around four times greater than the profits from Spain '82. They would lay grass fields on top of the artificial surfaces, and arrange the group games so that certain countries could play in cities or states where they would draw a large ethnic support. Indeed all this happened, but not until the 1994 tournament. In 1986, the US in reality had as much chance as Canada, and FIFA awarded the tournament to Mexico in May 1983.

A story in *Sports Illustrated* the following year blamed the USSF for the failed campaign. The magazine quoted Chicago Sting owner Lee Stern as saying that the USSF was 'jealous and disorganized', and in general offered no effective support to the NASL. The article described the USSF as, until recently, 'a small committee of little international prestige that was overtaken by the rise of the NASL and the boom in youth soccer. USSF members enjoyed their junkets to World Cups, voting in committees, mixing with the great ones of the sport. And then they found themselves riding a tiger.' It went on to quote sources close to Hermann Neuberger, the West German who was a member of FIFA's inner circle, as saying 'that at a critical stage of the negotiations [FIFA president] João Havelange ... received a call from a prominent USSF member. The US, Havelange was informed by the caller, was "not ready" to stage the World Cup. It is understood that the caller was a USSF official who was jealous of the NASL.'[48]

It certainly seems that the League was far keener to have the tournament than the US Soccer Federation. NASL Commissioner Howard Samuels called their failure to land the 1986 tournament 'an enormous setback. In one fell swoop we could have changed the sport. It was unconscionable in my view. It was handled absolutely abominably. In my view the decision was made beforehand. It's a club and we're not members of FIFA's club. It was a terrible business decision, and a terrible decision in the interest of developing the sport.'[49] By contrast, USSF president Gene Edwards was positively sanguine. 'In retrospect, what would have happened if we got it? We would have really messed it up,' he said, sounding more like a jaded pessimist at the bar on his fifth shot of bourbon than a man in charge of a major sports body. FIFA, he went on, depended on World Cup income to keep it going until the next tournament and had been 'concerned that the game was not popular enough here and would not generate the income it needed.' Despite the great stadiums and their infrastructure, 'there are none laid out just for soccer. They [FIFA] feel it's a little premature at this time.'[50] These sentiments, expressed in mid-1983, would certainly seem to back up *Sports Illustrated*'s story of that crucial, self-sabotaging call to Havelange from someone inside the USSF.

'Sure we can blame FIFA, but let's face it, we blew it ourselves,' said USSF treasurer Guy DiVencenzo, one of only two USSF members on the ten-man World Cup Organizing Committee. 'The application we presented to FIFA on March 11 was frivolous, glossy, and transparent, and probably deserved the treatment it received.' By then Edwards had been removed as chairman of the organizing committee, a move DiVencenzo cites as one of the biggest mistakes, as it 'gave FIFA the impression that something was wrong, and it confirmed their fears of political manoeuvring'. He also felt the NASL's role was 'counter-productive'.[51]

Over a decade and a half on from that contentious meeting with Sir Stanley Rous in Zürich, and US soccer's factions were still shooting each other in the foot and undermining their own interests through internecine feuding. Meanwhile, FIFA looked on, as tetchy as a distant uncle who is forced by family circumstances to deal with his querulous transatlantic cousins, but who would rather just cut them out of his life. For FIFA, the decision to award the 1986 World Cup to Mexico must have been an easy one. 'Mexico is a real soccer country,' said Havelange succinctly. 'The US and Canada are not ready for such a competition.'* The FIFA president cited the long travelling distances between host cities as another factor. Havelange also happened to be close friends with Mexican TV magnate Emilio Azcarraga, but of course that had nothing to do with the hosting rights going south. Gene Edwards was indignant at the very thought. 'I don't

---

* It took just over a year for FIFA to execute a swift U-turn on this. The huge success of soccer at the 1984 LA Olympics suddenly opened up Zürich's collective mind to the cash-generating possibilities of a World Cup hosted in the US.

buy that,' he said. 'I don't believe the president of an organization would subject himself to something like that.'[52] Why, the very idea. Indeed, if Edwards possessed any knowledge of that alleged USSF call to Havelange, he would also know for sure the real reason why the US bid was scuppered – it was the enemy within. Whatever the truth, the rest of the world barely cared. 'Call it corruption if you will,' wrote Richard Weekes in the *Guardian*, 'but in Latin America such connections raise not an eyebrow. They are the way of the world, the way to get things done.'[53]

'FIFA's looking at us and saying, "What the fuck are these guys doing to the game?"' says Bob Iarusci, who was playing with the New York Cosmos at the time of the US bid. He remembers how Cosmos vice-president Steve Ross, who was heavily involved with the bid, came back from Switzerland crushed. 'The US group goes to FIFA to get the World Cup, but FIFA would rather give it Mexico, in a state of national debt [Mexico's foreign debt had risen to $97 billion by the time the 1986 World Cup was over[54]], rather than give it to us. And that killed the North American Soccer League. Once that decision was made, Steve Ross lost his passion. Once Steve went, everybody went. You can check those timelines, because for me that was the moment in the NASL that killed the golden goose. It wasn't all that stuff about the GMs overspending – there was a lot of that, but the single biggest reason why the NASL collapsed was FIFA's refusal to give us the 1986 World Cup, and they should have. It was a big mistake.' If the 1986 bid had been successful, maintains Iarusci, 'the League would have exploded'.[55] In a good way, he means. As it was, the NASL was on the opposite plosive path.

Season-by-season overview

1976

Still at twenty teams, with Denver moving to Minneapolis/ St Paul,* and Baltimore heading west to San Diego. Rodney Marsh, George Best, Bobby Moore and Geoff Hurst all came to the NASL, and Chinaglia joined the Cosmos – he was two goals behind Tampa's prolific Smethurst at the top of the scorers' list. Crowds up on average from just over 7,500 the previous year to 10,300.

Fun facts: Out of eighteen players on the St Louis roster, fourteen were US citizens, the almost polar opposite of every other NASL team. They won five out of 24 games, but credit for trying. Journeyman English striker Tommy Tynan amassed goals almost everywhere he played – he scored over 250 in places like Plymouth, Torquay, Newport and Sheffield, but flopped in Dallas with just two goals in nineteen games, the sum of his NASL career. Dallas also had a player called Bob Hope, but he was a Scottish midfielder, not a singing, dancing, comic actor from Ohio. History has not recorded whether the Washington Diplomats' Yugoslav forward Stojan Trickovic was known to his fans and teammates as 'Tricky'. But surely he was.

1977

With Boston and Philadelphia dropping out, the League was down to eighteen teams, and there were lots of moves too. San Antonio went to Hawaii and San Diego to Las Vegas,† while Miami moved northwards up the Florida coast to Fort Lauderdale. Another short hop was made by the Bi-Centennials, who headed south from Hartford to New Haven and renamed themselves Connecticut. It didn't help – they had the worst record in the League and quit, but the bi-centennial was over anyway by then. Average gates took another bump, up to over 13,500 from 10,300 in 1976. An NASL franchise now cost a cool million.

---

* See Chapter 5.
† See Chapter 6.

Fun facts: Canadian Buzz Parsons played for the Vancouver Whitecaps, while American Buzz Demling turned out for the San Jose Earthquakes – this is stated merely to prove that in North America it is perfectly legal to name a child 'Buzz'. Both played when the Earthquakes lost 2–0 to the Whitecaps, and as Demling was a defender and Parsons a forward, it's feasible that Buzz was instructed to mark Buzz, leading to 90 minutes of Buzz-on-Buzz bump and bustle.

1978

Prior to this season, founding NASL members St Louis quit, as did Connecticut and one-season wonders Hawaii and Las Vegas. With expansion to 24 teams, there were almost a dozen newcomers and returnees: the California Surf (in Anaheim), Colorado, Detroit, Houston, Memphis, New England (in Boston), Oakland, Philadelphia (third attempt), San Diego (likewise) and Tulsa. Got all that? Average crowds fell slightly, to just over 13,000. Chinaglia (39 goals) and New England's Mike Flanagan (30) were on fire, way out ahead on the scoring list.

Fun facts: Canadian defender Bob Lenarduzzi scored ten goals and notched seventeen assists for the Whitecaps, finishing eleventh in the League's scoring list. He was also voted the NASL's North American Player of the Year, but still failed to make the Cosmos- and European-dominated All-Star Team. His teammate Alan Hinton, the former Derby County forward, managed just one goal all season, but registered a League record 30 assists (but he didn't make the All-Star team either). Lenarduzzi's brother Sam played sixteen games alongside him in defence, with neither a goal nor an assist to his name, which may have lead to some awkward family dinners that year. Or even on the pitch. 'Shall I go up for this corner, Bob?' 'Hmm, maybe best if you stay back here and cover, Sam. I'll take care of it, okay? Okay? Sam, look at me. It's okay, right?'

8

Broken teams in dysfunctional DC: Cruyff, the Dips, the Darts and the Whips

'Jimmy bloody Hill, Jesus wept. He bought Detroit, he and some people, screwed it up completely, then they moved to Washington, [and] screwed Washington up completely.'

—Clive Toye[1]

Washington DC is a city notorious for its inability to function. The capital of the free world should, at least in the mind of a utopian capitalist, be a spectacular showcase for the way that a wealthy, market-based society operates. Its politicians should be able to walk curious visitors down the steps of the Capitol building and out on to wide, clean streets that perfectly reflect the social and economic philosophies espoused by white settlers for the previous 400 years – hard work and self-belief will result in happiness and prosperity for all. Instead, what they will see is a city that symbolizes the country it governs. Half of Washington DC is mainly white and affluent, the other half is mainly black and, in a handful of city wards, grindingly poor, beset annually by dozens of unsolved drug- and gang-related murders in no-go areas for the tourists who flock to see the nation's magnificent museums on the Mall. Right here, almost literally on the doorstep of the national government, is overwhelming evidence that vehement long-term opposition to policies aimed at more integration and equality will lead to a nation divided down the middle. A nation that works for many, but excludes or marginalizes even more. One hundred and fifty years after the abolition of slavery, and over half a century after ending the iniquitous norms of segregation, DC might as well be the anti-town on a Soviet propaganda poster. The blatant split in privilege is so breathtaking that most of those politicians guiding you down the Capitol steps with a cracked smile choose to look far beyond the disparity and pretend it isn't there. Only creeping gentrification is slowly changing the face of some of the city's previously deprived areas, but it's not solving many social problems – merely edging them further out to the suburbs. Meanwhile, a lack of affordable housing pushed the city's homeless population to almost 12,000 in January 2014, a staggering figure for a city with a population of just under 650,000.[2]

Washington DC is a hard city to warm to, and you don't meet many people who laud it as their beloved home town. There is no city centre, as such, while a revolving cast of diplomats and politicians mean that much of its high-powered population remains fluid, and emotionally unattached to the capital. The statues and monuments that adulate former presidents give it the feeling of an old eastern European capital city that exists to at best commemorate, and at worst deify, bronze- and concrete-sculpted dead men. On the plus side, it boasts a jaw-dropping mile of mesmerizing museums and art galleries on the National Mall that almost make up for the fact that, in daily real life, the archetypal DC operator will be a lawyer or a lobbyist too busy to talk to you for more than 60 seconds at most. The political inertia is in stark contrast to the speed with which thrusting personal ambition can push smart and highly motivated individuals into positions of influence. It's hard to say what they end up influencing beyond their own personal wealth and reputation, but complain about this and you'll be met with a world-weary shrug. It's DC, what do you expect? Don't take it personally, it's just politics.

Bearing all this in mind, it's no surprise that during the seventeen-year span of the North American Soccer League, the city managed to consume and then spit back out no fewer than four soccer teams. Washington DC was the market that everyone believed was made to succeed. When one team failed, someone else came along and gave it another try, as though importing a fresh new ideology that would kick-start the political paralysis, or simply trying to pass some straightforward piece of legislation through Congress. No matter how obvious and logical that law might have seemed to a normal person standing on the outside, once it reached DC it was subject to wrangling, disputes, compromises, distortions, setbacks, and ultimate failure. *That's just DC.* Want to put money into a soccer team there? Sure, it's a potentially large and wealthy market. Best of luck! See you in a year on the bottom steps of the Lincoln Memorial dripping tears into your begging bowl.

For a town whose best efforts are invested in PR, image and shameless spin, it's a nice irony that the teams' names were so poorly thought through that soccer barely stood a chance from the moment each franchise was conceived and christened.

1. Whips, 1967–68

It's tempting to speculate that the Whips were so called because Washington DC teems with the kind of professional gentleman who would visit a whorehouse and demand to be sexually flagellated for the sins he was perpetrating against the

American people during the course of his day job. The idea of taking painful pleasure for being a bad person fits. Let's float the theory, disregard the rather dull political connotations, and move on.

In 1967 the Whips were in fact Scotsmen from Aberdeen, the United Soccer Association team rented for a season in DC; they lost the championship game 5–6 to the LA Wolves (from Wolverhampton, not California) in Los Angeles. The following year, in the newly united NASL, the Whips became a squad dominated by Danes and South Americans, attracting crowds of five to ten thousand. They didn't make the playoffs, and the Whips' owner Earl Foreman was one of several investors who pulled out of the League at the end of that season. He was a DC lawyer. If he enjoyed being whipped, he had his limits when it came to soccer, although the fact that he immediately took over an ailing basketball team and brought it to the DC region – where it struggled financially for several years – suggests that when it came to self-punishment, this man was not averse to baring his skin and letting the brandished leather do its thing.

The Whips' PR director Charlie Brotman later said that 'there was no personal identity with the players', which isn't that surprising given the lack of a Danish diaspora in DC. 'Foreign spectators were supposed to provide the nucleus of fans in a lot of cities until the Americans caught on,' said Brotman. 'Well, in Washington we figured embassy row would flock to the games. Instead, some of the kitchen help came, but the upper classes held out for free tickets.'[3] That's another thing about DC. No one in power expects to pay for anything. They think they should be treated with due dignity, respect and, above all, freebies. They're so busy and important that you should be grateful if they turn up at all, so don't expect His Excellency the Ambassador to actually fork out hard cash for deigning to grace the bleachers with his honourable arse.

2. Darts, 1970–71

If 'Whips' seemed too violent, the next Washington team decided to sound ... more violent still. At least a whip might, in the right sado-masochistic context, evoke the concept of satisfaction. Presumably a dart was intended to evince the idea of something fast and deadly. This is a city, after all, that while boasting one of the highest murder rates in the country, hosted a basketball team called the Bullets from 1973 until 1997, before finally bowing to public pressure and changing its name to the benign, child-friendly Wizards.* The Darts enjoyed no such longevity. Founded by Scotsman Norman Sutherland in 1961 as an amateur team called Washington Britannica, they had become a successful team in the semi-pro American Soccer League. After joining the NASL, though, they played for just two seasons at Catholic University in DC, usually on Sunday afternoons, in front of crowds in the low four figures. Their home shirt's primary colour was grey.

In their first season, 1970, they were coached by Trinidadian Lincoln Phillips, and consequently fielded a decent side dominated by his compatriots. In a six-team league

---

* Peak murder years in DC happened during the crack cocaine epidemic, 1988–96, generally around 400–500 per year in a city of around 600,000. During the Darts' years, the rates were a comparatively low 221 (1970) and 275 (1971), with a population of around 750,000. In 2012, the murder stat was down to 88, but a lot of crime had been pushed out of the city.

they won their three-team conference, then lost to Rochester in the championship final 4–3 on aggregate over two legs – DC's only championship game appearance throughout the NASL (if you exclude Aberdeen in 67's USA rent-a-team final, which we should). In 1971 they were coached by an Englishman, Alan Rogers, who added a few Scotsmen to the Trinidadian mix, but the fans continued to stay away. Their final game was at home to St Louis, a nine-goal thriller that the Darts won 5–4 in front of just 1,224.

Like the Whips before them, the Darts were all too notorious for giveaways, and consequently devalued their product. In a desperate marketing move, they hired a famous DJ, Murray 'the K' Kaufman, to play records during a home game to fit in with the mood and movement of the game. 'Eventually we hope to orchestrate the game to music,' Kaufman said at a press conference the day before the game. 'We expect to make a marriage between music and soccer. Anything new turns me on, maybe we'll even turn some soccer players on.'[4] Although he set up his equipment on the appointed day, rain tragically prevented the fulfilment of this experiment. At the end of the 1971 season, the Darts were moved to Miami, where you will recall they became the Gatos,* Spanish for 'cats'. Coincidentally, the last game that Miami played under this name was also at home to St Louis, in front of a crowd of 1,023. So, relatively speaking, the Darts were more successful than the Gatos, by 201 fans. After one season, the Cats became the manlier, more Hispanic-associated Toros ('Bulls').

---

* See Chapter 1.

3. Diplomats, 1974–81

> 'He [Washington Diplomats coach Dennis
> Viollet] was a wonderful man with a vast know-
> ledge of the game and he had a great vision for
> football in America. "Enjoy yourself for three
> months, play against Pelé and pull the birds." It
> sounded pretty good to me!'
>
> —Washington Diplomats' English striker
> Paul Cannell[5]

Although Washington DC's third coming in the NASL was
another cash drain, being passed from owner to owner like
a smouldering, dollar-burning hot potato, there's at least a
semi-golden era within this time frame. After DC somehow
managed to survive without professional soccer for two years,
a new group of owners gave the city another shot in 1974. The
name – the Diplomats – was at least Washington-related. True,
it conjured up images of stiff men in suits bowing slightly and
shaking hands for the sake of protocol, rather than a bird or an
animal with ruthless predatory skills, lofty pride, unstinting
vigour and inexhaustible strength. On the other hand, it really
was *very* Washington DC – underhand, cryptic and superficial
– and it could be shortened to the less formal-sounding Dips.

The first ownership group was not glamorous – it was
headed by a builder from Baltimore and the owner of an insur-
ance company. Although Manchester United legend Dennis
Viollet was drafted in as coach, the trend was a familiar one
of poor results and low crowds. Nonetheless, a franchise
they'd bought for $75,000 in 1974 was sold on the follow-
ing year for a League record $650,000 to a group headed

by Steve Danzansky, a supermarket magnate and horseracing enthusiast. The dramatic rise in value was not down to
any stunning soccer being played by the Dips; rather it was
because the Cosmos had just signed Pelé. Indeed DC's much-
vaunted potential as a soccer hotbed was finally tapped when
the Cosmos came to town in June of 1975, and almost 37,000
saw the Dips get whipped, 9–2. Crowds rose gradually through
1976 and 1977 as the League grew in size and notoriety, and
the Dips had a little time to establish themselves in the city
– clearly, there were soccer fans out there in the greater DC
area, they just had to be nurtured, courted and kept. However,
1977's results were mediocre, and included an 8–2 shellacking at the hands of the Cosmos. Viollet was finally replaced,
and former Cosmos coach Gordon Bradley took over for the
1978 season, while yet another new owner, the Madison Square
Garden Corp. (MSG), came in for the 1979 season and began
to invest the kind of money that brought bigger names to DC.
Danzansky's ownership group, San Juan Racing, had reportedly lost $2 million in the Dips, but Danzansky remained as
a minority investor and club president.

The team acquired a reputation for roughness on the field,
and partying off it. Former Newcastle United striker Paul
Cannell was a typical DC signing. Flamboyant but tough, he
became the face of the franchise by scoring lots of goals in
the late 70s, and for 'loveable rogue' antics that included, by
his own admission, consuming copious amounts of alcohol
and drugs in Georgetown night spots. 'Washington DC, you'd
see half the people who worked in the White House going
into bars at lunchtime and taking lines of coke,' he says. 'The
diplomats too [the actual diplomats, not the soccer team] –
drugs were everywhere in DC; same in New York; the same

in LA. That was the culture of the time. But the game was always taken seriously. Yes, there were after-game parties and that kind of stuff. A lot of the people thought players were coming over from England for a payday and a party. Some of them at the end of their careers, past their best – yes, they were there to enjoy themselves. But the majority, like myself, Bobby Stokes, Jimmy Steele, things were different.'[6] Though judging by the stories he tells in his frank autobiography *Fuckin Hell It's Paul Cannell*, Cannell, Steele and goalkeeper Bob Stetler spent a good deal of their time out on the lash, intoxicated to the extreme, and no one at the club seemed unhappy when these escapades were publicized.

At the time, Cannell was clear about his role. Discussing the time his challenge on Cosmos goalkeeper Bob Rigby put the New York player out for the season with a broken collarbone, Cannell said, 'I like to play it rough. It's part of my game. You've got to make things happen out there. I'm out there to stir up something and take advantage of it. It's a challenge to get people to come to the stadium by playing winning soccer as a team. It's my job to be controversial.'[7] Coach Gordon Bradley appeared to be accommodating to the publicity generators. 'I was concerned about Jim [Steele] when I first came to Washington,' he said. This was, after all, a player later described by the *Washington Post* as 'legendary for his capacity for beer'.[8] Bradley had 'heard in England that he liked the fast life a bit, and I wondered about his attitude. But there's been absolutely no problem with him. I found out his attitude towards the club and the game here were terrific.'[9]

There are two explanations for this quote. Either Bradley was prepared to turn a blind eye to Steele's social life because he was an important part of an improving team, or there were enough players leading similar lifestyles that it allowed them all to drink and play without anyone noticing too much. The third possibility is that reports of drinking, drug-taking and womanizing in the NASL were greatly exaggerated,* either by PR folk fostering an unsteady relationship with the truth, or by the perpetrators themselves bragging about their exploits in the time-honoured manner of males seeking approval and attention.

In spite of the distractions, the Diplomats under the corporate leadership of Madison Square Garden chairman Sonny Werblin had their two best seasons on the field in 1979 and 1980, and these years are still remembered fondly by many older DC area soccer fans as a fleeting but heady age of healthy crowds, eventful games and fairly decent results. In that first season, now under an ownership described by Cannell as 'a very professional operation', the English striking triumvirate of Cannell, diminutive and nippy ex-Coventry forward Alan Green, and former Southampton FA Cup winner Bobby Stokes scored 34 goals between them, supported by the huge and enigmatic Hungarian midfielder József Horváth, who registered seven goals and eighteen assists. Home crowds were round about the 10,000–12,000 mark – not high enough for the 20,000 average needed for the team to break even, but several thousand better than in previous years. In the playoffs, though, the team came up against a strong LA Aztecs side led by Johan Cruyff, who, like Pelé, had come out of retirement to play in the NASL. Also like Pelé, no one was quite sure about his real motivation. The player said he wanted to help US soccer. He too, though, had lost a lot of the fortune he'd made

---

* See Chapter 9.

in soccer through ill-advised financial decisions. 'He made a couple of bad investments early in 1979 ... and critics of Cruyff say he decided to play soccer again to make up for those losses,' wrote the *New York Times*. Cruyff himself hinted at such losses and said, 'I am a gambler and in football all along I took risks. The basic reason I came back was my feeling I had to do something in America for soccer.'[10]

Cruyff's impact at LA had been immediate. Rochester's Damir Šutevski was charged with marking the Dutchman when Cruyff made his debut a few games into the 1979 season. 'He played only one half and he scored two goals,' says Šutevski. 'I covered him but I couldn't stop him. He took me to the cleaners.'[11] In fact those two goals came within the game's first seven minutes, even though Cruyff claimed that he hadn't trained for six months. His arrival put a few thousand extra fans on the LA gate, but most home games still only pulled in around 10,000 to the massive Rose Bowl in Pasadena. The by-now-customary exceptions were the 4 July game (over 42,000 came to see the fireworks; Cruyff scored the only goal in a 1–0 win over Atlanta), and the Cosmos, when almost 39,000 were present for a 3–1 defeat. Cruyff played 23 games, scored thirteen goals, and assisted on a further sixteen. Only his Dutch teammate Leo van Veen came close to him on the scoring charts. Midfielder Thomas Rongen conceded that 'Cruyff is two or three levels above the rest of us. But he makes all of us better players.'[12]

Cruyff, reportedly earning £500,000 a year at LA, claimed he was 'saddened' that so many Americans didn't know soccer. 'I feel I owe the game something, and helping to spread the game in the US is the best way I can think of to pay it. I didn't go to the Cosmos because they don't need me. They were worried that their crowds would fall when Pelé retired. But they are still drawing 60,000 to 70,000. So my job is here on the west coast. To try and get the same kind of growth here.' He was happy to escape the long season and the non-stop pressure of the European game in the US, where 'the result is not of such great importance. Obviously you want to do well, but it's not important to win every game. You are trying to show people that soccer can give a lot of enjoyment, so you can take more time to try and entertain them. After the strain of Europe, that's a very nice feeling.'[13]

So Cruyff and LA met the Washington Diplomats in the first round of the post-season, two-leg playoffs. The Aztecs won the first leg at the Rose Bowl, 3–1. The Diplomats' Italian-Canadian midfielder Carmine Marcantonio, who had played in Toronto's championship winning side three years earlier in 1976, takes up the story of the second game:

'I had the pleasure and the duty to mark Cruyff because I was a central midfielder at the time. And I understood his greatness by playing against him. I remember the game we got knocked out, at RFK. I went up for a header at a corner kick, because I was good with my head, the ball was headed out, and Johan was just at the top of the penalty box in his own half. He got the ball, I caught up with him, and I tried to grab his shirt to hold him back, but I couldn't bring him down and I went down and dislocated my finger trying to hold him back. He went upfield with the ball, faked out two or three defenders and scored the winning goal. There's a picture with four of us on the ground and Johan putting the ball in the empty net. And because of that Sonny Werblin went out and signed Cruyff [for DC], and that was one of the best years I had, being teammates with Johan.'[14]

DC infighting: Cruyff vs the coach

> 'It happened at the Cosmos, Cruyff at the Dips,
> Eusebio at Toronto – the nod of approval goes to
> the great player.'
> —Bob Iarusci, Washington Diplomats
> defender, 1979–80[15]

Cruyff signed a three-year, $1.5 million contract with the Diplomats, having not been able to do for soccer on the west coast what Pelé had done for the game in the east. The Aztecs, who had been knocked out of the playoffs in 1979 by Vancouver one round after defeating DC, relieved themselves of Cruyff's burden on the payroll. Wherever Cruyff went, though, dressing-room discontent was sure to follow. The Dutchman disapproved of coach Gordon Bradley's approach to the game, and wasn't shy of showing it.

'Johan – I'll be very polite – at the time, he wasn't a great friend of British football,' says Marcantonio. 'So with a British coach, Gordon Bradley, and a British assistant coach in Joe Mallett, it was a clash of tactics. Johan had played total football with Ajax, and he was the consummate team player if you think about it, while at the same time being one of the greatest individual players ever. That's the school he grew up in. He took more pleasure in assisting and would pass to a teammate to score. He was the ultimate team player.'[16]

American defender Don Droege, an oak of a player who stood out on account of his uncompromising play and a shock of blond hair, played with the Diplomats during 1979 and 1980, and thinks that 'we had a better team in 79 than we did in 80 when Cruyff came. That first year there were a lot of

English players and we had a great camaraderie. I enjoyed that team better.'[17] His teammate Bob Iarusci agrees. 'On the 80 team, because of Johan and his powerful personality, that took a lot of the emphasis away from the dynamics of the team,' he says. 'In 79 we probably should have done better. We liked each other, we didn't have any pricks or problem players.'[18]

Cruyff, says Droege, certainly pissed a lot of players off. 'For me, he didn't piss me off,' he stresses. 'I'm just a lowly American player, and I'm just happy to be out on the field. You can stick me in goal if you want to. But the English players like Alan Green, Bobby Stokes, Jim Steele, Matt Dillon – you bring in a player like Cruyff and the whole dynamics are gone. I think that even Gordon Bradley was sort of afraid of Cruyff. He mixed the team around because MSG was paying money for all these players, so he had to play them, and so that did change the team and we just weren't as good as we had been the year before.' Is there any truth to the story that Cruyff once wiped Bradley's chalkboard clean so that he could give his own tactical talk? Droege laughs. 'I don't remember anything like that, but I do remember talking with Bradley in the bathroom and him checking under the stalls to make sure Cruyff wasn't in there listening to us.'[19]

Iarusci, who had come from the Cosmos to DC for the 1979 season, says that Gordon Bradley made him feel special, and that he joined the Diplomats because MSG was putting 'a whole lot of money into soccer. They went out and got Lozano from Belgium. We had a terrific team, and then the next year Cruyff joined us, and [Dutch midfielder] Wim Jansen. The trouble was that Cruyff and Bradley didn't get along. Cruyff went on television and they asked him why he wasn't play-ing well, because after half a season he only had a handful of assists. Bradley played him on the left side, and Cruyff being the player-coach that he was, he didn't want to say anything to Bradley, but he goes to the press and says, "I'm not playing well because I'm being asked to play on the left side. If the coach would listen to me, I would [play well]." So Gulf & Western [MSG's parent company] had a chat with Gordon and said, "You're a nice guy, but we think you should listen to this player." So Johan went central and in the back half of the season we ended up being the best team in the League, and he won MVP.'[20]

Marcantonio remembers Bradley's assistant, Joe Mallett, as 'a very knowledgeable man – he was instrumental in bringing the two sides together to settle the difference, and there was a compromise. Then the team started doing well, playing good football, we barely made the playoffs. But when Johan turned it on, he was like Messi today, the things I've seen him do. He was still very fit. Eusebio had had five operations on one knee. Eusebio was a team guy – he would call me and tell me to come to his room to play poker, he was one of the guys. Johan was more business-like, he didn't mingle much with the guys. Don't get me wrong – he would have dinner with us, but he was very professional, and when he was on his own he didn't spend too much time with us.'

The player also admits that when it came to the negotiations, 'I think Gordon had no choice. In 1980 Gordon's neck was on the block. And because Johan was such a big signing, it was to the advantage of both to start playing the same way. There was a change in tactics, we became more of a team, so you could say it was the two of them compromising and coming together. They didn't like each other, let's face it, they had different philosophies about football. There was even talk that Rinus Michels might come to Washington, so it was in Gordon's interest to change and get Johan on board, because Johan was the key man.'

On the field, says Marcantonio, Cruyff was a great professional who 'orchestrated the whole thing. Like any great player, he didn't shut up, Pelé was the same. Johan was very domineering. When it came to football he only knew one way, and that was his way – total football. He was a great individual in that he almost wanted to run the show on the field, but he wanted it done in a team concept.' Tension in the dressing room resulted from the fact that 'some of the British guys didn't like that Johan was such a big personality'.[21]

When the Cosmos came to RFK Stadium on 1 June 1980, the Diplomats had won only three of their first nine games, and Cruyff was yet to score. It was a Sunday afternoon game because of a live ABC broadcast, played in 95 degrees with that special level of intense humidity so enjoyed in summer by the DC residents who have no way of fleeing across the Chesapeake Bay for the coast. In spite of all these negatives, a record DC soccer crowd of 53,351 showed up – again, a genuine sign that the potential market was there. This was before Bradley and Cruyff had reached their 'compromise' (that is, the agreement to do things Cruyff's way), and all the tensions on the team were aired for the nation to see.

The game's first few seconds were remarkable. Cruyff received the ball straight from the kick-off and, with a sweeping left-foot pass, played the ball 40 yards with one touch into space on the right wing, where Sonny Askew took the ball, ran in on goal, and almost scored within moments of the starting whistle. It's as though Cruyff wanted to effortlessly make clear to Bradley what he was capable of when standing in the middle of the park. He then dropped to the left, where he was supposed to be playing, and within two minutes had beaten three men in the Cosmos penalty area before being tackled and winning a corner. It was in the centre, though, where he was most effective. He scored with a header directly from a corner kick, but the goal was belatedly disallowed when Alan Green was given offside. Cruyff told the referee, at some length, how much he disagreed with this verdict, while Green was in fact caught offside several times in the first half because he, Cruyff and Jansen were misreading each other. To show the English striker how it should be done, Cruyff again adopted a central position after 27 minutes and timed a run to put himself clean through on goal. He rounded the Cosmos goalkeeper Hubert Birkenmeier, but his shot was cleared off the line by Jeff Durgan. Just before half time he was finally booked for dissent, and then shortly afterwards escaped a clear second yellow when he took out Cosmos defender Andranik Eskandarian. The old NASL story: special dispensation for the world star.

At half time, Cruyff left the game with a knee injury, but his afternoon was far from over. The Dips had taken a 1–0 lead in the first half through an Iarusci penalty, but by the time Cruyff was interviewed by touchline reporter Verne Lundqvist during the second half, the Cosmos had equalized through a Giorgio Chinaglia header. Cruyff told Lundqvist that the referee should not have cancelled his headed goal (even though Green was clearly offside and obstructing the goalkeeper's view), and that the Dips should have had two additional penalties. This is no tendentious analysis – you look at Cruyff and you know he thinks that he is absolutely right.

As the game went on, and Lundqvist reported that the temperature on the field was 105 degrees, the play became slower and sloppier, and tempers started to fray. Droege and Johan Neeskens got in a brawl following a tussle at a corner kick, but neither player was booked when really both should have been ordered off. Marcantonio received a yellow card for a spectacular professional foul on the Cosmos' Vladislav Bogićević – he had to dive to pull Bogi's shirt and bring him down. Watching the tape, the Diplomats' József Horváth looks like an immensely gifted player, but was also utterly out of control, constantly fouling opponents, retaliating to fouls on himself, and remonstrating to anyone within hearing distance. In short, the Diplomats looked like a half-formed project with some core talent but no discipline whatsoever. Finally, it all imploded. Three minutes before the end, Alan Green had a goal disallowed for a clear foul by Ken Mokgojoa on Jeff Durgan – the former charged the latter from behind just as he was about to clear the ball off the line. It was the linesman Gordon Arrowsmith who made the call, and he was confronted by a bare-chested madman who rushed over and pushed him twice – at first glance it seems like a spectator, but it turned out to be Horváth, running from the substitute's bench having been replaced a few minutes earlier. Cruyff was there too, going nuts, and both he and Horváth were red-carded at last. Their fine example prompted a spectator to lob a rock from the crowd, which hit Arrowsmith and knocked him down again. The TV commentators Jim McKay and Paul Gardner muttered about English-style hooliganism, and how they had never seen any such thing at an NASL game.

The referee Toros Kibritjian finally restored order, a dazed Arrowsmith was checked for concussion and managed to continue, and after a goalless extra-time period the Cosmos won the shootout, when the players were clearly too exhausted to perform – only one of the ten attempts was converted. At the end, a spectator jumped on to the field and attempted to assault Durgan. Kibritjian tells the *Washington Post* that he gave Cruyff a second yellow, after having shown the red card to Horváth, because the Dutchman was 'using abusive language and inciting the other players. I gave him all the rope I could because of his stature. When he didn't stop, I gave him the card.'[22]

The Diplomats' tally for the afternoon: two red cards, one player assaulting a linesman, constant rough play and on-field dissent and brawling, and two incidents of serious spectator violence. Oh, and a seventh loss in ten games. The team was angry at the defeat, but they blamed it all on the match officials for disallowing their two 'goals'. That aside, they were full of praise – for themselves. Team president Danzansky said that 'as far as we all are concerned, we won this game 3–1'. The *Post*'s reporter Dave Kindred weighed in with his own comment: 'The Diplomats lost, yes, but they won more than they lost.' Cruyff called the crowd 'fantastic' and Iarusci, who had also confronted the linesman after the disallowed goal, said the full stadium meant 'my adrenalin was going all game'. To top it all, the club's PR director Jim Trecker called it 'the greatest day in our history'.[23] The team appealed the result, unsuccessfully, and Horváth was given a paltry two-match ban.

This extraordinary game tells us many things about the Diplomats' interpretation of the need to entertain. Only in Washington DC could you lose in such an ungracious, unsporting and quite frankly disgraceful manner, and then with the skilful mendacity of a politician spin the whole sorry event as the greatest day in the team's history. The huge crowd and the incident-packed game were used to cover up the fact that the team was borderline psycho, and lacking any coherent leadership. Not even the media was picking up on this, but it's significant that this game took place just before Cruyff's takeover, and his own renaissance as a player in the NASL. His knee injury meant that he missed the next four games after the loss to the Cosmos, including a 5–2 hammering in Chicago. Once he was allowed to resume his preferred central role, however, the team won thirteen out of its final nineteen games. Cruyff scored ten goals – including the NASL's Goal of the Season for a crunching, left-footed finish against Seattle following an explosive run from the halfway line that took him past four helpless opponents – and assisted on twenty. Alan Green scored 25 and was the beneficiary of Cruyff's impeccable team play. He may have been blind when it came to disputing a referee's decisions, but in this basic tactical change Cruyff was conclusively proven right. Not that it should have taken a genius to see that when you have a player like Cruyff on your hands, it's a good idea to let him control the play from the middle of the park and dominate the game.

'We had a good run and turned it around,' says Marcantonio, 'so when he was fit again and the tactics changed, things started clicking.' The team made the playoffs, but for the second year running were beaten by the Aztecs over two games, although this time it was much closer. 'I don't think we got outplayed in LA,' Marcantonio adds. 'We came pretty close to taking it all the way.'[24]

Not close enough for MSG. Although home crowds at RFK by the year's end were now regularly above 20,000, the team was still not making any money. Werblin and MSG wanted the NASL to contract to 20 teams from 24 – they felt that the weaker teams run by clueless businessmen were dragging the

League down. 'Sonny Werblin and Gulf & Western wanted to consolidate in 1980,' remembers Marcantonio, by then in his third year with the team. 'He wanted the League to weed out the weaker franchises and lose some of the teams. But Woosnam and the League wanted none of it, so Werblin pulled out.'[25] In fact at a meeting of League executives their proposal to shrink the NASL attracted a majority of support, but it needed a unanimous vote to pass, and the weaker owners weren't going to vote for their own execution.[26] So, having lost $2 million in two years, MSG pulled the plug on the Diplomats and returned its certificate of ownership. 'When a well-heeled, corporate-backed club in a prestigious city decides to fold, that's trouble,' remarked *Sports Illustrated*.[27] It quoted Werblin as saying the reasons were 'the recession, bigger operating expenses, and a geometrical leap in acquisition costs and salaries for players'. Paying Cruyff half a million per season had helped add 7,000 to the Diplomats' average gate, and eventually turned the team into contenders on the field. Yet when the sums were done, following the Cosmos model hadn't worked.

Jimmy Hill to the rescue!

In British school playgrounds during the 1970s, there was a special way of telling your classmates that you didn't wholly believe the claim that Bobby Charlton was their uncle, or that they'd seen Brigitte Bardot while shopping in Woolworths. You would stick out your chin, stroke an imaginary beard, and repeat the mantra 'Jimmy Hill, Jimmy Hill'. Eventually the words became superfluous, and the merest tickle of a slightly jutted jawbone would be the standard method of expressing scepticism. The former professional football player and manager turned club owner and television pundit, who could be seen every Saturday night pontificating about the ills of soccer on BBC1's *Match of the Day*, had become the symbol for all untruths, exaggerations and fanciful ideas.

Making Hill synonymous with bullshit was partially unfair, even if he came across on TV as hectoring, righteous, dogmatic and stern. In the late 1950s, as the chairman of the Professional Footballers' Association, he had successfully campaigned for the abolition of the maximum weekly wage of £20. In this respect he did more to usher English soccer into the modern age than any other individual, and as the manager of Coventry City in the 1960s he was also ahead of his time, 'rebranding' the team as the Sky Blues by changing their kit colour, presumably without the aid of a marketing consultancy and a PR firm. Hill expanded the club match programme to be more than just a team sheet, co-composed a club song, and introduced pre-match entertainment to get people into the stadium early. In themselves, these were not all necessarily *good* things (especially the club song – a variation on the Eton Boating Song – but then whoever composed an artistically acceptable club anthem?), but at least he was thinking things through and challenging the game's innate conservative core. As the same club's chairman in the 1970s, Hill advocated all-seater stadiums long before they became compulsory – Coventry's Highfield Road stadium became all-seater in 1981, the first in England to do so, although fans bemoaned a lack of atmosphere and eventually some of the seats were taken back out to create a standing area. On television, he regularly railed against hooliganism and the offside law, and many other things besides. Hill was strident and opinionated, and didn't give a shit what anybody thought about him. He could be funny and outrageous, and downright wrong, which was why he became the playground's object of derision, and his chin a symbol for perceived mendacity. He also had absolutely no qualms about making money, and that's how Hill and his son Duncan came to be involved in the NASL.

Hill had set up a company in the 1970s, World Sports Academy, that acted as a soccer advisor to Saudia Arabia, and over three years he and Duncan made a good deal of cash out of the oil-rich monarchy. Given his vision and reputation for innovation, Hill saw the US as a proving ground for the game's future, and that was where he decided to invest much of the profit he'd made in the Middle East. World Sports Academy bought into the Detroit Express in 1978 and made Trevor Francis its marquee player, on loan from England. Just as the Diplomats did with Cruyff in 1980, the Express used Francis to lure in the crowds and lead the team in scoring. It worked, up to a point – in 1978 and 1979, Francis was the team's leading scorer and the team built up a reasonable fan base.* In 1980, without Francis, a team of mainly British journeymen and the bare minimum of US players performed badly and crowds dropped. With the Express losing money, and the Diplomats leaving DC vacant, the Hills decided to move their franchise to the nation's capital instead where, like commissioner Phil Woosnam, they were convinced that the potential soccer market was much more lucrative in the long term. 'Washington is especially important to us internationally,' Woosnam said towards the end of the 1980 season, but before MSG had pulled out. 'I think the city has proven that

---

* See Chapter 5.

it is an excellent soccer city. I can't ever imagine us not having a team in Washington.'[28]

Former Diplomats striker Paul Cannell had been on his travels since leaving DC in 1979, playing in Tulsa and then Memphis, a team which moved to freezing Calgary to play in the middle of winter in the indoor league that had by now been established to try and keep income generated – and fans interested – all year round. 'I fucking hated Calgary,' he says. 'Oh my God. So I was dying to get away from there. I couldn't understand why Detroit suddenly wanted to sign me for their indoor season, which wasn't my kind of game at all – I was good in the air and all that. But even Detroit's a bit warmer than Calgary, so I went to Detroit and played about five or six indoor games. Then all of a sudden, out of the blue, MSG had given up the Dips, and lo and behold the Hills came up with the idea to move the Express to DC. And that's when I thought this must have been planned in advance. The contract I'd signed in Memphis came with me to Calgary, but I signed a new four-year contract with the Express. I thought this was great, moving back to DC, which I loved. I was suspicious, but I was more happy than suspicious because I was going to DC. So we relocated and I was held up as the pin-up boy because I was well known there already. But even as the season got under way there were strange goings on, players coming and going.'[29]

Cannell was indeed the Diplomats' new poster boy, as the entire 1980 Washington team had upped and left when MSG dropped out – they either returned to their home countries or became free agents and were picked up by other NASL teams. Initially, Detroit's move to DC was greeted with enthusiasm by local fans who had been heartbroken to see the team's previous incarnation pull out of the city. The Diplomats, while losing money for their parent company, had become very popular under MSG – not just because they were very good, but because they had, like so many NASL teams, been active in the community and continued the work of the Whips and the Darts in building what is still a massive youth soccer movement in the greater DC area. If anyone knew about serious debts left behind in Detroit, they kept quiet about it, and that included Woosnam and the League.

In early 1981, the Hills came to DC dropping all the right quotes about steady management and staying in town for the long term. 'I know we would never fold if we drew 19,000 a game,' said Duncan Hill, citing the previous year's average crowd. 'We're looking for stability, and the way to achieve stability is not to lose $3 million a year.'[30] Jimmy also aimed a shot at the previous owners. 'Unlike our predecessors, we don't want to flash for one, or for two years. We want to be a permanent part of this community.'[31] For anyone reading between the lines, though, there were already warning signs. 'We feel, as does the League membership, that Washington is an excellent soccer city,' said Duncan. 'That was proven last year by the Diplomats. We don't expect to draw the way they did because that was the result of months of planning and an excellent marketing effort. We've only got six weeks until opening day, so we can't expect those kinds of results.'[32] In another interview, Duncan spoke of how 'we pulled off a great coup in moving to Washington', but admitted that 'my weakness is that I don't yet understand the Washington area. And I'm trying to learn some marketing techniques.'[33]

As mentioned, Cannell was pushed as the team's face in the absence of the previous year's stars. A few of Detroit's British players like goalkeeper Jim Brown and former Sheffield United midfielder David Bradford had been shipped with the team to DC, while their promising Argentine youngster Pato Margetic had been sold by the Hills to Chicago for $200,000. There were, however, few names besides Cannell's that were familiar to the DC soccer-going public. 'He's dramatic, exciting and a good player, but some of the things he says really are what set him apart,' enthused Hill Jr. 'What did he say about playing in Calgary? "The weather was cold, and so were the women." Well, that's perfect. He's a character, but he rubs off well on others. People like him, he's infectious. He generates a good atmosphere.'[34] Cannell, though, was already unhappy in pre-season with the way that the team was being run. 'It was shambolic,' he says. Duncan was purportedly running the team as general manager, 'but you knew Jimmy was the one pulling the strings. At the end of the indoor season [in Detroit], before we moved to DC, we went on an end-of-season tour, and that's supposed to be a treat for the players. Normally you just relax, but they took us to Guatemala. We flew in – even the flight was dubious – we stayed in what was supposed to be a five-star hotel, but you could see five stars through the roof, it was atrocious.' When the 1981 season started, 'there was always a problem with the wages, there were always rumours about finances and stuff like that. There was a piece in the paper about Trevor Francis being owed a lot of money by them. Jimmy Hill would always come in and say it was a load of rubbish.'[35]

Nonetheless, the new Diplomats started the season well, and by the time the Cosmos came to town in late May, DC had won six of their first nine games. The downside was the attendance – Cannell alone wasn't enough to draw more than half of the previous season's average. A dramatic 3–2 win over the Cosmos, though, in front of almost 28,000 fans, was seen as the breakthrough game. 'Dips Can't Be Blamed for a Little Hyperbole' was the match report headline in the *Washington Post*, with Duncan Hill excitedly comparing the team's three first half goals to 'the second world war, with Patton leading the onslaught with his tanks'. *Post* reporter Ken Denlinger labelled the game 'a legitimate franchise saver', because the Dips had needed, and got, something 'mildly miraculous'. Phil Woosnam, who had attended the game, was described as 'ecstatic'. The only bum note came from the Dips' David Bradford, who observed of an opponent now shorn of all its household names bar Chinaglia, 'These aren't the Cosmos of old, are they?'[36]

Neither were these the Dips of old. Despite the unprecedented privilege of having a second home game against the Cosmos the following month, which pulled in almost 37,000 (a quirk of the fixture list, or blatant favouritism to help out the League's most consistent basket case?), the team began to fail, crowds remained stubbornly in four figures, and reports began to emerge of debts still outstanding in Detroit, as well as the now-tight budget in DC. In early June, Duncan Hill pointed out that, to the free-spending MSG, the Dips had been 'little more than a tax write-off', but now 'not one dollar is spent without thought, and there is a limit to the number of dollars available'. He admitted that the team should have tried to sign old favourites like Alan Green and József Horváth, who had moved to Jacksonville and San Jose respectively, but said that signing a star name like Trevor Francis or Kevin Keegan was unfeasible. Three of the players – Trevor Hebberd, Malcolm Waldron and Ross Jenkins – were only on loan from Coventry City, where Jimmy Hill was chairman, and would cost a transfer fee if they were to be retained permanently.[37]

Then later that month, having said they wouldn't be signing any stars, the Dips brought back Cruyff, who had been playing for Levante in the Spanish second division. 'I realized I enjoyed last season so much ... I really missed Washington DC,' Cruyff said. He dismissed talk of tension in the team due to his personality. 'I don't think there will be any trouble. Last year's team didn't have any problems during the last half of the season.' Jimmy Hill said Cruyff's salary was much lower then the previous year's,[38] but regardless of the amount involved, it was yet another mis-step. Cruyff barely played because he was injured (five appearances, two goals), and the Hills filed a complaint with the players' union saying they wanted some of their $175,000 back from Cruyff because he had misrepresented his fitness level.

In July, Jimmy Hill had to deny that he'd said he was selling the team, but his minority partner Gary Lemmen, a holdover from the team's Detroit days, told the *Post*, 'We would consider selling the whole thing if the price is right. I would definitely look at selling my 28%. But right now, we just need more investors.' Jimmy understood that 'some of the players are upset. I didn't *ever* say we'd outright sell the team. There isn't enough money on the table for us to consider that.'[39] However, should enough money come along ... Meanwhile, the team's public face, Cannell, had shown the public his discontent. 'This season? It's a joke,' he said. 'The people of Washington are the best. They deserve better and I just needed to say it.' Coach Ken Furphy had accused Cannell of not trying hard enough in practice. 'Hell, I'm 27 years old. I'm not going to run like a bull and kick people in the shins on that cabbage patch we practice on.'[40]

As the team's form worsened, so did the reports about

its financial status. In early August, more details came from Detroit about the money still owed in the city. Deferred back rent on the team's stadium, the Pontiac Silverdome, was overdue, while Express staff who had been promised severance payments had received nothing. Cannell tells a typical story of how the club was being run when he was told that the players were no longer insured against injury. 'I was the club captain and the players' union rep,' he says. 'So I thought *Bloody hell*. I pulled the players together and told them the situation. Ken Furphy comes down and says, "Are you causing trouble, Cannell?" I said we weren't insured and he said, "Don't be so bloody stupid." The Hills came down and said to me, yes, there have been a few problems, but don't worry, if anyone gets injured, we'll look after them. There were six or seven of us who refused to play, but the American kids filled in. Then a few weeks after that, pay wasn't going in, the players' union was trying to get hold of them [the Hills] but couldn't find them. And eventually we just didn't get paid and they disappeared.'[41]

New investors were sought, but the most promising lead – Andrew Mellon – backed out when he calculated the overall instability of the League. And so the Diplomats went bust once and for all and the Hills returned to England, their failed franchises leaving behind several hundred thousand dollars' worth of debts (newspaper reports from the time vary as to the exact amount, some put it at almost $2 million). Even before the team sank, the *Washington Post* had finally started quoting, albeit retrospectively, people who'd said the move from Detroit had been a mistake. Clive Toye had said back in May, 'I am sick and tired of our franchises chasing around the bloody country looking for stadiums in which to alight. There aren't many cities left for us to befoul.' Former Diplomats' general manager Andy Dolich had said when the Detroit-to-DC deal was done, 'That's the worst thing that could possibly happen to soccer in Washington. They're going to kill the market for the future.' A Diplomats marketing assistant, Diana Mergen, told the *Washington Post* that 'the budget absolutely hurt our sales and marketing efforts. We couldn't even get basic information out to the public. We advertised Johan so much, but he couldn't play. When he finally could play, it was like crying wolf. It didn't sink in.' Larry Dunn, a season ticket holder whose company had 25 season tickets, claimed that they had offered sales and marketing help to Duncan Hill several times. 'But he never responded.'[42]

Woosnam admitted that it was 'embarrassing for us and it's too bad for Washington' that the Hills had left the country without telling anyone.[43] Pay was owed to players and office staff, not to mention numerous local businesses. From the safety of old England, Jimmy Hill referred all questions to Duncan and he, according to the *Washington Post*, evaded all direct questions during an interview, blaming 'two very rich people' who had promised to invest in the Diplomats for backing out. 'That's why we moved to Washington in the first place,' he claimed. 'Let's face it. We were about $15 million underfinanced. It takes an awful lot of money to launch a soccer team.' He declared himself 'very, very disappointed', but 'not bitter. You learn something from every experience. In this case, no one has benefitted; everyone's lost out.' Though not everyone upped and left leaving behind a ream of unpaid bills and broken promises ('Everyone will be paid,' Duncan had pledged, 'whoever it is.').[44] Jimmy, meanwhile, continued his career as a TV pundit. No one in the UK cared that he had overseen the extinction of two soccer teams – that was far away in stupid America, after all. 'Mr. Hill is a private individual and the matter has nothing whatsoever to do with us,' said a spokesman for the English FA.[45] In December, Hill confessed to Coventry City FC's annual meeting that the team had lost £600,000 thanks to his investments in the Express and the Diplomats. 'It was an investment to improve Coventry's finances,' Hill told the meeting, 'but it did not pay off. It was not to make me any richer. In fact my loss is worse than the club's, but I don't see why we should cry. Coventry City's future is too big for us to worry about last year.' The reaction? He was unanimously voted back in as club chairman 'without being questioned about his American connections'.[46]

The Hills were no exception in being investors who lost money in the NASL, of course, but the manner in which they operated seems to have been particularly amateurish and slapdash, and their treatment of the people who worked for them shabby at best. While Jimmy seamlessly continued his TV work and involvement in English club football, whatever happened to Duncan? If you guessed 'used car salesman', go to the top of the business class. With brother Graham, he started a second-hand automobile business in south London that went under in the 1990s owing £842,000. Six former employees sued not only the brothers, but dad Jimmy too, because his name was on the company's headed notepaper. Jimmy professed ignorance, even though he had invested several thousand pounds in the firm. 'I know absolutely nothing about cars,' he told an industrial tribunal seeking restitution for the unpaid former employees. 'I do know how to drive one, but I have neither the interest, time or desire to become involved in the business.'[47]

It could be that he was telling the truth. It could also be

that, while reading his claim, former schoolboys of the 1970s find their right hand moving irresistibly towards their chin, fingers stroking a well-trimmed but imaginary beard.

4. Team America, 1983

> 'We are ready. We have the players. What we're talking about today is an historic new beginning.'
> —NASL Commissioner Howard Samuels on the world-conquering, bionic new Team America.[48]

You thought we were done with Washington DC? Not so fast. Yes, that was effectively four teams, but we'll be generous and count the Diplomats and their serial owners as one franchise, even though the 1981 operation was moved lock, stock and barrel from Detroit, debts and all. Former Dips' coach Gordon Bradley tried to raise funds from area fans for a new team in 1982, but could only muster a few thousand dollars. Not because there was no enthusiasm for soccer in the city; there was just no enthusiasm for seeing more money drained by a badly run professional team. Given the number of cities now dropping out of the NASL, few investors, either large or small, could be convinced that they would ever see any return. Still, even in 1982 League sources were still being quoted as saying that they would love a franchise to return to Washington because 'it's one of maybe five cities where we've had real success. But it's still the same problem – finding a legitimate investor.' If the League's definition of 'real success' was a city that had chewed up and spat out multiple loss-making teams and owners, it becomes increasingly clear why, by this point, the NASL's days were coming to a close.

Not before one final failure. Team America, sounding like a SWAT squad helicoptered in to blast down the bad guys and save the day (what a shame the Hills had long since fled town), brought soccer back to Washington in 1983. The idea was progressive, and in principle not a bad one at all. The US national team would play in the NASL regular season just like any other club, in order to help the players gel and prepare for qualification for the 1986 World Cup. It was backed by the League and the USSF and the money of Bob Lifton, who admitted that he knew nothing about the sport – just the sort of investor the League needed by now. Unfortunately, it was not backed by all the teams, many of whom did not want to let their best American players leave. By this point, clubs were obliged to field at least three US players, a rule that existed, as it had done from its introduction, in the interests of advancing the home cause and developing native talent. Why should they give up their strongest Americans and place themselves at a competitive disadvantage?

This being the NASL, there was some convenient bending of the definition of 'American'. So as well as a few established US internationals like Jeff Durgan and Arnie Mausser, there were a number of naturalized English-Americans such as goalkeeper Paul Hammond, striker Alan Green (you'll recall how the Hills regretted not signing him – now Team America lured him in with a passport), and former Minnesota defender Alan Merrick. They were joined by other staunch US patriots from Italy, South Africa, Yugoslavia, Costa Rica and Ecuador. The Cosmos, though, never known for caring about any team besides themselves, refused to relinquish their three talented US players, midfielders Ricky Davis and Angelo DiBernardo, and forward Steve Moyers. Seattle held on to striker Mark

Peterson and San Diego did likewise with forward Hugo Perez – little wonder that scoring goals was one of Team America's biggest problems.

'We were kind of doing alright,' says Arnie Mausser of the team. 'Some of the teams were keen to be part of it, some of the teams weren't. A lot of players didn't take to its philosophy and a lot of clubs didn't want to let players like Ricky Davies of the Cosmos go. Ricky would come to the national team games, but during the club season he'd be playing for the Cosmos. We had a problem scoring; we were tough defensively, but creating attacking players has always been a problem in the US.' Indeed, Team America quickly developed the same reputation as some previous Washington teams – they were rough. After losing 2–1 at RFK early in the season, the San Diego Sockers president Jack Daley labelled them Team Animal and called defender Jeff Durgan 'just a hatchet man for those butchers'.[49] Durgan, though, was one of the few star attractions, and TA marketed his physical reputation and punky haircut. A red-card suspension he was supposed to serve against the Cosmos was lifted by the League so that he could appear against his old club. Team America won the game in front of 31,000 fans, and as was now customary, the large crowd gave rise to hopes that the franchise had 'arrived'. Beckenbauer was back for New York, and obligingly scored in his own net to give TA their only open-play goal of the day. For journalist Paul Gardner, though, Durgan represented everything that was wrong with the development of US players.

Hardly any of the US players were good enough for the NASL, he reckons. 'And you saw that when they created Team USA. They wanted to get the best American players from around the League. Jeff Durgan was the best example. He came straight from high school, this great big clunky lad, and they put him on the back four at the Cosmos with Beckenbauer and Carlos Alberto – yeah, he looked good. But at Team America with his teammates from various teams he looked fucking terrible, and that was true of so many of the American players. They weren't good enough. The standard went down even more, and they saved money, and it contributed to the ultimate demise of the League, although it wasn't the cause.'[50]

By contrast, Alan Merrick calls the talent pool on Team America 'exceptionally good'. Merrick not only played for Team America, but won a single cap in the one international that the US played that year, against Haiti. He says that the team's rough reputation may have come from the treatment they dealt out to players who hadn't signed up for the cause. 'I must admit that when we played the Cosmos, Ricky Davis got "special treatment",' he says, laughing. 'Ricky's a good guy, and the resentment was short-lived – it was short-sightedness in some instances, and over-exuberance by some of the younger players. They felt a little bit cheated by not having all of their compatriots with them, but it wasn't that bad at all.' Merrick himself understood why a player like Davis would stay with the Cosmos. 'He was learning lessons from all of the great players they had, so you could make some exceptions to several of those players.'

Merrick's quibble was more with the appointment of Greek-American Alki Panagoulias as coach. Team America, he says, 'was a very good concept, but I was not particularly enamoured by the coaching selection. The USSF was in total disarray at that point. They were going through growing pains and hadn't put people in place who'd had worldwide experience of the game. They had administrators and personnel making decisions that were way above their heads.'

After a reasonable enough start, winning eight of their first thirteen games, form slumped and they won only two of their final seventeen fixtures, finishing bottom of the Southern Division. A defender, Dan Canter, was second top scorer with five goals. 'We caught a lot of teams by surprise who thought they were just playing a bunch of players who'd been thrown together,' says Merrick, 'but we organized ourselves pretty well initially, and had some great leadership from within the playing staff. Then there were some power struggles – I know that I was chastised for giving my opinions. The conversation [with Panagoulias] was: "Cease and desist. You're undermining my coaching ability." Although I was trying to supplement it, and also assist, because we'd only got a short time to get things right. It's very difficult to put a team on the field when the majority of your practices were playing head-throw-catch. He tried his best, but he was lacking.'[51]

The season had its moments of surreal farce and hokey patriotism. In spring the team went to the White House and met President Ronald Reagan in the Rose Garden, presenting him with an autographed team ball and a jacket that said 'Commander In Chief Team America' on the front. Reagan was either confused or badly briefed, because according to archives on the website 'The American Presidency Project', he told the players, 'We're very proud and happy to have this team and to be represented for the first time in the World Cup.'

The goal of qualifying for Mexico '86 was seen as another possible way of saving the League, but it was never attained. During the season, the team's soccer-ignorant benefactor Bob Lifton – who had started out by declaring that he loved to watch soccer for the sight of 'all those bodies spewing about the field'[52] (he was clearly not a man who liked to get too technical) – started to get pissed off. He wanted the best US players, or he'd quit backing the team. As a compromise, he was prepared to scrap a planned world tour during the off-season to allow players to return to their original clubs for the indoor season. Commissioner Samuels at the same time opted to get tough, and threatened to fine clubs who didn't give up their US players for Team America. In the end, though, all threats and compromises were immaterial.

'We'd only played one international match during that period [the 1983 season],' says Merrick, 'which was when I got my cap, and then at the end of the season we thought, "This is great. We're going to South America, to Europe, and we're going to play as the US national team, and the Olympic team in training." And we were going to bring in some of the other guys who hadn't joined us for the domestic year, like Ricky Davis and a couple of other players. That would have really bolstered the squad that we had, and put us on a very, very good road to producing some good results and turning some heads. But the doors were just completely slammed. It was right at the end of the season. "Here's your last pay cheque, bye bye." We had an hour's notice, and we were in the office, and we were told the doors would be shutting as soon as we'd left, never to be opened again. Take some souvenirs and walk out on to the street, I think it was just down from the White House. So we walked out, waved to Reagan, and said, boy oh boy, that was a short and sweet visit to the capital city.'[53]

Bruce Wilson points out how so many Canadian players being on teams like Vancouver and Toronto for long periods of time helped the Canadian national team. 'Looking back,' he says, 'the success we had in Canada – qualifying for the 84 Olympics and the 86 World Cup – that was due directly to us being able to play in a high profile pro league for ten to twelve years.'[54] Clive Toye, who was Toronto Blizzard GM in the early 1980s, agrees. 'What I really enjoyed about Toronto,' he says, 'apart from the fact you could get Cuban cigars there, was that we were really able to show that Canadian players could do it. We were helping produce some bloody good players.'[55]

Bearing that in mind, it seems like the grand but curtailed idea of Team America was another missed opportunity for US soccer. 'Oh yes, big time,' Merrick agrees. 'That shows the infancy of the game, and also some of the shortcomings of the Federation, and also the League, not realizing how good it was. It was hands-off management, because they'd given it to an individual [Panagoulias]. They didn't nurture it enough.' His view of the players' abilities is the direct opposite of Gardner's. 'There were players on that squad who could have gone into the English First Division, or into today's Premier League. There were seasoned players who had lots and lots of skill, physical attributes that were sometimes unmatched by European athletes, and all they needed was an opportunity and a format that allowed them to gain that credibility.'[56]

In the end, Lifton pulled out because of the old Washington problem – when the team started losing, gates dropped, although the dispute over the release of the best US players certainly didn't help. The team's final game at home to Fort Lauderdale was played in front of just 6,718 fans, and in previous games the attendance had dropped as low as 4,300. Right here on the President's doorstep, it seemed there was a perfect example of the failure of Reagan's much-espoused trickle-down economics. Those at the bottom couldn't be sustained by droplets from the top – instead, they were shut out and shut down.

Season-by-season overview

1979

The **Whitecaps** broke the Cosmos' domination in the second 24-team season, where the only changes were Colorado's move to Atlanta, and Oakland's to Edmonton, where they became the Drillers – *the* soccer team of choice for dentists and road workers across North America. Another network TV deal, another false dawn – a two-year contract with ABC provided for nine live broadcasts per season, including Soccer Bowl, but ratings were again too low and in the contract's second year only the final was broadcast. Average gates went up by 1,000 per game, though, to around 14,200.

Fun facts: Detroit's coach Ken Furphy signed up his own son, Keith, who'd failed to make the grade at Wealdstone, and that led to mutterings of nepotism. Keith scored fourteen goals and registered eight assists, second only to Trevor Francis on the team. 'The coach played his own son, which I didn't like,' says Steve David on why he left the team. But 'his son turned out to be a great player, and I apologized to him afterwards because I'd made a comment that the coach's son shouldn't be on the team.'[57] This season several players made their sole career NASL appearances on 14 April, the day of a players' strike. Hail the strike-breaking one-game wonders, many of whom were mysteriously called Joe: like Joe Salsamendi (Fort Lauderdale), Joe Porto and Joe Palumbo (New England), José Boyarizo (Memphis). Or the impressively named Fausto Foresto (Rochester). The Tulsa Roughnecks on a post-season tour of England yielded possibly the worst ever result for an NASL team abroad – a 9–2 defeat at the hands of mighty Lincoln City.

1980

Still 24 teams. No moves, no changes – stability! The playoffs were drawn out to a total of 29 games (only eight of the 24 teams didn't make the cut), after a 32-game regular season – all that just for the **Cosmos** to win again, 3–0 over Fort Lauderdale. Crowds averaged an all-time high of almost 14,500.

Fun facts: A team for once came close to outscoring the Cosmos in the regular season – the Chicago Sting netted 77 goals in open play to the Cosmos' 83. German striker Karl-Heinz Granitza, one of the League's least-loved personalities, scored 20, and his compatriot Arno Steffenhagen chipped in with sixteen from midfield. Granitza 'could hit the ball as hard as anyone I've ever seen', remembers Bruce Wilson. 'He was an asshole,' says Don Droege. 'I didn't like him at all. He was one of those guys who I thought treated the American players like a piece of shit.' Granitza, says Derek Spalding, 'could demoralize younger players. I knew how to handle the guy. He watched who he gave it to. He scored goals, no question, he was prolific, but if he went after you and you turned round and snapped back at him, he didn't like that.' Tim Twellman puts a more positive spin on the character of a man who was the League's third-placed all-time goalscorer (128 goals): 'He demanded perfection, which helped you play better.'[58] But it was rarely back to Karl-Heinz's place after practice for beer, bratwurst and a thigh-slapping sing-along.

9 Myths and memories: The Cosmos, the Fury and the rock 'n' roll lifestyle

'A lot of footballers are frustrated rock stars and
I think it works in reverse; a lot of rock stars are
frustrated footballers.'

—Frank Worthington

The stadium rock concerts of the 1970s had a lot in common
with NASL games. A young, mixed audience in celebratory
mood was there to socialize for the whole night in a huge arena
built to allow for noise, movement, drinking and smoking. The
team, or the band, were not necessarily the main event, because
going out on a Saturday night *was* the event. That the Beach
Boys played a number of double-headers with soccer teams in
50,000-seat stadiums was no surprise, and it did wonders for
the League's attendance averages. *Kick* magazine interviewed
Mike Love and asked him about the parallels between a soccer
player and a rock performer. 'In music nobody gets hurt,' he
said. 'By and large, you play a concert, people like it, they go
home happy, and there's no winner and loser. Everybody's a
winner.' Unless, like Rick Wakeman, you cross the path from
musician to investor and decide to put some of your winnings
in the NASL.

Yes keyboardist and prog-rocker Wakeman – whose band
you either deified for their epic compositions or vilified for
their self-indulgent tedium – was part of a group of people
connected with the music industry who decided to invest their

hard-earned royalties and commissions in the Philadelphia Fury in 1978. Paul Simon, Peter Frampton, music agent Frank Barsalona and Rolling Stones tour manager Peter Rudge were the others. Mick Jagger was reportedly on the verge of becoming part of the group until he was quite sensibly advised that the League was not a financially sound proposition – and this in a period when soccer was being widely touted by its league as the sport of the future. Wakeman, who had always been a huge soccer fan, tells the story of the Fury's inaugural game in April 1978 against the Washington Diplomats in one of his three autobiographies, *Further Adventures of a Grumpy Old Rock Star*.

Here's the short version: on the Saturday night before the game, the whole team – apart from Alan Ball who wasn't arriving until the following day – got steaming drunk when the mayor of Philadelphia threw a party for them. The next day, just before kick-off, Wakeman talked to Jimmy Hill, the owner of the Diplomats, who told him that his team was in the same position – the mayor of Washington had apparently also thrown a team party and got all his players wrecked too. The result was a terrible 0–0 draw because all the players were too hung over to function. Great story, except that it cannot possibly be true. In 1978, Jimmy Hill was still three years away from owning the Diplomats. By the time Hill took over the Diplomats, in fact, the Fury was already defunct. And the game was no 0–0 draw – it ended in a 3–0 win for Washington with goals from Ray Graydon and a Paul Cannell brace. And it took place on a Saturday.

One of the challenges in writing a book about a league that ceased to exist more than three decades ago – or indeed any book that involves narratives from the past – is to distinguish what parts of the beautifully told verbal anecdote differ from the truth. One former player related a neat story about the time his side played against the Cosmos, and he was ordered by his coach to man-mark Pelé. Unfortunately, he wasn't up to the job and Pelé scored a header directly from a corner kick. At half-time, the player was chewed out by the coach who then told him he would not be marking Pelé in the second half. (Pause for effect). Instead, he would now be marking Franz Beckenbauer. Another good yarn, sadly not backed by the stats. The only time this particular player could have played against the Cosmos, Pelé was out injured, and Beckenbauer left the game at half-time.

Does it matter? Surely the two stories reflect the *spirit* of the NASL, even if time and a murky memory may have distorted their content, which now fortuitously might help to sell a book or entertain an after-dinner crowd. The NASL was, after all, seen as being about players coming to the US for the party and getting boozed up (Wakeman), or having their moment in the sun against the world stars (our anonymous phantom marker of Pelé). Yet it's remarkable that for every player who tells you there was a whole lot of drinking and carousing in the NASL, there are four or five more who claim that if this was really the case then they missed out completely.

In 2006, a film called *Once in a Lifetime* professed to tell the story of the New York Cosmos, and by proxy the NASL too. It interviewed most of the major names still living at the time who had been involved with the team, with the notable exception of Pelé, who may have been glad that he refused association with what turned out to be a shoddy, selective and extremely slanted piece of cinematic work.

The film was built around two threads – that Pelé and

Giorgio Chinaglia didn't get along during the 1977 season, and that the Cosmos players were a decadent bunch of party animals who spent all their time being fêted in the Big Apple's nightclubs. Players Shep Messing and Bobby Smith were obligingly filmed in a stretch limo recalling the good old high times. Clive Toye, Jay Emmett and Chinaglia all bitched about each other to give the impression that the team was riddled with infighting, and that Warner Brothers ran it like some ancient imperial court where players, coaches and employees could fall in and out of favour at the whim of those pulling the strings. Chinaglia is painted as the Tony Soprano-style anti-hero.

While there is undoubtedly a great deal of truth in all of the above, you wonder what was left on the cutting room floor – as with most documentaries, the chosen footage has been clearly pieced together to forge the story that the film-makers wanted to tell. The revelation by a former Cosmos executive that during one flight on the team's chartered private jet 'at least two sex acts' took place is treated like the apogee of the movie's very reason for existing. What, wealthy people got drunk and had sex on private planes, *during the 1970s*? Who knew? It's hardly *Caligula*, or *The Wolf of Wall Street*.

'That movie was full of shit, it's all bullshit,' says Bob Iarusci, the Canadian defender who played for the Cosmos in 1977 and 1978. 'There may have been some rock and roll moments when we went to Studio 54, and maybe when Shep Messing was there. Shep was gone after 77, he played in the final, and then he was gone, and Werner Roth was gone after 78 – those two guys were the main spokesmen for the movie, which was skewed because Clive Toye felt he was done wrong by Giorgio, which he probably was. Clive and Giorgio didn't get along because Clive claimed the credit for signing Pelé, and

Giorgio used to say, "Clive didn't bring Pelé to the Cosmos, Steve Ross [Warner Communications CEO] bought Pelé, not Clive Toye." And Giorgio hated Clive for taking credit away from where it should have been, and that was on the players. So in the end Giorgio was the leader of the team, despite all those great stars we had around us.'[1]

Scottish defender Charlie Mitchell, who was at the Cosmos the year before Iarusci, says that *Once in a Lifetime* 'really disappointed me. I was married at that time, and Keith Eddy and a lot of the British players were married too. Shep, you know, all that stuff about the 21 Club and smoking dope, I was completely unaware of that. I wasn't aware that we could apparently walk into any nightclub in New York. I know Shep was in that environment, he was in the Playboy mood, and Bobby Smith, but when I saw that movie, and Clive was running down Chinaglia and so forth, I was very disappointed. As far as going into all the clubs and being accepted like the New York Jets or the New York Giants or Yankees ... I don't think so. Of course I can only speak for myself, [but] I was never aware of all that, I never heard about that. Usually in the dressing room people talk about what they did the night before and have a bit of a laugh about it. We used to drive to training together every day and I never heard about any of this, but I'll let other players speak for themselves. We just weren't aware of it. All the British players lived out on Long Island and we'd end up at the local pub and talk about the game. Having been there in 76 I was a little disappointed in that movie, but what happened in 77 or 78, I can't comment.'[2]

Another player not included in the party crowd was Gary Etherington, who after moving to the US from England as a boy had signed for the Cosmos in the mid-70s straight out of college. 'I think I must have missed out on all that was going on!' he says, laughing. 'They were probably stretching the truth on some things, but I thought it [the film] was a pretty good laugh, to be honest with you.' English striker Alan Willey, who was invited to play as a guest on the Cosmos' post-season tour of 1978, says that even when touring around Europe for exhibition games, 'you couldn't be a party team and get results like they did all the time. They were in the Soccer Bowl nearly every year: they had to be doing something right, and I'm sure they were worked hard during the week, and partied as much as they wanted to after the games. I think players like Carlos Alberto and Beckenbauer were probably the first ones to bed; they were getting on a bit.'[3]

There's plenty of photographic evidence that Beckenbauer and Pelé, for example, were willing participants in the New York nightlife. The German especially was enjoying the freedom of being young, single and largely unrecognized in Manhattan after news of his alleged extra-marital affairs had been splashed all over the tabloids back in West Germany. He became mates with the ballet dancer Rudolf Nureyev, who lived in his apartment building, and the two would regularly hit the town together, although the Kaiser politely rejected the dancer's amorous advances.[4] Yet it can hardly be disputed that the image of the Cosmos as a party team was something that Warner Brothers, as giants of the entertainment business with a host of celebrity actors and rock stars on their books, consciously cultivated for publicity. It's probably not a coincidence that players like Iarusci, Mitchell and Etherington were unaware that Studio 54 was the place to hang out – no one at Warners told them to be there at an appointed time to hold up a drink and smile for the camera. The Cosmos' PR lackeys knew exactly how much the NFL's New York Jets had thrived on the social reputation of star quarterback 'Broadway Joe' Namath during his years on the team from the late 60s up until 1976.

The movie also makes much of a reported dressing-room dispute between Pelé and Chinaglia during the 1977 season. Iarusci plays down the differences on the team. 'We didn't have any problems in the dressing room, we really didn't,' he says. 'In 77 there was some tension because Giorgio said to Pelé, "We're not going to win because you're not giving me the ball". The interpretation was that Giorgio was an egotist and a prick, but in all honesty he was saying if you want to win you've got to give me the ball, and I'll score.'[5] In that respect, he wasn't wrong. When the two players started working together, the team set out on a run that took them to the Soccer Bowl, where, in a 2–1 win against the Sounders, the pair linked up throughout the game. Etherington hardly paints a picture of harmony, though, describing the atmosphere in the Cosmos dressing room as merely 'okay'. On the other hand, he doesn't think it was that different to any other club. 'The first-choice pros – Chinaglia, Beckenbauer, Pelé, etc. – were on one side of the locker room, and the Americans on the other side of the locker room: we called it American Alley. They weren't separate locker rooms, but there was kind of a divide in the group; but that's typical of most pro teams when you've got the youngsters and the seasoned pros. There were only two US players allowed on the field at that time. So there wasn't too much interaction with them apart from training, and the road trips, and on game day.'[6]

Whether they played, starred or were merely on the bench, it's hard to find any players who regretted going to New York, which was without exception a step up from where they'd been before. 'Everything at New York was first class,' says Bruce Wilson, who played there for just one season in 1980 after being signed from Chicago. 'Huge crowds, there was pre-season in the Bahamas and tours in South America and Mexico, we win the Soccer Bowl, then a post-season European tour. It was a fully professional team and it was run first class.'[7] Charlie Mitchell 'was on $10k at the Lancers and I tripled it at the Cosmos and went full time. It was comparable with the English First Division. You stayed in the best hotels, it was first class all the way; you're travelling with Chinaglia and Pelé, class guys, so I must admit I really enjoyed that environment. We had a great training facility at Hofstra University, sharing with the Jets. I was living in Long Island at the time, so we got a *per diem* [daily allowance] for housing and a car.'[8]

Alan Willey recalls how 'we went to Europe and played in the Olympic Stadium against Bayern, we went to Italy and Spain for a month, staying in all these high-class hotels'.[9] The extravagant way that the Cosmos treated their players was not just in contrast to most other NASL teams, but to any professional British side too. Being owned by a record label really did mean getting the rock star treatment. The staggering split in standards (and wages) is perfectly illustrated by Bob Iarusci's engaging tale of how he came to move from Toronto to the Cosmos during the 1977 season.

Iarusci had been in protracted contract negotiations with Toronto. He was on a basic wage of $100 per game, plus bonus payments of $100 per point, and $100 per win. The year before, he'd got an extra $1,200 for winning the 1976 Soccer Bowl. This brought him close to an annual salary of $4,000, a barely living wage at the time, and having been voted League

Rookie of the Year he was hoping to negotiate a rise to around $6,500. After six weeks of talks with the club, they settled on $5,800. The 1977 season started 'up and down', says Iarusci, with Eusebio and Wolfgang Sühnholz gone, 'but we'd picked up a few more Croatian guys and were still a good team'. The day after beating Portland, Iarusci played golf with goalkeeper Željko Bilecki, and then they went to his mum's house for some pasta.

'The phone rang and my mum looked at me with her sad eyes and said, "Somebody from New York wants to speak with you." So she had this fear, this premonition, and the gentleman on the line was Eddie Firmani, the Cosmos coach. He says, "This is Eddie Firmani, I'm pleased to tell you you're now a Cosmos player. There's a pre-paid ticket for you at the airport; someone will pick you up tomorrow at LaGuardia airport. Someone else will call you with further instructions." I couldn't say anything because I was in shock. Željko asked me what had happened and I told him, "They just sold me to New York." He made a quick escape after that, he didn't want to be in the same room as me, so I picked up the phone and called our GM Sam Parage. "Oh Bobby, I was just about to call you," he says. And I'm saying, "Oh, you were just about to fucking call me, were you? You pricks went and sold me just because I negotiated a few extra bucks on my salary this season. What's the matter with you guys?" And he says, "You don't understand Bob, we're doing you a favour. You're going to the Cosmos." So I'm saying, "You're doing me a favour? My mother's upset, I'm having a trauma and you're doing me a favour? Go fuck yourselves." And I slam the phone down.

'I called Aldo Principe, who was my mentor as a kid, and my former coach and manager, and someone I trusted, so

I told him he had to go to New York with me the next day because I didn't want to spend another six weeks negotiating a contract. So Aldo says, "I'll come with you, I'll be your agent." So we went to New York, and when we got off the plane there was a guy with a beautiful sign, it must have been three feet by three feet, saying "Bob Iarusci, NY Cosmos" – beautiful graphics, I remember that – and they ushered me into a limo with cold drinks, then we drove into New York with the club secretary and they checked me into the Americana Hotel. In my room there was a note saying to meet Eddie Firmani in the banquet room at six o'clock. There was a basket of fruit as well. Aldo and I sat in the room and didn't know what to make of it.

'Ten minutes before dinner I walk out of my room and this bronzed guy with curly hair walked out the room opposite to me and we both got in the elevator. I'm thinking he looks familiar, and then I realize it's Carlos Alberto. I didn't realize the Cosmos had just bought him too. He looked at me and said, "You a soccer player?" I said I was and he asked me where I was from. I told him Canada and he looks at me and says, "Oh, they play soccer in Canada?" I said, "Sometimes, a little bit." So we get into the banquet room and there's ten places set at our table. There's me, Aldo and Carlos Alberto, and Eddie Firmani would make four, but who are the rest for? Well then in walks Pelé with his entourage. So now I'm sitting with Carlos Alberto on my left and Pelé on my right in the Americana Hotel, and I'm thinking, maybe Sam did alright for me after all. I didn't say very much because I didn't think it was my place to talk. Next day I go to Giants Stadium for practice, and in the locker room, instead of that one little hook I had for my stuff at Lamport Stadium, there's a whole dressing area with my name up in lights; there was foot powder and tie-ups for my socks, and a brand new pair of boots. This guy with a beard comes up to me and says, "I work with Pony. Would you wear those shoes?" So I wore the shoes and after practice he asked me if I liked them, and I said "Yeah, they were fine, do you want them back?" He said, "No, I don't want them back, I want you to wear them." I said okay, and he gave me this contract. I said, "Why would I sign a contract to wear Pony shoes?" He said, "Because we're going to pay you $3,000." And I said, "Okay, where do I sign this?"

'Then Aldo and I went to meet the new GM of the Cosmos, Rafael de la Sierra, at Rockefeller Plaza, on the 25th floor. It was like that scene in *Wall Street* with Michael Douglas, the Manhattan city view out the window and de la Sierra with his hair slicked back, and there's Eddie Firmani, and I'm sitting there with Aldo. De la Sierra says, "Listen, we're very proud to have you here as part of our team. We don't want to waste any time, so I've got the contract here ready for you to sign and I expect to you to sign it straightaway." I kicked Aldo under the table to say, *We're not going to let these fucking guys push us around, right?* De la Sierra goes on: "It's a two-year deal, the first year we'll pay you $28,000, the second year we'll pay you $35,000. You'll get an apartment in New Jersey and a five-speed Toyota Celica to drive." There was a deafening silence, then Aldo was about to speak, so I kicked him again and said, "Mr de la Sierra, I just need to speak outside the room a moment with my agent." We went outside and I said, "Aldo, I don't know if this is a dream or not, but you'd better get fucking back to Toronto, I really don't need you here."'

Iarusci confesses that if they'd offered him $8,000, 'I would have signed. I had no idea what was coming. It was the most surreal moment of my life.'[10] He went on to spend five seasons with the Cosmos over two spells, playing in the 1978 Soccer Bowl win over the Tampa Bay Rowdies.

The Cosmos were also responsible for inflating wages around the League. Goalkeeper Alan Mayer had the chance to join the team after the Las Vegas franchise was relocated to San Diego in 1978, and New York were looking for a new keeper. 'I was on the US national team by this point,' says Mayer, 'and so I talked to Eddie Firmani about ten times. They offered me a contract, so I just went to Las Vegas and said, "I'm a free agent", because I always had a free agent clause in my contract, and I told them the Cosmos were interested in signing me, and here's what it would take if I'm going to San Diego. I said it as a joke, but they went for it. At that particular time I was making $15k at Las Vegas. The Cosmos offered me $65k, so I went to San Diego and said unless you give me $95k I'll sign for the Cosmos, and I wanted eight plane tickets to New York to see family, then I asked for health club membership and four or five other things. They came back and said we'll give you $95k for one year, and a raise for the second year and guarantee the contract, and you can be a free agent the second year. And all the other perks they threw in too. I went from $15k to around $100k. Most other players were earning around $7,500 to $20k.'

Mayer felt 'pretty honoured' that the Cosmos wanted to sign him. 'I wanted to play for the Cosmos,' he adds, 'but then you wouldn't be sure of your playing time. And, being the Cosmos, they might kick you out at any time. I didn't have any regrets, I went out to San Diego and loved it there.'[11]

One more NASL player may feel a twinge of regret at reading those figures. Arsenal goalkeeper Geoff Barnett, who'd played in the 1972 FA Cup final defeat to Leeds and later joined the Minnesota Kicks, was all set to be transferred to the Cosmos from the north London side at the end of 1975. 'Do you want to hear a really strange story?' he asks. 'My dad was ex-military. He always had this thing that, if you've got a clean white shirt and your shoes are shiny, you're halfway towards being smart. If you remember the rules at the time, you were the possession of the club, and they could sell you to who the hell they liked, but not if they were selling you outside the country. So me and Ken Friar, the Arsenal secretary, drove out to Heathrow when the Cosmos were coming in to start a world tour, with Pelé and [GM] Clive Toye and Warner Brothers and the whole travelling roadshow.

'Everybody's nicey-nicey, as you would be when you're trying to sign a new player, and Clive Toye says, "I'd like to introduce you to our coach Gordon Bradley." I went over; he'd just got off the plane. His shirt was totally scruffy around the neck, and his shoes were dirty, and I took one look at him and thought to myself, my dad would never agree with me playing for a guy with a dirty shirt and dirty shoes. I turned to Ken and said, "Let's go back to Highbury, I'm not signing." He asked me why, and I said, "There's just something that's not right about this deal." I never told him the real reason. It's only years after that you can tell a story like that. There's Pelé and the whole team about to go on a world tour that I could have been part of, and I'm saying, "I'm not going, his shoes are dirty!"'

When Barnett signed for the Kicks the following year, did Barnett check out Minnesota coach Freddie Goodwin's shoes? 'Freddie wasn't exactly the best dresser, but at least his shoes were clean,' says the goalkeeper.[12] His initial instincts were probably right, though – like many former Kicks players who moved there from England, Barnett still lives in Minnesota today.

Toye with the thorn in his side

The thorn in the side of the Cosmos' general manager was Giorgio Chinaglia, the League's all-time top scorer, a striker with a gargantuan ego that was partly justified by his remarkable record with the Cosmos. Chinaglia wasn't just an opportunist poacher, he could score from all ranges and angles, with his head and with both feet, and often with spectacular scissor kicks or overhead moves. His goal celebrations may have been what needled a lot of people. There's something entirely selfish about the way he runs off and salutes the crowd, or the bench, or Warner Communications president and Cosmos boss Steve Ross, while mainly ignoring his teammates – even those who set him up. His naked self-glorification is almost admirable in its shameless, internally directed focus.

Although the infighting and personality wars at the Cosmos were overplayed in the *Once in a Lifetime* movie, there's no doubt that they were real, even if – for the vast majority of players and fans – they were largely a sideshow, and irrelevant to the team's success. Clive Toye still nurtures strongly resentful views on his time at the team, and on Chinaglia in particular, and claims that the only way to work within such a celebrity-driven organization was 'by ignoring a lot of the shit. I didn't realize early on that they [the owners] were as dumb as they turned out to be.'

Toye says that the team's first owner, Alan Cohen, 'wasn't bad to deal with', but when he sold the club he was never seen again. 'So I had enormous resistance to Warner as business partners. Nesuhi Ertegun was in the music business and wanted to call them the New York Blues. Someone else wanted to call them the New York Hearts, with pink hearts painted down the sides of their shorts. And from the very start I came up with the New York Cosmos. "Cosmopolitans" was too long.' Toye staged a competition to name the team and then 'pretended we had lots of letters' suggesting that 'Cosmos' was the best name. 'That was an early indication of the kind of crap that was going to continue over the years,' he says. The late Chinaglia (who died in 2012 aged 65) he still describes as 'unspeakable', and says that the striker's relationship with Steve Ross 'was something to behold. Even Jay Emmett said to me, "What is it about Chinaglia and Steve Ross?" So the only way I could handle it was by ignoring the lot of them.'[13]

Toye says that when Chinaglia signed for the Cosmos he was on $40,000 a year, but that later, when the Italian became so close to Ross, 'I'm sure it was a lot more'. As Bob Iarusci tells it, Chinaglia 'got Gordon Bradley fired as coach, and Gordon and Clive were buddies, so then Clive went.'[14] Toye says he left the Cosmos after he wrote a memo 'saying that so far I'd run the club, and asking: do we carry on like that? The answer was: we don't. And that was it.'[15] In his book *A Kick in the Grass*, Toye describes Bradley's successor, Eddie Firmani, as someone Chinaglia 'could manipulate and control'.

After Toye left, though, the problems around the dominant Chinaglia continued. 'Jay Emmett, the vice-president, became jealous because Giorgio and Steve [Ross] became blood brothers,' says Iarusci. 'And so then Giorgio had Steve's ear, and Steve knew that with Giorgio, they'd win.' There was no disputing this truth. On the field, Chinaglia just scored and scored:

1976: 19 goals (NASL leading scorer, counting assists).
1977: 15 goals (Cosmos champions).

1978: 34 goals (NASL top goalscorer; Cosmos champions).

1979: 26 goals (NASL top goalscorer).

1980: 32 goals (NASL top goalscorer; Cosmos champions).

1981: 29 goals (NASL top goalscorer).

1982: 20 goals (NASL joint top goalscorer; Cosmos
champions).

1983: 18 goals (in just 17 games).

He wasn't just a goal hog, he tallied plenty of assists too –
even though he didn't act like much of a team player when he
scored, he wasn't a selfish striker.

'The bottom line,' Iarusci continues, 'was that with Giorgio
in the team, the Cosmos won. They won four NASL Soccer
Bowls [when Chinaglia was playing] and he scored the winning goal in each of them. Was Giorgio in an uncompromising position with Jay Emmett and Clive Toye? Yes, and those
were the guys who gave Giorgio the bad reputation, right? The
other thing that nobody understands is that Giorgio loved
the North American players. He didn't hang out with Franz
Beckenbauer and Carlos Alberto, though Carlos was a good
guy. When he hung out before and after games he hung out
with myself, Bob Smith and Freddie Grgurev.'[16]

Gordon Bradley wasn't the only Cosmos coach whose
firing was rumoured to have been instigated by Chinaglia
reporting directly upstairs to Ross. Eddie Firmani's firing
two years later was also reported in the media as having been
at Chinaglia's behest. 'It's been in the air,' Chinaglia said at
the time, but denied that Firmani's sacking had anything to
do with him. 'There's always been a conflict between Eddie
and management. I'm not really shocked, but I didn't think
it would come this soon. Eddie hasn't done a bad job at all,'

he added, possibly damning the coach with faint praise. 'But you know, and I know, this is New York.'[17] Then again, listening to Firmani's team talks that were filmed for the official Cosmos 1977 end-of-season review leaves the viewer wondering what special skills the coach possessed that qualified him for the job. In one clip, Firmani tells the team at half-time in the home playoff game against the Rowdies, with the score at 0–0: 'The people up front – let's give them the ball as much as we can.' Admittedly, the Cosmos went on to win 3–0, so you could argue that this was sound tactical advice. Before the semi-final game against Rochester, Firmani is recorded telling Franz Beckenbauer to knock the ball ahead of Chinaglia for him to run on to. He illustrates his point with an arm motion indicating 'in front' and 'not behind'. Chinaglia is told to 'just get on with the game, we'll try to get the balls [to you]'.

It could be that these scenes were staged for the benefit of the film crew, perhaps asking for something not too technical because they wanted some dressing-room interaction to break up the endless footage of Chinaglia and Pelé scoring goal after goal. Then again, they could easily be real. What new football knowledge could a coach possibly impart to players like these? As we've seen, thanks to its unprecedented array of all-star names, the NASL was unique in terms of player power. Chinaglia, it seems, was running the Cosmos off the field, while on the field a player like Cruyff went public to the media when his coach instructed him to play wide on the left. In his short post-season spell with the Cosmos in 1978, Alan Willey says that although Firmani was the coach, 'most of the talking was done on the field, what with all those great players'. When interviewed, the majority of former players talk about their coaches in terms of either respect or disdain. When it comes to their superstar teammates, though, they mostly talk in terms of nothing but awe.

'I was very happy,' says Bruce Wilson of his time in New York. 'Beckenbauer, Carlos Alberto, Chinaglia, fourteen different nationalities, a lot of them captains of their World Cup teams at one point. It was quite an experience.'[18] Iarusci says of Carlos Alberto that 'you wouldn't dare to be on his team during a practice game and lose, because he wouldn't talk to you, you'd be a piece of shit.' This was not, however, a negative. On the contrary, it helped keep less established players like Iarusci on his toes and up to scratch, as well as making it clear what was expected. On one occasion, even though Iarusci was playing left-back, Carlos Alberto told the right-footed player after one misplaced pass into the crowd with his wrong foot: 'You play it with the left foot one more time and you don't play on this team any more.'

'We never played the ball from the back directly to the forwards, we always played it through the midfield,' says Iarusci, 'and that was back in the 70s, way before the current Barcelona team. We knocked the ball around and didn't give it up. If you lost the ball, someone would give you shit because you were the weak link in the team. And I was one of four or five guys who was on trial every game. Though I believed in myself, I had a confidence in myself as a player, and I was able to build strong relationships with those players on the field – if those big-name players like you and believe in you, then they'll put you in situations where you don't look bad. That's how good those players were. And I knew that they would make me better, but I would have to sacrifice for them, and that was during games, practice, or off the field – a favour here or there. It sounds like I'm kissing their rear ends, but it isn't that;

it's creating situations that will eventually end up benefiting you.'[19] Etherington concedes too that playing for the Cosmos 'was a little bit intimidating. They'd certainly let you know about it if you made a bad pass or a wrong decision.'[20]

When Firmani was sacked he claimed the dismissal was unfair given his winning record, and that the Cosmos board had only given him 'a few excuses'. The same report quoted an unnamed Cosmos player as saying, 'They wanted Firmani to make a bunch of superstars play like a world-class side. But no star side plays like a team, and they never will, and the people who run this team will never realize that. We have all craftsmen waiting to be served. Eddie wanted a combination, which usually constitutes a team.'[21] This was surely fair comment, but it ignored what made the Cosmos unique. They were so good that they didn't need to play like your run-of-the-mill team eking out results through graft, industry, stamina and a nine-man defence. They went out to score more goals than the other team. 'The Cosmos added so much adventure, and they played that dazzling, sparkling champagne sort of soccer,' says Paul Gardner.[22] It brings us back to the same discussion about style versus results, and Rodney Marsh's belief that the best way to win is with entertaining soccer. The Cosmos did this for several years as a follow-through to signing Pelé and Beckenbauer. Abnormally huge crowds didn't just turn out to watch them around North America because they wanted to see a particular famous face. They wanted to see the famous face, and his feet, *perform*, and they were never disappointed – either the Cosmos turned it on, or the home team enjoyed a rare victory over the League's loved-and-hated rich kids.

'Make no mistake, when a team is winning, they don't give a shit what anybody thinks,' says Iarusci. 'They [the players] don't care that the fans are booing Giorgio after every goal. We just know that guy makes the beer taste better after every win.' Questions about teamwork and intra-club politics become irrelevant. After Pelé left the Cosmos in 1977, Vladislav Bogićević came in as Chinaglia's provider, 'then the focus was on Giorgio. From then on the team was happy because we were winning. Bogi and Giorgio were a machine. Those two guys had this telepathy between them. Giorgio knew exactly where Bogi was going to put the ball, and Bogi knew exactly where Giorgio was going to make his runs. And we continued to win, because in the end, winning disguises everything, right?'[23]

In other words, when the Cosmos won the Soccer Bowl in 1977, 1978, 1980 and 1982 by playing champagne soccer, what did it matter if Clive and Jay hated Giorgio and Steve, and if Giorgio and Pelé weren't the best of friends, and someone had sex on a plane?

'When you look back at it,' says Gary Etherington, 'it's pretty incredible what was going on. I always say about the Cosmos that it was a circus, but it was a good circus.'[24] The bad thing about a circus, of course, is that it can always pack up its tents and leave.

Philly Fury – the downside of rock 'n' roll soccer

Frank Worthington in his prime looked like the archetypal rock 'n' roll soccer player with his long hair, his gritty good looks, and the attitude of a smiling, laid-back Jack the Lad who could perform on the field with character and live the high life off it. In his autobiography he describes the perks of playing for the Philadelphia Fury and its music biz owner-ship in 1979 by reeling off a list of concerts that he attended because the Fury's Veterans Stadium was 'just across the road from the Spectrum concert hall, where I spent many a happy evening backstage in the company of bands like AC/DC, Bad Company and Humble Pie thanks to the free passes which were always readily to hand'. On another night, he goes to see John Conteh box and sits next to Diana Ross, then gets a table watching her perform afterwards. Mick Jagger once came to watch the Fury and his wife Bianca gave Worthington a 'red silk tour shirt'. One night he dreams that he's chatting with Elvis about personal stuff in Elvis's dressing room ('We were talking about life, just bumping things off one another.'). He pulls lots of women, and tells us about them – George Best's sister-in-law, for example, and a 30-something divorcee who takes him home and gets him stoned and then they have sex for three hours. Then Frank decides that you can keep your recreational drugs, they're not for him – maybe three hours was too much for a man not exactly known for running his heart out for the whole 90 minutes. Still, 'here was I, a free spirit in a new country where the girls went mad for the accent. I was going to make the most of my time.' Like those private plane 'sex acts' performed by the Cosmos' entourage, there's more detail than we could possibly want to know, but when you're writing your life story you usually have to sell yourself the way that the public wants to know you.

'If only the rock 'n' roll influence had permeated the play-ing side of the club,' Worthington laments after outlining the considerable upsides to life off the field. 'The squad was a mixture of downbeat and cliquey Yugoslavs, a smattering of English and Scots lads, and young Americans who were just learning the game. Our Yugoslav coach Marko Valok could have made Alan Hansen look cheerful.' Worthington falls out with Valok, and even smacks a soccer ball into his face one time in the changing room after the coach has ordered him to stop juggling the ball. It was the coach who had to compromise, though – the team's general manager, Tom McAdam, calls Valok in and orders him to 'relax his approach to western players'.[25]

The Fury was a team invented to be a copy of the Cosmos, but they tried to build it overnight, despite the claims of its co-investor, the Stones' tour manager Peter Rudge, that the club was planning for the long term (something most new owners in the NASL claimed as a matter of course). In early 1979 – the second year of the club's short existence – Rudge stressed the club's professionalism by saying that it 'sent home three players last summer because they tried to take advantage of us. The club won't stand for it. Three years ago, America may have been the land of the fast buck. Not now.' In spite of signing players like Johnny Giles at 38 and ageing pros like Alan Ball, Peter Osgood and Worthington (all in their 30s), Rudge said that the NASL was 'improving all the time, and people realize America is not some sort of retirement home for those past their best, nor a place for young "rejects" to receive another chance.' He saw the Fury as a business venture. 'We won't make money just yet,' he declared, 'but we shall. The "deadwood" is being replaced by clubs who have a lot to offer, and I expect the 1979 season to be even more competitive than the last.'[26]

Clive Toye saw the Fury, however, as a typical example of the NASL's new wave of clueless ownership who didn't know how to run a franchise and who typified the League's impetuous expansion to 24 teams in 1978. Toye may have had enough grievances about the Cosmos to fill his short and highly entertaining book, but his real contempt is reserved for the League's latecomers. 'I remember they were bought at one stage by these famous rock stars,' he says, 'and we went down there to play a game. We went to breakfast and all the Philadelphia players were there at the hotel, Peter Osgood and the like, all sitting at different tables with different owners, and we were wondering what's going on. And we were told this is where the players live. And we were asking, "You mean they're not living out as part of the community?" And they were saying, "Well, they're all famous players." Not here they're not. No one's ever heard of Peter bloody Osgood. Get out there and start working, but no, they sold the club to Montreal [in 1981]. It was that kind of rubbish that was going on.'[27]

Indeed, after the 1978 home opener against the Diplomats, which pulled in 18,000, and the obligatory higher gate against the Cosmos (19,000 – modest compared with the numbers that the Cosmos usually drew on their travels), most of the team's home games saw crowds of only around 6,000–7,000 fans, who were inevitably lost in the huge stadium built for 65,000. The soccer that the Fury played was hardly of Cosmos standard during that first season either – just 40 goals in 30 games as the team finished bottom of their four-team Eastern Division. Yet Tony Glavin, the young Scot from Queen's Park who played in Philadelphia for all of its three seasons, counters Toye's image of a haphazardly run team, and also speaks highly of Worthington – though perhaps not in a way that the English striker would expect.

'Frank brought so much charisma to the team,' says Glavin, who nowadays runs his own soccer complex in St Louis. 'For me as a young player I could only look at him with awe. He wasn't quite the party kind of guy that he was made out to be, at least from what I saw. He was a class act, both on and off the field. Alan Ball was more the kind of guy to take everyone out for beers. Frank was actually quite reserved in groups of people.'[28]

Wait a second. If Worthington wasn't leading the party, then surely all those rock stars and their managers were snorting coke off the halfway line. 'I'm sure there was a certain element that went out partying,' says Glavin. 'I was a young lad myself and enjoyed the time, but I've never really been into that scene. The ownership group was a class group. The main guy, Frank Barsalona, a promoter, was one of the most wonderful, level-headed people you could ever meet.' Two lawyers who were also part of the ownership group 'were just class people, they were just so good to us, and it wasn't about a wild scene; they'd take you to lunch, dinners, to rock concerts – they took care of you, that kind of thing. They protected their investment and they treated us very well. If anything, they went overboard for us. So I wouldn't say it was a wild party scene, definitely not. Peter Rudge, he was a bit of a character; he was a party man – I didn't party with him; maybe some of the other players did, I don't know.'

In an imaginary press room filled with everyone who ever played in the NASL, the reporters have long since stopped writing and are looking over Glavin's shoulder for Best, Ball and Worthington. There's no story in professionalism. This kid can't even have been there, he was way too straight. Maybe that was the problem with the Fury. They just weren't rock 'n' roll enough, despite Worthington's claims. There was no *fury*, no wild nights out like Paul Cannell and his well-publicized Quaalude-popping soirees in DC, no riding en masse with Pelé in a limo to the famous downtown clubs of ... Philadelphia. Just a few boozy British lads watching AC/DC from the VIP seats being carefully monitored by the team's owners in case they leaned too far over the balcony. Then they were yelled at in the morning by a stern Yugoslav coach who'd been schooled in hard eastern European values like discipline and the importance of the collective.

In 1978, Alan Ball had taken over coaching duties after Englishman Richard Dinnis was sacked midway through the season. Valok's year was 1979, but results didn't improve much, although thanks to Worthington the team was at least scoring more goals. Crowds were falling, though, down to around 4,000–5,000. Glavin cites a 'cultural difference' between the Yugoslav and his players. 'Marko's style was very militaristic, which suited me because if you tell me to do something, I'll do it,' he says. 'To a point he didn't want too much creativity, but he did encourage it as well. If he thought a player was creative he'd allow you to do things. I like fitness, but he was very technical, I loved that about his coaching style – so it was very regimented, but technical too.' In its final year, 1980, the Fury jettisoned Valok and took on the much-travelled former Tampa and Cosmos coach Eddie Firmani, but the team – now shorn of all its maturing British players – didn't even make the playoffs, and several home gates fell below the 4,000 mark. Just 2,309 watched the 2–0 home win over Atlanta in May after the team had lost seven of their eight opening games. Finally, like so many owners, the music businessmen did their sums, cut their losses, and sold the team on to Montreal. Worthington claimed he was never paid a $40,000 bonus that he'd been due at the end of the 1979 season. He was hardly the only NASL import lured over by the dollar sign, but who ended up getting less than he was promised.

'It did cost me a lot of money,' Rick Wakeman admitted

of his time as an NASL investor, 'but I don't regret one penny of it. I had the most wonderful time and made the most wonderful friends.'[29] As Mike Love would have said, no one got hurt, and everyone went home happy. Except for Frank Worthington, short-changed out of 40 grand.

Rock 'n' roll soccer – the bottom line

> 'To get the best [soccer] athletes you have to pay for them. And in order to pay for them, you have to gross enough money and draw enough people to pay for them, it's kind of like the record business.'
>
> —Beach Boy Mike Love[30]

Of the parallels drawn so far between soccer and rock 'n' roll, Love's in the above quote is perhaps the least romantic, but most pertinent. All the glamour, the debauchery, the characters, the risks, the drugs and the limousines are not possible without money. Once the money runs short, there will be no entertainment for its own sake. Entertainment is an indulgence, something to spend your excess cash on as a reward. Rick Wakeman had a great time and made lots of friends, but he looks back on his time in US soccer as he might look back on a tour of North America in the 1970s. Oh man, the drugs and drink and groupies, you wouldn't believe it. The wrecked hotel suites, the sex acts on the private planes, the smashed guitars and ... oh, here comes an accountant and he's telling us that's enough. We've exhausted the budget. It's time to head back to the studio and record a new album and get ready for the next tour. Great times, man, but we've gotta generate some new revenue.

Almost every issue of the retro-nostalgic UK rock magazine *MOJO* recounts tales of bands in the 1970s who rose, rocked and then split apart, usually with a death or two on the way. The ones who survived are usually the ones who quit drinking or taking drugs – or both, like Wakeman did after surviving three heart attacks in his 20s. Ultimately, it's another way to make a living, and you have to show up for work. Even Alice Cooper, at the zenith of their shock-rock infamy in 1973, often had to turn guitarist Glen Buxton's amplifier off during concerts because he was too fucked up on drink to perform, or hadn't bothered to learn the guitar parts to start with (Mick Mashbir covered his solos instead).[31] Musicians recounting the standard 30- and 40-year-old tales of Bacchanalian indulgence tend to do so matter-of-factly, without any great relish, but sometimes with a hint of embarrassment, as though having to listen to one of their own seventeen-minute guitar runs or two-hour rock operas that seemed daring at the time, but now comes across as a meandering, aimless conceit.

Worthington's quote on page 317 about rock stars wanting to be soccer players, and vice versa, surely stems from the envy of sportsmen for the apparent freedom of the rock star, who doesn't have to get up in the morning to train, and who can consume vast amounts of drugs whenever he or she wants, even right before going out on stage. They can express themselves liberally, without some coach or manager getting on their back. They can party anytime, anywhere, and they make tons of cash. The rock star, meanwhile, envies the soccer player precisely because his form of entertainment requires discipline. The natural vanity of a superstar strutting around on stage would cause him to look at the body of a professional sportsman and think that he would want to look as good as

that too when he ripped off his shirt and showed the screaming girls more than just a puny, muscle-deficient torso edging
into flabbiness.

To the outsider, of course, it all seems like a life of glitz
and glamour. 'The titillation over sex and drugs on rock and
roll tours is largely an obsession of civilians, not the musicians
and their handlers,' wrote Michael Walker in his superb book
about The Who, Alice Cooper and Led Zeppelin on tour in
1973, *What You Want is in the Limo*. The reality of rock 'n' roll
soccer in the NASL was summed up in a 1980 *Washington Post*
feature that followed the Diplomats on the road, headlined
'On The Road With The Dips: Boredom, Loneliness.' 'There
is nothing romantic about airports, hotel lobbies and dingy
stadium locker rooms,' wrote John Feinstein. 'They all look
the same. Most of the time they are all the sights an athlete
sees.'[32] He quotes a grumpy Johan Cruyff as saying that 'the
only good thing about a road trip is coming home. The bad
thing is there's always another one after that.' Cruyff, who was
rumoured to have missed the 1978 World Cup because his wife
was still pissed off at the images of Dutch players cavorting
with unknown girls in a swimming pool at the 1974 tournament, won't even smile at girls in the hotel bar. 'Why give them
the wrong idea?' he asks.

Non-stop hard living is unsustainable, whether you're a
musician or a soccer player. Our rock 'n' roll soccer players
– Best, Marsh and Worthington, for example – had to either
slow down or face addiction and early death. What we mean by
rock 'n' roll soccer is something a little different from drinking and womanizing. It embraces more a carefree attitude
and approach to the actual game, not a literal adoption of
the music business lifestyle. The Washington Diplomats team

of 1980 aimed to entertain fans and keep them coming to the game, but that meant long, tedious road trips as part of their job, not endless long nights in the fleshpots of Minnesota and Memphis. Ultimately, the acts of entertainment performed by musicians and sportsmen are of no practical use to society, and only of limited use economically – that is, their use depends on how much they can be sold. If the performer is too drunk or hung over to make the solo (guitar) run, then the reputation of the performer suffers, and so does his or her market value.

Having said that, perhaps the Philadelphia Fury would have been better served as a truly rock 'n' roll team, rather than trying to treat their players like professionals and building up what Peter Rudge hoped would be a long-term business. They should have strategically sent Worthington and a squad of notorious bad boys out on the town every night and ordered them to get trashed in the city's bars and restaurants. Even bad publicity might have brought in more than the crowds that dwindled to the low four figures over the course of three seasons. Rick Wakeman, Peter Frampton and Paul Simon (whom, incidentally, no one ever claims to have seen at a single Philly game) would still have lost money, and the team would probably still have crashed after three years, maybe less. At least, though, they'd have maintained the image that *Once in a Lifetime* wants you to believe was the decadent, orgiastic reality of the NASL.

Season-by-season overview

1981

Numbers dropped from 24 to 21 teams, the start of the slide. Calgary came in, New England went to Jacksonville, Philly to Montreal, and Rochester, Memphis, Detroit and Houston all packed it in. **Chicago** were again rampant, this year finally outscoring the Cosmos (thanks once more to the lovely Granitza, supported still by Steffenhagen), and beat the Cosmos at Soccer Bowl in a shootout after a dull 0–0 final.

Fun facts: Racial high jinks at the Vancouver Whitecaps, where black English forward Carl Valentine told of having previously shared a flat with Bruce Grobbelaar, formerly in the Rhodesian army 'fighting native revolutionaries in the jungle'. Valentine joshed: 'We got a lot of mileage out of the situation. I think everyone thought Bruce was going to murder me in my bed one night.'[33] *Kick* magazine explained the thrilling story of how the Montreal Manic came to be so named: 'The name Le Manic was chosen through scientific survey, reflecting a major source of pride in Quebec – the pioneering Manicougan (shortened to le manic) hydroelectric project, which sent the province on the road to energy self-sufficiency.' Strangely, it worked – the team drew huge crowds. In the playoffs, 58,542 saw them beat Chicago 3–2, though they eventually lost the best-of-three series. 'They were owned by Molson Breweries,' says former Manic striker Alan Willey. 'They looked after us. Once a month you'd get five or six cases of Molson beer dropped off at your door.' Needlessly, he adds, 'I enjoyed my time there.'[34]

10 Crash

> 'I don't believe in this league. I stopped believing
> in it last summer, and the quicker it goes down
> the better. When you lose fourteen franchises in
> three years, that speaks for itself.'
> —Montreal Manic President Jacques Burrelle after
> folding his team in 1983.[1]

Thanks to the Beach Boys, David Chadwick knew that the
North American Soccer League was about to die.

The English coach of the Minnesota Strikers – a team
transferred from Fort Lauderdale earlier that year in 1984
to try and capitalize on the remaining support of the extinct
Minnesota Kicks – walked out with his team for a home game
against the Golden Bay Earthquakes at the Metrodome in
Bloomington, and found themselves faced with a crowd of
just over 6,000. Eleven days previously, in the same stadium,
they had played against the Tampa Bay Rowdies in front of
52,261 people. Except that night the Strikers had been part
of a double bill with those willing NASL co-headliners the
Beach Boys.

'We'd beaten the Rowdies 1–0,' Chadwick recalls. 'We'd
played well, it was a good game. The week before the papers
had been full of what a great night, what a great team. Where
the hell did everybody go? You could see the players come out
and they're entertainers, they want to feel good, they're top of
the league, and there's just 6,000 people. That's when it kicks

you in the guts. Does that mean they just came to watch the Beach Boys, and that the game in itself isn't enough to sell it? You could see the wind was knocked out of their sails. That's when I realized I'd been in it ten years, and I thought, the game is still not good enough to stand on its own merits, there still has to be all this razzmatazz, and that was the hard thing to take. It really hurt me a lot. I came home and it just killed me.'[2]

The general consensus among former players and coaches is that the NASL's end came as not exactly a shock, but it was still somehow unexpected. They were holding out hopes that the League could struggle on in some form or other, even if it was on a hugely reduced scale. 'As players we were hoping to get a contract, basically, that we'd still have a job, but by 1984 things looked pretty bleak,'[3] says Carmine Marcantonio. In general, their view was narrowed to their immediate playing field – they weren't too worried as long as they were getting paid by somebody to kick a ball. They were less focused on the big picture, no matter how many teams went down, and no matter how the crowds were dwindling in the stands around them as they travelled around the country. By the 1980s there were two indoor soccer leagues too – one run by the NASL, and the rival Major Indoor Soccer League – so there were still possibilities to make a living out of the game even if the NASL went bust.

For those involved in the ownership and administrative side, however, the NASL's demise was much more inevitable. Many trace the League's defining, declining moment back to the decision to expand from eighteen to 24 teams in 1978, which Clive Toye terms as the coming of 'the six arseholes'.

In 1982, the League finally removed the perennially optimistic, but by now utterly unrealistic Phil Woosnam as commissioner. His replacement was Howard Samuels, a civil rights activist and former US undersecretary for commerce with little background in soccer, who realized that the only way for the NASL to survive was to make drastic cuts, everywhere. Samuels offered none of Woosnam's vim or vision, but by this point the League had seemingly had enough of both.

Woosnam's final love child was the Trans-Atlantic Challenge Cup (TACC), an international club competition mostly played between the previous season's Soccer Bowl finalists and – initially – two randomly invited top European clubs. South American teams came later. It ran from 1980 until 1984, and most years the competition was played at the end of May, just as the European season ended. Played in group format with each team meeting the other once, the last round of two games was a double-header at Giants Stadium in New York, home of the Cosmos. It helped that the Cosmos played every year, regardless of whether or not they'd 'qualified'. No European club was going to be lured in a transatlantic direction without the prospect of meeting the NASL's flagship team, and a sightseeing tour of Manhattan. In the competition's final year, 1984, neither of the previous year's Soccer Bowl finalists – Tulsa or Toronto – played in the TACC. It was just the Cosmos against Barcelona, Udinese of Italy, and the Brazilian side Fluminense. The Cosmos won in a reduced knockout competition, beating the Catalans 5–3 in the semi-final and Udinese 4–1 in the final. As the League was dying around it, the Cosmos were busy beating world-class opponents, but by that time the question of whether or not the New Yorkers could compete with the best in the world was moot.

'We've created tremendous credibility in the last five

years,' said Woosnam at the competition's launch in 1980. 'Now we have to get North America tuned in to soccer as an international sport. The time has come to see how we stack up against the rest of the world.' He also spotted a potential opportunity long before FIFA. 'There is a void in terms of a world club championship,' said the commissioner, once again decades ahead of his time. 'We think we may be able to fill that void.'[4] As usual, though, he over-reached and declared that the TACC could become 'the major soccer competition of the world because of the rapidly improving quality of our clubs and the reputations of the Europeans'.[5] Participating clubs were also enthusiastic. John Best, the president of the Vancouver Whitecaps – who had qualified for the first tournament through having won the 1979 Soccer Bowl – said, 'We've always known that the NASL has to expand its horizons. It's always been our feeling in Vancouver that sooner or later North Americans have to tackle the best teams in the world.'[6]

The tournament was to be played by the prevailing FIFA rules of the time, which meant two points for a win, a single point for a draw, and offside being called beyond the halfway line. Suddenly this wasn't an issue now that major international names were on the invite list. 'The tournament will enhance the level of play in our league in the eyes of the rest of the soccer world,' gushed Cosmos president Ahmet Ertegun. 'These will not be exhibition games. We're playing for high stakes, and this will be the first test for the NASL internationally. It's our chance to answer those questions about whether or not the North American teams are really as good as the European and South American teams.'[7]

It takes two teams to take a game seriously, though. Paul

Gardner is not convinced that the visiting teams saw the stakes as being quite so high as Ertegun would have wished. 'They were off-season tours by European teams,' he says. 'Why couldn't they bring in [South American teams like] Boca Juniors? And they did eventually. I don't think these things ever produced a serious competition.' In its first incarnation, the NASL won convincingly – New York finished as champions, topping the group with five points, and Vancouver were second with four. Their two European opponents were hardly of the highest calibre. Manchester City had just finished in seventeenth place in the English First Division, six points clear of the relegation zone, and were hammered 5–0 by the Whitecaps. Roma had finished sixth in the chronically dull Serie A, although they could at least boast having won the Italian Cup.

Nonetheless, the cultural contrast between top-flight European soccer and the NASL at that time is highlighted by the goalscoring stats. Roma scored 40 goals in 34 Serie A games in the 1979–80 season. The Cosmos scored almost three goals a game in 1980 League play during their 32 regular-season games. The Italians did loosen up a little when they came to New York, though. Having drawn 1–1 in Vancouver, they entered into the spirit of the competition and lost 5–3 at Giants Stadium to the Cosmos. It's unlikely that they were happy at allowing former Lazio hero Giorgio Chinaglia to score a hat-trick against them.

It was a similar story in the following years. In 1981 Southampton (featuring Kevin Keegan, Alan Ball, Charlie George and Mick Channon) and Celtic both lost their two games against the Cosmos and eventual winners Seattle. The final attracted 20,000 fewer fans than the previous year, with almost 41,000 seeing the Cosmos and the Sounders share six goals in what Sounders coach Alan Hinton described as 'a magnificent soccer game'.[8] Nacional Montevideo of Uruguay added South American flavour in 1982, but neither they nor Napoli could overcome the Cosmos or the Chicago Sting, who triumphed in another climactic thriller – a 4–3 win for the Sting over the Cosmos that saw them lift the cup. It seemed that the competition's best games were always between the two NASL sides. It wasn't until 1983, the competition's fourth year, that outsiders managed to beat the hosts when Fiorentina won 1–0 in Seattle in early June, and São Paolo beat the Cosmos 3–2 the following night. The Cosmos, though, were still crowned champions when they trounced Seattle 4–1 in the final game, having beaten Fiorentina in the opener by the same scoreline.

In the truncated 1984 tournament mentioned above (see page 349), when the Cosmos beat Diego Maradona and Barcelona 5–3 in front of 37,629 fans, the victory must have seemed a little hollow. As they had been knocked out of the 1983 NASL playoffs in the first round, the Cosmos had no right to be there at all. By this point, the team was starting to trade off its name only, which led to the announcement in late 1984 (as the League was in its death throes) that they were leaving the NASL to play exhibition games. That was not only the noose on the gallows of the NASL, but a way for the Cosmos to hang themselves too. FIFA would not sanction soccer's equivalent of the Harlem Globetrotters, and the Cosmos' name and logo went into hiding for the next quarter of a century.

'I'd forgotten all about that,' says Clive Toye of the Trans-Atlantic Challenge Cup. 'It wasn't bad, it wasn't the end of the world. We had said to ourselves, we have to establish a relationship with Europe. Did we really want to establish a strong relationship with Mexico and the Caribbean? No, you know, we wanted the best of Europe.' Toye says that the League proposed to UEFA that 'one or two of our clubs should play in the UEFA Cup, not just friendlies. UEFA informally agreed this could happen, and we were working out how. It never happened, and I don't know why, or when this was exactly, but that was our idea, to form a competitive relationship with Europe.'[9]

The perception problem for the North American sides was the same as they face now, and the same that the Atlanta Chiefs faced when they beat Manchester City way back in 1968. When NASL teams beat foreign sides, especially Europeans, the latter would just claim that they were on an off-season tour. Either they were tired from a long season back home, or they weren't yet in shape because they'd only just started preparations for the coming year. Furthermore, they had to play on artificial turf, or baseball fields, in very hot weather, and the European teams weren't used to that kind of thing. In contrast, when the North American sides lost to foreign opposition, well, that just proved how far they still had to come in order to compete with the rest of the world.

Hammering Hamburg at 'operetta soccer'

If the standard and motivation of the NASL's visiting opponents in the Trans-Atlantic Challenge Cup was open to debate, there was no such doubt about the quality of the team that came to play the Cosmos in an exhibition game in the middle of June 1983. Reigning Bundesliga champions SV Hamburg had just one month earlier been crowned European champions after deservedly beating Juventus 1–0. To put that victory into context, Juventus had featured six starters from the Italy team that had won the World Cup against West Germany twelve months earlier – Dino Zoff, Marco Tardelli, Paolo Rossi, Claudio Gentile, Antonio Cabrini and Gaetano Scirea – not to mention Michel Platini at his peak, and the seasoned Italian international Roberto Bettega (signed by Clive Toye one year later for the Toronto Blizzard). Hamburg themselves boasted the poised playmaker Felix Magath, who scored the glorious winning goal against Juventus, and the penetrating right-back Manny Kaltz, who had featured on the other side in that World Cup final, along with his Hamburg teammate, the striker Horst Hrubesch.

Hrubesch, though, was one of three first-choice Hamburg players who skipped the trip, along with defender Ditmar Jakobs and Danish forward Lars Bastrup. Key midfielder Jürgen Milewski was also missing, and coach Ernst Happel had taken a trip home to Vienna, allowing general manager Günther Netzer to coach the team. Hamburg had won the Bundesliga on the final day of the season, eleven days earlier, with an away win at Schalke. Presumably, in the meantime, they had been celebrating and perhaps resting up a little after a long domestic and European campaign. Yet in the first half of the game against the Cosmos, in front of 30,000 fans, the Germans dominated completely, and took a 2–1 lead by the interval. The Cosmos repeatedly fell prey to the Hamburg offside trap, and Hamburg's two goals – scored by another Dane, Allan Hansen, and Jimmy Hartwig – reflected their domination. New York had levelled briefly through Paraguayan forward Roberto Cabanas.

After half-time, the Cosmos came back into the game, directed by Franz Beckenbauer, who had just returned to

New York after two years with ... Hamburg. Cosmos midfielder Vladislav Bogićević said after the game he remembered when they had lost 6–2 to Stuttgart and 7–1 to Bayern Munich on a tour of West Germany in 1978. 'So tonight I said, *These people are going to have to pay*, and they did. Motivation is very important for this team. Say anything you want, but don't tell me I have no pride.'[10] Chinaglia equalized ten minutes into the second half, and another ten minutes later Johan Neeskens put the Cosmos in front. Then in the final thirteen minutes came the deluge – Chinaglia converted a penalty after Wim Rijsbergen was fouled, Ricky Davis beat the German offside trap by dribbling through on his own and rounding keeper Uli Stein to make it 5–2, Cabanas got his second, and Bogićević rounded things off two minutes from time for a final score of 7–2. They had not only beaten the champions of Europe, they had absolutely thumped them. Netzer was furious, and spoke after the game of 'a humiliation, for which there will be consequences'.[11]

The German acknowledged that the artificial turf and the high humidity were unfamiliar to his team, but refused to accept these two standard excuses of touring European teams as reasons for the heavy defeat. Netzer, though, was partly to blame. He hadn't even inspected the surface before the game, let alone arranged a training session on it to allow the players to adjust. As one unnamed player told the *Hamburger Abendblatt*, 'We players only saw the city from the tourist's point of view. That is, a shopping trip, and then New York by night.' The paper reported that the Cosmos had handed over the $120,000 match fee with 'a bitter smile' (luxury hotel accommodation and round-trip first-class flights had also been part of the deal). An anonymous Cosmos source said,

'We always hear from the Europeans that apparently we only play operetta soccer*, but in that respect we can't trump what Hamburg offered tonight.' Hamburg's president Wolfgang Klein immediately challenged the Cosmos to a revenge match in Hamburg (it never happened) and said his players had gone on holiday a day too soon. The following day, though, there was no more talk of 'consequences' – Netzer flew with his girl-friend to Hawaii, three other players to Florida, and the rest back to Hamburg.[12] It's likely that the game had been more or less forgotten, or at least brushed under the carpet, by the time the new Bundesliga season kicked off two months later.

For the Cosmos, this was certainly a proud moment in their history, but a fleeting one too. It was, ultimately, just a friendly, and would thus go unmarked in the record books. There were match reports in the New York papers, but scant further coverage. Domestic concerns soon overrode any sense of celebration – the win over Hamburg was sandwiched between League losses to Golden Bay and Team America. Rijsbergen said that 'people are going to make us world champions all of a sudden. One day we can't beat Golden Bay and the next we do this. Sure, we played well, but 7–2 is not a realis-tic score.'[13] Rijsbergen's analysis is accurate, except that people did not actually start calling the Cosmos world champions – the result caused barely a ripple in the NASL, and nothing beyond. International competition for most Americans still

---

* Another translation for 'operetta soccer' is 'Mickey Mouse soccer'. The entrenched European prejudice against the NASL is such that they were still using the term in Germany in 2014 – Lars Jensen of the normally sound magazine *11 Freunde* described the NASL as 'a Mickey-Mouse league without foundations, in which the public lost interest as soon as Pelé and Franz Beckenbauer had left'. (January 2014)

meant the Olympics and individual sports like golf, boxing and tennis. The Cosmos could lose to Bayern 7–1 and beat Hamburg 7–2, but beyond the players and a few excitable fans it didn't mean a thing because the results were in isolation. Despite Ahmet Ertegun's prognosis, few people cared about measuring the NASL against the rest of the world, except in negative terms. It was both too soon – even now the World Club Championship is a fledgling competition deemed by many as another unnecessary burden on the fixture-heavy calendar – and too late, because the League was on its way down, even as the Cosmos were annihilating Europe's top team and showing them that the NASL wasn't just operetta soccer.

The NASL's closing years: the optimists vs reality

In sport, as in life, there are optimists and realists. Most teams boast a section of fans who are bug-eyed with hope and excitement no matter how mediocre the soccer they see week after week, while a separate conglomerate will refuse to accept even a 20-game winning streak as evidence that their side is anything other than a clutch of failures about to crash into an abyss of misery and defeat. Both sets of supporters are inevitable, and necessary to counterbalance their respective hubris and despair. In between, though, is a small gaggle of fans capable of striking a middle ground and making an objective, realistic assessment of their team. The NASL's twilight years reflect a pattern where the realists tried to keep a check on those who thought the glass was not just half full, but overflowing. That is, the League didn't freewheel downhill towards bankruptcy without brakes, on a screaming high until it belatedly realized that it was about to veer off the edge of a very steep cliff. On its path to extinction, there were several warning signs, and a lot of voices advocating caution. Woosnam's momentum, though, carried him through that caution (or at least it did until he was ousted in 1982), with the single-mindedness of a stockbroker buying up shares in only one company – a company he believes is just going to get bigger and better. When the price crashes, there is no safety net.

Let's look at the League year by year from around the time when it seemed the NASL was booming, in 1977, and track the contrast between the positive propaganda from the League's HQ, and the owners and officials who were beginning to suspect that the NASL's rapid growth was not just unsustainable, but also potentially damaging to US soccer's long-term prospects.

1977: Ignoring the Strategic Plan

The Optimists: Commissioner Woosnam was in the habit of making grossly unsubstantiated forecasts about the growth of the NASL. At this time, if you excluded the Cosmos, the average budget of an NASL team was $600,000, he told the *New York Times*. By 1985, he said, that figure would be $4 million, and NASL salaries would be on a par with those in the NFL, and 'we will have 32 clubs, and each will be worth plenty of money. A lot of people want to join now, but we are not taking anyone who is under-financed. We can afford to be choosy.'[14]

The Realists: Later that same year, the League's planning committee, which consisted of various owners and general managers such as Steve Danzansky (Washington Diplomats), Walter Daggatt (Seattle Sounders), Lee Stern (Chicago Sting) and Clive Toye (Cosmos) produced a very sensible Strategic

Plan as a blueprint for the NASL's future. This report is crucial to understanding where the NASL went wrong because it is packed with rational recommendations that were largely ignored. Two particularly sensitive areas warranted the League's attention. First, the need to stop a single team dominating the NASL. Second, the need to expand slowly and carefully.*

Clearly aware that the Cosmos, even in 1977, were starting to upstage the rest of the League, the committee recommended a players' union as a collective bargaining agent to help standardize salaries and working conditions. It also pointed the League towards 'upgrading the ownership of existing franchises and carefully screening the ownership of expansion franchises'. The plan proposed something very similar to the English Football Association's current vaguely defined 'fit and proper persons' test for new owners. The FA has aped the NASL in its negligible execution of this test.

The Strategic Plan classified the League's eighteen teams from 1977 as follows: ten were 'standard' and eight were 'below standard'. It recapped poetically, and pertinently, that 'the history of NASL territorial occupancy and vacancy, accordion-like in movement, exemplifies a decade of uncertainty and instability.' In the post-Pelé era, the demand for franchises was increasing, and future expansion had to be 'accomplished with discretion, patience and concern for the effects of dilution'. It pointed out, 'assuming continued growth', that the longer the

---

* Other posited long-term goals included the establishment of a reserve league (or 'farm teams'), a need to end the reliance on imported professionals so as to boost the number of home-grown players, better referees and coaches, improved training facilities, and the recognition of a players' union to help standardize salaries.

NASL held off on increasing the number of its teams, the more it would be able to demand for expansion fees. It worked out that if the League expanded to 24 teams in 1978 and 28 teams in 1979, the existing eighteen franchises would each receive $236,111. On the other hand, if the League expanded to 24 teams in 1980 and 28 in 1984, the existing eighteen franchises would receive $700,000.

The committee looked at the cautious rate at which America's other major league sports had expanded: the NFL expanded to 28 teams over 52 years; baseball to 26 teams over 101 years; the NBA to 22 teams over 20 years; and the NHL to 18 teams in 59 years – all much, much slower rates of expansion than the NASL. Those four simple figures should have been the markers of sanity that held the League in check. The League's executive committee, the report concluded, 'in considering the rate of expansion ... shall be generally governed by principles of caution, moderation and deliberation and shall consider: present versus future franchise value, saturation of markets, dilution of existing NASL member franchises, and the capacity of the League front office to deliver services, new and existing.'

The planning committee's report was circulated in October 1977. In March of 1978, despite objections from several of the established team owners, the NASL kicked off its new season with 24 teams.[15]

1978: Getting high in a helicopter

The Optimists: At the start of the new season, Woosnam predicted that all three major TV networks will be 'involved in televising NASL games in the not too distant future'. He also forecast that 'television will bring the sport to every corner of

North America and contribute enormously to our continued growth'.[16] The Minnesota Kicks' Alan Merrick believed that the NASL 'has improved itself with the introduction of the six new teams. I feel the League has more financial stability, and that the new people on the field and in the front offices are of high calibre.'[17]

Woosnam tells the story of the famous night the previous summer when the Cosmos sold out Giants Stadium. He had been in a helicopter with the League's director of operations, Ted Howard, having just come back from a playoff game in Minnesota that had drawn almost 36,000. 'We had just flown into LaGuardia, and Warners sent their helicopter to fly us out to the Meadowlands. We passed over Randall's Island and I remembered that just two years ago, the Cosmos were playing there before a couple [of] thousand people. Then we crossed the river into New Jersey and as we came up to Giants Stadium, I turned to Ted and said, "My God, there are five thousand people just waiting to get in." Then I saw the crowd inside, the 77,691, a tremendous crowd, a crowd that may never be beaten there. Yes, that certainly was the high point.'[18] Unfortunately, that remained the NASL's high point until the very end, and Woosnam's high from up on high in the Warners' swanky helicopter may have played a major role in his delusion that the NASL was already huge, and was only going to grow and grow and grow until accorded the necessary respect from the NFL.

The Realists: At this stage, the realists weren't getting much of a say. They were possibly hoping that the expansion to 24 teams might just work. Now that it had happened, they maybe thought that there was no point in talking it down. Nonetheless, Tulsa Roughnecks owner Ward Lay confessed, 'I don't like very rapid expansion, and I hope we haven't done that. We still can't think we have solved all our problems just because we have expanded. The six teams we took in are going to still have some problems, and some of the other teams are not yet strong.'[19] In fact there were in all ten new teams in 1978 – six starting from scratch, and four that were moved from elsewhere. Six of these ten new teams – California, Detroit, Houston, Memphis, New England and Philadelphia – lasted just three years in those cities. Colorado and Oakland moved after just one. Out of this new group, only Lay's Tulsa and the San Diego Sockers made it through to the League's end.

Seattle's general manager Jack Daley was also careful in looking to the future. Soccer was not yet major league, he said, and the Sounders were still a 'faceless' team in other cities. 'I honestly believe soccer will be a great sport in this country,' he went on. 'The only question is when. But you have to build viable franchises. Winning games isn't the only answer. It takes promotion, marketing, winning, player appearances, all orchestrated to work together.'[20] Can the League support 24 teams, Cosmos president Ahmet Ertegun was asked. 'I think it's alright,'[21] he replied, most unconvincingly. This was in the League's official publication, *Kick* magazine, so you can imagine his views in private. 'They expanded the League to 24 teams? HAVE THEY GONE COMPLETELY FUCKING CRAZY?' This fabricated quote remains unsourced, of course, but is plausible nonetheless.

1979: Onwards to world domination by 1985!

The Optimists: 'The three key factors which will result in our clubs, and the League itself, becoming major forces in the world of soccer are the quality of soccer provided by the teams, the ability of the managements to increase attendance each year until we emulate the success of the NFL teams, and the increased involvement of major companies at the local and national levels.' Woosnam, of course, and his customary obsession with drawing parallels to the NFL. Paraphrased: we just need world-class players at every team, massive crowds, and huge corporate investment. A sign from the heavens that the NASL was God's Own League would be nice too. 'There is no doubt in my mind,' Woosnam went on, 'that the NASL, due to the efforts of its individual members, can become the dominant league in world soccer by the mid-80s.'[22]

Chicago Sting owner Lee Stern was also looking to the long term. 'If you look at what we're doing,' he said, 'you can see that this club is not just being built for this season. It's being built for many years to come. We've increased the worth of our franchise by more than $1m from what it was at the end of last season. If the Toronto Metros organization can be sold, like it was, for $2.5m, what does that make the Sting worth with players like Karl-Heinz Granitza and Arno Steffenhagen?'[23] This idea of investing in a sports team to make a future profit was, at the time, almost completely alien to soccer club owners outside the US. In the UK, benevolent, wealthy fans generally resigned themselves to pouring thousands, if not millions, into their pet projects without any hope of a return. They did it for the purposes of prestige and self-promotion, and sometimes even out of love for the club they'd supported as a kid, and because they cared about the game. Only in the 80s did unscrupulous asset-strippers start taking over teams and selling their grounds to supermarket chains, taking advantage of fans' naivety and faith that no one would ever be so nasty to their beloved, century-old clubs. Americans were of course upfront and blunt about their motivation when it came to money. No US owner would have been wooed by the League saying, 'Hey, you should invest in soccer so that the fans will love you, and you get to take part in the beautiful game and be part of one big, hand-holding, global sporting community!'

The Realists: In 1979 the League remained at 24 teams, and only two teams moved – Colorado to Atlanta, and Oakland to Edmonton. So everyone was either swept up with the hype, or continuing to hold their breath. Might this just work? Ted Turner thought so – the CNN founder revived the Atlanta Chiefs franchise six years after its first incarnation, buying the Colorado Caribous for $1.5 million. The Chiefs' former chief executive, Dick Cecil, was still involved with Atlanta's baseball team, the Braves, when he received a call from Turner. He remembers that the conversation went as follows: '"Cecil, tell me about soccer," he [Turner] said. I tell him, and he says, "Let's buy a team. I'll put up my own money."'[24] In Europe, teams were built on a century of tradition, glory and hardship. In the US, all it took was a phone call from a wealthy man.

1980: 'We are not socialists, we are businessmen'

The Optimists: As the years went by, Woosnam's forecasts became ever more fantastical. Focused as ever on the importance of a long-term, lucrative network TV contract (like the NFL's, of course), he greeted the new decade by repeatedly declaring soccer as *the* sport of the 80s, and claiming: 'We really believe that before the end of the 80s most, if not all, of our franchises will be attracting average attendances in excess of 40,000 for the six-month summer season and filling the arenas for three months of indoor soccer. At that point, decisions in regard to TV format will not be too difficult.'[25] Just let the crowds come en masse, week after week, and a gargantuan TV deal will take care of itself.

In his defence, the NASL retained all 24 teams from the previous season. Nobody moved, and nobody went under. Even those teams that were hurting decided to give it at least one more year. Woosnam conceded that it was too soon to talk about *further* expansion, but that didn't stop him dreaming. There were still lots of places in Canada you could put a team – Ottawa, Calgary, Winnipeg. And then in the US there was St Louis, Cincinnati, Kansas City, Milwaukee, New Orleans, Denver, Pittsburgh, Cleveland, Indianapolis and 'probably quite a few others you could name'.[26] He was even willing to admit to the *Washington Post* that 'we may have made a mistake expanding when we did. But we had several reasons for doing it. Basically, we wanted to influence you people, the media. We wanted to be sure we would be taken seriously. Having a 24-team coast-to-coast league was one way of doing that.'[27] The NASL expanded to 24 teams because it wanted to show the media its balls. Given that the expansion was the main reason the NASL failed, this sounds like brittle reasoning, at best. Big balls are all very well, but put them out on display for the world to see and they make a tempting target for a severe kicking. While the Cosmos were pulling in almost 47,000 per game, nine teams were attracting average four-figure crowds of between five and ten thousand.

The Realists: Dennis Wit, a US midfielder with the New England Tea Men, lamented how difficult it was to play in front of low crowds. 'It's tough to play in front of only two or three thousand people,' he said. 'This is a tough town. There are so many successful teams here, the Red Sox, the Celtics, the Bruins, the Patriots. All those teams are well established. We have to compete against them.'[28] He knew what he was talking about. On a wet, windy and freezing night on 28 April 1980, the Tea Men beat the visiting Memphis Rogues 3–1 in front of just 254 soaked spectators inside Schaefer Stadium, Foxboro (capacity: 60,292), the lowest gate in NASL history. 'Maybe we should always play in bad weather in front of bad crowds,' said their sardonic Irish coach, Noel Cantwell.[29] At the end of the season the team's owners, Liptons, opted for warmer weather and better crowds by moving the team to Jacksonville, Florida. In Boston they'd not only had to compete with all the teams Wit mentioned, but a conflict with the adjacent Foxboro Raceway meant the team could never play at home on Saturday nights. President Derek Carroll admitted the Tea Men management had 'made mistakes' during the team's three years in New England, but claimed, with some justification, that they were 'never given a chance to succeed'.[30]

The Atlanta Chiefs also threw in the towel after just two seasons back. Ted Turner had little patience for an operation losing $2 million a year, according to Dick Cecil. 'The League was foundering, there were some real problems,' says Cecil. 'Phil [Woosnam] lost control of it.' The Cosmos and Time Warner were great for the League, but they were also bad for it, he adds. 'The Cosmos – it was like Snow White and the Seven Dwarves, or rather Snow White and the Fifteen Dwarves. No one could keep up with them. If they wanted to do something, they did it. The cast of characters [at NY] were very unlike Lamar [Hunt, Dallas Tornado owner] and some of the other owners. It was tough, and I think Phil had to battle that a lot. The League became very high maintenance, it was bleeding dollars. Franchises were going. The League just didn't agree on the way to go forward. We got out; there was just no sense in keeping on.'[31] Detroit, Memphis and Rochester joined them, along with Houston, whose team president and GM Hans von Mende had said a few months earlier: 'I despair from time to time. But I have to pick myself up. I'm convinced we'll make it here.'[32] One of Woosnam's hoped-for Canadian cities, Calgary, started a new team, the Boomers. Possible memo from Woosnam to new Calgary team: 'Think of a positive name! Preferably the opposite of "bust".'

The figures at the end of the year made for grim reading. 'The League's 24 franchises lost an estimated $30 million this season,' reported the *New York Times* in December, 'and none of the teams showed a profit despite a 4% overall increase in attendance.' Rafael de la Sierra, the Cosmos' executive vice-president, said, 'Any move to shrink the League is a move in the right direction.' Clive Toye, by now chairman of the Toronto Blizzard, said the League 'bit off more than we could chew when we expanded'. Team owners had now abandoned their policy 'of helping the League's weaker franchises. "We're not a socialist group, we're businessmen," said Bob Bell of the San Diego Sockers. "If an owner can't make it, we won't go to the well any longer."'[33]

This was also the year when long-time NASL owner Robert Hermann sold the California Surf, which he'd moved to the west coast from St Louis in 1977. Hermann later explained that he thought owners buying expensive but unknown players from abroad 'would spend the League into oblivion'. Such owners 'raised the salaries to where teams with individual owners, like myself, couldn't compete any more. When I saw that coming I sold my team.'[34]

1981: Debit does Dallas

The Optimists: 'Many people say the game will finally reach its peak in the next decade when all the youngsters now playing soccer grow into adulthood and attend NASL games, when they become the first generation of fans who have actually grown up playing the game. We can't agree more with that theory.'[35] Woosnam likely agreed with that theory because its realization, or not, was a generation away. It was a reasonable but also somewhat shallow supposition, ignoring the multiple distractions that these nascent fans would face – all those other major league sports, for starters. Major League Soccer is faced with the same conundrum 30 years later – the number of youths in the US who play soccer is still many times more than the number that go to watch it. Geography, time and expense all play a role, while many of those who watch the game prefer to learn from the English, Spanish, Italian or German top flights, all available at the touch of a digital button.

The Realists: ABC's failure to renew its contract with the League due to poor ratings, and the demise of the Dallas Tornado were two particularly painful moments for the NASL. Lamar Hunt's Texan team was the only one to have been there from the start. Hunt was the old-school investor referred to above by Dick Cecil (page 366), one of the few who really did stay in soccer for the long term (he later did the same in MLS, helping that league through several lean years). 'I'm sure it was the right business decision, but it hurts me a lot,' said US midfielder Kyle Rote, who had played for Dallas for six seasons up until 1978. 'I'm sad for Lamar because he did so much to keep it alive – and the antithesis of his philosophy did him in. Lamar could have bought a championship team from the beginning, but he wanted balance. He always had the little guy on his mind – how would this affect Rochester. Then the League turned on his experience and his philosophy and developed the Cosmos philosophy – spend dollars that don't make good business sense.'[36] This cuts again to the paradox at the heart of the NASL. Without the Cosmos it's possible that few people would remember this league, and all the ways that it eventually influenced modern soccer. Its obituary might have been a footnote hidden at the bottom of the sports pages as a News In Brief item. Alternatively, with enough owners like Hunt, it might have slowly but progressively grown at a rate that would have allowed its steady but unspectacular survival. By now, it might have been fifteen years ahead of where MLS currently stands.

The League did itself few favours at this critical point. It held the 1981 Soccer Bowl between the Chicago Sting and the Cosmos in Toronto, and ABC neglected to show the game live in either home city. Sting fans would see the game delayed later that evening, while Cosmos fans had to wait until the following afternoon. Even though Chicago won, 1-0, their coach Willy Roy said, 'I think it would be better if we repeat this game, better for US soccer. We could've gone to New York or Chicago and replayed this game in front of 70,000 or 80,000.'[37] The game did attract a gate of almost 37,000, though, including 4,000 travelling Chicago fans. Giorgio Chinaglia was reportedly out of sorts because, according to *Sports Illustrated*, 'as the Cosmos' bus waited to leave the hotel before the game [...] an unruly Sting fan yelled insults at Chinaglia in Italian. Giorgio charged out the bus and a short fracas followed. A historic moment, perhaps: the first touch of soccer hooliganism to reach North America. The game is clearly maturing here.'

1982: Boomers going bust

The Optimists: The League's drastic reduction to fourteen teams wasn't enough to dampen Woosnam's spirit. 'I believe that 1982 is going to be our best season ever,' he swaggered. 'We've got a schedule that will greatly appeal to the fans, because they'll have a chance to see every other team in the League.'[38] Nice spin – 24 teams good, fourteen teams better. 'The best thing for the NASL was to get rid of the weak sisters,' said a Darwinistic Amy Rankin, a former League executive who had moved to the Jacksonville Tea Men. 'There is a lot of enthusiasm around the League because we have stronger squads.' San Jose general manager John Carbray believed that players 'are more concerned with signing contracts as opposed to signing *big* contracts. Also there will be more established players and less of an influx of new foreign players.'[39]

The Realists: The Calgary Boomers had gone bust, along with Dallas, DC, Minnesota, LA and the California Surf. Former Aztecs player and coach Peter Short said, 'Reality caught up to the NASL. What happened was that the management started to believe some of their own press releases, which tended to paint a picture that was optimistic but not quite factual. They ran ahead of what they actually could do.' By mid-season, average gates were down 22.3 per cent across the League compared with the year before.[40] The first moves to sideline Woosnam were mooted by the League's owners at a secretive March meeting in Chicago – they voted unofficially to remove him and set up a three-man committee to find a replacement. One unnamed club executive cited the reasons as: 'Expansion too soon; the constant chasing after ABC-TV; the huge build-up of the marketing arm and its copying of the NFL.'[41] The owner of the Edmonton Drillers, Peter Pocklington, said in May he had lost $10.5 million in three years, and that he would dissolve his team if the players didn't accept a 50 per cent pay cut.[42]

There was one more newcomer to the realist camp. In the middle of the gloomy season, Woosnam blamed unusually wet weather and the moribund economy for the League's decline, but reiterated his conviction that the sport would prevail in the US. 'We will be third behind football and baseball by the end of the '80s,' he said, downgrading his previous forecasts of global domination by the mid-1980s.[43] By this point it's doubtful that anyone was listening to even such a comparatively modest forecast.

1983: Optimists out, doom-mongers in

The Neo-Optimists, who had become the Realists: Howard Samuels was the new commissioner, and as such took over Woosnam's role as optimist-in-chief, except that he was firmly in the realist camp. In fact, he was putting a real downer on the whole project. 'This past season [1982] was terrible,' he said. 'Our attendance was down 18 per cent. Teams lost a lot of money. If we can't cut our losses by 25 to 50 per cent, I could be out of a job. We've had bad management of teams, the failure of Americanization, the failure to create excitement, and the failure to prove to American sports fans that soccer is an American sport.'[44] Apart from that, everything looked great. This was the single year of the failed Team America experiment in DC. Elsewhere, more clubs folded as the League was reduced to twelve teams. Edmonton had gone, as Pocklington had threatened, helping to fulfil his own declaration that, 'The NASL is dead.' Jacksonville and Portland also closed their doors, and the San Jose Earthquakes rebranded themselves the Golden Bay Earthquakes. Only in California could you polish an earthquake and resell it as gold.

1984: Sorry for your losses

Realists only: 'Everybody thinks we're dead,' said Howard Samuels on the eve of the new season, 'and let me tell you, we're sick.' The League was now down to nine clubs – Seattle had collapsed in internal acrimony, Team America had flopped, and the Montreal Manic threw in the towel. Each club now had a salary cap of $825,000, squads were reduced from 28 to nineteen players, and Samuels himself took a salary cut of 50 per cent to 'barely six figures'.[45] Owners were trying to outdo each other by announcing how much they'd lost. San Diego Sockers president Jack Daley said his team had lost $10 million since 1978. In 1983 alone, the Chicago Sting lost $1 million and the Earthquakes $3 million, while the oilmen who ran Tulsa claimed to have lost $8 million in four years. Losses could have been exaggerated as an excuse for bailing out, though that would hardly help attract any potential buyers of ailing teams. Not that there were reams of suitors lining up to invest in soccer by this stage. The Cosmos lost money too, as they always had done, but their losses were easily absorbed by Warner Communications, as they always had been. Except that the parent company was taking a hit from its struggling Atari subsidiary, which had been severely affected by the crash in the computer games market. With a plummeting share price, Warner could no longer afford a plaything like the Cosmos in a declining league – the team's lavish budget was slashed, and by July Giorgio Chinaglia had bought a majority interest in the team. Their final competitive game at the Meadowlands against Golden Bay pulled in just 7,581 fans, their lowest crowd since the pre-Pelé era. They lost, 1–0, the anti-Cosmos scoreline.

The owners' litany of woes were now becoming a familiar refrain. 'Our hype tried to present the NASL as the new NFL when we weren't ready,' said Daley. 'It became fashionable to chase the Cosmos. Everyone had to have a Pelé. Coaches went around the world on talent searches, forcing the prices up.' Chicago's Lee Stern said, 'We spent too much money trying to market teams as if they were instant big league franchises before the attendance and money justified it.' Coach Ron Newman, now with San Diego, could barely contemplate life without the NASL. 'If the NASL had gone, it would have been like losing a leg. I've put 17 years of my life into this league.' He put the blame on management, and said the League 'changed direction so many times, you didn't know what would happen next. We'd shift from foreign superstars to grass roots and back again.' *Sports Illustrated* judged, very harshly, that 'in the market place of pro sport, hype is no crime so long as the product has quality. The NASL's product was a slowed down, pre-digested, bland, dull copy of the real thing.'[46] And this was all while the League was still alive.

Samuels himself failed to outlive his dying league. In October – three and a half weeks after the last ever game in the NASL, between Chicago and Toronto – he died of a heart attack, aged 64, in his Manhattan apartment. Clive Toye gamely took over what could at that moment have been fairly described as the worst job in US sport.

1985: Toye story – the end

One last Optimist/Realist: Toye, Woosnam's old sidekick from the League's founding years, shared some of the Welshman's inherent optimism, but only on a foundation of realism. He'd gone to Toronto three years earlier as chairman, convinced that he could make the team work and attract regular crowds up to 30,000. Although the team did well – losing finalists in both 1983 and 1984 – the crowds weren't good enough and were usually in the 10,000–12,000 range. The month before Samuels' death, Toye had produced a sensible report on how to save the NASL, advocating a six-team league playing a sixteen-game season, with gradual expansion over the following years. Toye didn't think there was anything wrong with soccer, just with the NASL. Unfortunately, even this modest blueprint was beyond what now seemed like a league on a suicide mission.

'Howard Samuels,' says Toye. 'You don't want to speak ill of the dead, but what a moron.' When Toye took over as acting president of the League following Samuels' death, 'I found in the office absolute idiocy and incompetence. There was this demand on teams that if they wanted to play in the next season [1985] they had to find a half-million dollar performance bond. If you don't play next year, then you lose your half a million. But I found that Howard had allowed various clubs until March or April of the next year to think about whether they were going to post their performance bond. Brilliant! So we're going to plan the League's future without knowing how many teams are going to be in the League?'[47]

Toye called up the other remaining teams, and one or two prospective owners, to see where their cash was. Tampa,

Toye says, told him, 'We were waiting for you to get back to us.' There was a formal meeting with the Cosmos, with Toye's nemesis Giorgio Chinaglia now retired as a player but installed as president. 'When we told him the rules of the League and that they'd be out if they didn't post the bond, he threatened to throw the lawyer Marc Bernstein out of the window, charming fellow. And before that I was in Vancouver, and one of the guys had to take a phone call, then he came back in and said, "We've just heard the Cosmos are not going to post their performance bond." End of the Whitecaps. Then another guy, Peter King, was going to take Houston, then he heard the Cosmos weren't in. Little bang, little bang, little bang, until it was gone.'

What is he talking about? Toye explains that he subscribed to the big bang and little bang theories expounded by Madison Square Gardens chairman Sonny Werblin when discussions were under way in the late 70s about expanding the League to 24 teams from eighteen. Werblin, who was involved with the NASL through MSG's ownership of the Washington Diplomats, said the big bang theory to stabilize the League was to get rid of its six weakest teams now, 'and leave ourselves with twelve clubs that are going somewhere, and expand later on. The little bang theory was that if we don't get rid of those six clubs, you get rid of them one by one as time goes by, a little bang here, a little bang there, and not only will you lose the ones you *want* to get rid of, but you'll also lose some of the good guys who'll say, "To hell with this, this is not the league it was, I'm out." And he was 100 per cent right. I went to a League meeting [ahead of the 1978 season]; there were six applicants, each prepared to pay $3 million for a franchise. We lost the vote [opposing their acceptance]. So now we had six good, six okay, and twelve bad, and that led to the dissolution of the League. The Robin Hood business model never lasted long enough to get the owners their money back. But what it did do, it made the game arrive in America and made Americans love the game.'[48]

In 1985 that left just Toronto and Minnesota, 'who had done what they were supposed to do and posted their bond,' says Toye. 'You can not plan a bloody season when you don't know who's going to bloody well play in it two weeks before the season starts. Everyone agrees with that. So that is how the League declined, because our success, or our apparent success, led to idiots being allowed into the League, idiots running the League. And you couldn't have a league where the Strikers play the Blizzard 24 times a year.'[49]

Lack of (tele)vision

> 'We prostituted ourselves for a little money, and
> when the ratings were low and they dropped us,
> that was another negative story.'
>
> —Tulsa GM Noel Lemon on
> the League's television deals.[50]

Two other factors played a role in the NASL's decline – television and the rise of indoor soccer. Cable television, which many believe would have been perfect for soccer (that is, those who wanted it could have subscribed), arrived across the whole of America just a few years too late. Without it, as Noel Lemon bluntly states in the above quote, the focus on the need for a national TV contract was both misguided and rather pathetic. ABC producers like Chet Forte would make grand announcements at the start of a new contract like, 'We're all soccer nuts, we all love soccer. We're all big believers in this. We all love the sport and there's no reason why we shouldn't do well with it.'[51] Wahay! Except that there were lots of reasons, such as lousy ratings from games shown on Sunday afternoons in the middle of summer. The US home viewing public was simply not interested enough in soccer to watch it in large enough numbers across the whole country. No one in Miami much cared about a game between San Jose and Portland. It was the opposite case with American football, but gridiron's TV success had coincided with the post-Second World War economic boom, the establishment of a country-wide league thanks to the ease of air travel, and the fact that the sport had been part of North American culture for several decades.

Remember the League's sensible Strategic Plan from 1977? It also recommended focusing on local TV contracts, and stated: 'Having a national TV contract not properly thought through leads to poor ratings and the risk of the national TV contract being axed for the third time in the League's history.'[52] This is exactly what happened when big believers ABC, despite being 'soccer nuts', dropped the League in 1980, the year after proclaiming their faith in the sport. Nothing against soccer, of course, it's just business. 'Madison Avenue started screaming that the NASL had bad ratings,' said Lemon. 'The NASL got a black eye again. We should have stayed off network TV until we could command prime time. Then we could have thoroughly examined the ratings and seen where we stood.'[53]

It wasn't the lack of a stable, long-term and lucrative network TV contract in itself that led to the NASL's demise.

Rather, it was the focus of too many parties in the League on that possible contract as a panacea to the NASL's money problems, and clubs spending as though the wished-for TV deal really did exist.

Take it indoors

> 'I didn't decide not to play outdoors. The fans decided for me by not coming. I couldn't continue to take the losses I had been taking and I saw the only chance to keep the team alive was to play indoors.'
>
> —Chicago Sting owner Lee Stern[54]

Stern announced he was taking his Chicago team out of the NASL even before they'd played the two-leg Soccer Bowl against Toronto in 1984, creating some bitterness in the League. He'd lost at least half a million dollars per season, he said, and was disillusioned that when they'd played the Cosmos that season, 'We had 8,000 people, the smallest Cosmos crowd in our history. Three years ago, we had 40,000. Where did they go? It has me stumped.'[55] The final was further denigrated by officials and players on both teams criticizing the other's style and tactics. There were twelve yellow cards in the first game, which Chicago won 2–1. They won the second leg in Toronto 3–2. New champions, on their way out to play in the Major Indoor Soccer League (MISL).

The MISL had started in 1978. Its co-founder Earl Foreman had been burned by the NASL in the early 1970s as an investor in the Washington Whips. 'I died for two years with 5,000 people rattling around the [RFK] Stadium in Washington,' he said. 'But put that same number in the Spectrum [Philadelphia's indoor arena] and they'll sound like 50,000. We have to draw only 10,000 to accomplish the same thing outdoor teams accomplish with 35,000.'[56] The game in itself didn't threaten the NASL, because the MISL played in winter. It was more the fact that one year later the NASL founded its own indoor league, and couldn't decide whether or not to make it mandatory for member clubs. First it was, then it wasn't, then it was again. The thinking was to keep contracted players busy all year round, gain extra income, and further market the game and keep it in the public consciousness.

The indoor game had its advocates all right. 'We have a faster game, higher scoring, easier to see,' said Foreman. 'You're close to the action with us. You don't sit up in the rafters wondering who has the ball. And we are going to have American players – we can develop identification because at the end of the season, our players won't go home.'[57] Ron Newman recalls that 'it was all promotion, it was easy to sell, the fans loved it, they were close to the players, they could watch three games a week.'[58] Steve David thinks the indoor game helped bring about the end of the outdoor game. 'That's one of the reasons why I left [the NASL]: indoor was taking over the game,' he says. 'Americans loved the physicality of the game, a lot of goals, there was goal-to-goal action, so I thought that was the future. I felt that would also bring about the demise of the NASL. It did affect the NASL because of the nature of the game and the action.'[59] Gary Etherington had 'thirteen good, fun years out of it. It did seem like the future of US soccer at that point. There were hardly any teams that were struggling for crowds.'[60]

The dissent tended to come from traditionalists horrified at the presentation. As *Sports Illustrated* summarized a few years into the MISL's life: 'Where the league has succeeded, it has been the first sport consciously to try to market itself as a product, as if it were a soap or a tire. The audience has been carefully targeted, the Show professionally choreographed, the entire image packaged.'[61] There was rock music, lots of smoke and dry ice, and a participating compere encouraging the crowd – this was a blatant attempt to encroach on the ice hockey market. Clive Toye termed it 'a different sport',[62] Brian Glanville called it 'a crude reduction of the real thing, much easier to understand and relate to in its vulgar banality'.[63] A BBC documentary about the MISL's Baltimore Blast was narrated in the customary tone of distanced condescension.

After years of back and forth, merger talks between the two leagues broke down, and the MISL ended up taking teams from the NASL's indoor league. The NASL had no choice but to allow its teams to go, or face losing them for the outdoor season. In terms of rock 'n' roll soccer, it was outdone by a concept more overtly garish than anything it could have staged in an outdoor stadium, with what *World Soccer* magazine described as 'the peculiar combination of pin-ball action and half-time laser shows'. Little wonder that Ron Newman, when he heard that the NASL was going out of business, could do nothing more than 'sit there in my office crying my eyes out'.[64]

Season-by-season overview

1982

League down to fourteen teams, all of whom had to have at least seven North Americans in the squad, and two on the field at any time. Cue the 'naturalizing' of lots of long-term foreign players. Toronto signed Manchester United and Northern Ireland international Jimmy Nicholl, who by a fortunate coincidence had been born in Canada and had dual citizenship. The **Cosmos** took the championship for the final time, but again the flagship game was a disappointment, a 1–0 win over Seattle. Average crowds down almost 7 per cent to just above 13,000.

Fun facts: Steve Hunt – who'd returned to England from New York in 1978 declaring 'British is best' – returned to the Cosmos on loan from Coventry City, a little older and balder. Maybe he just came to tell everyone how much better it was in England, to which his teammates retorted, 'So how come you're losing your hair?' Talking Heads singer David Byrne scored eight goals in 32 appearances for the Toronto Blizzard. Yes, it really was him. Really. Why else do you think they called that crappy Cosmos documentary *Once in a Lifetime*? Alright, it wasn't him.

1983

Twelve teams left. The rough **Tulsa Roughnecks** won.* Crowds steady at still just over 13,000, but largely thanks to Montreal, New York and, especially this year, Vancouver, who pulled in over 60,000 for a June home game with Seattle on the inaugural night for the spanking new BC Place Stadium (at least it wasn't a double-header with the Beach Boys). The same venue hosted Soccer Bowl with a similarly huge crowd. The Canadians tried their own pro soccer league, a strange time to do so given that Montreal, Toronto and Vancouver were three of the strongest remaining teams in the NASL. It folded after two months with the season incomplete.

* See Chapter 5.

1984

Nine teams, in a dying league. **Chicago**, already having announced they were leaving the NASL to concentrate on indoor soccer, won the championship against Toronto over two games. Montreal's crowds had plummeted in 1983 when they had announced that, in 1984, they would become Team Canada – an ill-considered marketing move in Quebec, where French-language separatists were quite prevalent. That, and Molson were losing millions of dollars every year on the team, despite healthy crowds. Neither Montreal nor Team Canada showed for 1984. Five North American players had to be on the field now at all times, but it was way too late to be thinking about the development of native talent. The only real world star names left in the League were Roberto Bettega at Toronto and Johan Neeskens at the Cosmos. The latter team played a few exhibition games in 1985, but with paltry crowds lost inside Giants Stadium showing little enthusiasm, even they realized when it was time to call it a day. The final game was against Lazio, with both teams now owned by Giorgio Chinaglia, but fewer than 9,000 turned out and Chinaglia announced that the game had made a loss of $60,000. 'We can no longer continue to offer something to our fans that they no longer want,' said Chinaglia's former agent Peppe Pinton, now the Cosmos general manager.[65]

It wasn't complete gloom. The USSF was so encouraged by the massive soccer crowds at the 1984 LA Olympics that it decided to make a serious bid for the 1994 World Cup. That meant reinvigorating the men's national team programme, and the laying of plans for an eventual new professional men's outdoor soccer league.

Conclusion

Learning from your alcoholic dad: the NASL legacy

> 'There is a place for good, major league soccer in this country, with sensible budgets, sound management, and sound ownership.'
>
> —Noel Lemon, former Tulsa Roughnecks GM, 1985

When the North American Soccer League folded, most of the people involved had long been able to pinpoint the reasons, even as they were helpless to prevent its rapid, inexorable slide into liquidation. In spite of the gloom that inevitably shrouded the shutting of all doors and the long-term mothballing of logos and team identities, some could see that the endeavour had not been a complete waste of time and money. Out-of-pocket owners probably disagreed, but in retrospect there is no debating the importance of the NASL to both the US and the world game. At home, it laid the foundation for a nationwide soccer infrastructure that continues to move from strength to strength – from millions of tottering infants of both sexes bee-hiving around the ball in recreational games all the way up to a competitive national team that has taken part in seven successive World Cups, and an established professional league that is gradually expanding towards the size of the NASL at its peak.

'You see this once glamorous machine brought to a state of morgue-like existence,' said Clive Toye a few months after the

League shut down, 'and you say, "What a bloody shame." But it was an equal part of "Let's put all this rubbish to rest and get on with it. This league doesn't deserve to go on." My loyalty is to the game of soccer, not to any single entity.' Toye already believed the NASL had laid a secure enough foundation for soccer to survive and that, somewhere down the line, it would eventually thrive again. He foresaw a league that would conform to FIFA laws, with many more North American players, and 'a league prepared to spend reasonable but not outrageous sums of money and grow naturally, rather than comparing itself with the NFL or any other league.'[1] He envisioned the game being played 'in stadiums that seat under 30,000. We must pay more attention to the aesthetics of the game. For example, playing in rectangular stadiums where it looks like a soccer game.'[2] In short, he foresaw Major League Soccer, founded in 1996.

In the shorter term, the NASL also hugely influenced the world game. No one would have admitted it at the time, but the League gave FIFA and the European game a hard kick in the arse. True, during the NASL's peak years many in Europe feared an Americanization of the game that would trample upon its hallowed traditions. Yet even as they gasped in horror at the sight of cheerleaders, fireworks and artificial turf, many were looking anew at how the game was being marketed. In an era of widespread stadium violence and diminishing but predominantly white, male, working-class crowds, English league clubs especially began to quietly examine the possibilities of the American match-day experience. They were tired of hooliganism and the threat of imminent bankruptcy. The 1980s stadium disasters in Brussels, Bradford and Sheffield would in any case have prompted the process of change, but the NASL had begun to affect the way that British teams looked at the game long before that. In 1976, while playing in the Second Division, Fulham FC signed George Best and Rodney Marsh – both of whom had just completed their first seasons in the NASL – to join Bobby Moore in their line-up, initially doubling home crowds. Wasn't this an attempt to bring North American-style soccer to grey little England?

'It was,' Rodney Marsh confirms, 'and it was intentional. The chairman, Ernie Clay, he said that was our brief. He signed George and myself and said, "I want you to entertain the fans." I can remember that meeting in Claridge's Hotel, and Ernie said, "I'm paying you a lot of money, George – much more than you, Rodney."' He laughs. 'George was the big hit and I was the deputy big hit – we had a fantastic eight or nine months, then we both went back to America.'[3] Fulham, however, only finished seventeenth that season. Fulham supporters of a certain age may cherish the memory of a unique season where they had the opportunity of watching two flair players bring a little style to games against the likes of Hereford United and Notts County. The televised home game against Hereford saw Fulham win 4–1, and its highlights should appear in any dictionary as the definitive synopsis of the word 'showboating'. It didn't happen every week, though, and with Marsh injured for long stretches, they were almost relegated. Would the fans have preferred more functional soccer, and a challenge for promotion?

Historically, though, the idea of entertainment eventually won out for the English game's top level. There are regularly skewed results in the Premier League nowadays that were an extreme rarity in the 1970s and 1980s. From the past few seasons alone, and this is between the top teams, there have been the following scorelines: Manchester United 8 Arsenal 2; Chelsea 3 Arsenal 5; Manchester United 1 Manchester City 6;

Manchester City 6 Arsenal 3. There are regular 4–4 draws and one-sided hammerings where lowly teams ship five, six, seven or eight goals against the Champions League regulars – fans barely blink at these results now, even as the TV presenters try to affect an expression of shock upon announcing them. It's not that coaches have suddenly become cavalier about defence and told their teams not to worry about letting in goals. It's more that the emphasis of the game in the television age has broadly shifted towards attack. These results do wonders for the image of the game in the far-flung places where the Premier League is now broadcast – Asia, Africa and North America. Goals mean talking points and fattened highlight reels, while the purists who mutter about the lost art of defending represent an increasingly archaic, irrelevant voice. These are high-class, attacking games played on perfect surfaces in sold out, all-seater stadiums, and they are played by some of the biggest names in world soccer. This is the easily sellable TV product that the NASL wanted to be – a round-ball version of the NFL, with globally known brands and massive sales of merchandise in every country where the absolutely-crucial-to-human-destiny Manchester derby is transmitted.

'If television had backed the NASL, the Premier League would now be the NASL,'[4] says Marsh. It's a leap of the imagination, but not without substance. If you transpose today's TV market back to the 1970s, you can imagine the eye-watering cost of the global broadcasting rights for a league featuring Cruyff, Pelé, Best and Beckenbauer. If MLS had the money, the will and the persuasive powers to sign Lionel Messi, Cristiano Ronaldo, Wayne Rooney, Franck Ribery and Luis Suarez, then selling global TV rights would be the only way to recoup their outlay. This is why the NASL was the prototype league for the modern game – the Premier League and the UEFA Champions League depend on their worldwide TV audience to sustain them. That audience will not be satisfied watching Stoke and Sunderland kick each other on the way to a grim 0–0 draw where both teams are happy to take a point in the fight against relegation. It's the big games and the big names that sell the Premier League, and those games must be sold on the back of their stars, their stories, and an endless drum-roll of pre-match hyperbole that dramatizes the entire spectacle as an epic showdown. Possibly to the annoyance of some who used to prefer Stoke and Sunderland in a grim, goalless mud-battle, the product more often than not delivers on its promise. In the same way that mass-marketed fast food often tastes gratifyingly good, the Premier League and the Champions League – the latter at least during its knockout stages – can be fantastically entertaining to watch.

Going back to the summer of 1979, more than a dozen British clubs came over to the US during their pre-season to play NASL teams, and several of them were interested in how North American clubs were approaching the game off the field. 'When we [the Cosmos] were at our best,' says Clive Toye, 'we were constantly being visited by executives from English clubs to see what we were doing, asking why we were doing it.'[5] Two teams in particular tried their hand at US-style razzmatazz – Bristol City and Aberdeen. 'I was so impressed with what I saw in America,' said City's promotions manager Jim Evans, 'as soon as I got back I put together a marketing booklet which was sent round the English League.' The club introduced pre-match and half-time entertainment that included performing animals, live music, Wild West shootouts, marching bands, and golf and archery contests. On top of that came the team of eighteen cheerleaders, The Great Western Girls. 'They've done very, very well,' claimed Evans. 'We send our girls out to the centre of the field fifteen minutes before kick-off. They do a dance routine to some rock and roll music for about five minutes. After that they line up for the team to come on to the field, just like they do in the States.'[6]

After Aberdeen secretary Ian Taggart returned home from a trip to the US he started to send out players to make personal appearances at youth clubs, social groups and local teams. 'We've even organized coaching sessions in local parks,' he said. Both Aberdeen and Bristol City began allowing fans in for organized stadium tours. At this point in time, no new soccer stadium had been built in England since Southend United's Roots Hall in 1955. 'It's got to come,' said Evans. 'Only finance at present stops it. We're going to make a move on this next season.'[7] In fact, Bristol City today still play at Ashton Gate, their home for over a century, with plans for a new stadium at Ashton Vale – years in the making – about to be dropped at the time of writing in favour of redeveloping their current stadium. It would be another nine years from Evans's 1979 forecast before England boasted a new soccer stadium – Scunthorpe United's functional, modest Glanford Park, built on the edge of town to replace the Old Showground, which was a stadium with history and character, but standing on desirable city centre land with a high real estate value. It's now a supermarket with a concrete plaque on an outer wall commemorating the place where Kevin Keegan used to play.*

---

* In early 2014 Scunthorpe unveiled plans for yet another new stadium – a 12,000-capacity ground not far from their current home as part of a leisure complex.

Blandly christened Glanford Park did, however, kick off a busy new era of remodelling and brand-new construction. The rebuilding during the 1970s of Rangers' Ibrox Park in Glasgow following 66 deaths and 200 injuries at the Ibrox disaster of 1971 had already showcased what could be done, and pointed to UK soccer's future – there were three new, all-seater stands with clear sightlines of the entire pitch, no matter where you sat. In the US, such a stadium would be classed as the norm. In Britain, this was radical, but soon afterwards attendances at Ibrox slumped – the team were doing poorly as the club spent more money meeting the cost of redevelopment at the expense of new players, while many fans complained that the atmosphere had suffered due to the redesign from an oval, enclosed stadium (where most fans had stood) to a rectangular ground with open corners where 85 per cent of the fans were sitting down.

In the long run, though, such fans would have little or no say in British football once standing was outlawed in the top two divisions following the Hillsborough disaster. New or redeveloped stadiums at all levels in the UK boast the following: wide and accessible exits (good – minimal chances of any more stadium disasters); vast concourses filled with a wider choice of concession stands for food and drink (broadly good, though usually extortionate); a club shop (or shops) selling every conceivable object imprinted with the team's name (good if you like that sort of thing); more and better toilets (good unless the smell of piss takes you back to the good old days); and neat rows of seats overseen by stewards who will threaten to throw you out of the stadium if you don't sit down (for many fans, very bad). The archetypal example would be Arsenal's move from Highbury to the Emirates Stadium. Decades of nostalgia, sentimentality, history and tradition were shunned in favour of a bigger stadium to accommodate more people buying significantly more expensive tickets (partly to help pay for the new stadium). A visit to the new Arsenal Stadium will feel familiar to anyone who's ever been to an NFL game at FedEx Field just outside Washington DC, or Lincoln Financial Field in Philadelphia – all that concrete, that long walk to the upper tier, and that utter absence of the club's soul. Every brick has been laid with the sole intention of maximizing income. Anyone who'd feared the Americanization of soccer in the 1970s could now stand before the Emirates Stadium with a grimace and say, 'I told you so.' Their envious north London neighbours Tottenham Hotspur plan to build one just like it.

More legacy: points, women, offside, stats, jerseys and pass-backs

There are a number of other ways that the NASL has influenced soccer to a larger or lesser degree. However much FIFA disliked the League's innovations, at least they got the conversation rolling in the following areas, most of them covered in chapter seven.

To recap, the NASL's **point-scoring system** aimed simply to encourage attacking soccer. In 1981, on the recommendation of an investigative panel headed by none other than former NASL team owner Jimmy Hill, England became the first country to introduce three points for a win, with precisely the same aim. Hill had seen for himself in the US what a more incentivized points system could produce, and this would undoubtedly have influenced his report. Only up to a point, though – neither the FA nor FIFA had the courage to follow through and actually reward goalscoring in terms of extra points. FIFA incorporated 'three points for a win' into its laws in 1995 after using it for the first time at the 1994 World Cup, but in truth it has never really been determined whether or not the change has made any positive difference to the game at all. In fact an extensive Spanish study concluded quite the opposite – three points for a win was actually detrimental to the game because it encouraged teams that took a one-goal lead to play more defensively.[8]

The NASL experimented with three **substitutes**, with FIFA's permission, and that is now the international norm. **Names and squad numbers on jerseys** are now universal in the professional game around the world. The NASL was the first league in the world to recognize that you could double your potential audience by appealing to **women**. It's true that FIFA never adopted the **35-yard offside line** and eventually forced the NASL to drop it, but the NASL's willingness to try and combat the insidious interference of offside prompted everyone to look long and hard at this attack-killing side effect. By fiddling with the law on and off down the years, and with an increase in the speed of play, the dreaded sight of four lump-headed defenders moving out and raising their arms in sync has become another image left in the 1980s.

Time-wasting by the goalkeeper Americans were baffled that something as tedious as the **back pass** to the goalkeeper was tolerated, and that the keeper could hang on to the ball until he was chivvied by the ref to kick it upfield. The NASL talked about forbidding the keeper to pick up the ball, but FIFA wouldn't listen until the early 1990s, long after the League's demise. Maybe by then they hoped that everyone would have forgotten it wasn't their idea. Then there was Carl Berg, maligned as one of the generation of NASL owners who knew nothing about the game – indeed, when he took over the Golden Bay franchise in San Jose, he had never even seen a soccer game in his life – but sometimes it takes a fresh pair of eyes. Once he'd watched a game or two, he wanted to abolish offside, have 'more scoring', but also to make the goalkeeper release the ball within five seconds.[9] When FIFA finally introduced such a ruling several years later, they made it seven seconds. It's also very rare to see referees actually enforce it – Thierry Henry is fond of standing next to a referee and counting down the seconds on his fingers when he thinks a goalkeeper is wasting time, and he's yet to come across an official who pays him a second's notice.

Like them or not (and you probably don't), **statistics** have become a huge part of soccer's television coverage, because you have to somehow fill in all that airtime before the game, at half-time, and after the game. It's arguable that in Europe few people really care, but there are also fans among us who read the possession stats, and the corner kick stats, and the offside and fouls stats with at least a smidgen of interest. This all started in the NASL, because Americans love a lot of stats with their sports – if you've ever overheard two baseball fans discussing numbers at any length, you'd probably assess the conversation as some kind of pernicious penalty on mankind for developing the power of speech. *Kick* once devoted an entire issue to statistics, surmising that 'it's not too far down the road when fans can argue that a ratio of shots to saves is the only way to rate a goalkeeper rather than goals against average.'[10] One team official, former Dallas Tornado PR man Dick Berg, invented new stats called the Involvement Ratio (IR) and Box Penetrations (BP). IR measured the average of a player's frequency in shooting, passing, tackling, intercepting and clearing the ball. BPs counted the number of times the ball made it into the eighteen-yard box, while Danger Zone Penetrations measured the number of times the ball made it into the 35-yard area. Box Penetration stats have come to pass in their own way – a Californian company called Match Analysis has been providing clients such as the German national team with scrupulously detailed statistical breakdowns of their opponents for over a decade.

MLS: 'We are not the NASL'

The re-establishment of a professional league was one of the conditions set by FIFA for awarding the 1994 World Cup to the USA, and when Major League Soccer kicked off two years later it made a point of identifying itself as the antithesis of the NASL. Even now, almost two decades on, the teams and their player transfers are still centrally regulated by MLS (the so-called 'single entity' structure), each team must stick to a salary cap, and any potential new owners and cities are subject to a rigorous examination of their suitability (i.e. their wealth, and how much of it they're prepared to plough into a soccer team). Starting out in 1996, a year later than planned, the new league survived an early antitrust suit from its own players, who objected to the central planning and the salary cap, and in 2000 a contraction back to ten teams from the twelve it had increased to two years earlier. Despite a handful of foreign semi-stars, such as Jorge Campos of Mexico, Carlos Valderrama from Colombia, and the Bolivian Marco Etcheverry, the league concentrated far more than the NASL on nurturing US players, although a fair number of Caribbean, Central and South American hopefuls have always made up the numbers. In 1999, the soccer-dedicated stadiums foreseen by Clive Toye in 1985 began to spring up, starting with the Columbus Crew. There is no chance now of a new team joining MLS if it does not have plans for a stadium, preferably in a downtown location – new soccer stadiums stuck out in the suburbs, such as in Dallas and Chicago, have been far less successful at pulling in fans than city centre sites like Houston and Toronto.

MLS at first did, however, retain a few American-style features held over from the NASL. It kept the time off-field, so that the game was over when the scoreboard said so, not when the ref blew his whistle. For drawn games, it stuck with the NASL shootouts for the first few years, then changed to a ten-minute period of sudden-death extra time (although with no tie-breaker if there were no further goals). Finally, it conformed to FIFA norms. As in the rest of the world, the referee kept time, and a drawn game after 90 minutes was just that – a drawn game, with one point each. Teams have come and gone (Tampa Bay, Miami*), and a couple have moved (San Jose to Houston in 2005, but then San Jose was reborn a couple of years later), but there's been nothing like the perennial mobility and bankruptcy in the NASL. On the whole, Major League Soccer was a completely new start for professional soccer in the US, and the new league ignored any overtures from old NASL hands keen to give advice or land a job with this slim, austere new body. 'Clive [Toye] has a very jaundiced view of everything that happens in MLS, particularly with the team here in New York,' says Paul Gardner. 'He thinks he could have handled them much better,

---

* Miami is scheduled to return to MLS in 2017 under the auspices of David Beckham and other investors, contingent upon finding a location for a new stadium downtown.

and who's to say he's wrong? The NASL was bad news for MLS, a failure. They understood, possibly correctly, that you didn't throw good money after bad. You could argue they've done it better, though I'm not sure I would argue that.'[11]

In terms of its stability, there would appear to be little room for argument. The aim of MLS is to expand from its current nineteen teams (for the 2014 season) to 24 by 2020 – if that happens it will have taken MLS 24 years to manage what the NASL achieved in less than half that time. This is not, of course, to the detriment of MLS, which has made starting a new franchise an attractive proposition under the canny management of commissioner Don Garber. Under his leadership, MLS has landed television rights deals worth $90 million annually (including coverage of US national team games), significantly increased sponsorship, upped match-day revenues thanks to most teams having their own stadiums, and allowed its marketing arm to invest some of the league's income through a private equity firm. Yet many MLS teams are still losing money, only no one knows exactly how much. The NASL owners, as we have seen, were keen to broadcast their losses, usually just before locking the doors and running for cover. MLS refuses to issue any financial figures, leaving journalists to speculate on the scale of losses – it was widely estimated that between 1996 and 2004 the league lost $350 million. Over half of its teams are, though, according to *Forbes* magazine,[12] now running at a profit, yet still Garber conceded at the end of 2013, 'Major League Soccer still loses money as an enterprise. We've got to find a way that we can get closer to a break-even enterprise.'[13]

Superstars have also found their way into MLS, thanks to a change in the financial rules announced late in 2006 that allowed teams to sign Designated Players (that is, expensive players with mind-blowing salaries), paving the way for David Beckham to sign for LA the following year, and Thierry Henry for New York in 2010. Beckham's signing became The Pelé Moment for MLS, but it did not usher in a rush of world stars because there were not enough teams prepared to put up the kind of money that LA was paying him – in 2007, Beckham's *basic* annual salary of $6.5 million was nine times more than the combined wages of the league's 57 developmental players (apprentices). In 2014, Toronto FC moved to counter seven years of failure since its inception by signing Tottenham's Jermain Defoe and Roma's Michael Bradley, both for huge sums and huge wages in MLS terms. It was a massive risk (or a 'bold move', if you want to be more generous) for a team in a 20,000-seater stadium, but that stadium was no longer close to selling out as it had been during the team's vibrant early years. Toronto tried several changes in coaches and management, but in the end it opted for the NASL way – expensive, foreign stars. At the time of writing, the result of their gamble is not yet known.

Former NASL goalkeeper Alan Mayer agrees that the negative aspects of the NASL had a positive influence on MLS, like the young boy looking at his alcoholic father and deciding that he will become the opposite. 'The kid grows up to be a success,' he says. 'The dad has a big effect, whether positive or negative.'[14] Other former players are not so generous to the current league. 'MLS is still a bush league to me,' says Bob Iarusci. 'They still run games during the World Cup qualifiers. For me they're still a renegade league. They still treat the Canadians as second-class citizens, even though they had to come to Canada to save their league. If they hadn't come to Toronto seven years ago [in 2007], the league wouldn't be where it is today.' He maintains that if the US had been awarded the 1986 World Cup, 'the NASL would still be here today, and there'd be no MLS'.[15] Rodney Marsh finds the idea of MLS competing with the Premier League for the attention of television viewers as 'disheartening'. People will be watching New York play Seattle, 'and then it'll be City vs United on television. One is dross and the other is world-class football, so why would you go to the games when you can watch on TV the best players in the world?' Having two teams in New York – as MLS will when the Manchester City-backed New York City FC starts play in 2015 – he calls 'suicidal'.[16]

Others are more generous to MLS, and view the numerous other foreign leagues on TV as beneficial to the US game. 'I think MLS is doing very well and is on the right path,' says Arnie Mausser. Soccer in the US, he says, 'would have exploded a little bit sooner' if there had been the same TV exposure back in the 1970s as there is now.[17] Tim Twellman, whose son Taylor thrived in MLS with the New England Revolution, says the NASL 'laid the groundwork for fans in this country to understand the sport. The fans are educated now, they really are. The good thing is that it [the NASL] brought a lot of good players into this country, and a lot of them stayed here and helped the sport as well. I do think the NASL players of my era need to support MLS in a better way. You hear a lot of snide remarks like, "Oh, we were better than them".'

That may have resulted from MLS consciously cutting the NASL out of history. Twellman agrees, but adds that 'they were not necessarily cutting themselves off, but didn't want to be seen as having the same voices speaking. I get that, because the sport has moved on, and you can't hang on to the past the whole time.'[18] On the other hand, it was not only Canada, but the Pacific North West that MLS finally turned to in order to help it expand. The three regional rivals that were a vital part of NASL's peak years – the Seattle Sounders (joined MLS in 2009), the Portland Timbers (2011), and the Vancouver Whitecaps (also 2011) – all signed up for the latter-day league using their old names, having continued or reformed as semi-pro clubs in the years after the NASL collapsed. MLS finally acknowledged the soccer-rich legacy that the NASL had bequeathed to the region. Crowds have not only been healthy, but have blessed MLS with the kind of devoted fan culture and heady atmosphere it has long yearned for to assimilate itself with the world game, and in contrast to the less spontaneous, tannoy-generated noise that fans experience in other US sports.

'I look at the northwest and Seattle and Vancouver and Portland and that pretty much describes the NASL legacy right there,' says former Whitecap Bob Lenarduzzi, who is now president of the team's MLS incarnation. 'I know for a fact we have supporters that look back with fuzzy memories to the NASL days. When MLS started out they didn't want us, because they wanted a fresh start, but if you look at the northwest now it's living proof that there is a material leftover from the old NASL days.' Why did it take MLS so long to catch on to the fact that there were three teams in the Pacific North West with ready-made fan bases? 'You'd have to ask them that,' he says. 'I guess that cosmetically it might have been good to have separation from a league that failed, and that's what they thought at the time. But give them credit, they maybe realized eventually that it was important to reconnect, and that the NASL was a positive rather than a negative.'[19]

Should MLS have revived the Cosmos?

While MLS belatedly tapped into the ready-and-waiting Pacific North West fans of its predecessor league, it ignored the Cosmos from the start. Aside from the legal question of who actually owned the Cosmos name and logo (Giorgio Chinaglia's associate Peppe Pinton claimed it was him, and eventually he sold them on), the Cosmos represented all that MLS wanted to avoid – a dominant team with overpaid stars run at a chronic loss. Most Cosmos lovers refused to align themselves with the city's new MLS team in the Meadowlands, the woefully named New York/New Jersey MetroStars, who won themselves few fans and few games while rattling around in the Cosmos' former home. A corporate takeover and rebrand as the New York Red Bulls in 2006, a smart new soccer stadium in Harrison, New Jersey, and the signing of Thierry Henry have gone some way to rectifying a mediocre first decade, but for many New York area soccer fans this team is still primarily 'not the Cosmos'. Neither will New York City FC be the Cosmos, even though they will be playing (somewhere as yet unspecified) in Manhattan or Queens, after starting out at Yankee Stadium. And neither are the revived New York Cosmos, playing semi-pro in the reformed, ten-team North American Soccer League along with exhumed entities like the Tampa Bay Rowdies* and the Fort Lauderdale Strikers.

---

* Rodney Marsh: 'I'm not at all involved with the new Tampa Bay Rowdies. I have no time in my life for bollocks. I went to a game two seasons ago and it looked like the Dog and Duck playing the Kings Arms, it was horrendous. I live in Tampa most of the year – a Tampa Bay team playing again is great for the community, but I just can't do that. I'd rather go on Twitter.' (Author interview)

When the revived Cosmos were interested in joining MLS in 2011 – under a secretive new ownership group headed by bankrupt British businessman Paul Kemsley – league commissioner Garber warned, 'They need to believe in the MLS system, which is not about one team dominating everybody else like the Cosmos did 30 years ago. And if they don't believe in our system, we won't sell them the team.'[20] The Cosmos did not join MLS, possibly baulking at the league's demand for a $100 million expansion fee, and had to wait until the summer of 2013 before playing in the second-tier NASL, which itself had begun again in 2011. Playing out in Long Island in a 12,000-capacity stadium at Hofstra University – where the original Cosmos started out – the neo-Cosmos stated that they still aim to join MLS one day, and want to build a new $400 million stadium on the border of Queens and Nassau County on Long Island. Given the arrival in MLS of New York City FC – the aforementioned team being backed not only by Manchester City but also the New York Yankees, and which thus naturally *could* afford the $100 million expansion fee – this seems like a distant pipe dream.

One of the recurring clichés of the NASL era was that if a league could get a team to succeed in the New York market, then it could get a team to succeed anywhere. In the modern era, the best chance a team had of succeeding in New York would have been a revived Cosmos in 1996. That moment having long since passed, there will now be three teams with a New York name fighting for soccer prominence in the notoriously capricious city. It's possible that soccer's future will one day look so bright in the US that all three teams will compete as rivals, London-style. In the meantime, the debate is still open on whether or not MLS could do with a giant team like the

Cosmos to dominate its moribund league just a little bit. It would be a terrible thing, of course, to have an outstanding team, but then this is exactly what the league lacks. A hated bogey team, an obnoxious monster to be vilified for the same reasons that big teams in other leagues and other sports are despised – because of their success. MLS abjures any such notion, and that is why the championship usually changes hands on a season-by-season basis. This is all very equitable, and democratic, and commendable too. Yet, is it interesting? Is it exciting and entertaining? The LA Galaxy, with its four MLS titles and its signing of Beckham and, ahem, Robbie Keane, came slightly close to becoming a glamour team, and therefore the fans' whipping boy, but it was never quite convincing. MLS and most of its players, including the ever-courteous Beckham, were in the end just too *nice*. The Cosmos had that allure of the despicable, of the evil rich – they would bring in the crowds wherever they played, who all wanted to see the arrogant, demon-eyed Chinaglia and his colleagues fail. They were a spectacle, a travelling fairground of multifarious talents and attractions. Even now, though, the idea of another Cosmos provokes ambivalent reactions.

Former Tulsa Roughnecks coach Charlie Mitchell cites his team as a typical example of an NASL club that were obscured by the long shadow of the Cosmos. 'My budget as a coach was the same as Beckenbauer and Chinaglia alone,' he says. 'How are you meant to compete? We *did* compete, in that we beat them once, but if you played them ten times they'd beat you nine times, because they had the money to spend. Eventually you can only spend so much, and you can't buy a championship. It wasn't a good match-up between Tulsa and the Cosmos, for example. One run by a couple of oil men, the other run by Warner Brothers. There was no structure as far as salaries were concerned to keep it even, it was just buy, buy, buy.'

In that respect, the Cosmos really did foreshadow the current trend in global soccer. The domination of a single or small handful of teams in Europe has been accentuated by the wealth generated at the game's top end by the Champions League, and the touted best four leagues in the world (England, Italy, Spain, and Germany) have become predictable to the point of tedium. Every year, Barcelona and Real Madrid dominate in Spain, although in 2014 Atlético Madrid made a welcome and successful challenge for the title. The once egalitarian Bundesliga is succumbing to the Champions League-instigated economic model too, with CL regulars Bayern Munich and Borussia Dortmund pulling away from the rest of the German league. The same teams in England – the Manchester duo, Chelsea, Arsenal and Liverpool – now dominate the top positions of the Premier League pretty much year in, year out. Smaller leagues in countries like Scotland, Switzerland, Holland and many eastern European nations lack new names on the championship trophy due to the perennial economic and sporting dominance of one or two clubs who benefit from annual Champions League cash. It's true that there have always been bigger names that were more prominent than others, but other teams always had the chance to build a side and emerge as challengers. Even when Liverpool dominated English and European soccer in the 1970s and early 1980s, teams like Derby County, Nottingham Forest, Leeds United, Aston Villa and Everton were able to rise up and have their championship moments too. The best that any of those teams can now hope for is to hold down a Premier League spot, or maybe launch a sporadic challenge for the coveted fourth place that would edge them into the Champions League qualifying round. To do that, however, they would almost certainly have to risk borrowing and investing large amounts of money for new players. The days of one club producing a golden generation of exciting players brought up through the ranks of its youth teams are probably gone for good.

So Major League Soccer has clearly got it right by excluding the possibility of a New York Cosmos. Yet at the same time, Major League Soccer could really, really use a team like the New York Cosmos.

What is rock 'n' roll soccer?

At its peak, the North American Soccer League in the form of teams like the Kicks, the Cosmos, the Rowdies and the Sounders boasted a rock 'n' roll swagger that was new to the sport. The League was brash, cocky and prepared to bend the laws and explore garish gimmicks. It attracted the adventurous, the curious, the money-hungry and the wandering mavericks. The attention-seeking NASL was so keen to sell its product that it would happily stand up on centre stage and make a fool of itself just for the media coverage, and to lure in the doubtful passers-by. Unshackled from the burdens of history and tradition, too many of those involved in the League cared only about the moment, not enough about the future. Whatever worked NOW was most important. If that meant spending, they'd worry about the consequences later. The important thing was to fill the stadiums, milk the applause, and enjoy the present. In 1977 the band was at its peak, and no one wanted to listen to the accountant in a grey suit warning that all the excess would have to be paid for down the line. Fuck it, we're young and wild and free, and we're playing champagne soccer. Just listen to the crowd!

The NASL had its rock 'n' roll owners and its celebrity rock star hangers-on in LA and New York, and some of its players undoubtedly thought they were leading the lives of rock stars, or at least wanted to give that impression. But rock 'n' roll soccer is, if you'll forgive the cliché, more to do with an attitude that works as an over-arching catchphrase to reflect the crash-and-burn ethos of the League. That applied of course more to the Tampa Bay Rowdies of 1976 than it did to the Rochester Lancers of 1971, say. It's not the Rochester Lancers in 1971 that anyone really remembers the NASL for, though. The memorable moments are down to its daring, its dash, its mischievous spirit, and its conscious distance from the serious business of winning in favour of allowing players and fans to indulge in, dare we say it, good times. The NASL lived fast and died young, like any rock star worth mythologizing. It played with a smile, albeit a sometimes drunken smile. And like the young rock geniuses who accidentally OD'd or crashed or killed themselves before they could realize their full potential, the NASL had the courage to create, experiment and innovate, and to inspire enough people to ensure the continuity and evolution of its art. 'We know what we did,' says Clive Toye, 'and we know what's happening now.'[21]

Appendix A

North American cities and their NASL teams

Note: In 1967 the foreign teams representing US cities in the United Soccer Association league are stated. Other 1967 teams were in the National Professional Soccer League.

Anaheim – California Surf (1978–81)

Atlanta – Chiefs (1967–73 and 1979–80)

Baltimore – Bays (1967–70), Comets (1974–75)

Boston – Rovers (1967, Shamrock Rovers in the USA), Beacons (1968), Minutemen (1974–76), New England Tea Men (1978–80)

Calgary – Boomers (1981)

Chicago – Spurs (1967), Mustangs (1967–68, Cagliari in the USA in 67), Sting (1975–84)

Cleveland – Stokers (1967–68 – Stoke City in the USA in 67)

Colorado – Denver Dynamo (1974–75), Caribous (1978)

Dallas – Tornado (1967–81, Dundee United in the USA in 67)

Detroit – Cougars (1967–68, Glentoran in the USA in 67), Express (1978–80)

Edmonton – Drillers (1979–82)

Fort Lauderdale – Strikers (1977–83)

Hartford – Bi-Centennials (1975–76)

Honolulu – Team Hawaii (1977)

Houston – Stars (1967–68, Bangu in the USA in 67), Hurricane (1978–80)

Jacksonville – Tea Men (1981–82)

Kansas City – Spurs (1968–70)

Las Vegas – Quicksilvers (1977)

Los Angeles – Toros (1967), Wolves (1967–68, Wolverhampton Wanderers in the USA in 67), Aztecs (1974–81)

Memphis – Rogues (1978–80)

Miami – Gatos (1972), Toros (1973–76)

Minneapolis/St Paul – Minnesota Kicks (1975–80), Minnesota Strikers (1984)

Montreal – Olympique (1971–73), Manic (1981–83)

New Haven – Connecticut Bi-Centennials (1977)

New York – Skyliners (1967, Cerro in the USA), Generals (1967–68), Cosmos (1971–84)

Oakland – Clippers (1967–68), Stompers (1978)

Philadelphia – Spartans (1967), Atoms (1973–76), Fury (1978–80)

Pittsburgh – Phantoms (1967)

Portland – Timbers (1975–82)

Rochester – Lancers (1970–80)

St Louis – Stars (1967–77)

San Antonio – Thunder (1975–76)

San Diego – Toros (1968), Jaws (1976), Sockers (1978–84)

San Francisco – Gales (1967, ADO Den Hague in the USA)

San Jose – Earthquakes (1974–84, renamed Golden Bay Earthquakes 83–84)

Seattle – Sounders (1974–83)

Tampa Bay – Rowdies (1975–84)

Toronto – City (1967, Hibernian in the USA), Falcons (1967–68), Metros (1971–74), Metros-Croatia (1975–78), Blizzard (1979–84)

Tulsa – Roughnecks (1978–84)

Vancouver – Royals (1967–68, Sunderland in the USA in 67), Whitecaps (74–84)

Washington DC – Whips (1967–68, Aberdeen in the USA in 67), Darts (1970–71), Diplomats (1974–81), Team America (1983)

Appendix B

North American Soccer League championship games

Champions in bold, home team listed first unless venue neutral (1975–83).

1967 (NPSL):　Baltimore Bays 1 Oakland Clippers 0; **Oakland Clippers** 4 Baltimore Bays 1 (Clippers won 4–2 on aggregate)

1967 (USA):　**LA Wolves** 6 Washington Whips 5

1968:　San Diego Toros 0 Atlanta Chiefs 0; **Atlanta Chiefs** 3 San Diego Toros 0 (Chiefs won 3–0 on aggregate)

1969:　No championship game, **Kansas City Spurs** won five-team league

1970:　Rochester Lancers 3 Washington Darts 0; Washington Darts 3 **Rochester Lancers** 1 (Lancers won 4–3 on aggregate)

1971:　Atlanta Chiefs 2 Dallas Tornado 1; Dallas Tornado 4 Atlanta Chiefs 1; Atlanta Chiefs 0 **Dallas Tornado** 2 (Dallas won two games to one)

1972:　**New York Cosmos** 2 St Louis Stars 1

1973:　Dallas Tornado 0 **Philadelphia Atoms** 2

1974:　Miami Toros 3, **LA Aztecs** 3 (Aztecs won on penalties AET)

1975 (*in San Jose*):　**Tampa Bay Rowdies** 2 Portland Timbers 0

1976 (in Seattle): **Toronto Metros-Croatia** 3 Minnesota
Kicks 0

1977 (in Portland): **New York Cosmos** 2 Seattle Sounders 1

1978 (in East Rutherford, NJ): **New York Cosmos** 3 Tampa
Bay Rowdies 1

1979 (in East Rutherford, NJ): **Vancouver Whitecaps** 2
Tampa Bay Rowdies 1

1980 (in Washington DC): **New York Cosmos** 3 Fort
Lauderdale Strikers 0

1981 (in Toronto): **Chicago Sting** 0 New York Cosmos 0
(Sting won shootout AET)

1982 (in San Diego): **New York Cosmos** 1 Seattle Sounders 0

1983 (in Vancouver): **Tulsa Roughnecks** 2 Toronto
Blizzard 0

1984: Chicago Sting 2 Toronto Blizzard 1; Toronto Blizzard
2 **Chicago Sting** 3 (Sting won two games to nil)

Notes

Introduction

1. *Sports Illustrated* 30/5/77
2. *Kick* magazine, Issue 4, 1978
3. *The Observer*, 9/10/77
4. *The Guardian*, 12/2/79
5. *Sports Illustrated*, 3/7/78

Chapter 1

1. *Birmingham Evening Mail* 23/11/68
2. *Atlanta Journal*, 24/5/68
3. *ibid.*
4. *Atlanta Journal*, 23/5/68
5. *Atlanta Journal*, 24/5/68
6. *Atlanta Constitution*, 28/5/68
7. *Atlanta Constitution*, 28/5/68
8. *Atlanta Journal*, 28/5/68
9. 'It Made the Kop Sound Like a Cathedral Choir ...!', *Football Monthly*, August 1968
10. *MCFC – We Are The Champions* (brochure), 1968
11. Author interview
12. For the full story, see chapter 2 of *Soccer in a Football World*, David Wangerin (WSC Books, 2006)
13. 'Baseball Concerned: Soccer Gets Attention of Eckert', Associated Press, 20/2/67
14. *Fair Game: Myth and Reality in Sport*, Eric Midwinter (George Allen & Unwin, 1986)
15. *Soccer USA* by Chuck Cascio (Robert B. Luce, Inc., 1975)
16. Letter from Sir George Graham to Willie Gallagher, 31/10/66 (Dick Cecil private archive)
17. Author interview
18. 'Two Soccer Leagues One Too Many?' *New York Times*, 16/4/67
19. 'TV Gives Boost to High Hopes of New NPSL', *Atlanta Journal*, 2/11/66

20. Author interview
21. Letter from Phil Woosnam to Dick Cecil, 12/12/66 (Dick Cecil private archive)
22. Author interview
23. Author interview
24. Author interview
25. *Atlanta Journal*, 6/1/67
26. Author interview
27. 'Duel at Boleyn Ground', *Atlanta Constitution*, 10/2/67
28. *Atlanta Journal*, 11/1/67
29. 'Never seen a game, watched Chiefs' 3–2 opening win over the Bays', *Atlanta Journal*, 5/4/67
30. Author interview
31. *Atlanta Journal*, 27/11/67
32. 'Woosnam to Return', *Atlanta Constitution*, 4/10/67
33. *Atlanta Journal*, 16/2/68
34. *Atlanta Journal*, 17/1/68
35. 'City Shuns the World?' *Atlanta Journal* 6/2/68
36. 'Mixed Feelings For Chiefs', *Atlanta Journal*, 1/4/68
37. *Atlanta Journal*, 13/5/68
38. 'US Pro Soccer Faces Extinction', *Atlanta Journal*, 10/5/68
39. *Atlanta Constitution*, 4/6/68
40. 'No Foolin' ... City Is Serious', *Atlanta Journal*, 12/6/68
41. *ibid*.
42. *Atlanta Journal*, 15/6/68
43. *ibid*.
44. 'City's Barbs Rile Chiefs', *Atlanta Journal*, 11/6/68
45. Author interview
46. *ibid*.
47. *Atlanta Constitution*, 16/5/68
48. *Atlanta Journal*, 1/7/68
49. Author interview
50. Author interview
51. Author interview
52. Author interview
53. Author interview
54. Author interview

Chapter 2

1.   *Sports Illustrated*, 30/8/76
2.   *Soccer USA*, Chuck Cascio (Robert B. Luce, Inc., 1975)
3.   *Boston Globe*, 21/6/75
4.   *Boston Globe*, 12/6/75
5.   Author interview
6.   Author interview
7.   *New York Times*, 22/6/75
8.   *Boston Globe*, 21/6/75
9.   *ibid*.
10.   *New York Times*, 22/6/75
11.   *Soccer USA*, Chuck Cascio (Robert B. Luce, Inc., 1975)
12.   *ibid*.
13.   *Newark Star Ledger*, 10/7/75
14.   Author interview
15.   *New York Times*, 4/6/75
16.   Author interview
17.   Author interview
18.   *Soccer Digest*, July 1978
19.   Securities & Exchange Commission vs An-Car Oil Co., Inc. (1979)
20.   Author interview
21.   Author interview
22.   Author interview
23.   Author interview
24.   Author interview
25.   Author interview
26.   Author interview
27.   Author interview
28.   Author interview
29.   Author interview
30.   Author interview
31.   Author interview
32.   Author interview
33.   Author interview
34.   Author interview
35.   Author interview

Chapter 3

1.   *Soccer Digest*, September 1978
2.   *Soccer Digest*, August 1981
3.   Author interview
4.   *Erich Mielke, die Stasi und das runde Leder*, Hanns Leske (Verlag die Werkstatt, 2004)
5.   *Soccer Fever*, Richard B. Lyttle (Doubleday & Company, Inc., 1977)
6.   Author interview
7.   Author interview
8.   *One Hump or Two*, Frank Worthington (ACL & Polar Publishing Ltd, 1994)
9.   Author interview
10. *ibid.*
11. *ibid.*
12. Author interview
13. 'PROCUREMENT PROGRAMME: COACHES, PLAYERS, REFEREES', undated internal NASL memo (Dick Cecil private archive)
14. *ibid.*
15. Author interview
16. *Soccer Fever*, Richard B. Lyttle (Doubleday & Company, Inc., 1977)
17. Author interview
18. Interview with Gary James, 2005
19. *Kick* magazine, Issue 3, 1978
20. *Kick* magazine, 21/4/79
21. *Soccer Digest*, September 1981
22. 'From the Commissioner' *Kick* magazine, 12/5/79
23. 'A Passion or a Parade?' *Soccer Monthly,* October 1978
24. Author interview
25. *Kick* magazine, Issue 10, 1980
26. *Soccer Monthly*, September 1978
27. Author interview
28. Author interview
29. Author interview
30. *The Guardian*, 16/8/78
31. *Kick* magazine, Volume 6, Number 12, 1981
32. *Kick* magazine, Issue 2, 1978
33. *Kick* magazine, 24/6/79
34. *Kick* magazine, Issue 10, 1980

35. *Kick* magazine, Issue 10, 1980
36. *Kick* magazine, 7/6/78
37. *Kick* magazine, Volume 6, Number 15, 1981
38. *Soccer Digest*, September 1978
39. Author interview
40. *Soccer Monthly*, January 1980
41. *Soccer Monthly*, March 1979
42. Author interview
43. *Soccer Monthly*, December 1978
44. *New York Times*, 31/5/78
45. Author interview
46. *Soccer Digest*, Issue 1, 1978
47. *Sports Illustrated*, 6/8/79
48. Author interview
49. *Kick* magazine, 7/6/78
50. Author interview
51. Author interview
52. *Soccer Digest*, August 1981
53. *Trevor Francis: Anatomy of a £1 Million Player*, Rob Hughes with Trevor Francis (World's Work Ltd., 1980)
54. *Kick* magazine, Conference Finals issue, 1978
55. *Soccer Digest*, October 1978
56. *Kick* magazine, 8/9/79
57. *Kick* magazine, Issue 1, 1978
58. Kick magazine, 8/9/79
59. Associated Press, 16/7/79
60. *New York Times*, 1/9/79
61. *Sports Illustrated*, 6/8/79
62. Author interview
63. Author interview
64. Author interview
65. Author interview
66. *Soccer Digest*, August 1981

Chapter 4

1. *Kick* magazine, 7/4/79
2. Author interview
3. Author interview

4. *Priceless*, Rodney Marsh (Headline, 2001), chapter 8
5. Author interview
6. *ibid.*
7. *ibid.*
8. *ibid.*
9. *Kick* magazine, 7/4/79
10. *Kick* magazine, 17/5/78
11. Author interview
12. *St Petersburg Times*, 12/7/77
13. *Soccer Monthly*, November 1978
14. Author interview
15. Author interview
16. Author interview
17. Author interview
18. Author interview
19. *Sarasota Herald Tribune*, 2/4/79
20. *Blessed,* George Best (Ebury Press, 2001)
21. Author interview
22. *Kick* magazine, 17/5/78
23. *Kick* magazine, 7/4/79
24. *Kick* magazine, 17/5/78
25. Author interview
26. *Soccer Digest*, September 1978
27. *The Working Man's Ballet*, Alan Hudson (Robson Books, 1997)
28. Author interview
29. Author interview
30. *Evening Independent*, 24/8/78
31. *New York Times*, 14/7/76
32. Author interview
33. *Soccer Digest*, June 1979
34. *Kick* magazine, 7/4/79
35. *ibid.*
36. Author interview
37. Author interview
38. *St Petersburg Times*, 12/7/77
39. Author interview
40. Author interview
41. *San Jose Mercury News*, 5/7/81

42. Undated column written by John Lindblom, *San Jose Mercury News* (Alan Merrick private archive)
43. Author interview
44. Author interview
45. *Blessed*, George Best (Ebury Press, 2001)
46. Author interview

Chapter 5

1. 'Fans Frolic Outside Met', *Minneapolis Star* 7/6/79
2. 'Kicks Games Inherit Spirit of Rock Festivals', *Minneapolis Star*, 16/6/78
3. Author interview
4. *How We Got Our Kicks!* Allan Holbert (Ralph Turtinen Publishing Company, 1976)
5. *ibid.*
6. Author interview
7. Author interview
8. Author interview
9. Author interview
10. Author interview
11. Author interview
12. *Minnesota History* (Volume 63, No. 3), Timothy D. Grundmeier
13. *Minnesota Star*, 11/8/78
14. Author interview
15. *News World*, 20/6/77
16. Author interview
17. *New York Times*, 28/6/77
18. *Kick* magazine, 7/6/78
19. *ibid.*
20. *Kick* magazine, 7/7/78
21. *Kick* magazine, Issue 6, 1978
22. *Soccer Fever,* Richard B. Lyttle (Doubleday & Company, Inc., 1977)
23. *Kick* magazine, Issue 6, 1978
24. *Kick* magazine, Conference Championships edition, 1979
25. Author interview
26. *Soccer Monthly* (US edition), April/May 1979
27. *ibid.*
28. *ibid.*
29. *ibid.*

30. *Kick* magazine, Issue 4, 1978
31. *Kick* magazine, Issue 3, 1978
32. *Kick* magazine, Issue 4, 1978
33. *Soccer Fever,* Richard B. Lyttle (Doubleday & Company, Inc., 1977)
34. *Kick* magazine, Issue 4, 1978
35. *Soccer USA,* Chuck Cascio (Robert B. Luce, Inc., 1975)
36. Author interview
37. *Soccer Digest,* July 1978
38. *Soccer USA,* Chuck Cascio (Robert D. Luce, Inc., 1975)
39. *Soccer Digest,* July 1978
40. Author interview
41. *Soccer Digest,* July 1981
42. *Soccer Digest,* August 1979
43. *Trevor Francis: Anatomy of a £1 Million Player,* Rob Hughes with Trevor Francis (World's Work Ltd., 1980)
44. *Sports Illustrated,* 8/8/77
45. *Fuckin Hell, It's Paul Cannell,* Paul Cannell (Kindle)
46. *ibid.*
47. Author interview
48. *One Hump or Two?* Frank Worthington (ACL & Polar Publishing Ltd, 1994)
49. Author interview
50. *Trevor Francis: Anatomy of a £1 Million Player,* Rob Hughes with Trevor Francis (World's Work Ltd., 1980)
51. *ibid.*
52. *ibid.*
53. Author interview
54. Author interview
55. *Sports Illustrated,* 8/8/77
56. *ibid.*
57. Author interview
58. Author interview
59. Author interview
60. *Minneapolis Star,* 15/8/78
61. Author interview
62. *Minneapolis Star,* 15/8/78
63. *Minneapolis Star,* 17/8/78
64. *Minnesota History* (Volume 63, No. 3), Timothy D. Grundmeier

65. Joe Soucheray in the *Minneapolis Star*, undated 1981 cutting from Alan Merrick's private archive
66. *The Guardian*, 21/11/81
67. Author interview
68. *Minneapolis Star*, 16/7/81
69. Joe Soucheray in the *Minneapolis Star*, undated 1981 cutting from Alan Merrick's private archive
70. *Minneapolis Star*, 16/7/81
71. Author interview
72. Author interview
73. *Sarasota Journal*, 11/11/81
74. IN RE MINNESOTA KICKS, INC. *BANKRUPTCY NO. 4-81-2310*. 19/3/85. Leagle.com
75. *Minneapolis Star*, undated 1981 cutting from Alan Merrick's private archive
76. *The Guardian*, 21/11/81
77. *Sarasota Journal*, 5/11/81
78. Author interview
79. Author interview

Half-time

1. *UPI*, 15/7/81
2. *Evening Independent*, 7/6/84
3. *Soccer Monthly* (US edition), March/April 1978

Chapter 6

1. *New York Times*, 17/10/76
2. Author interview
3. Author interview
4. Author interview
5. Author interview
6. Author interview
7. Author interview
8. Author interview
9. *Kick* magazine, Issue 4, 1978
10. Author interview
11. *Associated Press*, 9/4/77
12. Author interview
13. Author interview

14. *Las Vegas Sun*, 14/4/09
15. *Las Vegas Sun*, 14/5/14
16. *Soccer Digest*, August 1979
17. *Soccer America*, 26/11/12
18. Author interview
19. *Soccer Digest*, July 1981
20. *Soccer Digest*, July 1981
21. Author interview
22. *World Soccer*, November 1983
23. *New York Times*, 30/09/83
24. *New York Times*, 2/10/83
25. *New York Times*, 3/10/83
26. *United Press International*, 3/10/83
27. Author interview
28. *A Kick in the Grass*, Clive Toye (St Johann Press, 2006)
29. Author interview
30. Author interview

Chapter 7
1. 'Absolutely Confidential', Ken Macker memo to NPSL team directors, 20/12/67 (Dick Cecil private archive)
2. *ibid.*
3. Author interview
4. *New York Times*, 30/8/70
5. Author interview
6. Author interview
7. Author interview
8. Author interview
9. Author interview
10. *New York Times*, 27/6/72
11. *Observer*, 30/3/80
12. *Kick* magazine, Issue 3, 1978
13. Author interview
14. *Kick* magazine, Issue, 3, 1978
15. *One Hump or Two?* Frank Worthington (ACL & Polar Publishing Ltd, 1994)
16. Author interview
17. *Kick* magazine, Issue 10, 1980

18. *Soccer Monthly*, September 1978

19. *Trevor Francis: Anatomy of a £1 Million Player*, Rob Hughes with Trevor Francis (World's Work Ltd, 1980)

20. *Observer*, 5/4/81

21. *World Soccer*, October 1982

22. *World Soccer*, October 1983

23. *Kick* magazine, 21/6/78

24. Author interview

25. Author interview

26. Author interview

27. Author interview

28. *Kick* magazine, Issue 10, 1980

29. *Kick* magazine, 24/6/78

30. Author interview

31. Author interview

32. *Kick* magazine, 24/6/78

33. *Tagesspiegel*, 23/10/05

34. Author interview

35. Author interview

36. Author interview

37. 'The Last Days of the NASL', Dan Herbst, *Soccer Digest*, Dec/Jan 1987

38. 'Phil Woosnam: The Commissioner's View', Dave Hirshey, Kick magazine, Issue 1, 1978

39. *New York Times*, 26/10/80

40. Author interview

41. *NASL – A Strategic Plan, 1978–1987*

42. *Soccer Digest*, October/November 1983

43. *Soccer Digest*, August 1981

44. *Soccer Digest*, October 1981

45. *Kick* magazine, 8/9/79

46. 'World Cup: Why Fifa Turned Down the United States', Michael Lewis, *Soccer Digest*, Oct/Nov. 1983

47. *World Soccer*, May 1983

48. *Sports Illustrated*, 5/7/84

49. 'World Cup: Why Fifa Turned Down the United States', Michael Lewis, *Soccer Digest*, Oct/Nov. 1983

50. *ibid.*

51. *ibid.*

52. *ibid.*
53. *The Guardian*, 14/5/83
54. *LA Times*, 30/6/86
55. Author interview

Chapter 8
1. Author interview
2. *Washington Post*, 15/5/14.
3. Soccer USA, *Chuck Cascio (Robert B. Luce, Inc., 1975)*
4. *Washington Post*, 29/4/71
5. *Fuckin Hell It's Paul Cannell*, Paul Cannell (Kindle, 2012)
6. Author interview
7. *Kick* magazine, Issue 6, 1978
8. *Washington Post*, 16/8/80
9. *Kick* magazine, Issue 3, 1978
10. *New York Times*, 23/5/79
11. Author interview
12. *Soccer Monthly*, September 1979
13. *ibid.*
14. Author interview
15. Author interview
16. Author interview
17. Author interview
18. Author interview
19. Author interview
20. Author interview
21. Author interview
22. *Washington Post*, 2/6/80
23. *ibid.*
24. Author interview
25. Author interview
26. *New York Times*, 26/10/80
27. *Sports Illustrated*, 1/12/80
28. *Washington Post*, 18/9/80
29. Author interview
30. *Washington Post*, 15/3/81
31. *Washington Post*, 2/4/81
32. *Washington Post*, 28/2/81

33. *Washington Post*, 15/3/81
34. *Soccer Digest*, September 1981
35. Author interview
36. *Washington Post*, 25/5/81
37. *Washington Post*, 6/6/81
38. *Washington Post*, 20/6/81
39. *Washington Post*, 19/7/81
40. *Washington Post*, 25/7/81
41. Author interview
42. *Washington Post*, 25/8/81
43. *Washington Post*, 28/8/81
44. *Washington Post*, 26/9/81
45. *Washington Post*, 11/11/81
46. *The Guardian*, 8/12/81
47. *The Mirror*, 17/8/96
48. *Soccer Digest*, April/May 1983
49. *World Soccer*, October 1983
50. Author interview
51. Author interview – *US Soccer Players* (website), 12/12/07
52. *World Soccer*, October 1983
53. Author interview – *US Soccer Players* (website), 12/12/07
54. Author interview
55. Author interview
56. Author interview – *US Soccer Players* (website), 12/12/07
57. Author interview
58. Author interviews

Chapter 9

1. Author interview
2. Author interview
3. Author interview
4. *11 Freunde* Spezial 4, 'Fussball und Pop'
5. Author interview
6. Author interview
7. Author interview
8. Author interview
9. Author interview
10. Author interview

11. Author interview
12. Author interview
13. Author interview
14. Author interview
15. Author interview
16. Author interview
17. *Soccer Digest*, September 1979
18. Author interview
19. Author interview
20. Author interview
21. *Soccer Digest*, September 1979
22. Author interview
23. Author interview
24. Author interview
25. *One Hump or Two?* Frank Worthington (ACL & Polar publishing Ltd., 1994)
26. *Soccer Monthly*, April 1979
27. Author interview
28. Author interview
29. *Four Four Two* magazine, January 2014
30. *Kick* magazine, Volume 6, No. 14, 1981
31. *What You Want is in the Limo*, Michael Walker (Spiegel & Grau, 2013)
32. *Washington Post*, 16/8/80
33. *Kick* magazine, Volume 6, No. 12, 1981
34. Author interview

Chapter 10
1. *Soccer Digest*, April/May 1984
2. Author interview
3. Author interview
4. *New York Times*, 30/1/80
5. *Kick* magazine, Issue 3, 1980
6. *ibid.*
7. *ibid.*
8. *New York Times*, 20/7/81
9. Author interview
10. *New York Times*, 16/6/83
11. *Hamburger Abendblatt*, 18/6/83
12. *ibid.*

13. *New York Times*, 16/6/83

14. *New York Times*, 22/5/77

15. *NASL – A Strategic Plan, 1978–87* (adopted: 14/10/77)

16. *Kick* magazine, Issue 1, 1978

17. *Kick* magazine, Issue 2, 1978

18. *Kick* magazine, Issue 1, 1978

19. *Kick* magazine, Issue 4, 1978

20. *Kick* magazine, Playoffs 1st Round issue, 1978

21. *Kick* magazine, 3/6/78

22. *Kick* magazine, 7/7/79

23. *Soccer Digest*, August 1979

24. Author interview

25. *Kick* magazine, Issue 2, 1980

26. *Kick* magazine, Issue 12, 1980

27. *Washington Post*, 18/9/80

28. *Kick* magazine, Issue 9, 1980

29. *Boston Globe*, 29/4/80

30. *Boston Globe*, 17/11/80

31. Author interview

32. *Kick* magazine, Issue 10, 1980

33. *New York Times*, 1/12/80

34. *Soccer Digest*, August/September 1986

35. *Kick* magazine, Volume 6, No. 11, 1981

36. *Soccer Digest*, August 1982

37. *Sports Illustrated*, 5/10/80

38. *Boston Globe*, 6/4/82

39. *Soccer Digest*, May 1982

40. *Evening Independent*, 16/6/82

41. *New York Times*, 25/4/82

42. *New York Times*, 19/5/82

43. *Evening Independent*, 16/6/82

44. *Soccer Digest*, April/May 1983

45. *Sports Illustrated*, 7/5/84

46. *ibid.*

47. Author interview

48. Author interview

49. Author interview

50. *Soccer Digest*, Aug/Sep. 1985

51. *Kick* magazine, 22/4/79
52. *NASL – A Strategic Plan, 1978–87* (adopted: 14/10/77)
53. *Sports Illustrated*, 7/5/84
54. *Soccer Digest*, Aug/Sep. 1985
55. *ibid.*
56. *Soccer Digest*, June 1979
57. *ibid.*
58. Author interview
59. Author interview
60. Author interview
61. Sports Illustrated, 28/2/83
62. *Soccer Digest*, April/May 1984
63. *World Soccer*, May 1985
64. Author interview
65. *The Day*, 18/6/85

Conclusion

1.   *Soccer Digest*, Aug./Sept. 1985
2.   *Soccer Digest*, April/May 1985
3.   Author interview
4.   Author interview
5.   Author interview
6.   *Kick* magazine, 1/8/79
7.   *ibid.*
8.   *Sabotage in Tournaments: Making the Beautiful Game a Bit Less Beautiful*,
     Luis Garicano and Ignacio Palacios-Huerta (2005)
9.   *Sports Illustrated*, 7/5/84
10. *Kick* magazine, 7/7/78
11. Author interview
12. *Forbes.com*, 20/11/13
13. *Kansas City Star*, 3/12/13
14. Author interview
15. Author interview
16. Author interview
17. Author interview
18. Author interview
19. Author interview
20. *New York Times*, 15/4/11
21. Author interview

Acknowledgements

First and foremost I would like to thank my original co-author J Hutcherson, who had to drop out of writing this book for work reasons (that is, he has a proper job). Not only did he conduct much of the initial research, but many of his original thoughts and theories on the NASL helped form the backbone of *Rock 'n' Roll Soccer*.

I would also like to thank all the former NASL players, coaches and administrators who gave up their time to be interviewed. I'm particularly grateful to Dick Cecil, Alan Merrick, Dave Chadwick and Paul Gardner for inviting me into their homes and making me feel so welcome, and to Geoff Barnett for making a 260-mile round trip to meet me during a harsh Minnesota winter. A huge thanks also to Rodney Marsh, Clive Toye, Alan Birchenall, Peter McParland, Joseph Fink, Bruce Wilson, Winston DuBose, Arnie Mausser, Ron Newman, Don Droege, Tony Glavin, Bob Iarusci, Carmine Marcantonio, Bob Lenarduzzi, Damir Šutevski, Steve David, Derek Spalding, Paul Cannell, Gary Etherington, Ray Bloomfield, Charlie Mitchell, Alan Willey, Alan Mayer, Tim Twellman, John Best, Jimmy Gabriel, Freddie Goodwin, Joanna Olszowska, Rachel Green at Leicester City FC, and Ken Adam.

Dave Brett Wasser at the NASL Alumni Association provided invaluable contacts and DVDs of NASL games, and was both patient and timely in dealing with my numerous questions and requests – thank you for being the curator of this incredible league, Dave. In Atlanta, Drew Whitelegg, his psychotic dog and his even stranger cat provided accommodation, vinyl and welcome distraction as I sifted through boxes of cuttings and documents. Thank you in Atlanta also to Andy Goldsmith for contacts. Gary James provided invaluable material about late 1960s Manchester City, and thank you to Tony Curran for the contact. Thank you also to Chuck Cascio for permission to quote from his book, to Jason Goldman for invaluable feedback on some early draft chapters, and to Thomas Kaufhold for trips to the post office in Dresden. The friendly and always efficient staff at the Library of Congress were a huge boon during my countless forays to a place of wonder that made me think I should have become a librarian or an archivist.

I would also like to especially thank Anne Price, wife of the late and much missed football writer David Wangerin, who responded movingly and graciously when I told her that I was writing a book which, by all rights, should have been written by David. Anyone who has enjoyed this book would, I am sure, also love David's final US soccer book, *Distant Corners* (Temple University Press, 2011).

Much gratitude is also due to Icon's commissioning editor Ian Preece for taking this book on, and to both him and Rob Sharman for their observant, diligent editing, which has significantly improved the final text. Also at Icon, the unstinting support and enthusiasm of Duncan Heath, Stacey Croft, Andrew Furlow, Henry Lord and Philip Cotterell allowed me to write this book in the knowledge that it would not be a wasted endeavour.

And finally, my thanks and endless love to my wife Conny, and daughters Nina and Natascha, my staunchest critics who keep me grounded and allow me to bang on about long-forgotten football names and games at the dinner table. For a few minutes, at least.

Washington DC, June 2014

Index